WINNING RECIPES
FROM
THE JUNIOR LEAGUE
OF INDIANAPOLIS

JLI Publications
The Junior League of Indianapolis, Inc.
Indianapolis, Indiana

The purpose of the Junior League is exclusively educational and charitable and is to promote voluntarism; to develop the potential of its members for voluntary participation in community affairs; and to demonstrate the effectiveness of trained volunteers. Proceeds from the sale of WINNERS will be returned to the community through the community projects of the Junior League of Indianapolis, Inc.

To order additional copies of WINNERS, use the order blanks in the back of the book or write:

JLI Publications
3050 North Meridian
Indianapolis, Indiana 46208

Checks should be made payable to JLI Publications for $14.95 plus $2.00 shipping and handling. Indiana sales tax is $.75 (if applicable) per book.

Copyright © 1985
by
The Junior League of Indianapolis, Inc.
Indianapolis, Indiana
All Rights Reserved
First Edition
First Printing: May 1985   15,000 copies

ISBN 0-9614447-0-3
Library of Congress Catalogue Card Number 85-060333
Printed in the United States of America
by
R.R. Donnelley & Sons Company
Crawfordsville, Indiana

Indianapolis is a city of

From the blue ribbons proudly adorning the judges' picks at the bustling Indiana State Fair to the checkered flags jubilantly signaling the victory lap of another world-renowned 500 Mile Race, winning is a time-honored tradition in Indiana's capital city.

Rising in recent years to global recognition as a major center of amateur sports, Indianapolis hosted the 1982 National Sports Festival and was selected as the site for the International Pan American Games of 1987. The phenomenally successful first International Violin Competition, held here in 1982, captured the attention of music devotees everywhere, and will be repeated on a quadrennial basis.

Accordingly, when we set out to produce a cookbook representing our winning city, we determined that it must be of first place, blue ribbon quality. Our book, *Winners*, delineates the full variety of foods and techniques which blend deliciously to create our city's distinctive culinary legacy. It stresses ease of preparation and use of only the freshest ingredients, and presents a spectrum of sophisticated recipes which lend themselves to elegant and memorable meals.

Preceding inclusion, each recipe went through an exacting selection and triple-testing process. Only the very best of the 3,500 submitted were accepted for final use. This collection includes hearty harvest favorites from the bounty of Hoosier farmlands alongside prized ethnic specialties introduced by the many nationalities which have fused to form the cosmopolitan Indianapolis community.

One additional notation is necessary. Indianapolis is and always has been a community known for the warmth of its hospitality—and the best of that hospitality is the wonderful food for which Hoosier hostesses are deservedly famed. Now we hope to share our traditions and heritage with you in a cookbook of our Indianapolis *winners*.

The Committee
1983-1985

Jane Judkins McCabe   Anne Ewing Smith
Co-Chairmen

Recipe Testing
Kathryn Gloin Betley
Mary Ann Gunter Buckley
Dinny Trubey Cochran
Deborah Mitchell Falk
Cynthia Winters Fisher
Nancy Milligan Frick
Carol Gartland
Jane Teixler Hebert
Deborah Berg Nell
Celestine Donnelly Sipe
Elizabeth Miller Smith
Barbara Feck Stayton
Anita Booth Stewart

Computer Typists
Janet Neal Patton
Margaret Myers Sullivan

Secretary
Gloria Vehling Scott

Marketing
Cheryl Longardner Lynn
Barbara Anderson
Barbara Lewis Coles
Gayle Geisler Crouse
Nancy Morris Pugh
Kate Lee Steele
Jane Polivka Stone
Hannah Hofherr Ten Eyck
Nancy Nichols Williams

Proofing
Jan Moore Eveleigh
Amy Karatz-Weisz
Catharine Shipley Singleton

Art and Graphics
Kathryn Wilsey Lerch
Susan Peck Van Huss

Business Manager
Bobbie Martin Yencer

Table of Contents

Appetizers and Beverages	7
Soups and Sandwiches	41
Salads	71
Eggs, Cheese and Pasta	105
Meats	123
Poultry and Game	157
Fish and Seafood	187
Vegetables	205
Breads	233
Desserts	257
Best of the Basics	303
Party Pastiche	309
Metric Conversions and Pan Sizes	316
Terms and Procedures	317
Index	322

Acknowledgements

Hoosier Photo Supplies and Sheryl Hanson for their contribution of time, expertise and equipment for computerizing the recipes and index; L. S. Ayres & Company for underwriting the celebration of the publication of WINNERS; Marge Hanley of *The Indianapolis News* and Donna Segal of *The Indianapolis Star* for their technical assistance and marketing ideas; Fran Shine for sharing her unlimited knowledge of foods and of creative presentations; Jim Crahan of Pearson, Crahan and Fletcher for his guidance in developing theme and marketing concepts; a special thank you to Cheryl English for her extensive hours of paste up.

A heartfelt thanks to the hundreds of volunteers from the Junior League and from the Indianapolis community who submitted, tested, retested, proofread and promoted the recipes included in this book. This two-year project demanded countless hours and sacrifices, and we are indebted to those who volunteered their time and to their families who supported their efforts. These unselfish contributions have given WINNERS the elements necessary for an outstanding and classic cookbook.

The Graphic Designer

Richard Listenberger, founder of Listenberger Design Associates, is a graduate of John Herron School of Art, Indiana University, and has more than 18 years of in-depth experience in the advertising agency business. His design work has spanned a diversity of business, professional and cultural areas and a wide spectrum of graphic creations.

Mr. Listenberger is the recipient of numerous important local, state and national awards for excellence in the field of design, and his work has been reproduced on nationally distributed posters and international magazine covers.

Appetizers and Beverages

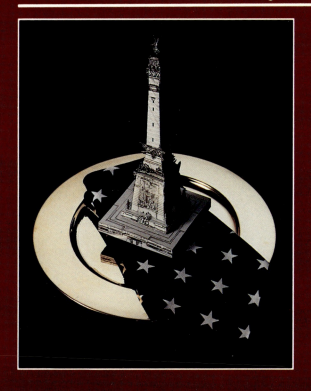

The Circle—Heart of the City

All roads to Indianapolis converge on "The Circle." There, the graceful Soldiers and Sailors Monument soars 284 feet above the heart of the surrounding city.

Commissioned in 1888 to commemorate the veterans of the Civil War, the massive limestone column is encircled by bronze sculptures and bordered on two sides by a series of broad stone steps. On the remaining two quadrants, gently curved, cascading fountains splash their waters into tranquil pools. The thirty-foot crowning figure of the Monument, holding aloft a sword and a torch, was designed to represent "Victory," but has come to be popularly known as "Miss Indiana."

With the approach of warm weather, Monument Circle becomes a focal point for a buzz of activity. Sidewalk vendors and open air cafes, reminiscent of those in European cities, ring the Monument in all directions. Horse-drawn carriages, available for hire, clatter gaily over its red-bricked circumference. Downtown workers and shoppers stroll its perimeters and loll on its steps.

An annual summer "Strawberry Festival" attracts throngs to feast on fresh Indiana strawberry shortcake and confections, and is replicated each fall with a similar "Apple Fest." At yuletide, twinkling, multicolored lights, strung from the Monument's pinnacle to its foundation, transform it into "the world's largest Christmas tree." Caroling choirs send music into the chill air and vividly garbed skaters trace figure 8's on a small ice rink at the Monument's base throughout the winter.

Within a moment's stroll of the Circle are a host of metropolitan attractions—major arenas for sports and entertainment events, a host of fine shops and restaurants, and the acclaimed Indianapolis Symphony Orchestra and Indiana Repertory Theatre, both housed in exquisitely renovated early-century theater buildings.

A winning city—absolutely—with the Circle and the Monument at its hub.

APPETIZERS AND BEVERAGES

First Course
Croustades (Toast Cups) . . . 8
Mushroom Croustades . . . 8
Westmoreland Asparagus Puff . . . 7
Ratatouille Pie . . . 9
Shrimp-Filled Salmon Rolls . . . 7

Dips and Spreads
Boursin Cheese . . . 13
Caper Cheese Spread . . . 14
Chicken Liver Pâté . . . 16
Fresh Fruit Dip . . . 12
Herbed Pâté . . . 17
Mushroom Spread . . . 15
Pesto Torta . . . 12
Polly's Fancy Liptauer Cheese . . . 14
Tex-Mex Dip . . . 13
Tuna Cheese Ball . . . 16
Zippy Beef and Olive Spread . . . 15

Cold Appetizers
Caviar Tart . . . 10
Crab-Filled Snow Peas . . . 19
Elegant Appetizer Tart . . . 11
Marinated Mushrooms . . . 11
Miniature Cucumber Pinwheels . . . 18
Roquefort Stuffed Shrimp . . . 10
Surprise Sandwich Loaves . . . 19
Vegetable Grab Bag . . . 18

Hot Appetizers
Apricot Brie . . . 30
Artichoke Appetizer . . . 32
Cheese Squares Florentine . . . 23
Chicken Kabobs . . . 26
Chinese Sweet and Sour Meatballs . . . 27
Crab Meat Wrapped in Phyllo . . . 31
Crab Puffs Supreme . . . 22
Crab Rangoon . . . 26
French Bread Appetizers . . . 28
George's Mushrooms . . . 24
Golden Chicken Nuggets . . . 25
Gouda Cheese Round . . . 30
Gouda Wheels . . . 32
Ham Sensations . . . 23
Hot Mustard Sauce . . . 25
Hot 'n Sweet Mustard Sauce . . . 25
Oriental Chicken Wings . . . 28
Party Roll Ups . . . 20
Ripe and Rye Appetizers . . . 20
Sausage and Leek Tarts . . . 33
Sausage Surprise Balls . . . 21
Spinach Balls . . . 22
Stuffed Mushrooms . . . 24
Swiss Onion Squares . . . 29
Texas Torte . . . 29

Snacks
Cheese Pennies . . . 34
Chinese Fried Walnuts . . . 35
Granola . . . 34
White Chocolate Party Mix . . . 35
Zesty Nibbles . . . 33

Beverages
Apricot Brandy Slush . . . 38
Banana Fruit Punch . . . 36
Berry Good Hot Cider . . . 39
Champagne Punch . . . 37
Citrus Frappé . . . 40
Claire's Almond Punch . . . 36
Hummers . . . 40
Kahlúa . . . 39
Miss Ora's Mint Cooler . . . 38
Spiced Tea Special . . . 37
Wassail . . . 40

Shrimp-Filled Salmon Rolls
Unusual and elegant first course.

Place mayonnaise in small bowl. Fold in Tabasco, paprika and tomato purée. Cut shrimp into small pieces. Add to mayonnaise and mix gently.

Lay salmon slices flat. Divide shrimp mixture equally among slices. Spread mixture evenly over the salmon and roll up. Place, seam down, on individual plates with lemon wedge. Serve with brown bread and butter, if desired.

½ cup mayonnaise
3–4 drops Tabasco sauce
½ teaspoon paprika
½ teaspoon tomato purée
10 ounces shrimp; cooked, shelled and deveined
8 uniform slices fresh salmon, about ½ pound (may substitute frozen smoked salmon, thawed)
8 wedges fresh lemon

Serves: 8
Preparation: 30 minutes

Westmoreland Asparagus Puff
Outstanding as a first course or as a luncheon entrée.

Snap off tough portion of each asparagus spear. Steam 6 of the spears for 2 minutes. Drain and finely chop. Cut remaining spears into 4-inch lengths. Steam for 3–5 minutes or until bright green and crisp tender.

Combine finely chopped asparagus, olives, Swiss cheese, cream cheese, bread crumbs, egg yolks and lemon juice. Beat with electric mixer at low speed until well combined. Divide into 6 equal portions.

Spread 1 filling portion over bottom ⅔ of a puff pastry square. Filling must not touch the edges. Place 3 cut-up asparagus spears on top. Moisten edges of pastry with water. Fold square over to cover the spears. Crimp edges together with a fork. Repeat with remaining 5 puff pastry squares. Cover and refrigerate for 1 hour to set cheese mixture.

Preheat oven to 350°.

Brush each pastry square with small amount of milk. Bake at 350° for 30–40 minutes or until pastry is golden.

24 asparagus spears, divided
½ cup chopped pimiento-stuffed olives
4 ounces Swiss cheese, grated
4 ounces cream cheese, softened
¼ cup dry bread crumbs
2 egg yolks
Juice of ½ lemon
6 (5-inch) squares puff pastry
Milk

Yield: 6 puffs
Preparation: 30 minutes
Chilling: 1 hour
Baking: 30 minutes
Temperature: 350°

Appetizers

24 croustades

4 tablespoons (½ stick) butter
3 tablespoons very finely chopped shallots
½ pound mushrooms, very finely chopped
2 tablespoons all-purpose flour
1 cup heavy (whipping) cream
½ teaspoon salt
⅛ teaspoon cayenne pepper
1 tablespoon finely chopped fresh parsley
1½ tablespoons finely chopped chives
½ teaspoon fresh lemon juice
2 tablespoons freshly grated Parmesan cheese
Butter

Yield: 24
Preparation: 15 minutes
Cooking: 20 minutes
Baking: 10 minutes
Temperature: 350°

48 slices thin-sliced white bread [3½ (1-pound) loaves]
⅔ cup butter, melted

Yield: 48 cups
Preparation: 1 hour
Baking: 10 minutes
Temperature: 350°

Mushroom Croustades

A marvelous appetizer.

Preheat oven to 350°.

Melt butter in medium-size skillet. Sauté shallots over medium heat, for about 4 minutes, stirring frequently. *Do not let shallots brown.* Stir in mushrooms. Continue to cook until all moisture has evaporated, about 10–15 minutes. Remove from heat. Add flour and stir until smooth and bubbly. Add cream gradually, stirring until blended. Return to heat. Bring mixture to a boil, stirring constantly. Remove from heat; stir in salt, cayenne, parsley, chives and lemon juice. Pour into bowl; cool. (May be covered and refrigerated until ready to use.)

Fill croustades, mounding slightly. Sprinkle with Parmesan and dot with speck of butter. Place on ungreased cookie sheet. Bake at 350° for 10 minutes, then place under broiler briefly. Be careful not to burn.

Croustades (Toast Cups)

Preheat oven to 350°.

Cut rounds from bread slices, using 2½-inch cookie cutter. Brush both sides with butter. Press into 1¾-inch muffin-tin cups. Bake at 350° for 10–15 minutes or until golden around edge. Gently lift out of pans; cool on wire racks.

Store, lightly covered, at room temperature.

Note: Use larger cookie cutter for bread rounds to fill regular-size muffin-tin cups. These edible serving dishes lend themselves to many uses. Fill with creamed chicken for a luncheon entrée, chipped beef for a supper dish, eggs for a brunch. Fill miniature croustades for hors d'oeuvres.

Ratatouille Pie
A tantalizing introduction to a meal.

Preheat oven to 425°.

Heat olive oil in large oven-proof skillet over medium-high heat. Add eggplant and cook for 5 minutes. Add zucchini, onion, green pepper, garlic, thyme, bay leaf, salt and pepper. Cook for 4 minutes, stirring constantly. Add tomatoes and parsley; cook 5 more minutes. Place skillet into oven and bake, uncovered, at 425° for 30 minutes. Stir in olives and bake 10 more minutes. Cool thoroughly. Remove bay leaf.

Divide pastry into 2 equal parts. Roll out 1 part and fit into 9-inch deep-dish pie plate. Reserve remaining pastry. Sprinkle Parmesan on bottom, add ratatouille and top with Fontina. Roll out remaining pastry and fit on top of pie. Fold edge over bottom crust. Crimp edges to seal. Brush with egg white and cut several slits in the top to vent steam. Bake in lower third of oven at 425° for 30 minutes. Reduce heat to 375° and bake 15 more minutes. Let stand for 15 minutes before serving.

Serving Suggestion: Good served as a first course with grilled chicken or lamb or as a luncheon entrée with salad.

Appetizers

- ¼ cup olive oil
- 1 eggplant, peeled and cut into 1½-inch cubes
- 2 small zucchini, cut into ¾-inch pieces
- 1 large onion, cut into ½-inch pieces
- 2 green peppers, seeded and cut into 1½-inch pieces
- 2 tablespoons minced garlic
- 1 teaspoon chopped fresh thyme (may substitute ½ teaspoon dried thyme)
- 1 bay leaf
- Salt
- Freshly ground pepper
- 1 pound tomatoes, peeled and cut into pieces
- 1 cup chopped fresh parsley
- ½ cup pitted Greek olives

- Pastry for (9-inch) double crust deep-dish pie
- ¾ cup freshly grated Parmesan cheese
- 2 cups grated Italian Fontina cheese
- Egg white

Serves:	8–10
Preparation:	1 hour, 30 minutes
Baking:	1 hour, 25 minutes
Standing:	15 minutes
Temperature:	425°

Appetizers

Caviar Tart
Unique way to serve caviar.

- 2 (8-ounce) packages cream cheese, softened
- 1 (3-ounce) package cream cheese, softened
- 1 small onion, grated
- 1 tablespoon Worcestershire sauce
- Dash of Tabasco sauce
- Pinch of garlic powder
- 1 tablespoon fresh lemon juice
- 1 cup mayonnaise
- 4 hard-cooked eggs
- 1 (3-ounce) jar black caviar
- Finely chopped fresh parsley
- Melba rounds

Combine cream cheese, onion, Worcestershire, Tabasco, garlic powder, lemon juice and mayonnaise in large bowl. Spread cheese mixture evenly on a 12-inch round plate, making a lip around the edge like a pizza crust. Finely chop eggs and sprinkle over cream cheese. Sprinkle with caviar then with parsley. Cover lightly and chill for 2 hours. Serve with melba rounds.

Serves: 12–15
Preparation: 15 minutes
Chilling: 2 hours

Roquefort-Stuffed Shrimp
A delectable showpiece.

- 2 quarts water
- 1 tablespoon (3 teaspoons) salt
- 24 large shrimp, uncooked
- 1 (3-ounce) package cream cheese, softened
- 1 ounce Roquefort cheese, softened
- ½ teaspoon prepared mustard
- 1 teaspoon finely chopped green onions
- 1 cup finely chopped fresh parsley

Place water and salt in large saucepan or Dutch oven and bring to boil. Add shrimp. Return to a boil and cook for 3–5 minutes. Drain; shell and devein shrimp. Split the shrimp down the spine about halfway through. Chill.

Mix cream cheese, Roquefort, mustard and onions. Fill the split of the shrimp with cheese mixture, using a knife or small spatula. Roll cheese-filled area of shrimp in parsley. Spear with toothpicks and serve chilled.

Yield: 24 large shrimp
Preparation: 30 minutes
Chilling: 2 hours

Elegant Appetizer Tart
Savor this showpiece.

Preheat oven to 425°.

Place pastry on large baking sheet and pat it into an 11-inch circle. Crimp the edges and pierce well with fork. Bake at 425° for 8 minutes or until lightly browned. Cool. Place on a flat serving platter.

Beat together cream cheese, blue cheese, sherry, mayonnaise and garlic salt until fluffy. Spread on top of pastry. Cover and chill at least 4 hours.

Before serving, place a circle of cherry tomatoes on outer rim of pie, followed by increasingly smaller rings of mushroom slices, chopped onion or parsley, chopped egg and then sliced olives. Place a cherry tomato half in the center. Cut into wedges and serve.

Pastry for a (9-inch) deep-dish pie
12 ounces cream cheese, softened
2 ounces blue cheese
2 teaspoons dry sherry
½ cup mayonnaise
½ teaspoon garlic or onion salt
Cherry tomato halves
Sliced fresh mushrooms
Chopped green onions or chopped fresh parsley
Finely chopped hard-cooked eggs
Sliced green or black olives

Serves: 10–12
Preparation: 30 minutes
Baking: 8 minutes
Chilling: 4 hours
Temperature: 425°

Marinated Mushrooms
These marinated mushrooms are the best.

Clean mushrooms. Remove stems and reserve for another use. Cut mushroom caps into quarters, if large.

Place oil, vinegar, onion, salt, parsley, mustard and brown sugar in medium-size saucepan and bring to a boil. Reduce heat to low and add mushroom quarters. Cook, stirring frequently, for 5–6 minutes. Refrigerate in marinade for 24 hours before serving.

8 ounces fresh mushrooms
⅓ cup olive oil
⅓ cup red wine vinegar
1 small onion, sliced and separated
1 teaspoon salt
2 teaspoons finely chopped fresh parsley
1 teaspoon prepared mustard
1 teaspoon firmly packed brown sugar

Serves: 4–6
Preparation: 15 minutes
Chilling: 24 hours

Appetizers

12 Appetizers

Pesto Torta
Lovely to look at and even better to eat.

Moisten 2 (18-inch) squares of cheesecloth. Wring dry. Place the two squares together to make a double thickness. Line 5–6 cup, straight-sided mold or loaf pan with cheesecloth. Place 1 clean basil leaf on bottom.

Place basil leaves, Parmesan, oil, garlic, salt and pepper in blender or food processor. Blend until well combined. Transfer to another container. Clean blender or processor bowl.

Place cream cheese and butter in blender or food processor. Blend until thoroughly combined. Spread 1/6 of cheese mixture in bottom of a prepared mold. Spread 1/5 of pesto mixture over cheese mixture. Repeat layers, ending with cheese mixture. Fold cheesecloth over torta and use hand to press down to compact.

Chill for 1 hour or until torta feels firm.

Invert onto a serving plate and gently pull off cheesecloth. (If allowed to stand, the cheesecloth will act as a wick and cause the filling color to bleed onto cheese.) Serve with crackers or French bread.

Wrap leftovers tightly in plastic wrap. Will keep for 5 days in refrigerator.

- 1 clean fresh basil leaf, if available

Pesto:
- 2½ cups fresh basil leaves (may substitute ¾ cup dry basil leaves)
- 1 cup freshly grated Parmesan cheese (may substitute Romano cheese)
- ⅓ cup olive oil
- 1 clove garlic, crushed
- Salt
- Freshly ground pepper

Torta:
- 2 (8-ounce) packages cream cheese, softened
- 2 cups (4 sticks) butter, softened

Serves: 14–16
Preparation: 20 minutes
Chilling: 1 hour

Fresh Fruit Dip
Easy, pretty and delicious summer dip.

Melt butter in small saucepan over medium heat. Add brown sugar; stir until smooth. Remove from heat and cool. Add sour cream and vanilla to cooled mixture. Serve with fresh fruit.

- ½ cup (1 stick) butter
- 1 cup firmly packed brown sugar
- 1 cup sour cream
- 3 teaspoons vanilla
- Fresh fruit

Yield: 2½ cups
Preparation: 10 minutes
Cooling: 10 minutes

Tex-Mex Dip
Great eye appeal and taste.

Combine sour cream, mayonnaise and taco seasoning in medium-size bowl. Set aside.

Peel, pit and mash avocados in medium-size bowl. Add lemon juice, salt and pepper.

Spread bean dip on bottom of a 13-inch pizza pan. Spread sour cream mixture evenly over the top. Spread avocado mixture over sour cream. Sprinkle with tomatoes, onions, olives and cheese.

Note: To avoid excess moisture, drain chopped tomatoes on paper towels before adding to dip.

- 1 cup sour cream
- ½ cup mayonnaise
- 1 (1.25-ounce) package taco seasoning mix
- 3 medium-size ripe avocados
- 2 tablespoons fresh lemon juice
- ½ teaspoon salt
- ¼ teaspoon pepper
- 2 (10½-ounce) cans plain or jalapeño bean dip
- 2 cups fresh tomatoes; cored, seeded and coarsely chopped
- 1 cup chopped green onions
- 2 (3½-ounce) cans black olives, chopped
- ½ pound sharp Cheddar cheese, grated
- 1 (16-ounce) bag tortilla chips

Serves: 12
Preparation: 45 minutes

Boursin Cheese
Like imported cheese at a fraction of the cost.

Blend all ingredients in blender or food processor. Chill at least 24 hours. Serve with crackers of choice.

Variation: May be used as dip by adding ½ cup sour cream.

Variation: Stuff mushroom caps with boursin and bake at 350° for 15–20 minutes.

- 1 (8-ounce) package cream cheese, softened
- 1 small clove garlic, crushed
- 2 teaspoons finely chopped fresh parsley
- ½ teaspoon snipped chives
- 1 tablespoon dry vermouth
- Pinch of lemon pepper
- Freshly ground pepper
- Salt

Serves: 8
Preparation: 10 minutes
Chilling: 24 hours

Appetizers

2 (8-ounce) packages cream cheese, softened
½ cup (1 stick) butter, softened
1½ tablespoons finely chopped green onions (including tops)
1½ tablespoons finely chopped capers
1 teaspoon garlic powder
1 teaspoon paprika
Dash of cayenne pepper (optional)

Yield: 2 cups
Preparation: 5 minutes
Chilling: 24 hours

Caper Cheese Spread
Capers add a nice "new" flavor.

Place cream cheese, butter, green onions, capers, garlic powder, paprika and cayenne in large bowl. Beat with electric mixer at medium speed for 2–3 minutes. Cover and refrigerate for 24 hours or more. Serve with melba toast or crackers.

Note: Capers, garlic powder, paprika and cayenne pepper may be increased "to taste." Spread keeps for 2–3 weeks in refrigerator or may be frozen. If frozen, thaw and mix with electric mixer.

---

2 (8-ounce) packages cream cheese, softened
¼ cup (½ stick) butter, softened
2 tablespoons milk
½ teaspoon paprika

Toppings:
    Chopped green onions
    Chopped cucumber
    Bacon, cooked and crumbled
    Capers
    Chopped radishes
    Anchovies

Serves: 8–10
Preparation: 10 minutes
Chilling: 4 hours

Polly's Fancy Liptauer Cheese
Create your own taste experience.

Grease a 2-cup mold with mayonnaise or oil.

Beat cream cheese, butter, milk and paprika until light and fluffy. Turn into mold and chill at least 4 hours. Unmold and place on serving platter. Surround mold with onions, cucumber, bacon, capers, radishes and anchovies. Serve cheese on crackers or party rye. Guests may select preferred toppings.

Mushroom Spread
Convenient to make ahead and reheat in microwave.

Cook bacon in large skillet until crisp; drain, reserving 2 tablespoons of the drippings. Crumble bacon and set aside.

Add mushrooms, onion and garlic to reserved drippings in skillet. Cook over medium heat until tender and most of the liquid has evaporated. Stir in flour, salt and pepper; cook until smooth and bubbly. Add cream cheese, Worcestershire and soy sauce. Stir until cheese is melted. Stir in sour cream, lemon juice and crumbled bacon. Heat through. *Do not boil.* Serve warm with crackerbread or Bremner wafers.

- 4 slices bacon
- 2 tablespoons bacon drippings
- 8 ounces fresh mushrooms, chopped
- ½ cup finely chopped onion
- 1 clove garlic, minced
- 2 tablespoons all-purpose flour
- ¼ teaspoon salt
- ⅛ teaspoon freshly ground pepper
- 1 (8-ounce) package cream cheese, cubed
- 2 teaspoons Worcestershire sauce
- 1 teaspoon soy sauce
- ½ cup sour cream
- 1 tablespoon fresh lemon juice
- Crackerbread or Bremner wafers

Yield: 2 cups
Preparation: 20 minutes

Zippy Beef and Olive Spread
Celery with a new look.

Combine cream cheese and mayonnaise; mix until well blended. Stir in remaining ingredients. Chill at least 3 hours. Spread in celery stalks and serve.

Note: May also be spread on crackers.

- 1 (8-ounce) package cream cheese, softened
- 2 tablespoons mayonnaise
- 4 teaspoons minced onions
- 1 teaspoon dry sherry
- 1 (3-ounce) package dried beef, finely snipped
- ¼ cup chopped pimiento-stuffed green olives
- Celery

Yield: 1½ cups
Preparation: 15 minutes
Chilling: 3 hours

Appetizers

Chicken Liver Pâté
Subtle blend of flavors.

- ⅓ cup margarine
- 1 pound chicken livers
- ¼ pound fresh mushrooms, chopped
- ⅓ cup chopped fresh parsley
- ¼ cup chopped green onions
- ½ teaspoon salt
- Freshly ground pepper
- ½ teaspoon dried thyme
- ¼ cup red wine
- 2 tablespoons light (coffee) cream
- 1 cup (2 sticks) butter, softened

Melt margarine in large skillet over low heat. Add chicken livers, mushrooms, parsley and onions. Sauté over medium heat until chicken livers are slightly pink inside, about 8–10 minutes. Stir in salt, pepper, thyme and red wine. Simmer until all liquid is absorbed. Remove from heat. Cool liver mixture completely.

Purée mixture in food processor. Add cream and butter by chunks, processing until smooth. Pour into terrines or small ramekins and refrigerate overnight. Serve on crackers or toast rounds.

Yield: 4 cups
Preparation: 30 minutes
Chilling: Overnight

Tuna Cheese Ball
Crunchy goodness.

- 1 (8-ounce) package cream cheese, softened
- 1 (7-ounce) can white tuna, drained and flaked
- 4–6 ounces macadamia nuts, chopped
- ½ cup finely chopped fresh parsley
- ¼ teaspoon Tabasco sauce
- 1 small onion, chopped (may substitute 4 green onions, chopped)
- 1 (8-ounce) can water chestnuts, drained and chopped
- Salt
- Freshly ground pepper
- Finely chopped fresh parsley

Combine cream cheese, tuna, nuts, ½ cup parsley, Tabasco, onion and water chestnuts in large bowl; mix well. Add salt and pepper. Roll mixture into a ball and then roll in chopped parsley. Refrigerate at least 2 hours. Serve with crackers or Triscuits.

Serves: 12–15
Preparation: 20 minutes
Chilling: 2 hours

Herbed Pâté
The ultimate in rich elegance.

Line the bottom and sides of a 1½-quart terrine or loaf pan with bacon strips.

Combine parsley, onion, garlic, basil and olives in small bowl. Set aside.

Chop and wash spinach. Place in large saucepan. Cook spinach in its own moisture over low heat for 3–5 minutes or until just wilted. Squeeze to remove excess moisture. Chop spinach again until it is very fine; place in large bowl. Stir in ½ the parsley mixture and set aside.

Combine pork, salt, pepper, eggs and the remaining parsley mixture in another large bowl. Add rosemary, thyme, nutmeg, Tabasco and cognac; mix well.

Preheat oven to 350°.

Place ⅓ of the pork mixture in bottom of terrine. Cover with ½ of the sliced ham, then with ½ of the spinach mixture. Spread another ⅓ of the pork mixture evenly over spinach mixture and layer with remaining ham. Spread remaining spinach mixture over ham. Top with last ⅓ of the pork. Press mixture down and place bay leaves on top. Cover with foil and place heavy lid on top.

Place terrine in a 9x13-inch baking dish. Pour hot water into the baking dish until water comes to ⅔ the height of terrine. Bake at 350° for 1 hour and 30 minutes.

Remove lid; cool for 15 minutes. Place a 3-pound weight on top of pâté. Refrigerate overnight. Invert onto a plate and slice into 1-inch thick slices.

Variation: Pâté may also be served warm. Cover terrine and heat at 300° for 30 minutes.

- 1 pound lean bacon strips
- 3 tablespoons freshly chopped parsley
- 1 medium onion, finely chopped
- 3 cloves garlic, finely chopped
- 1 teaspoon dried basil
- 1 cup finely chopped pitted Italian olives (black and green)
- 3 pounds fresh spinach
- 1½ pounds ground pork
- 1 teaspoon salt
- ½ teaspoon freshly ground pepper
- 2 eggs, slightly beaten
- ½ teaspoon dried rosemary
- ½ teaspoon dried thyme
- ⅛ teaspoon ground nutmeg
- ⅛ teaspoon Tabasco sauce
- ⅓ cup cognac
- ½ pound boiled ham, thinly sliced
- 2 large bay leaves

Serves:	10
Preparation:	1½ hours
Baking:	1½ hours
Cooling:	15 minutes
Chilling:	Overnight
Temperature:	350°

Appetizers

- 1 cup sour cream
- 1 cup mayonnaise
- ½ cup prepared horseradish
- ½ teaspoon monosodium glutamate (optional)
- 2 teaspoons dry mustard
- ½ teaspoon salt
- 1 tablespoon fresh lemon juice
- Cherry tomatoes
- Fresh mushrooms
- Black olives
- Water chestnuts
- Avocado cubes
- Cucumber cubes

Serves: 8–10
Preparation: 20 minutes

- 1 cucumber (unpeeled), grated
- 1 small onion, grated
- 4 ounces cream cheese, softened
- Salt
- 2 tablespoons mayonnaise
- 1 (20-ounce) loaf white bakery bread, sliced horizontally by bakery

Yield: 36 rolls
Preparation: 20 minutes
Chilling: 24 hours

Vegetable Grab Bag
Unique and fun to eat.

Mix sour cream, mayonnaise, horseradish, monosodium glutamate, dry mustard, salt and lemon juice in large serving bowl.

Add any or all of the vegetables to sauce and toss gently to cover. Use long bamboo skewers to spear vegetables.

Variation: Fresh cooked shrimp is a wonderful addition to the vegetable mixture.

Miniature Cucumber Pinwheels
Refreshing anytime of year.

Mix cucumber and onion together. Drain in sieve lined with paper towels, pushing to squeeze out all excess liquid. Place cucumber mixture in bowl. Add cream cheese, salt and mayonnaise; mix well.

Work with a few slices of bread at a time to keep it from drying out. Remove crusts from bread. Lightly roll each slice with a rolling pin to flatten. Spread filling to edges of bread slices. Starting at wide end, roll each slice tightly in jelly-roll fashion. Wrap in wax paper like a party favor, twisting ends. Refrigerate for 24 hours.

Unwrap and cut into ½-inch slices. Serve chilled.

Note: Only very fresh bread will flatten properly.

Crab-Filled Snow Peas
Crisp and savory.

Remove the stems from the pods and very carefully slit the seed-side of the pods with a small sharp knife, making a pocket.

Beat filling ingredients together in a large bowl until well combined. (This may be done in a food processor.)

Stuff each pod by spreading filling into the pocket with a knife. Stuffed pods may be covered and refrigerated for several hours.

60	snow peas (approximately ¾ pound), washed
2	(6½-ounce) cans crab meat, drained
4	ounces cream cheese, softened
1	green onion (including top), finely chopped
1	teaspoon fresh lemon juice
1	teaspoon curry powder

Yield: 60 pods
Preparation: 1 hour

Surprise Sandwich Loaves
A delicious and intriguing finger food.

Scoop out the center of each loaf half with spoon; leave ½ inch around the edges. Spread mayonnaise in each of the bread halves; sprinkle with parsley.

Stir together cream cheese, Cheddar, celery and onion in large bowl. Pack ½ of the cheese mixture into each loaf half. With a knife handle, make a narrow lengthwise groove in the center of the cheese filling. Roll each pickle quarter in 2 slices of ham and place end to end in groove. Place halves together again, closing tightly. Refrigerate until cheese sets, about 1½ hours. Cut each loaf across the width into 1-inch slices and serve.

6	small individual loaves of Italian or French bread, sliced in half horizontally
½	cup mayonnaise
¼	cup chopped fresh parsley
1	(8-ounce) package cream cheese, softened
3	(3-ounce) packages cream cheese, softened
½	cup grated Cheddar cheese
½	cup finely diced celery
2	tablespoons finely chopped onion
3	whole dill pickles, quartered lengthwise
½	pound boiled ham, thinly sliced

Serves: 8–12
Preparation: 30 minutes
Chilling: 1½ hours

Appetizers

- 12 thin slices, fresh soft white bread, crusts removed
- 2 (3-ounce) packages cream cheese, softened
- 8 slices bacon, cooked and crumbled
- 12 fresh asparagus spears, cooked and chilled (may substitute canned asparagus spears)
- ½ cup (1 stick) butter, melted

Yield: 36 pieces
Preparation: 30 minutes
Chilling: 1 hour, 30 minutes
Baking: 15 minutes
Temperature: 400°

Party Roll Ups
Pretty, easy and delicious.

Flatten bread slices with rolling pin. Work with a few slices at a time to keep bread from drying out.

Beat cream cheese until smooth. Stir in bacon; spread evenly on bread. Place an asparagus spear on each bread slice and roll up. Brush outside of bread with melted butter. Place, seam down, on ungreased baking sheet and place in freezer until firm, about 1 hour and 30 minutes.

Preheat oven to 400°.

Remove rolls from freezer. Thaw slightly and cut into thirds. Bake at 400° for 15 minutes or until golden brown. Serve hot.

Note: If making ahead, store frozen rolls in freezer bags until needed. Thaw slightly and follow baking instructions.

Variation: Combine 1 (5-ounce) jar Old English cheese spread, ½ cup butter, 1 tablespoon minced onion and dash of Worcestershire sauce. Substitute for cream cheese and bacon mixture.

- 3–4 ounces sliced smoked beef, snipped into small pieces
- 1 cup grated Cheddar cheese
- 1 (4¼-ounce) can pitted ripe olives, drained and sliced
- 1 cup mayonnaise
- 1 (8½-ounce) package Rye Krisp

Yield: 36
Preparation: 20 minutes
Baking: 5 minutes
Temperature: 375°

Ripe and Rye Appetizers
A real crowd pleaser.

Preheat oven to 375°.

Combine beef, cheese, olives and mayonnaise in large bowl. Spread 1 tablespoon on each Rye Krisp. Bake at 375° for 5–8 minutes.

Sausage Surprise Balls

The sauerkraut remains a mystery in these balls.

Crumble sausage in large skillet; add onion. Brown over medium heat until meat is thoroughly cooked. Drain fat. Add sauerkraut and 2 tablespoons bread crumbs.

Combine cream cheese, parsley, mustard, garlic salt and pepper. Stir into sausage mixture and chill for about 30 minutes.

Shape chilled mixture into ¾-inch balls. Coat with flour. Combine eggs and milk. Roll floured balls in egg mixture and then in bread crumbs. Deep fry a few balls at a time in hot oil until lightly browned, about 3–5 minutes. (The balls may be frozen at this point and warmed in oven before serving.) Serve hot with Mustard Sauce.

Mix sour cream and mayonnaise. Stir in dry mustard, onion, vinegar and salt.

Note: *Sauce keeps well in refrigerator.*

- ¾ pound bulk sausage (may substitute ½ mild and ½ hot sausage)
- ⅓ cup finely chopped onion
- 1 (16-ounce) can sauerkraut, drained and minced
- 1⅓ cups dry bread crumbs, divided
- 1 (3-ounce) package cream cheese, softened
- 2 tablespoons chopped fresh parsley
- 1 teaspoon prepared mustard
- ¼ teaspoon garlic salt
- ¼ teaspoon pepper
- ¼ cup all-purpose flour
- 2 eggs, well beaten
- ¼ cup milk
- Oil

Mustard Sauce:
- ⅓ cup sour cream
- ⅓ cup mayonnaise
- 1 tablespoon dry mustard
- 1 tablespoon finely chopped green onions
- 1½ teaspoons cider vinegar
- Salt

Yield: 3 dozen
Preparation: 1½ hours
Cooking: 30 minutes

Appetizers

- 2 (10-ounce) packages frozen chopped spinach
- 3 cups herb-seasoned stuffing mix
- 1 large onion, finely chopped
- 6 eggs, well beaten
- ¾ cup (1½ sticks) butter or margarine, melted
- ½ cup freshly grated Parmesan cheese
- 1 teaspoon pepper
- 1½ teaspoons garlic salt
- ½ teaspoon dried thyme

Yield: 7–8 dozen
Preparation: 30 minutes
Baking: 20 minutes
Temperature: 325°

Spinach Balls

Just plain good.

Preheat oven to 325°.

Lightly grease cookie sheets.

Cook spinach according to package directions; drain well. Squeeze spinach to remove excess moisture. Combine spinach with remaining ingredients in large bowl; mix well. Shape mixture into ¾-inch balls and place on cookie sheets. Bake at 325° for 15–20 minutes.

Note: Can be frozen before baking. Place on cookie sheet to freeze. Store frozen balls in plastic bag. Thaw slightly and bake at 325° for 20–25 minutes.

Variation: May fill mushroom caps with spinach mixture. Place 2 tablespoons oil in baking dish. Place mushroom caps in dish and bake at 350° until heated through.

- 1 (6½-ounce) can crab meat, drained and flaked
- ½ cup grated sharp Cheddar cheese
- 3 green onions (including tops), chopped
- 1 teaspoon Worcestershire sauce
- 1 teaspoon dry mustard
- 1 cup water
- ½ cup (1 stick) butter
- ¼ teaspoon salt
- 1 cup all-purpose flour
- 4 eggs

Yield: 4 dozen
Preparation: 20 minutes
Baking: 25 minutes
Temperature: 400°

Crab Puffs Supreme

Delicate puffs that melt in your mouth.

Preheat oven to 400°.

Combine crab meat, cheese, onions, Worcestershire and mustard in medium-size bowl; mix well. Set aside.

Combine water, butter and salt in large saucepan; bring to a boil. Remove from heat and immmediately add flour. Beat with electric mixer at low speed until mixture leaves the sides of the pan and forms a ball. Add eggs, 1 at a time, beating thoroughly after each addition. Stir in crab mixture. Drop by teaspoonfuls onto ungreased baking sheet. Bake at 400° for 15 minutes. Reduce heat to 350° and bake 10 more minutes.

Ham Sensations
Indeed, they are.

Preheat oven to 450°.

Grease a cookie sheet.

Combine flour, cheese, cayenne and butter in large bowl or food processor. Add water gradually, mixing until dough forms into a ball. Knead on floured surface 12 times.

Divide dough in half. Roll ½ of dough into a 10x14-inch rectangle (approximately). Cut the rectangle into 4 (5x7-inch) pieces. Place a piece of ham on each small rectangle and sprinkle onions over ham. Start with 7-inch side and roll up each rectangle jelly-roll fashion. Seal edges by pinching with fingers. Prepare the remaining ½ of dough in the same manner. Place the pieces, seam down, on prepared cookie sheet. Brush with milk. Bake at 450° for 10–12 minutes. Remove from oven and cut each roll into 5 slices. Serve warm.

1½ cups all-purpose flour
1 cup grated Cheddar cheese
¼ teaspoon cayenne pepper
½ cup (1 stick) butter, softened
¼ cup cold water
8 thin slices boiled ham
1 (2.8-ounce) can French fried onions, crumbled
Milk

Yield: 40
Preparation: 45 minutes
Baking: 10 minutes
Temperature: 450°

Cheese Squares Florentine
Terrific pick-up hors d'oeuvres.

Preheat oven to 325°.

Grease a 9x13-inch baking dish.

Mix flour, salt and baking powder in large bowl. Add eggs, milk, butter, cheese and onion. Squeeze spinach to remove all excess moisture. Add to cheese mixture; mix well. Spread spinach mixture evenly in prepared baking dish. Bake at 325° for 30–35 minutes. Cool slightly. Cut into small squares.

Note: Baked squares freeze well. Bake frozen squares at 350° until heated through, about 15 minutes.

1 cup all-purpose flour
1 teaspoon salt
1 teaspoon baking powder
2 eggs, slightly beaten
1 cup milk
3 tablespoons butter, melted
1 pound sharp Cheddar cheese, grated
½ cup finely minced onion
1 (10-ounce) package frozen chopped spinach, thawed and drained

Yield: 5 dozen
Preparation: 20 minutes
Baking: 30 minutes
Temperature: 325°

Appetizers

24–30 large mushrooms
2 tablespoons butter
1 medium onion, finely chopped
½ cup finely diced pepperoni
¼ cup seeded and finely chopped green pepper
1 small clove garlic, minced
½ cup finely crushed Ritz crackers
3 tablespoons freshly grated Parmesan cheese
1 tablespoon finely chopped fresh parsley
½ teaspoon seasoned salt
¼ teaspoon dried oregano
Freshly ground pepper
⅓ cup chicken stock or broth

Yield: 24–30
Preparation: 35 minutes
Baking: 25 minutes
Temperature: 325°

1 pound large mushrooms
1 cup fresh lemon juice
Shrimp to equal number of mushroom caps; cooked, deveined and shelled
¼ cup Italian salad dressing
10 ounces cream cheese with chives, softened
Chopped fresh dill

Yield: About 18
Preparation: 30 minutes
Marinating: 4 hours

Stuffed Mushrooms
Pepperoni adds just the right spice.

Preheat oven to 325°.

Clean mushrooms. Remove caps and set aside. Chop stems finely; set aside.

Melt butter in large skillet over medium heat. Add onion, pepperoni, green pepper, garlic and chopped stems. Cook until tender but not brown. Add crackers, cheese, parsley, seasoned salt, oregano and pepper. Mix well. Stir in chicken broth. Remove from heat.

Spoon stuffing mixture into mushroom caps. Place caps in shallow baking dish. Add ¼ inch of water to cover bottom of dish. Bake, uncovered, at 325° for 25 minutes.

George's Mushrooms
An attractive presentation with an interesting meld of flavors.

Clean mushrooms and remove stems. Place mushrooms and lemon juice in medium-size bowl. Toss gently to coat. Cover and marinate in refrigerator for 4 hours or overnight.

Place shrimp and Italian dressing in medium-size bowl. Toss gently to coat. Marinate in refrigerator for at least 4 hours or overnight. Drain mushrooms and shrimp.

Stir cream cheese in small bowl until smooth. Fill each cap with about 1 tablespoon cream cheese. Arrange shrimp on top and garnish with dill.

Hot 'n Sweet Mustard Sauce
Delicious dip for chicken nuggets or egg rolls.

Combine preserves, jelly, horseradish and mustard in large bowl. Beat with electric mixer at medium speed until well combined. Spoon over boursin or cream cheese. Serve with crackers.
Note: Will keep in airtight jar in refrigerator for 6 months.

- 1 (18-ounce) jar pineapple preserves
- 1 (10-ounce) jar apple jelly
- 1 (5-ounce) jar prepared horseradish
- 4 tablespoons dry mustard

Yield: 4 cups
Preparation: 5 minutes

Hot Mustard Sauce
Versatile and delicious.

Mix mustard and vinegar in a jar. Cover jar and refrigerate overnight.

Beat egg in top of double boiler. Stir in sugar. Add vinegar-mustard combination and stir. Cook the mixture in double boiler over hot (not boiling) water until thick enough to coat a spoon. Cool. Add mayonnaise equal to the amount of the mixture. Serve chilled. Store in jar in refrigerator.
Serving Suggestion: Tangy sauce for ham, egg rolls or sandwiches.

- ½ cup dry mustard
- ½ cup cider vinegar
- 1 egg
- ⅓ cup granulated sugar
- Mayonnaise

Yield: 1½ cups
Preparation: 25 minutes
Cooling: 30 minutes
Chilling: 2 hours

Golden Chicken Nuggets
Tender, juicy and just the right spice.

Preheat oven to 400°.

Cut chicken into 1-inch pieces.

Mix salt, bread crumbs, basil, thyme and Parmesan in medium-size bowl.

Melt butter in small saucepan. Dip chicken pieces into melted butter, then roll in crumb mixture. Place chicken in 9x13-inch baking dish. Bake at 400° for 10 minutes.

- 4 large chicken breast halves, skinned and boned
- 1 teaspoon salt
- 1 cup fine dry bread crumbs
- ½ teaspoon dried basil
- ½ teaspoon dried thyme
- ¼ cup freshly grated Parmesan cheese
- ½ cup (1 stick) butter

Serves: 8–12
Preparation: 30 minutes
Cooking: 10 minutes
Temperature: 400°

Appetizers

Chicken Kabobs
Great for cocktail buffet.

Cut chicken breasts into ½-inch cubes.

Clean mushrooms and remove stems. (If mushrooms are large, they will need to be quartered.) Toss with chicken and set aside.

Combine oil, corn syrup, soy sauce, vinegar, garlic and ginger. Stir until well mixed. Pour marinade over chicken and mushrooms. Refrigerate for 3 hours in an airtight container. Drain.

Preheat oven to broil.

Arrange a piece of pepper, a cube of chicken and a mushroom on a toothpick or skewer. Broil for 8–10 minutes, turning once. Serve immediately or keep warm on a warming tray.

Note: Marinade may be reused within 12 hours.

Variation: Cherry tomatoes may be added to skewers.

- 4 chicken breast halves, skinned and boned
- 8 ounces small fresh mushrooms (may substitute 8-ounce can button mushrooms, drained)
- ½ cup oil
- ½ cup corn syrup
- ¼ cup soy sauce
- 2 tablespoons red wine vinegar
- 1 clove garlic, halved
- ¼ teaspoon ground ginger
- 1 green or red pepper, seeded and cut in small pieces

Yield: 30
Preparation: 30 minutes
Marinating: 3 hours
Broiling: 10 minutes
Temperature: Broil

Crab Rangoon
Delightful finger food.

Heat oil in deep fat fryer to 375°.

Combine crab meat, cream cheese, Worcestershire and garlic.

Separate Won Ton papers. Place 2 teaspoons of crab mixture on each Won Ton paper. Brush edges of Won Ton with water. Roll diagonally and twist edges of each Won Ton to keep mixture in shell. Deep fry rolls, about 6 at a time, for 3–5 minutes or until golden brown. Serve immediately.

Note: May be frozen and reheated at 350° for 20 minutes.

Serving Suggestion: Serve with Hot Mustard Sauce or Hot 'n Sweet Mustard Sauce.

- Oil
- 1 (6-ounce) package frozen crab meat, thawed and drained
- 2 (8-ounce) packages cream cheese, softened
- 2 tablespoons Worcestershire sauce
- 1 clove garlic, minced
- 1 (16-ounce) package frozen Won Ton papers, thawed
- 1 small bowl water

Yield: 40–45
Preparation: 1 hour

Chinese Sweet and Sour Meatballs

Pork and water chestnuts add a new twist to meatballs.

Mix water chestnuts, onions and ground pork in large bowl. Add soy sauce, eggs, salt and bread crumbs. Mix with hands until well combined. Chill for 30 minutes.

Shape mixture into round balls the size of a walnut. Roll lightly in cornstarch. Place enough oil in electric skillet or deep heavy skillet to allow meatballs to float freely. Heat oil to 370°. Fry meatballs in batches until thoroughly browned. Transfer to chafing dish.

Heat vinegar, pineapple juice, sugar, consommé, soy sauce and ginger in large saucepan.

Add cornstarch to cold water. Stir until smooth. Gradually add to heated mixture and cook over medium heat, stirring constantly until thickened. Pour over meatballs in chafing dish.

Variation: May also be served as a main dish over rice.

Meatballs:
- 5 (8-ounce) cans water chestnuts, drained and finely chopped
- 2 bunches green onions (including tops), finely chopped
- 5 pounds lean ground pork
- ¼ cup soy sauce
- 6 eggs, slightly beaten
- 1 tablespoon (3 teaspoons) salt
- 2½ cups fine dry bread crumbs
- Cornstarch
- Oil

Sauce:
- 1 cup white vinegar
- 2 cups pineapple juice
- ¾ cup granulated sugar
- 2 cups beef consommé
- 2 tablespoons soy sauce
- 3 tablespoons freshly grated ginger (may substitute 1½ teaspoons ground ginger)
- ½ cup cornstarch
- 1 cup cold water

Yield: 300 meatballs
Preparation: 1 hour
Chilling: 30 minutes

Oriental Chicken Wings
Oh my, are these good!

10 chicken wings
½ cup oil
1 small piece ginger root, peeled and sliced
1 tablespoon dry sherry
2½ tablespoons soy sauce
3 tablespoons oyster sauce
1 teaspoon granulated sugar
1 cup water

Yield: 20 pieces
Preparation: 40 minutes
Cooking: 20 minutes

Cut wings at joints. Discard wing tips or third joint. Pat dry with paper towels.

Heat oil in large skillet over medium heat. Add ginger root and ½ the wings. Brown both sides of wings. Remove browned wings; set aside. Repeat process with remaining wings. (The oil tends to spatter so remove skillet from heat about 1 minute before turning or removing wings.)

Drain oil from skillet. Return wings to skillet and add sherry, soy sauce, oyster sauce, sugar and water. Bring to a boil. Cover and simmer for 10 minutes. Remove cover and cook another 10 minutes, basting and turning occasionally. Serve warm in chafing dish.

Note: Oyster sauce can be found in food stores carrying international foods.

Variation: The wings make a wonderful entrée when served with rice.

French Bread Appetizers
Crisp bread with a bite.

2 loaves soft French bread
1 cup (2 sticks) butter, softened
8 ounces Monterey Jack cheese, grated
1 teaspoon Worcestershire sauce
½ teaspoon garlic salt
1 (4-ounce) can chopped green chilies, drained
Mayonnaise

Yield: 3–4 dozen
Preparation: 15 minutes
Broiling: 5 minutes
Temperature: Broil

Preheat oven to broil.

Slice bread into ½-inch slices.

Beat butter in medium-size bowl until creamy. Add cheese, Worcestershire, garlic salt and chilies; combine. Add enough mayonnaise to bind mixture together. Spread each slice of bread heavily with cheese mixture. Place bread, cheese side up, on ungreased cookie sheet. Place cookie sheet on rack in middle of oven and broil until bubbly and lightly browned.

Note: Cheese mixture may be prepared a day ahead. Bring to room temperature before spreading on bread.

Variation: For a fancier looking appetizer, use party rye instead of French bread.

Swiss Onion Squares
Perfect cocktail fare for a hungry crowd.

Preheat oven to 375°.

Combine cracker crumbs and butter in small bowl; press into 8-inch or 9-inch square pan.

Cook bacon until crisp. Drain and crumble. Reserve 2 tablespoons drippings. Sauté onion in drippings until transparent.

Combine bacon, onion, Swiss cheese, sour cream, eggs and pepper in medium-size bowl. Pour over crust.

Bake at 375° for 30 minutes. Top with Cheddar cheese and return to oven for 2–3 minutes. Let stand for 10 minutes before cutting into squares. Serve hot or cold.

- 1 cup crushed saltine crackers
- 4 tablespoons (½ stick) butter, melted
- 6 slices bacon
- 1 cup chopped onion
- 8 ounces Swiss cheese, grated
- ¾ cup sour cream
- 2 eggs, slightly beaten
- Freshly ground pepper
- ½ cup grated sharp Cheddar cheese

Serves: 10–12
Preparation: 15 minutes
Baking: 30 minutes
Standing: 10 minutes
Temperature: 375°

Texas Torte
Rich and spicy.

Preheat oven to 375°.

Mix all ingredients together in large bowl. Pour into an 8-inch square baking dish or a quiche dish. Bake at 375° for 40 minutes. Let stand for 10 minutes. Cut into squares or wedges. Serve warm.

Note: These freeze well after baking. Reheat at 300° until warmed through.

- ¾ pound Monterey Jack cheese, grated
- ¾ pound mozzarella cheese, grated
- 1 (4-ounce) can chopped green chilies, drained
- 3 eggs, beaten
- ⅓ cup milk
- 3 tablespoons all-purpose flour

Yield: 24 squares
Preparation: 15 minutes
Baking: 40 minutes
Standing: 10 minutes
Temperature: 375°

Appetizers

Apricot Brie
Heavenly—melts in your mouth!

12 sheets phyllo dough
1–1½ cups (2–3 sticks) butter, melted
1 (5-pound) whole Brie cheese, not fully ripe
1 (12-ounce) jar apricot preserves

Serves: 20–24
Preparation: 30 minutes
Baking: 20 minutes
Standing: 30 minutes
Temperature: 350°

Preheat oven to 350°.

Butter a 9x13-inch baking sheet.

Layer 6 sheets of phyllo on baking sheet (stagger layers to create a circle), brushing each layer with melted butter. Place Brie in center of phyllo and spread top and sides with apricot preserves. Fold phyllo up around the cheese.

Cover top of cheese with 6 sheets of phyllo, again staggering layers and brushing each with butter. Smooth top and sides. Tuck ends under Brie. Brush top and sides with butter. Bake at 350° for 20–30 minutes or until golden brown. Let stand for 30–45 minutes before serving. Cut into small wedges.

Note: The same procedure may be used on a smaller round of Brie by decreasing the amount of preserves. This may be made a few hours before serving if covered with a barely damp linen towel, then baked according to directions.

Gouda Cheese Round
A elegant package with a zesty taste.

½ cup (1 stick) butter or margarine, softened
2 (3-ounce) packages cream cheese, softened
1 cup all-purpose flour
1 small Gouda cheese round
4 ounces mild chili peppers, drained and chopped

Serves: 10–12
Preparation: 20 minutes
Chilling: 1 hour
Baking: 25 minutes
Temperature: 425°

Preheat oven to 425°.

Combine butter, cream cheese and flour to make a dough. Form into a ball and chill for at least 1 hour.

Pat or roll out dough until it reaches a size sufficient to encase cheese round. Place cheese round in middle of dough. Spread chili peppers over cheese. Bring edges of pastry up to cover cheese and peppers; seal edges. Excess pastry may be used to decorate top. Place in round or square baking dish that is close fitting. (The appetizer will take the shape of its container.) Bake at 425° for 25 minutes. Serve hot with crackers or cut and serve with forks.

Crab Meat Wrapped in Phyllo
Outstanding—definitely worth the effort.

Melt butter in large saucepan over low heat. Add onion; sauté until transparent. Stir in flour; cook until smooth and bubbly. Add milk slowly and mix until creamy. Remove from heat and add parsley, dill, mushrooms, pimiento, eggs, Tabasco, A-1, Maggi, sherry, basil, salt, crab meat and bread crumbs. (Add more bread crumbs if mixture is too loose, more milk if too thick.)

Preheat oven to 350°.

Cut long dough sheets into 3-inch wide, lengthwise strips. Keep strips wrapped in wax paper covered with a damp towel. Work with a single strip at a time.

Brush strip with melted butter. Place 1 teaspoon of crab meat mixture in the center of strip, 1 inch from bottom. Fold bottom of strip over mixture, then fold enclosed mixture upward 2 times. Fold right side ⅓ over and roll upward 2 more times. Fold the left side ⅓ over and roll upward until entire strip is folded into a square. Brush with butter. Repeat for remaining pastry.

Bake at 350° on an ungreased baking sheet for 15–20 minutes or until golden brown.

Note: These may be frozen before baking if fresh or canned crab meat is used. Partially thaw before baking as directed above. They also may be frozen after baking and then reheated, but the phyllo loses some of its crispiness.

- 5 tablespoons butter
- 1 small onion, chopped
- 2 tablespoons all-purpose flour
- 2 cups lukewarm milk
- 1 tablespoon chopped fresh parsley
- 1 tablespoon chopped fresh dill (may substitute 1 teaspoon dried dill weed)
- ½ cup chopped fresh mushrooms
- 1 tablespoon chopped pimiento
- 2 hard-cooked eggs, chopped
- Dash of Tabasco sauce
- 1 tablespoon A-1 sauce
- Dash of Maggi seasoning
- 1 teaspoon dry sherry
- Pinch of dried basil
- Salt
- 1½ pounds lump crab meat
- ½ cup fine bread crumbs
- ½ pound phyllo dough sheets
- ¾ cup (1½ sticks) butter, melted

Yield: 6 dozen
Preparation: 1½ hours
Baking: 15 minutes
Temperature: 350°

Artichoke Appetizer
Little effort—great reward.

1 tablespoon butter
¼ cup chopped onion
1 clove garlic, crushed
4 eggs
2 tablespoons finely chopped fresh parsley
4 dashes Tabasco sauce
Salt
Freshly ground pepper
12 saltine crackers, crushed
½ pound sharp Cheddar cheese, grated
1 (14-ounce) can artichoke hearts, drained and chopped

Preheat oven to 350°.

Grease an 8-inch square baking dish.

Melt butter in small skillet over low heat. Add onion and garlic; sauté over medium heat until tender but do not brown. Set aside.

Blend eggs, parsley, Tabasco, salt and pepper in blender or food processor. Pour into large bowl. Add onions and garlic, crackers, cheese and artichokes. Stir to mix. Pour into prepared baking dish. Bake at 350° for 40–45 minutes. Cut into bite-size squares. Serve warm.

Note: Can be frozen and reheated.

Yield:	28 squares
Preparation:	20 minutes
Baking:	45 minutes
Temperature:	350°

Gouda Wheels
Zesty and so easy to prepare.

6 slices bacon, cooked and crumbled
2 cups grated Gouda cheese
2–3 tablespoons mayonnaise
6 drops Tabasco sauce
1 loaf cocktail rye bread (may substitute small loaf French bread, thinly sliced)

Preheat oven to broil.

Mix bacon, cheese, mayonnaise and Tabasco in small bowl. Spread mixture thickly on slices of bread. Place on baking sheet. Broil for 3–5 minutes or until cheese melts and bubbles.

Yield:	25–30
Preparation:	15 minutes
Broiling:	5 minutes
Temperature:	Broil

 | 33

Sausage and Leek Tarts
These extraordinary tarts are easy to prepare in stages.

Preheat oven to 350°.

Cut out 30 rounds from bread using a 3-inch biscuit cutter. Press rounds firmly with fingers into muffin tin cups (without liners), molding to shape of cups. Melt butter and brush over sides (not bottoms) of bread. Bake at 350° for 25 minutes or until golden brown. Remove from pan and cool. (Toast cups may be made ahead and stored, lightly covered, in container.)

Cut off green tops and root ends from leeks and discard. Split stalks in long thin pieces and wash well. Combine leeks with chicken broth in large saucepan. Bring to a boil; lower heat and simmer for 5 minutes or until leeks are tender. Add browned sausage. Stir in cream; mix well. Process mixture, a little at a time, in food processor or blender until mixture is slushy. Transfer mixture to large bowl and cool.

Spoon cooled sausage mixture into toast cups. Place filled cups on cookie sheet and bake at 350° for 15 minutes. Garnish with parsley, if desired.

Toast Cups:
- 30 slices white bread
- 4 tablespoons (½ stick) butter

Filling:
- 2 leeks
- ¾ cup chicken broth or stock
- 1 pound bulk pork sausage; cooked, drained and crumbled
- ⅓ cup heavy (whipping) cream
- Finely chopped fresh parsley

Yield:	30 tarts
Preparation:	1 hour
Baking:	40 minutes
Temperature:	350°

Zesty Nibbles
Great and quick to fix. Good gift item.

Place oyster crackers in a large plastic container. Warm the oil and pour over crackers.

Combine salad dressing mix, lemon pepper, garlic powder and dill weed in small bowl. Add to crackers and rotate container to gently toss. Let stand in covered container for 24 hours. Shake several times. Place in bowl and serve.

Note: May be made 1½ hours before serving. Will keep for 2 weeks.

- 14 ounces oyster crackers
- ⅓ cup oil
- 1 package buttermilk salad dressing mix
- ½ teaspoon lemon pepper
- ¼ teaspoon garlic powder (more if desired)
- ½ teaspoon dried dill weed

Yield:	1 quart
Preparation:	5 minutes
Standing:	24 hours

Snacks

10 cups quick oats
1 cup sliced almonds
1 cup sesame seed
1 cup unsalted sunflower kernels
1 cup shredded coconut
1 cup soy granules
1 cup dried milk
1 cup wheat germ
1 cup chopped pecans
2 cups bran
1½ cups honey
1 cup oil
2 cups raisins

Yield: 2 pounds
Preparation: 30 minutes
Baking: 40 minutes
Cooking: 1 hour
Temperature: 275°

Granola

This is delicious as a breakfast cereal.

Preheat oven to 275°.

Combine oats, almonds, sesame seed, sunflower kernels, coconut, soy granules, milk, wheat germ, pecans and bran in large bowl.

Heat honey and oil together in medium-size saucepan until blended together. Mix with dry ingredients.

Spread in 2 (11½x17-inch) baking pans. Bake at 275° for 40 minutes. Stir 2 or 3 times. Cool completely. Add 2 cups raisins after mixture cools.

Note: Store in refrigerator. Freezes well.

---

2 cups all-purpose flour
2 cups grated sharp Cheddar cheese
1 cup (2 sticks) butter, softened
1 teaspoon salt
2–4 tablespoons cold water
2 cups Rice Krispies
Dash of Worcestershire sauce

Yield: 3–4 dozen
Preparation: 30 minutes
Baking: 15 minutes
Temperature: 400°

Cheese Pennies

Good as a snack or as alternative to bread.

Preheat oven to 400°.

Combine flour, cheese, butter and salt in large bowl. Add cold water as needed to moisten. Add cereal and Worcestershire. Form into 1-inch balls and place on ungreased cookie sheet. Flatten balls with a fork. Bake at 400° for 12–15 minutes. Serve warm.

Note: These freeze well after baking. Reheat at 300° until warm.

Chinese Fried Walnuts
Terrific to give as a gift.

Place water in 4-quart saucepan; bring to a boil over high heat. Add walnuts and bring back to a boil. Cook for 1 minute; drain. Rinse walnuts under running hot water; drain. Wash saucepan and dry well.

Combine warm walnuts with sugar in large bowl; stir gently with rubber spatula until sugar is dissolved. (If necessary, let mixture stand for 5 minutes to dissolve sugar.)

Pour oil in same 4-quart saucepan until it measures about 1-inch. Heat oil, according to manufacturer's directions or heat until it registers 350° on a deep-fat thermometer. Add about ½ the walnuts to oil with slotted spoon. Fry for 5 minutes or until golden, stirring often.

Remove walnuts with slotted spoon. Place in coarse sieve over bowl to drain. Sprinkle very lightly with salt. Toss gently to keep walnuts from sticking together. Transfer to paper towels to cool. Fry remaining walnuts. Store in tightly covered container.

- 6 cups water
- 4 cups whole walnuts, shelled
- ½ cup granulated sugar
- Oil
- Salt

Yield: 4 cups
Preparation: 30 minutes

White Chocolate Party Mix
Terrific and really different.

Slowly melt white chocolate in top of double boiler over simmering water.

Combine Rice Chex, Corn Chex, Cheerios, pretzels, peanuts and M&M's in large bowl. Slowly pour chocolate over mixture and stir to evenly coat. Spread the mixture on wax paper and cool. Break into small pieces. Store in airtight container and refrigerate to keep fresh.

- 1 pound white chocolate
- 3 cups Rice Chex cereal
- 3 cups Corn Chex cereal
- 3 cups Cheerios cereal
- 2 cups stick pretzels
- 2 cups dry roasted peanuts
- 1 (12-ounce) package M&M's plain candy

Yield: 12–14 cups
Preparation: 15 minutes

Claire's Almond Punch

The almond and vanilla give this a delightful taste.

3 lemons
2 cups granulated sugar
1 quart water
2 cups strong tea
20 ounces pineapple juice (approximately 2½ cups)
1 teaspoon vanilla
1 teaspoon almond extract
1 quart ginger ale, chilled

Yield: 3½ quarts
Preparation: 10 minutes
Chilling: 4–6 hours

Squeeze juice from lemons into a small bowl. Set aside. Reserve rinds.

Place sugar, water and reserved lemon rinds in large saucepan or Dutch oven. Boil for 3 minutes. Add lemon juice, tea, pineapple juice, vanilla and almond extract. Strain into 4-quart bowl or container. Chill.

Add ginger ale when ready to serve.

Note: The base for this punch can be kept in the refrigerator for up to a week and be combined with ginger ale as needed.

Banana Fruit Punch

Fruity liquid refreshment.

6 cups water
4 cups granulated sugar
Juice of 5 oranges
Juice of 2 lemons
52 ounces pineapple juice
5 medium bananas, puréed
2 (1-liter) bottles club soda, chilled

Yield: 50 (4-ounce) servings
Preparation: 30 minutes
Freezing: 4–6 hours

Combine water and sugar in medium-size saucepan. Boil for 5 minutes. Cool. Pour into large freezer container. Add orange juice, lemon juice, pineapple juice and banana purée. Freeze for several hours. Scoop into punch bowl and add club soda. Stir to a slushy consistency.

Note: Frozen mixture may be kept in the freezer and small portions used as desired.

Champagne Punch
A lovely complement to any luncheon.

Combine concentrates, apple juice and water. Chill for 4–6 hours. Serve by adding chilled champagne to juice mixture in large punch bowl.

1	(12-ounce) can frozen orange juice concentrate, thawed
1	(12-ounce) can frozen lemonade concentrate, thawed
1	quart apple juice
6	cups water
2	bottles champagne, chilled

Yield: 5 quarts
Preparation: 5 minutes
Chilling: 4–6 hours

Spiced Tea Special
Light and refreshing.

Combine tea, allspice, cinnamon and nutmeg in medium-size container. Pour boiling water over tea and spices. Cover and steep for 5 minutes. Strain into 2-quart jar or other container. Add sugar and cool. Add cranberry juice, water, orange juice and lemon juice. Chill. Serve over ice. Garnish with lemon slices.

2	tablespoons loose tea
¼	teaspoon ground allspice
¼	teaspoon ground cinnamon
¼	teaspoon ground nutmeg
2½	cups boiling water
¾	cup granulated sugar
1	pint cranberry juice
1½	cups water
½	cup fresh orange juice
⅓	cup fresh lemon juice
	Lemon slices

Yield: 6 (8-ounce) servings
Preparation: 30 minutes
Cooling: 30 minutes
Chilling: 4–6 hours

Beverages

Juice of 6 lemons, reserve rind of 2 lemons
Juice of 6 oranges, reserve rind of 1 orange
½ cup crushed fresh mint leaves
2 cups granulated sugar
2 cups water

Suggested Mixers:
Water
Club soda
Ginger ale
Unsweetened ice tea

Yield: 3 quarts
Preparation: 25 minutes
Cooling: 1 hour

4 tea bags
2 cups boiling water
2 cups granulated sugar
5 cups cold water
1 (12-ounce) can frozen lemonade concentrate, thawed
1 (12-ounce) can frozen orange juice concentrate, thawed
1 pint apricot brandy
2 (1-liter) bottles club soda, chilled

Yield: 1 gallon
Preparation: 10 minutes
Cooking: 20 minutes
Cooling: 30 minutes
Freezing: 4–6 hours

Miss Ora's Mint Cooler
Thank you, Miss Ora!

Grate reserved lemon rinds and orange rind. Set aside.

Combine lemon juice and orange juice in a 2-quart, heat-resistant container. Add crushed mint leaves.

Combine sugar and water in medium-size saucepan. Boil for 5 minutes. Pour hot syrup over juices and mint leaves. Add orange and lemon rinds. Cool. Strain to remove mint leaves and rind.

Serve by pouring equal parts juice mixture and mixer over ice.

Apricot Brandy Slush
Oh, so tasty.

Steep tea in boiling water in large bowl for 20 minutes. Add sugar and stir until dissolved. Stir in cold water. Cool.

Stir in lemonade and orange juice concentrates and brandy. Pour into 1 or 2 plastic containers. Freeze.

Serve by scooping 1 cup of frozen mixture into a 12-ounce glass. Fill with club soda and stir to a slushy consistency.

Kahlúa
Spoon over ice cream for a real taste treat.

Combine sugar, water, coffee and salt in medium-size saucepan. Bring to a boil. Reduce heat and simmer for 1 hour or until syrupy. Add vodka and vanilla. Store in covered container for 10 days before serving.

Note: This boils over easily. Watch carefully while heating.

- 4 cups granulated sugar
- 3 cups water
- 1 cup instant coffee
- ¼ teaspoon salt
- 2½ cups vodka
- 3 tablespoons vanilla

Preparation: 5 minutes
Cooking: 1 hour
Standing: 10 days

Berry Good Hot Cider
It is the berries!

Combine apple cider, berries, cinnamon and cloves in a large saucepan. Heat to boiling; reduce heat. Cover and simmer for 10 minutes. Strain through sieve lined with cheesecloth.

Serve by pouring into heat-proof cups. Float an apple wedge in each cup.

- 8 cups apple cider
- 1 (10-ounce) package frozen unsweetened red raspberries (may substitute 10-ounce package frozen unsweetened sliced strawberries)
- 1 (4-inch) cinnamon stick
- 1½ teaspoons whole cloves
- 1 medium apple, cut into 8–10 wedges

Serves: 8–10
Preparation: 10 minutes
Cooking: 10 minutes

Beverages

2 quarts cranberry juice
4 (6-ounce) cans frozen orange juice concentrate, thawed
8 cups water
4 tablespoons granulated sugar
1 teaspoon ground allspice
13 cups (104 ounces) sauterne
Red food coloring
Thick orange slices studded with whole cloves

Yield: 7 quarts
Preparation: 30 minutes

¾ cup Kahlúa
½ cup light rum
¼ cup creme de cacao
½ gallon vanilla ice cream, divided

Yield: 2 quarts
Preparation: 5 minutes

½ cup fresh orange juice
¼ cup fresh lemon juice
½ teaspoon freshly grated lemon rind
1 cup lemon sherbet
10 ice cubes, crushed
2 tablespoons dry sherry (optional)

Yield: 4 servings
Preparation: 5 minutes

Wassail
Christmas merriment.

Combine cranberry juice, orange juice concentrate, water, sugar and allspice in a large pot or Dutch oven. Heat to almost simmering. Add sauterne. Continue heating but *do not boil*. Add food coloring to desired color. Float clove-studded orange slices on top.

Hummers
Creamy and so delicious.

Place Kahlúa, rum, creme de cacao and ½ the ice cream in blender. Blend until smooth. Add remaining ice cream gradually and blend until smooth.

Citrus Frappé
Very refreshing.

Combine orange juice, lemon juice and lemon rind in blender. Blend for 5 seconds. Add sherbet and ice cubes. Blend for 1 minute or until frothy. Add sherry, if desired, and blend for 5 seconds. Serve immediately in parfait or sherbet glasses.

Note: Lemon sherbet is usually available at ice cream specialty stores.

Soups and Sandwiches

Historic Preservation

Indianapolis stands as a leader among American cities winning their battles to restore and preserve their architectural legacies.

Internationally famed architect Nathaniel Owings, a native of Indianapolis whose ancestral roots in this city go back to its founding in 1821, said of his hometown: "Indianapolis shaped my point of view for life. Tree-lined vistas, broad boulevards, and solid buildings with granite, marble and stone, bronze and copper, confirmed from birth my instinct for permanence and a predilection for style." Indianapolis is determined to save these buildings.

Union Station, the nation's first centralized railway station, still stands intact in downtown Indianapolis. A splendid example of Romanesque revival architecture, the building is constructed of pink granite and brickwork. A planned total renovation will place beneath its spectacular 70-foot barrel-vaulted ceiling, a complex of fine shops and restaurants. Soon, this magnificent building will once more resound to the bustle of activity that characterized it in its heyday.

Our centrally located City Market which dates from 1821, was scheduled for destruction in 1958. Saved by a public outcry, the handsomely renovated structure continues to serve the purpose for which it was designated by city planners 165 years ago. Throughout Indianapolis's downtown area, historic buildings have been rescued for a variety of innovative adaptive uses, reappearing as condominiums, offices, restaurants and theaters.

This regard for tradition is widely visible in Indianapolis's diverse residential neighborhoods. The stately homes lining Meridian Street, our major north-south artery, always attract the admiring comments of visitors. Areas like Lockerbie Square, a singular downtown residential enclave, are bases of authentic Victorian charm in the very core of a modern metropolis.

In Indianapolis, the best of our distinguished past has become a symbol of our aware present and a key to our promising future. Our "instinct for permanence" is a winning attitude.

SOUPS AND SANDWICHES

Hot Soups
Bloody Mary Soup . . . 53
Boothbay Chowder . . . 41
Brie Soup au Sherry . . . 58
Cauliflower-Cheese Soup . . . 48
Cheese Dumplings in Tomato Soup . . . 45
Chicken Cheese Chowder . . . 41
Cock-a-Leekie Soup . . . 49
Cream of Broccoli Soup . . . 57
Cream of Parisian Vegetable Soup . . . 53
Cuban Black Bean Soup . . . 63
Curried Pea Soup . . . 49
Curry Soup . . . 62
Harvest Moon Chowder . . . 42
Hearty Mushroom Barley . . . 47
Hearty Potato Soup . . . 52
Italian Mushroom Soup . . . 60
Italian Vegetable Soup . . . 54
Kielbasa Soup . . . 51
King's Arm Tavern Cream of Peanut Soup . . . 57
L.S. Ayres Chicken Velvet Soup . . . 56
Old-Fashioned Vegetable Soup . . . 55
Pumpkin Soup . . . 56
Shrimp Bisque . . . 42
Sour and Hot Soup . . . 61
Spicy New England Clam Chowder . . . 43
Spinach-Lentil Soup . . . 60
Springtime Soup . . . 45
Tomato Bisque . . . 44
Tortilla Soup . . . 59
Watercress Soup . . . 58
Wiener Kalbseinmachsuppe (Veal Soup) . . . 50
Winter Soup . . . 46

Cold Soups
Chilled French Pea Soup . . . 66
Cold Carrot-Potato Soup . . . 65
Cold Cream of Cucumber Soup . . . 64
Hungarian Cold Sour Cherry Soup . . . 66
Quick Spinach Soup . . . 65
Squash Soup . . . 63

Sandwiches
Avocado-Pita Sandwich . . . 70
Family Favorite . . . 68
Hot Avocado Crab Sandwiches . . . 67
Mushroom Delights . . . 68
Pita Pockets with Steak and Mushrooms . . . 70
Shrimp and Camembert en Croissant . . . 69
Stroganoff Steak Sandwich . . . 67
Tijuana Tidbits . . . 69

Boothbay Chowder
Excellent flavor and consistency.

Cook bacon in heavy Dutch oven until crisp. Drain bacon on paper towel. Set aside. Add onion to bacon drippings. Sauté over medium heat until transparent. Add potatoes, water, salt and pepper. Cover and simmer for 12 minutes or until potatoes are tender. Remove pan from heat.

Drain liquid from clams into a 4-cup measure. Reserve clams. Add bottled clam juice and cream to liquid. Stir flour briskly into clam liquid in cup. Add to potato mixture in Dutch oven. Cook, stirring constantly over medium heat, until chowder thickens. Let bubble for 1 minute. Add clams and heat until piping hot. Sprinkle with parsley and bacon.

Variation: *May sauté ½ pound sliced mushrooms in 3 tablespoons butter. Add drained mushrooms to chowder with clams and heat through.*

- 3 strips bacon, diced
- 1 large onion, chopped
- 4 medium potatoes, peeled and diced
- 2 cups water
- 1 teaspoon salt
- ¼ teaspoon pepper
- 2 (10½-ounce) cans minced clams
- 1 (8-ounce) bottle clam juice
- 1 cup light (coffee) cream
- 3 tablespoons all-purpose flour
- 2 tablespoons finely chopped fresh parsley

Serves: 6–8
Preparation: 30 minutes
Cooking: 20 minutes

Chicken-Cheese Chowder
Delicious way to remove winter's chill.

Sauté carrots and onions in butter in large saucepan until tender but not brown. Stir in flour and cook until smooth and bubbly; add milk and chicken broth. Cook, stirring constantly until thickened. Stir in chicken, wine, celery seed and Worcestershire. Heat through. Add cheese; stir until melted. Garnish with snipped chives.

Note: *If soup is not thick enough, thicken further by mixing 1 tablespoon flour with ½ cup chicken broth until combination is watery. Add to soup and cook until thickened.*

Variation: *For a spicier soup, add ¼ cup seeded and diced green peppers when cooking the carrots and onions. Add ¼ cup chopped pimientos along with cheese.*

- 1 cup shredded carrots
- ¼ cup chopped onion
- 4 tablespoons (½ stick) butter
- ¼ cup all-purpose flour
- 2 cups milk
- 1¾ cups chicken broth or stock
- 1 cup diced cooked chicken
- 1 tablespoon dry white wine
- ½ teaspoon celery seed
- ½ teaspoon Worcestershire sauce
- 1 cup grated, sharp processed American cheese
- Freshly snipped chives

Serves: 8
Preparation: 30 minutes

Harvest Moon Chowder

A family favorite.

- 1 large onion, finely chopped
- 1 cup peeled and thinly sliced carrots
- 1 cup broccoli flowerets
- 1 cup peeled and finely diced potatoes
- ½ cup finely diced celery
- 2 cups chicken broth or stock
- ¼ cup (½ stick) butter or margarine
- 4 tablespoons all-purpose flour
- 1 (13-ounce) can evaporated milk
- 2 cups milk
- 1 cup grated Cheddar cheese
- Croutons (optional)

Serves: 6
Preparation: 25 minutes
Cooking: 30 minutes

Place onion, carrots, broccoli, potatoes, celery and chicken broth in large kettle or Dutch oven. Simmer for 10–15 minutes or until vegetables are tender.

Melt butter in small saucepan over low heat. Stir in flour. Cook, stirring constantly until bubbly. Add evaporated milk gradually, stirring constantly until thick and smooth. Add to vegetable mixture. Simmer over low heat until thickened. Add cheese; stir until melted. Serve garnished with croutons.

Variation: For a thicker soup, add 1 cup mashed potatoes. May also add 1 cup chopped, cooked chicken.

Shrimp Bisque

Easy and so good.

- ¾ cup (1½ sticks) butter
- ¾ cup all-purpose flour
- 7½ cups milk
- 3 (10¾-ounce) cans shrimp soup, undiluted
- 3 cups heavy (whipping) cream
- 2½–3 pounds shrimp; cooked, shelled, deveined and chopped
- ¾ cup dry sherry
- Salt
- Freshly ground pepper
- Worcestershire sauce

Serves: 8–12
Preparation: 30 minutes

Melt butter in Dutch oven over low heat. Stir in flour; cook until smooth and bubbly. Add milk gradually and stir until thickened. Add soup, cream, shrimp and sherry. Season with salt, pepper and Worcestershire to taste. Stir until heated through.

Note: May be made ahead and reheated on low.

Spicy New England Clam Chowder
A real winner.

Melt butter in 4-quart saucepan over medium heat. Add flour, salt and cayenne. Stir until smooth. Remove from heat. Add milk all at once and whisk thoroughly. Add remaining ingredients. Simmer for 1 hour, stirring occasionally.

Note: This is better made the day before. It freezes well.

- ½ cup (1 stick) butter or margarine
- ½ cup plus 3 tablespoons all-purpose flour
- 1½ teaspoons seasoned salt
- ½ teaspoon cayenne pepper
- 3 cups milk
- 5 (6½-ounce) cans minced clams, undrained
- 2 medium carrots, coarsely grated
- 2 medium red potatoes; boiled, peeled and diced
- 1 medium onion, diced
- ¼ cup chopped fresh parsley
- 1 teaspoon dried sweet basil
- 1 teaspoon dried rosemary leaves
- 1 cup sour cream
- 1 teaspoon coarsely ground pepper

Yield: 12 cups
Preparation: 30 minutes
Cooking: 1 hour

Soups

- ¼ pound bacon, sliced
- 4 large cloves garlic, minced
- 1½ onions, finely chopped
- 6 celery stalks, finely chopped
- 1 bay leaf
- 1 teaspoon dried thyme
- 1 (28-ounce) can tomatoes, diced (reserve juice)
- 1 (6-ounce) can tomato paste

- 2 tablespoons butter
- 3 tablespoons all-purpose flour
- 1 quart heavy (whipping) cream, at room temperature
- ½ onion, finely chopped
- 1 small bay leaf
- 2 whole cloves
- Salt
- Freshly ground pepper

Serves: 8–10
Preparation: 30 minutes
Cooking: 1½ hours

Tomato Bisque
Rich and creamy.

Cook bacon in large skillet until fat is rendered; remove bacon and reserve for another use. Add garlic to fat and sauté lightly. Add onion, celery, bay leaf and thyme; sauté over medium heat until onion is transparent. Add tomatoes with juice and tomato paste. Bring to a boil, stirring occasionally. Reduce heat; cover and simmer for 30 minutes.

Melt butter over low heat in large saucepan. Stir in flour; bring to a boil, stirring constantly. Remove from heat and slowly add cream. Add onion, bay leaf and cloves. Place over medium heat and cook, uncovered, for 45 minutes, stirring occasionally. Strain through fine strainer into tomato mixture. Add salt and pepper. Cover and simmer, stirring occasionally, about 15 minutes. Add milk, if thinner consistency is preferred.

Cheese Dumplings in Tomato Soup
Easy supper for two.

Combine tomato juice, cheese, dry milk, Worcestershire and water in large saucepan. Cook over low heat until cheese melts.

Place bread in blender. Blend until crumbled. Combine bread crumbs, egg, cheese, salt and pepper in a small bowl; mix well. Drop by teaspoonfuls into hot soup. Simmer, covered, for 10 minutes.

Note: May easily be doubled or tripled.

1	cup tomato juice
1	cup grated Cheddar cheese
½	tablespoon non-fat dry milk
¼	teaspoon Worcestershire sauce
¼	cup water

Dumplings:

1	slice coarse white bread
1	egg, slightly beaten
⅓	cup grated Cheddar cheese
¼	teaspoon salt
⅛	teaspoon pepper

Serves: 2
Preparation: 10 minutes
Cooking: 10 minutes

Springtime Soup
Easy, creamy vegetable soup.

Heat butter until frothy in large Dutch oven. Add onions and sauté over medium heat until tender. Add cream and broth. Beat with fork or whisk until well blended. Add potatoes, carrots and rice; bring to a boil. Lower heat; cover and simmer for 15 minutes. Stir in asparagus and spinach. Cook for an additional 15 minutes. Add salt and pepper before serving.

6	tablespoons butter
1	cup chopped green onions
2	cups light (coffee) cream
5	cups boiling chicken broth or stock
2	potatoes, peeled and sliced
2	medium carrots, peeled and sliced
¼	cup long grain rice
1½	cups fresh asparagus, cut into 1-inch pieces (may substitute 10-ounce package chopped frozen asparagus)
1	pound fresh spinach, chopped (may substitute 10-ounce package chopped frozen spinach)
1	teaspoon salt
	Freshly ground pepper

Serves: 6
Preparation: 30 minutes
Cooking: 30 minutes

Soups

Winter Soup

Satisfies a winter appetite.

- 3 medium onions, chopped
- 1 pound ground beef
- 1 clove garlic, minced
- 3 cups beef stock or broth
- 1 (28-ounce) can tomatoes
- 1 cup sliced celery
- 1 cup peeled and diced potatoes
- 1 cup sliced carrots
- 1 cup trimmed and cut-up green beans
- 1 (12-ounce) can corn, drained
- 1 cup dry red wine
- 1 tablespoon chopped fresh parsley
- ½ teaspoon dried basil
- 1 tablespoon (3 teaspoons) salt
- ¼ teaspoon dried thyme
- Freshly ground pepper

Cook onions, beef and garlic together in Dutch oven over medium heat until beef is browned. Drain grease completely. Add remaining ingredients. Bring to a boil. Reduce heat and simmer for 1 hour. Season to taste.

Serves: 6
Preparation: 25 minutes
Cooking: 1 hour

HINT:
Season soups and other dishes with lemon juice for no-salt cooking.

Hearty Mushroom Barley Soup
Sherry is the perfect touch.

Melt butter in large saucepan or Dutch oven. Sauté onion, carrots and mushrooms over medium heat for 10 minutes. Stir in flour. Add stock and heat, stirring constantly until mixture comes to a boil. Add barley.

Cover and simmer soup until barley is cooked through, about 20 minutes. Stir in milk, poultry, Worcestershire, sherry, salt and pepper. Heat thoroughly and serve.

3	tablespoons butter
½	cup diced onion
½	cup peeled and diced carrot
½	pound fresh mushrooms, sliced
1	tablespoon all-purpose flour
3	cups chicken broth or stock
½	cup medium barley
2	cups milk
1½	cups diced cooked turkey or chicken
2	teaspoons Worcestershire sauce
1	tablespoon dry sherry (optional)
	Salt
	Freshly ground pepper

Serves: 8
Preparation: 25 minutes
Cooking: 25 minutes

HINT:
Cornstarch or arrowroot can be substituted for flour as a thickener, but use only half as much.

Soups 47

Soups

- 3½ cups cauliflowerets, divided
- 2 cups peeled and diced potato
- 1 cup chopped carrots
- 3 medium cloves garlic
- 1 cup chopped onion
- 1½ teaspoons salt
- 4 cups chicken stock or broth
- 1½ cups grated Cheddar cheese
- ¾ cup milk
- ¼ teaspoon dried dill weed
- ¼ teaspoon caraway seed (optional)
- ¼ teaspoon dry mustard
- Freshly ground pepper
- 2 tablespoons butter
- ¾ cup buttermilk
- Chopped green onions

Serves: 6
Preparation: 25 minutes
Cooking: 40 minutes

Cauliflower-Cheese Soup

Buttermilk is the magic in this hearty soup.

Combine 2 cups cauliflowerets, potatoes, carrots, garlic, onion, salt and chicken stock in large kettle or Dutch oven. Bring to a boil; cover and simmer for 15 minutes. Let cool for 10 minutes. Purée mixture in blender until smooth and creamy.

Transfer mixture to large kettle or Dutch oven. Whisk in cheese, milk, dill weed, caraway seed, mustard and pepper. Heat soup slowly over low heat.

Cut remaining 1½ cups cauliflowerets into small bits. Sauté in butter in small skillet over medium heat until tender. Add to soup mixture. Whisk in buttermilk. Heat through. Serve topped with chopped green onions and extra grated cheese.

Note: May be prepared ahead and may be frozen.

Cock-a-Leekie Soup
Top ratings and rightly so.

Combine chicken and water in large kettle or Dutch oven. Add carrots, celery, onion, parsley, salt, pepper and bay leaf. Cover and simmer for 25 minutes or until chicken is tender.

Remove chicken, bay leaf and parsley from broth. Discard bay leaf and parsley. Cool chicken until it can be easily handled. Skin and bone chicken. Cut into small pieces and set aside.

Add leeks (reserving a few for garnish), potato and barley to soup. Bring to a boil. Reduce heat and simmer, covered, for 15–20 minutes.

Stir in cream and chicken. Heat through. Top with sliced leeks, if desired.

Curried Pea Soup
Soup is even more distinctive when served cold.

Place peas, onion, carrot, garlic, celery, potato, salt, curry and 1 cup of chicken broth in medium-size saucepan. Bring to a boil; cover and simmer for 15 minutes or until peas are tender.

Place vegetables and liquid into container of blender. Cover and blend on high speed for 6 seconds. Remove cover and with motor on, add remaining cup of chicken broth and the cream.

Serve hot or chill overnight and serve cold.

Soups | 49

- 2½–3 pounds chicken pieces
- 4 cups water
- ½ cup finely chopped carrot
- ½ cup finely chopped celery
- ¼ cup finely chopped onion
- 2 sprigs fresh parsley
- 2 teaspoons salt
- ¼ teaspoon white pepper
- 1 bay leaf
- ½ pound leeks, washed and thinly sliced (about 1½ cups), divided
- 1 small potato, peeled and chopped (about ½ cup)
- ½ cup quick-cooking barley
- 2 cups light (coffee) cream

Serves: 8
Preparation: 35 minutes
Cooking: 25 minutes

- 1½ pounds fresh peas, hulled (may substitute 10-ounce package frozen peas)
- 1 medium onion, sliced
- 1 small carrot, sliced
- 1 clove garlic
- 1 stalk celery with leaves, sliced
- 1 medium potato, peeled and sliced
- 1 teaspoon salt
- 1 teaspoon curry
- 2 cups chicken stock or broth, divided
- 1 cup heavy (whipping) cream

Serves: 6
Preparation: 15 minutes
Cooking: 15 minutes

Soups

Wiener Kalbseinmachsuppe (Veal Soup)

A specialty of the house at the Glass Chimney.

6	tablespoons butter, divided
1	pound boneless veal shoulder, cut into ¾-inch cubes
2	medium carrots, chopped
½	large onion, chopped
1	celery stalk, chopped
1	small leek; washed, trimmed and chopped
¼	cup coarsely chopped pimiento
6	cups veal or beef broth (preferably homemade)
1	tablespoon chopped fresh parsley
¼	teaspoon dried marjoram, crumbled
¼	teaspoon dried thyme, crumbled
1	bay leaf
⅛	teaspoon freshly grated nutmeg
	Salt
	Freshly ground pepper
¼	cup all-purpose flour
2	eggs
	Chopped fresh parsley

Serves: 6–8
Preparation: 1 hour
Cooking: 50 minutes

Melt 2 tablespoons butter in heavy Dutch oven over medium-high heat. Pat veal dry with paper towels. Add veal and sauté until lightly browned on all sides. Stir in carrots, onion, celery, leek and pimiento. Sauté for 5 minutes. Add broth, parsley, marjoram, thyme, bay leaf, nutmeg, salt and pepper; bring to a boil. Reduce heat and simmer until meat is tender, about 45 minutes. Taste and adjust seasoning, if necessary.

Melt remaining 4 tablespoons butter in small saucepan over low heat. Whisk in flour; cook and stir for 3 minutes. Gradually whisk roux into soup. Continue simmering for 5 minutes.

Beat eggs in small bowl and gradually whisk 1½ cups hot soup into eggs. Return egg mixture to soup and stir through. Remove from heat; taste and adjust seasoning. Ladle soup into heated bowls. Sprinkle with parsley and serve.

Kielbasa Soup
A hearty winter meal.

Melt ¼ cup butter in large kettle or Dutch oven over low heat. Add carrots and celery; sauté until vegetables are softened. Add leeks and cabbage; sauté for 3 minutes. Stir in chicken stock. Bring to a boil. Reduce heat and simmer for 15 minutes.

Melt remaining ¼ cup butter in large skillet over low heat. Add flour, stirring constantly for 3 minutes. Remove skillet from heat; whisk in 2 cups hot soup. Pour flour mixture into kettle, stirring continuously. Add potatoes and marjoram. Simmer for 10 minutes. Stir in kielbasa; simmer for 15 minutes or until vegetables are tender. Add salt and pepper to taste. Garnish each serving with parsley and dill, if desired.

Note: *The soup improves each time it is reheated.*

- ½ cup (1 stick) butter, divided
- ½ cup coarsely chopped carrots
- ½ cup minced celery
- 3 cups leeks, washed and sliced into ½-inch pieces
- 2 cups shredded cabbage
- 2 quarts chicken stock or broth
- 5 tablespoons all-purpose flour
- 2 cups peeled and cubed potatoes
- ½ teaspoon dried marjoram
- ¾ pound lean Polish kielbasa, skinned and thinly sliced (about 2 cups)
- Salt
- White pepper
- Finely chopped fresh parsley
- Fresh dill weed (optional)

Serves: 8
Preparation: 1 hour, 10 minutes

Soups

3–4 medium potatoes, peeled
3 cups peeled and cubed potatoes
1 cup peeled and sliced carrots
½ cup sliced celery
4 tablespoons (½ stick) butter
3 tablespoons all-purpose flour
3 cups milk
½ pound bacon
1–2 cups washed and sliced leeks
Salt
Freshly ground pepper
Garlic salt
Chopped fresh parsley

Serves: 6–8
Preparation: 1 hour
Cooking: 45–60 minutes

Hearty Potato Soup

This soup requires many pans but it is well worth the effort.

Place 3–4 medium potatoes in large saucepan. Cover with water and boil until tender. Drain and mash thoroughly, using some of liquid in which the potatoes were cooked.

Cover cubed potatoes, carrots and celery with water in large saucepan and boil until tender. *Do not drain.*

Melt butter over low heat in 8-quart saucepan. Stir in flour and cook until smooth and bubbly. Add milk slowly and stir until sauce thickens. Combine sauce with vegetable mixture and liquid in saucepan. Add mashed potatoes and mix until well combined. (If thicker soup is desired, combine 1 tablespoon flour with small amount of hot soup. Stir until blended. Return to soup pot and stir until thickened.)

Cut bacon into small pieces and fry in medium skillet until crisp. Remove bacon with slotted spoon. Set aside. Sauté leeks in bacon drippings. Remove leeks with slotted spoon and add to soup. Season to taste with salt, pepper, garlic salt and parsley. Cook over low heat until warm. Be careful not to scorch. Pour soup into bowls and sprinkle with crumbled bacon.

Note: Leeks have a distinctive flavor and should be used if possible. Onion is not an equal substitute.

Soups

Cream of Parisian Vegetable Soup
Great supper with salad and bread.

Place frozen vegetables and water in large saucepan. Cook over medium heat until tender. Remove from heat; add fresh mushrooms and cover. Set aside. *Do not drain.*

Melt butter and margarine over medium heat in 6-quart Dutch oven. Add celery and onion; sauté until tender. Stir in flour and cook until bubbly. Stir in crushed bouillon cubes. Add cold milk, stirring until thick and smooth. Add ham, pepper and monosodium glutamate. Stir in vegetables and their liquid. Heat until steaming.

Note: May be frozen.

1	(20-ounce) package frozen cauliflower/broccoli/carrot combination
2	cups water
¼	pound fresh mushrooms, sliced
½	cup (1 stick) butter
½	cup (1 stick) margarine
½	cup chopped celery
½	cup chopped onion
1	cup all-purpose flour
4	chicken bouillon cubes, crushed
6	cups cold milk
1–2	cups cubed cooked ham
1	teaspoon white pepper
1	teaspoon monosodium glutamate (optional)

Yield: 12 cups
Preparation: 30 minutes

Bloody Mary Soup
Perfect for tailgate parties—served hot or cold.

Melt butter in large saucepan. Sauté onion and celery in butter over medium heat. Add tomato purée and sugar. Cook for 1 minute. Add V-8 juice and simmer for 8 minutes. Stir in remaining ingredients. Strain. Serve hot or well chilled.

2	tablespoons butter
1	medium onion, diced
3	celery stalks, diced
2	tablespoons tomato purée
1	tablespoon sugar
5	cups V-8 juice (may substitute tomato juice)
1	tablespoon (3 teaspoons) salt (optional)
2	teaspoons Worcestershire sauce
¼	teaspoon pepper
1	tablespoon fresh lemon juice
4	ounces vodka

Serves: 6
Preparation: 20 minutes

Soups

¼ pound bacon, diced
¼ pound ham, chopped
¼ pound Italian sausage, chopped
2 cloves garlic, minced
1 large onion, sliced
2 stalks celery, diced
1 medium-size zucchini, sliced
1 leek, thoroughly washed and sliced
    Ground allspice
    Freshly ground pepper
2 quarts beef consommé or soup stock
½ cup kidney beans, drained
2 cups shredded cabbage
1 cup red wine
1 pound tomatoes, peeled and chopped
½ cup macaroni or small noodles
¼ cup fresh basil (may substitute 1 tablespoon dried basil)
    Freshly grated Parmesan cheese

Serves: 8
Preparation: 30 minutes
Cooking: 2 hours

Italian Vegetable Soup

Great flavor gets even better with reheating.

Place bacon, ham, sausage and garlic in large skillet. Cook over medium heat until bacon is crisp and sausage is cooked. Add onion, celery, zucchini, leek, pinch of allspice and pepper. Simmer for 10 minutes.

Heat stock in large soup kettle. Add contents of skillet and beans. Stir in cabbage and wine. Simmer for 1½ hours. Add tomatoes and macaroni; cook for 15 minutes. Add basil about 3 minutes before serving and top with cheese.

Old-Fashioned Vegetable Soup
Wonderfully rich flavor.

Brown all meat in hot fat in large kettle. Add water and soup bone; simmer for 1½–2 hours. Remove bone and skim fat from top of soup. Add remaining ingredients. Cook an additional 20–30 minutes or until vegetables are tender. Remove peppercorns and serve.

Note: Soup gets better every time it is reheated.

- 1 beef soup bone, meat removed and cut into small chunks
- 1–1½ pounds stew meat, cut into bite-size chunks
- 1–2 tablespoons fat
- 6 cups water
- 1 medium onion, chopped
- 1 cup peeled and cubed potatoes
- 1 cup peeled and sliced carrots
- 1 cup sliced celery
- 1 (16-ounce) can tomatoes, cut-up
- 3 sprigs parsley, finely chopped
- 1 tablespoon (3 teaspoons) salt
- ½ bay leaf, crumbled
- 3 peppercorns, tied in cheesecloth bag
- ¼ teaspoon dried marjoram
- ¼ teaspoon dried thyme
- ¼ teaspoon chili powder
- 2 teaspoons Worcestershire sauce
- 2 cups tomato juice

Serves: 6–8
Preparation: 30 minutes
Cooking: 2 hours

Soups

Pumpkin Soup
Perfect for fall luncheon or holiday dinner.

Cut off top of pumpkin; remove pulp and seeds. Cut enough meat from inside pumpkin to make 3 cups. Set aside pumpkin shell and top to use as serving container.

Heat butter in large saucepan over low heat. Add pumpkin and tomatoes. (If using canned tomatoes, add after pumpkin has cooked.) Cook over low heat for 5 minutes. *Do not brown*. Add water, chicken broth, rice, potatoes, salt and pepper. Simmer for 40–60 minutes.

Purée soup, a little at a time, in blender or food processor. Return soup to saucepan and keep warm until ready to serve. Pour soup into pumpkin shell and garnish with nutmeg. Replace pumpkin top to keep soup hot. Ladle soup from pumpkin to serve.

Note: Soup may be made ahead and reheated. Keeps for several days in the refrigerator.

- 1 medium-size pumpkin (about 8–9 inches in diameter)
- 4 tablespoons (½ stick) butter
- 1 cup chopped ripe tomato (may substitute 16-ounce can tomatoes, drained)
- 1 quart boiling water
- 1 quart rich chicken stock or broth
- 1 tablespoon long grain rice
- 2 cups peeled and sliced potatoes
- Salt
- Freshly ground pepper
- Freshly grated nutmeg

Serves: 6–8
Preparation: 30 minutes
Cooking: 1 hour

L.S. Ayres Chicken Velvet Soup
A local favorite.

Melt butter in Dutch oven over low heat. Stir in flour; cook until smooth and bubbly. Combine milk, 2 cups chicken stock and cream; gradually add to flour mixture. Cook and stir until well blended. Add remaining 4 cups stock, chicken, salt and pepper. Heat through.

- ¾ cup (1½ sticks) butter, softened
- ¾ cup all-purpose flour
- 1 cup warm milk
- 6 cups hot chicken stock or broth, divided
- 1 cup warm light (coffee) cream
- 1½ cups chopped cooked chicken
- ¾ teaspoon salt
- Freshly ground pepper

Yield: 10 cups
Preparation: 45 minutes

Cream of Broccoli Soup
Elegant and full flavored.

Remove tough stems from broccoli. Split each stalk lengthwise into halves. Combine broccoli, onion, celery, salt, pepper, nutmeg and bay leaves in 6-quart Dutch oven or heavy kettle. Add water and enough chicken broth to make 6 cups; add to broccoli. Bring to a boil; simmer, covered, until broccoli is tender, about 30 minutes. Drain; reserve broth. Remove bay leaves. Purée vegetables in blender or food processor with 1 cup broth.

Melt butter in Dutch oven. Add flour, stirring until smooth. Remove from heat. Gradually add remaining broth, stirring constantly. Cook over medium heat, stirring until mixture boils.

Add puréed vegetables and half and half. Continue stirring until soup is hot and well blended. Whip cream in medium-size bowl.

Top each serving with whipped cream and nutmeg.

- 2½ pounds broccoli
- ½ cup chopped onion
- ¾ cup sliced celery
- ¾ teaspoon salt
- ¼ teaspoon pepper
- ¼ teaspoon ground nutmeg
- 2 bay leaves
- 1½ cups water
- 3 (13¾-ounce) cans chicken broth (may substitute 1 quart plus 2½ cups rich chicken stock and omit the water)
- 4½ tablespoons butter
- 4 tablespoons all-purpose flour
- 3 cups half and half

Suggested Garnishes:
- 1 cup heavy (whipping) cream
- Freshly grated nutmeg

Yield: 12 cups
Preparation: 15 minutes
Cooking: 35 minutes

King's Arm Tavern Cream of Peanut Soup
Rich and different.

Melt butter in large skillet over low heat. Add onion and celery; sauté over medium heat until vegetables are soft but not brown. Stir in flour until well blended. Add chicken broth gradually, stirring constantly. Bring to a boil. Remove from heat; rub through a sieve. Add peanut butter and cream to sieved mixture, stirring to blend thoroughly. Return to low heat. *Do not boil.* Garnish with peanuts.

- ¼ cup (½ stick) butter
- 1 medium onion, chopped
- 2 ribs celery, chopped
- 1 tablespoon all-purpose flour
- 2 quarts chicken stock or broth
- 1 cup smooth peanut butter
- 2 cups light (coffee) cream
- Chopped peanuts

Serves: 10–12
Preparation: 20 minutes

Watercress Soup

A lovely complement to any meal.

- 3 tablespoons butter
- ⅓ cup minced onions
- 3–4 cups fresh watercress leaves and tender stems, washed and dried
- ½ teaspoon salt
- 3 tablespoons all-purpose flour
- 5½ cups boiling chicken stock or broth
- 2 egg yolks
- ½ cup heavy (whipping) cream
- 2 tablespoons butter, softened

Serves: 6–8
Preparation: 30 minutes

Melt butter in large kettle or Dutch oven over low heat. Add onions. Sauté over medium heat until tender. Reserve a few watercress leaves for garnish. Stir in remaining watercress and salt. Cover and cook slowly for 5 minutes or until leaves are tender and wilted. Sprinkle flour over vegetables. Cook and stir over medium heat for 3 minutes. Remove from heat. Whisk in boiling stock. Simmer for 5 minutes. Purée in food processor or blender and return to Dutch oven. (Soup may be prepared ahead to this point.)

Combine egg yolks and cream in large bowl. Slowly beat in 1 cup of hot soup to equalize temperature. Whisk yolk mixture into soup. Stir over low heat for 1–2 minutes to poach egg yolks. *Do not allow soup to simmer.* Remove from heat.

Stir in butter, 1 tablespoon at a time. Drop reserved watercress leaves into 1 cup boiling water. Cook for 30 seconds, drain and refresh with cold water. Decorate soup with these leaves.

Variation: Spinach may be substituted for watercress. Cut leaves into shreds and do not purée.

Brie Soup au Sherry

This unusual soup is rich and wonderful.

- ½ large wheel (about 2½ pounds) Brie cheese, crust removed
- 1 quart hot chicken stock or broth
- 1 cup sliced fresh mushrooms
- 1 cup julienne carrots
- 1 cup sliced green onions
- 2 tablespoons butter
- ¼ cup dry sherry
- 2 cups heavy (whipping) cream

Serves: 4–6
Preparation: 30 minutes

Dissolve Brie in hot chicken stock in large heavy saucepan; strain.

Melt butter in Dutch oven over low heat while cheese is dissolving. Add mushrooms, carrots and green onions; sauté until tender. Add cheese mixture. Stir in sherry and cream.

Note: *If thicker soup is desired, gradually stir 1 cup hot soup into 1 tablespoon flour. Return to soup and stir until thickened.*

Tortilla Soup
A spicy soup to excite your taste.

Place oil in large skillet. Add onion, chilies and garlic; sauté over medium heat until soft. Add tomatoes, beef broth, chicken broth, water, tomato-vegetable juice, cumin, chili powder, salt, pepper, Worcestershire and steak sauce; bring to a boil. Lower heat and simmer for 1 hour. Add tortilla strips and cheese; simmer for 10 minutes. Garnish with additional grated cheese, if desired.

- 2 tablespoons oil
- 1 small onion, chopped
- 1 (4-ounce) can green chilies, drained and chopped
- 2 cloves garlic, crushed
- 1 cup peeled and chopped tomatoes
- 1 (14-ounce) can condensed beef broth, undiluted
- 1 (14-ounce) can condensed chicken broth, undiluted
- 1½ cups water
- 1½ cups tomato-vegetable juice
- 1 teaspoon ground cumin
- 1 teaspoon chili powder
- 1 teaspoon salt
- ⅛ teaspoon pepper
- 2 teaspoons Worcestershire sauce
- 1 tablespoon steak sauce
- 3 flour tortillas, cut into ½x1½-inch pieces
- ¼ cup grated Cheddar cheese

Serves: 6–8
Preparation: 40 minutes
Cooking: 1 hour, 10 minutes

Soups

- 1 pound lentils, washed
- 10 cups chicken broth or stock
- 2 tablespoons olive oil
- 1 tablespoon butter
- 1 large onion
- 4 cloves garlic, crushed
- 2 stalks celery, finely chopped
- 2 pounds fresh spinach, chopped [may substitute 2 (10-ounce) packages frozen chopped spinach, unthawed]
- ¾ cup fresh lemon juice
- Salt
- Freshly ground pepper

Serves: 10–12
Preparation: 30 minutes
Cooking: 4½ hours

Spinach-Lentil Soup

This one hit the top of the scale.

Combine lentils and broth in large kettle. Simmer for 3–4 hours.

Heat oil and butter in medium-size skillet. Add onion, garlic and celery; sauté over medium heat until tender. Add to cooked lentils. Add spinach, lemon juice, salt and pepper. Cook gently for 30 minutes or more to blend flavors.

Note: Even better the next day.

- 4 tablespoons (½ stick) butter
- ½ cup chopped onion
- 1½ teaspoons minced garlic
- 12 ounces fresh mushrooms, sliced
- 2 tablespoons all-purpose flour
- 2 cups half and half or light cream
- ½ cup chicken stock or broth
- 3 tablespoons dry Marsala wine or sherry
- 1 teaspoon salt
- ⅛ teaspoon ground nutmeg
- ⅛ teaspoon pepper
- Chopped fresh parsley

Serves: 4
Preparation: 30 minutes

Italian Mushroom Soup

Freezing actually improves the flavor of this soup.

Melt butter in large saucepan or Dutch oven over low heat. Add onions; sauté until transparent. Add mushrooms and garlic; sauté until tender, about 5 minutes. Add flour; cook and stir until smooth and blended. Gradually add cream and chicken broth, stirring constantly. Stir in wine, salt, nutmeg and pepper. Cook until thickened, about 5 minutes. Garnish with chopped parsley.

Sour and Hot Soup
Very different and so good.

Soak dried mushrooms for 30 minutes in warm water; drain. Cut away and discard tough stems. Cut mushroom caps horizontally into paper-thin slices, then into thin strips.

Drain and rinse bean curd and bamboo shoots. Shred as fine as mushrooms.

Trim pork of all fat. Shred by slicing meat as thin as possible and cutting the slices into narrow strips about 1½ to 2 inches long.

Combine mushrooms, bamboo shoots, pork, stock and soy sauce in large heavy saucepan or wok. Bring to a boil over high heat. Reduce heat immediately to low; cover and simmer for 3 minutes. Add bean curd, salt, pepper and vinegar. Bring to a boil.

Combine cornstarch and cold water. Stir until smooth. Add to soup; stir until soup thickens. Add beaten egg slowly, stirring gently. Transfer soup to bowl or tureen. Stir in sesame oil. Sprinkle soup with green onions and serve.

- 4 dried chinese mushrooms, 1½ inches in diameter (may substitute 6 fresh mushrooms, but omit soaking process)
- ½ cup warm water
- 2 (3-inch) squares tofu (chinese bean curd), about ½-inch thick
- 6 tablespoons canned bamboo shoots
- ¼ pound boneless pork
- 1½ pints chicken stock or broth
- 2½ teaspoons soy sauce
- Salt
- ¼ teaspoon ground white pepper
- 5 teaspoons white vinegar
- 5 teaspoons cornstarch
- 2½ tablespoons cold water
- 1 egg, slightly beaten
- 1½ teaspoons sesame oil
- 1 green onion (including top), finely chopped

Serves: 4–6
Preparation: 30 minutes

Soups

Curry Mix:
- 1 tablespoon whole cumin seed
- 4 inch stick cinnamon
- 5 whole cloves
- 1 teaspoon cardamon seeds
- 1 teaspoon peppercorns
- 2 bay leaves
- 4 teaspoons coriander seeds
- ¼ cup dried parsley flakes
- 2 tablespoons instant minced onion
- 2 tablespoons ground turmeric
- 1 teaspoon ground ginger
- 3 cups non-fat dry milk powder

Soup:
- 6 tablespoons butter
- ⅔ cup Curry Mix
- 3 tablespoons all-purpose flour
- 29 ounces chicken broth or stock
- 1½ cups diced cooked chicken
- ¾ cup dry white wine

Serves: 6
Preparation: 15 minutes
Cooking: 1 hour

Curry Soup

Most unusual—Curry Mix makes a great gift.

Combine cumin, cinnamon, cloves, cardamon, peppercorns, bay leaves and coriander in blender (not food processor). Blend until well ground. Place in small bowl. Add parsley, onion, turmeric, ginger and dry milk. Stir well to combine. Store in airtight container.

Melt butter in large saucepan. Stir in Curry Mix and flour. Cook and stir for 3 minutes over medium heat. Add chicken broth gradually. Cook and stir until bubbly. Stir in chicken and wine; simmer for 1 hour.

Note: Soup is spicy. Serve with something bland.

Cuban Black Bean Soup
A marvelous soup.

Soak beans in water overnight in large Dutch oven.

Add salt; boil beans for 2 hours until soft. Drain and reserve water.

Marinate rice and chopped onions in 5 tablespoons oil and 5 tablespoons vinegar.

Crush garlic, cumin, oregano and 2 tablespoons vinegar in a mortar. Heat remaining 5 tablespoons oil in large saucepan or Dutch oven over medium heat. Add onions and peppers; cook until onions are tender. Add crushed ingredients. Add beans and enough reserved bean-water to achieve desired consistency. Cook slowly until ready to serve. To serve, spoon ¼ cup rice into each bowl of soup. Pour hot soup into each bowl and serve.

- 1 pound black beans
- 2 quarts water
- 2 tablespoons (6 teaspoons) salt
- 1½ cups cooked long grain rice
- ½ cup finely chopped onions
- 7 tablespoons white vinegar, divided
- 10 tablespoons olive oil, divided
- 5 cloves garlic
- 1½ teaspoons ground cumin
- 1½ teaspoons dried oregano
- ½ pound onions, diced
- ½ pound green peppers, seeded and diced

Serves: 6
Preparation: 30 minutes
Soaking: Overnight
Cooking: 2 hours

Squash Soup
Rich in color and smooth tasting.

Combine squash, onion and 1 cup of chicken broth in large saucepan. Cook over low heat until squash is soft. Purée in blender or food processor. Add remaining ½ cup of chicken broth and sour cream. Chill. Serve with sprinkle of dill weed.

- 1 pound yellow squash, peeled and cut into pieces (may substitute butternut)
- 1 medium onion, diced
- 1½ cups chicken broth or stock, divided
- ½ cup sour cream
- Dill weed

Serves: 4–6
Preparation: 30 minutes
Chilling: 3 hours

Cold Cream of Cucumber Soup

Delightfully refreshing—great as a first course.

- 2 tablespoons butter
- ½ cup chopped green onions (including tops)
- 2 cups diced cucumber (about 1 large cucumber)
- 1 cup fresh watercress or fresh spinach (pack into measuring cup)
- ½ cup peeled and diced potato (about 1 medium)
- 2 cups chicken stock or broth
- ¾ teaspoon salt
- ½ teaspoon white pepper
- 1 cup heavy (whipping) cream

Suggested Garnishes:
Thinly sliced radishes
Thinly sliced cucumber
Snipped chives

Serves: 4–6
Preparation: 15 minutes
Cooking: 15 minutes
Chilling: Overnight

Melt butter in large saucepan over low heat. Sauté onion over medium heat for 5 minutes. Add cucumber, watercress, potato, broth, salt and pepper. Bring to a boil and simmer over low heat for 15 minutes. Cool.

Purée cooled mixture in blender, 1 cup at a time. Stir in cream and chill thoroughly several hours. Overnight is best. Serve cold. Garnish with radish or cucumber slices and chives, if desired.

Cold Carrot-Potato Soup
A League favorite.

Place potatoes, carrots, leek and chicken stock in large heavy saucepan. Bring to a boil; simmer for 25 minutes or until vegetables are tender. Purée vegetables and liquid, a little at a time, for 30 seconds on high speed in blender or food processor. Empty into bowl or pitcher. Add white pepper, salt and cream. Mix well. Chill. Serve icy cold. Top with shredded raw carrot, if desired.

- 2 cups peeled and diced potatoes
- 1¼ cups peeled and sliced carrots
- 1 leek, washed and sliced (white part only)
- 3 cups chicken stock or broth
- Pinch of white pepper
- 1 teaspoon salt
- 1 cup light (coffee) cream
- Shredded raw carrot

Serves: 8
Preparation: 20 minutes
Cooking: 25 minutes
Chilling: 4–6 hours

Quick Spinach Soup
Everyone raves about this one.

Squeeze spinach to remove all excess moisture.

Melt butter in Dutch oven over low heat. Add onions and sauté over medium heat until tender. Add spinach slowly. Add remaining ingredients; stir until heated and well combined. Chill. Serve chilled with a lemon slice on top.

- 1 (10-ounce) package frozen chopped spinach, thawed and drained
- 3 tablespoons butter
- 1½ cups chopped green onions
- 21 ounces chicken broth or stock
- ½ cup sour cream
- 1 cup half and half
- 2 (10½-ounce) cans cream of potato soup
- 2 tablespoons fresh lemon juice
- ¼ teaspoon pepper
- Salt
- Lemon slices

Serves: 8–10
Preparation: 30 minutes
Chilling: 2–4 hours

Hungarian Cold Sour Cherry Soup
So colorful and refreshing.

- 3 cups cold water
- 1 cup granulated sugar
- 1 cinnamon stick
- 4 cups fresh pitted sour cherries (may substitute canned cherries, drained)
- 1 tablespoon arrowroot (may substitute 2 tablespoons flour)
- 2 tablespoons cold water
- ¼ cup heavy (whipping) cream
- ¾ cup dry red wine, chilled

Serves: 6
Preparation: 20 minutes
Cooking: 40 minutes
Chilling: 4–6 hours

Combine 3 cups cold water, sugar and cinnamon stick in 2-quart saucepan. Bring to a boil. Add cherries; partially cover and simmer for 35–40 minutes. (Simmer for 10 minutes, if cherries are canned.)

Remove cinnamon stick.

Mix arrowroot with 2 tablespoons cold water to make a paste; whisk paste into cherry soup, stirring constantly. Bring soup to a boil. Reduce heat; simmer about 2 minutes or until soup is clear and slightly thick.

Pour into shallow glass or stainless steel bowl and refrigerate until chilled. Stir in cream and wine just before serving.

Note: Freezes well. Stir, if separated.

Chilled French Pea Soup
Unusual and quick to fix.

- 1 tablespoon butter
- ½ cup chopped onion
- 1 teaspoon chopped fresh mint (may substitute ½ teaspoon dried mint)
- 1 cup chicken stock or broth
- 1½ pounds fresh green peas, hulled (may substitute 10-ounce package frozen peas)
- Salt
- 1½ cups light (coffee) cream

Suggested Garnishes:
  Thinly sliced cucumber
  Chopped chives
  Fresh mint

Yield: 4 cups
Preparation: 30 minutes
Chilling: 3–4 hours

Heat butter in large skillet. Sauté onion and mint over medium heat until onion is soft but not browned. Add stock, peas and salt. Heat over medium-high until mixture comes to a boil. Reduce heat to low; cover and cook until peas are tender. Pour mixture into blender; blend until smooth. Add cream and blend for a few seconds. Chill thoroughly. Serve garnished with thin cucumber slices, chives or mint sprig.

Stroganoff Steak Sandwich
Wonderful and elegant supper.

Combine beer, oil, salt, garlic and pepper in shallow dish large enough to accommodate steak. Marinate steak overnight in mixture.

Preheat oven to broil.

Melt butter in small saucepan over low heat. Stir in paprika and salt to taste. Add onions and sauté over medium heat until tender but not brown.

Remove steak from marinade and broil 3 inches from heat for 5–7 minutes, turning once. Cut meat diagonally across the grain into thin slices. Arrange meat on 2 slices toast and cover with onions. Serve with dollop of sour cream, if desired.

Hot Avocado Crab Sandwiches
Elegant and easy.

Preheat oven to broil.

Combine soup, milk, Worcestershire and Tabasco in medium-size saucepan. Cook over medium heat until hot, stirring occasionally. Add 1 cup cheese; stir until melted.

Place muffins on baking sheet. Spread a heaping tablespoon of sauce on each muffin half. Top with crab meat then avocado slices. Drizzle with remaining sauce. Sprinkle with remaining ½ cup cheese. Broil 4 inches from heat for 3–4 minutes or until golden brown and bubbly.

Sandwiches — 67

Marinade:
- ⅔ cup beer
- ⅓ cup oil
- 1 teaspoon salt
- 1 small clove garlic, crushed
- ¼ teaspoon pepper

Sauce:
- 2 tablespoons butter
- ½ teaspoon paprika
- Salt
- ⅓ cup sliced onions

- 2 pounds flank steak
- 12 slices French bread, toasted
- Sour cream (optional)

Yield:	6
Preparation:	15 minutes
Marinating:	Overnight
Broiling:	7 minutes
Temperature:	Broil

- 1 (10½-ounce) can cream of mushroom soup
- ¼ cup milk
- ½ teaspoon Worcestershire sauce
- Dash of Tabasco sauce
- 1½ cups grated sharp Cheddar cheese, divided
- 4 large English muffins; split, toasted and buttered
- 1 (6½-ounce) can crab meat, drained and picked clean
- 2 avocados, peeled and sliced

Serves:	8
Preparation:	15 minutes
Broiling:	4 minutes
Temperature:	Broil

Sandwiches

- 1 loaf French bread, unsliced
- 1 (8-ounce) package cream cheese, softened
- 1 (12-ounce) package bacon, cooked and crumbled
- ⅓–½ pound Cheddar cheese, sliced
- ⅓–½ pound turkey breast, sliced
- ⅓–½ pound baby Swiss cheese, sliced
- ⅓–½ pound peppered beef, sliced

Condiment Suggestions:
- Lettuce
- Sliced tomatoes (lightly marinated in Vinaigrette and fine herbs)
- Alfalfa sprouts
- Mayonnaise
- Mustard

Serves: 10
Preparation: 15 minutes

- 3 tablespoons butter
- 8 ounces fresh mushrooms, diced
- ½ cup (1 stick) margarine or butter, softened
- 1 (8-ounce) package cream cheese, softened
- 2 egg yolks
- 1 cup grated Cheddar cheese
- Diced cooked ham (optional)
- Salt
- Freshly ground pepper
- English muffins, split

Serves: 8–10
Preparation: 15 minutes
Broiling: 5 minutes
Temperature: Broil

Family Favorite
A tailgate winner.

Slice loaf of bread in half lengthwise. Hollow out top and bottom, leaving at least a 1-inch rim of bread in each piece.

Layer remaining ingredients on bottom half of bread beginning with cream cheese and ending with beef. Replace top and wrap tightly with foil or plastic wrap. Store in refrigerator until ready to serve. Serve by slicing loaves into serving pieces. Offer lettuce, tomatoes, alfalfa sprouts, mayonnaise and mustard as condiments.

Note: May be made day ahead. May also be frozen.

Variation: Warm in oven or microwave for a delicious hot melted sandwich.

Mushroom Delights
Mouth-watering goodness.

Preheat oven to broil.

Melt 3 tablespoons butter in medium-size saucepan over low heat. Add mushrooms and sauté over medium heat until tender. Drain and set aside.

Beat together remaining ½ cup butter and cream cheese in large bowl until creamy. Add egg yolks and beat well. Stir in mushrooms and cheese. Add ham, if desired. Spread mixture on muffins and broil for 3–5 minutes or until bubbly and golden.

Note: Mixture may be stored in the refrigerator in airtight container.

Tijuana Tidbits
A really different sandwich.

Combine dressing and taco sauce. Spread evenly on each slice of bread. Divide each ingredient into 4 portions and layer on 4 of the bread slices as follows: Monterey Jack cheese, peppers, onions, roast beef and American cheese. Top with slice of bread.

Combine eggs and sour cream. Dip each sandwich into the egg-sour cream mixture and then into crushed tortilla chips, coating each side.

Melt butter in large skillet over medium-high heat. Fry sandwiches until browned on both sides. Place prepared sandwiches on cookie sheet and freeze until solid, about 2 hours. Remove and cut each sandwich into 4 squares. Arrange in 9x13-inch baking dish; cover and return to freezer.

Preheat oven to 375°.

Bake tidbits for 15–20 minutes or until thoroughly heated.

Note: *Recipe may be kept frozen for 6 to 8 weeks.*

Serving Suggestion: Margaritas and avocado dip with tortilla chips complement the tidbits nicely.

- ¼ cup avocado or creamy garlic dressing
- 1 tablespoon taco sauce
- 8 slices coarse white bread, crusts removed
- 4 slices Monterey Jack cheese
- 2 small hot Mexican peppers, diced (optional)
- 1 large white onion, sliced
- ¾ pound shaved roast beef
- 4 slices American cheese
- 2 eggs, beaten
- 2 tablespoons sour cream
- 1 bag taco-flavored or regular-flavored tortilla chips, crushed
- 2 tablespoons butter, melted

Serves: 12–16
Preparation: 20 minutes
Baking: 20 minutes
Freezing: 2 hours
Temperature: 375°

Shrimp and Camembert en Croissant
A winner on all counts.

Combine avocado, milk and Tabasco. Spread each croissant half with avocado mixture. Layer cheese, tomato slices, shrimp and alfalfa sprouts on half of the split croissant. Place remaining croissant halves on top to make sandwiches.

Note: *Revitalize freshness by heating croissants in foil at 350° for 5 minutes before making sandwich.*

- ½ cup mashed avocado
- ¼ cup milk
  Dash of Tabasco sauce
- 4 whole wheat croissants, halved lengthwise
- 4 (1-ounce) slices Camembert or Havarti cheese
- 1 large tomato, sliced
- 4 ounces cooked shrimp, chopped
  Alfalfa sprouts

Serves: 4
Preparation: 20 minutes

Sandwiches

- 6 pita flat breads
- 2 (8-ounce) packages cream cheese, softened
- 3 ripe avocados, peeled
- 2 tomatoes, sliced
- ½ pound fresh mushrooms, sliced
- ½ pound bacon, cooked and crumbled
- Alfalfa sprouts
- Buttermilk dressing

Yield: 6 sandwiches
Preparation: 15 minutes

Marinade:
- ½ cup oil
- ¼ cup dry white wine
- 2 tablespoons vinegar
- 2 teaspoons granulated sugar
- 1 teaspoon dried basil
- ¼ teaspoon salt

- 1½ pounds sirloin steak, broiled to taste
- 8 ounces fresh mushrooms, sliced
- 2 tomatoes, peeled and chopped
- ½ cup sliced green onions
- 6 ounces fresh spinach, washed and well drained
- 1 cup sour cream
- ½ teaspoon dried dill weed
- 4–5 pita flat breads

Serves: 4–5
Preparation: 30 minutes
Marinating: 2 hours

Avocado-Pita Sandwich
Very light lunch.

Open pita bread by cutting across top of loaf. Spread inside with cream cheese. Insert into each pocket ½ avocado, sliced, and 2–3 tomato slices. Add mushroom slices and bacon. Top opening of sandwich with alfalfa sprouts. Serve with a buttermilk dressing.

Pita Pockets with Steak and Mushrooms
Light and tasty.

Combine all marinade ingredients in large bowl.

Slice steak into thin strips. Combine with mushrooms, tomatoes and green onions and place in marinade. Let stand at room temperature for 2 hours. Drain marinade from steak mixture; add spinach to steak mixture.

Combine sour cream and dill.

Open pieces of pita bread by cutting across top of loaf. Spread with sour cream mixture. Stuff pita bread with steak and spinach. Serve immediately.

HINT:
Pita pockets are easier to open without tearing if warmed slightly.

Salads

Music and Theater

Indianapolis has gained worldwide recognition for the strength of its musical achievements. Our superb Indianapolis Symphony Orchestra, conducted by Music Director John Nelson, played its premiere season in its new home, the exquisitely renovated Circle Theatre, in 1984-85. The orchestra, which recently celebrated its golden anniversary, features resident musicians and performing artists of world-class stature.

The first International Violin Competition, conceived in Indianapolis and presented here in 1982, attracted the attention of music devotees everywhere. Marvelously talented, aspiring violinists came from 22 countries to compete before an august panel of musically renowned judges. The phenomenally successful competition will be repeated quadrennially. A thriving Indianapolis Opera Company and critically hailed ballet and modern dance companies further testify to the appreciation of the musical arts in this city.

The history of theater in Indianapolis is almost as old as the city itself. The famed English Opera House, long a fixture of Monument Circle, attracted touring dramas featuring America's most acclaimed actors from Edwin Booth to the Barrymore clan. Today, our Indiana Repertory Theatre occupies the beautifully renovated Indiana Theatre Building, a rococco Italianate movie palace of the 20's. This nationally recognized repertory company performs on three stages, presenting a broad variety of classic and original productions, musical shows and revues.

Each summer our outdoor Starlight Musicals company books nationally famous performers for musical shows which regularly play to capacity audiences. Small community theaters abound here, offering a range of drama from popular to experimental, and an alfresco summer Shakespeare festival draws enthusiastic playgoers of all ages.

Music and theater in Indianapolis—contributing to the local scene and winning plaudits for themselves and for this city.

SALADS AND DRESSINGS

Green Salads
Caesar Salad . . . 73
Creamy Wilted Lettuce . . . 71
Eastwood Spinach Salad . . . 72
Strawberry and Spinach Salad . . . 71
Sue's Spinach Salad . . . 73
Zesty Tossed Salad . . . 74

Vegetable Salads
Asparagus Vinaigrette . . . 75
Broccoli Salad Supreme . . . 75
Carrots and Celery with Herbs . . . 78
Cheese and Potato Salad . . . 74
24-Hour Cabbage Salad . . . 76
Marinated Green Beans . . . 77
Sauerkraut Salad . . . 77
Sour Cream Green Beans . . . 76
Spiced Carrots . . . 79
Spicy Tomato Salad . . . 79

Main Dish Salads
Beef and Potato Salad in Sour Dough Round . . . 81
Cheese and Wurst Salad . . . 84
Chicken Cranberry Salad . . . 85
Chicken Tostada Salad . . . 86
Chicken-Wild Rice Salad . . . 87
Crab Salad Printanier . . . 90
Greek Salad . . . 83
Lamb and Bean Salad . . . 80
Mandarin Chicken Salad . . . 84
Potato Salad Deluxe . . . 82
Rice Salad . . . 88
Shrimp-Filled Cucumber Boats . . . 89
Shrimp Tomato Vinaigrette . . . 91

Pasta Salads
Garden-Style Seafood Salad . . . 92
Pesto and Pasta Salad . . . 93
Summer Pasta with Basil, Tomatoes and Cheese . . . 94

Molded Salads
Blueberry Layer Mold . . . 96
Crab Meat Mold . . . 95
Cucumber Aspic . . . 96
Pineapple-Lime Mold . . . 98
Two-Layer Cranberry Salad . . . 97
Wine Cherry Supreme . . . 98
French Fruit Salad . . . 101

Fruit Salads
French Fruit Salad . . . 101
Fruit Salad Olé . . . 100
Orange and Avocado Salad . . . 99
Pears with Cranberry Dressing . . . 100
Summertime Melon Salad . . . 99

Salad Dressings
Blue Cheese Salad Dressing . . . 102
Celery Seed Dressing . . . 102
Korean Salad Dressing . . . 101
New Orleans Salad Dressing . . . 102
Poppy Seed Dressing . . . 101

Relishes
Apple Chutney . . . 104
Green Pepper Jelly . . . 103
Indiana State Fair Peach Jam . . . 103
Pickled Beets . . . 103
Uncooked Cucumber Slices . . . 104

Strawberry and Spinach Salad

Strawberries and sweet-sour dressing make this a winner.

Wash and dry spinach. Arrange spinach and strawberries on individual plates or in clear glass salad bowl.

Place sugar, sesame seed, poppy seed, onion, Worcestershire, paprika and vinegar in blender. Add oil in a steady stream with blender on low speed. Blend until dressing is creamy and thick. Drizzle dressing over salad. Garnish with toasted almonds.

- ½ pound tender spinach
- 1 pint fresh strawberries, hulled and sliced
- 2 ounces almonds, toasted

Dressing:
- ½ cup granulated sugar
- 2 tablespoons sesame seed
- 1 tablespoon poppy seed
- 1½ teaspoons minced onion
- ¼ teaspoon Worcestershire sauce
- ¼ teaspoon paprika
- ¼ cup cider vinegar
- ½ cup oil

Serves: 4
Preparation: 15 minutes

Creamy Wilted Lettuce

Sour cream adds a pleasant variation.

Lay strips of bacon in 8x12-inch glass baking dish. Cover with wax paper. Microwave on High for 3½ minutes; turn bacon and microwave on High for 3 minutes. Remove bacon to paper towel; reserve 3 tablespoons grease. Crumble bacon and set aside.

Combine reserved grease, sour cream, egg, vinegar, sugar and salt in small microwave-safe container. Whisk until well blended. Microwave dressing on Simmer or Medium, uncovered, for 3 minutes. Stir with whisk and microwave for additional 3 minutes on Medium. The mixture should be thick and creamy.

Tear salad greens into bite-size pieces and place in large bowl. Sprinkle salad greens with green onion and bacon. Pour dressing over greens and toss. Serve immediately.

Note: Can adapt this to stove-top by using a non-stick pan. Cook over low to medium heat.

- 6–8 slices bacon
- ½ cup sour cream
- 1 egg, slightly beaten
- ¼ cup cider vinegar
- 2 tablespoons granulated sugar
- Salt
- 6 cups salad greens, washed and dried (may use combination of fresh spinach, leaf and romaine lettuce)
- 3–4 green onions, sliced

Serves: 4–6
Preparation: 20 minutes
Microwave: 10 minutes

Salads

Eastwood Spinach Salad

Exciting taste combination adds unusual twist.

- 1 pound fresh spinach
- 1 medium head lettuce
- 1 (16-ounce) can mandarin oranges, drained
- 1 cup peanuts (may substitute cashews)
- 1 (8½-ounce) can artichoke hearts, drained and cut-up
- 1 (8-ounce) can pitted ripe olives, sliced
- ¼–½ pound Swiss cheese, cubed
- Chopped green onion (may substitute red Bermuda onion)

Dressing:
- ⅓ cup granulated sugar
- 1 teaspoon dry mustard
- 1 teaspoon salt
- Freshly ground pepper
- ⅓ cup red wine vinegar
- 1 cup oil
- 1 tablespoon celery seed
- 1 tablespoon grated onion

Serves: 6
Preparation: 20 minutes

Tear spinach and lettuce into bite-size pieces. Layer spinach, lettuce, oranges, peanuts, artichokes, olives, cheese and onion in large salad bowl.

Combine dressing ingredients in blender. Blend well. Pour over salad ingredients just before serving. Toss gently until thoroughly coated.

Sue's Spinach Salad
Carrots and cabbage are a refreshing twist.

Combine dressing ingredients in shaker or jar. Shake well to mix.

Combine cabbage, carrots and spinach in large bowl. Add nuts and dressing just before serving. Toss well.

Dressing:
- 1 teaspoon garlic salt
- 1 teaspoon paprika
- ¼ cup white wine vinegar
- ⅓ cup catsup
- ⅓ cup granulated sugar
- ½ cup oil

- ½ head cabbage, grated
- 3–4 large carrots, peeled and grated
- 8 ounces fresh spinach, washed
- ¼ pound salted mixed nuts

Serves: 8
Preparation: 20 minutes

Caesar Salad
Classic salad to serve with a flair.*

Press garlic with garlic press into large salad bowl, preferably wooden. Add ½ of anchovy oil. Work garlic and oil up and around sides of salad bowl with a fork, until garlic is finely mashed and evenly distributed.

Add lemon juice, Worcestershire, Tabasco, mustard, pepper and anchovies. Mash anchovies thoroughly with fork and work around sides of bowl until evenly distributed.

Pour wine vinegar around top of bowl, repeat with olive oil. Break eggs into bowl. Mix thoroughly and work around sides of the bowl.

Add lettuce, cheese and croutons. Toss thoroughly and let stand for 5–10 minutes. Toss again and serve.

Note: Can be a meal in itself or a distinctive salad course.

*Entertain your guests by preparing the salad at the table. Premeasure and assemble ingredients prior to preparation. Best served with a Rhine, Mosel or Riesling wine.

- 2 cloves garlic
- 1 ounce anchovies in olive oil, drained (reserve oil)
- 1–2 teaspoons fresh lemon juice
- 1 tablespoon Worcestershire sauce
- Dash of Tabasco sauce
- ¼ teaspoon dry mustard
- ¼ teaspoon pepper
- 1 tablespoon red wine vinegar
- ¼ cup olive oil
- 2 large eggs (about ¼ cup)
- 2 pounds romaine lettuce, washed and dried
- 8 ounces freshly grated Parmesan cheese
- 3 ounces seasoned croutons

Serves: 2–4
Preparation: 10 minutes
Standing: 10 minutes

Zesty Tossed Salad

Basics withstand the tests of time.

Place vinegar and celery seed in a small saucepan. Bring to a boil. Remove from heat and let cool. Combine sugar, onion, mustard, salt and oil in blender or food processor. Add cooled vinegar and process until mixture is smooth and creamy.

Layer lettuce, onion, bacon, mushrooms and nuts in large bowl.

Pour dressing over layered salad just before serving and toss. Serve with dollops of sour cream.

Dressing:
- ½ cup white vinegar
- 1 tablespoon celery seed
- ½ cup granulated sugar
- 1 tablespoon chopped onion
- 1 teaspoon dry mustard
- 1 teaspoon salt
- 1 cup oil

- 1 large head lettuce, torn into pieces (may substitute spinach and other types of lettuce)
- 1 medium onion, sliced
- ½ pound bacon, cooked and crumbled
- 8 ounces fresh mushrooms, sliced
- 4 ounces sunflower kernels or pepita nuts
- ½ cup sour cream

Serves: 6–8
Preparation: 20 minutes

Cheese and Potato Salad

Flavor and texture of two cheeses elevate the basic potato salad.

Place potatoes in large saucepan; cover with water. Cook over medium-high heat until tender. Cut into ½-inch cubes. Place potatoes, cheeses and onion in large bowl.

Coarsely chop 5 eggs and add to potato mixture. Reserve 1 egg for garnish.

Combine mayonnaise, milk, salt and pepper in small bowl. Pour over potato mixture and toss gently. Slice remaining hard-cooked egg and arrange on top of salad. Refrigerate.

- 3 pounds red potatoes, peeled
- 2 cups grated Swiss cheese
- ¾ cup grated Cheddar cheese
- ⅓ cup sliced green onions
- 6 hard-cooked eggs
- 2½ cups mayonnaise
- 3 tablespoons milk
- 1½ teaspoons salt
- ½ teaspoon pepper

Serves: 8–10
Preparation: 45 minutes
Chilling: 2–4 hours

Asparagus Vinaigrette
Zest and herbs create elegant flavor.

Snap off tough ends of asparagus. Remove scales with a sharp knife or vegetable peeler. Steam or cook in ½ cup lightly salted boiling water for 8 minutes or until crisp tender. Drain well. Arrange asparagus in glass dish.

Combine remaining ingredients in medium-size bowl or jar. Mix well and pour over asparagus. Chill at least 1 hour.

Arrange asparagus spears on bed of lettuce and top with crisscrossed pimiento strips.

Microwave: Asparagus may be cooked in microwave according to manufacturer's directions.

1–1½	pounds fresh green or white asparagus spears
2	hard-cooked eggs, finely chopped
¾	cup olive oil
¼	cup white wine vinegar
2	tablespoons Dijon mustard
2	tablespoons shallots, minced
2	tablespoons chopped fresh parsley
1	tablespoon chopped fresh chives
1½	teaspoons chopped fresh tarragon (may substitute ½ teaspoon dried tarragon)
	Boston or red-tip leaf lettuce
	Pimiento strips

Serves: 4–6
Preparation: 15 minutes
Chilling: 1 hour

Broccoli Salad Supreme
Ingredients join in a wonderful surprise.

Cut broccoli flowerets and tender stalks into bite-size pieces. Discard woody stems. Place broccoli, bacon, onion, nuts, raisins and mushrooms in large bowl.

Mix together mayonnaise, sugar and vinegar. Pour over broccoli mixture. Toss gently. Chill for 2–4 hours before serving.

1	large bunch fresh broccoli
½	pound bacon, fried crisp and crumbled
½	medium red onion, chopped
1	cup sunflower kernels
½	cup raisins
½	cup sliced fresh mushrooms
1	cup mayonnaise
¼	cup granulated sugar
2	tablespoons cider vinegar

Serves: 4–6
Preparation: 20 minutes
Chilling: 2–4 hours

Salads

2 cups fresh green beans, trimmed (do not snap or cut)
1 medium red or white onion, sliced and separated into rings

Marinade:
2 tablespoons oil
1 tablespoon cider vinegar
Salt
Coarsely ground pepper

Sour Cream Dressing:
½ cup sour cream
½ cup mayonnaise
½–1 tablespoon prepared horseradish
½ teaspoon fresh lemon juice
¼ teaspoon dry mustard

Serves: 6
Preparation: 15 minutes
Marinating: Overnight
Chilling: 12 hours

Sour Cream Green Beans
Tangy dressing makes the beans especially good.

Steam or cook green beans until crisp tender. Combine with onion rings.

Whisk marinade ingredients together in medium-size bowl. Add beans and onion rings; toss gently. Marinate overnight.

Combine dressing ingredients in small bowl; chill.

Serve by draining beans and onions. Add enough dressing to coat lightly. Toss gently. Serve cold.

Note: Leftover dressing will keep in refrigerator.

Variations: The sour cream dressing is terrific on sandwiches. It also makes a great vegetable dip.

---

1 large head cabbage, cored and finely chopped
½ green pepper, seeded and chopped
1 small onion, finely chopped
1 carrot, peeled and grated

Marinade:
¾ cup oil
½ cup granulated sugar
½ cup cider vinegar
1 teaspoon celery salt

Serves: 8–12
Preparation: 20 minutes
Chilling: 24 hours

24-Hour Cabbage Salad
Crisp salad with a unique fresh taste.

Combine cabbage, pepper, onion and carrot in large heat-proof bowl.

Combine all marinade ingredients in small saucepan. Bring to full boil. Remove from heat and pour over vegetables. Toss gently. Cover tightly. Refrigerate 24 hours before serving.

Note: May use appropriate blades of food processor to prepare vegetables. Salad will keep at least two weeks in refrigerator.

Salads

Marinated Green Beans
These delicious beans keep in the refrigerator for several days.

Cook beans until crisp tender. Drain well. Cool slightly. Add onions and celery. Whisk together oil, vinegar, salt, pepper and mustard. Stir in eggs. Pour over green bean mixture; toss gently. Cover and chill thoroughly.

Line salad plates with lettuce. Arrange green beans on lettuce. Sprinkle with parsley.

1½ pounds fresh green beans
1 tablespoon finely chopped green onion
4 tablespoons finely chopped celery

Marinade:
¾ cup olive oil
6 tablespoons red wine vinegar
¾ teaspoon salt
Freshly ground pepper
1 teaspoon Dijon mustard

2 hard-cooked eggs, finely chopped
Boston or red-tip leaf lettuce
Finely chopped fresh parsley

Serves: 6–8
Preparation: 30 minutes
Cooking: 15 minutes
Chilling: 3–4 hours

Sauerkraut Salad
This hearty salad is a pleasant surprise.

Combine sauerkraut, green pepper, celery, onions, and pimiento. Whisk together vinegar, sugar and oil. Pour marinade over mixture; mix well. Refrigerate at least 24 hours.

Note: Can be stored in airtight jar in refrigerator for weeks.

1 (27-ounce) can sauerkraut, drained and rinsed
⅔ cup seeded and chopped green pepper
1 cup chopped celery
2 onions, chopped
1 (4-ounce) jar pimiento, chopped and drained
½ cup cider vinegar
½ cup granulated sugar
4 tablespoons oil

Yield: 1 quart
Preparation: 15 minutes
Marinating: 24 hours

Salads

½ cup water
1 teaspoon salt
5–6 medium carrots, peeled and cut into ½-inch slices
1 clove garlic, peeled and halved
2 stalks celery, sliced diagonally
1 tablespoon fresh lemon juice
⅛ teaspoon dry mustard
Salt
Freshly ground pepper
3 tablespoons sesame or sunflower oil
1 tablespoon minced fresh chives (may substitute 1 teaspoon dried chives)
2 tablespoons minced fresh dill (may substitute 1 teaspoon dried dill weed)

Serves: 6
Preparation: 10 minutes
Cooking: 8 minutes
Chilling: 1 hour

Carrots and Celery with Herbs
Lovely and tangy.

Combine water and salt in small saucepan. Bring to a boil. Add carrots and cook for 7–8 minutes. Drain immediately and plunge carrots into cold water to arrest cooking. Drain well.

Rub sides of medium-size serving bowl with garlic. Place carrots and celery in bowl and sprinkle with lemon juice, mustard, salt and pepper. Fold oil in slowly until lemon juice is absorbed and mustard is dissolved. Add chives and dill; stir. Chill for 1 hour before serving.

Variation: Parboiled zucchini or cauliflower may be added to carrots.

Spiced Carrots
Quick, attractive and delicious.

Whisk marinade ingredients together in large bowl until well combined. Add carrots and onions; toss gently. Marinate overnight or several hours. Drain marinade from vegetables and serve.

Marinade:
- ½ cup oil
- ½ cup granulated sugar
- ½ cup cider vinegar
- 1 teaspoon celery seed
- ¼ teaspoon dry mustard
- ¼ teaspoon salt

- 1½ pounds carrots; peeled, sliced, cooked and drained [may substitute 2 (16-ounce) cans small whole carrots, drained]
- 1 medium onion, thinly sliced

Serves: 4–6
Preparation: 20 minutes
Chilling: Overnight

Spicy Tomato Salad
Fresh and colorful.

Chill salad plates.

Alternate overlapping slices of tomatoes and cheese on each salad plate.

Sprinkle onions and olives over each plate.

Whisk together lemon juice and olive oil. Drizzle over tomatoes and cheese. Sprinkle with generous amount of fresh pepper. Garnish with coriander or fresh parsley.

- 4 small or 2 large garden fresh tomatoes, sliced
- ½ pound Monterey Jack cheese with peppers, thinly sliced
- 2 green onions (including tops), sliced
- 2 tablespoons sliced black olives

Dressing:
- 2 tablespoons fresh lemon juice
- ¼ cup olive oil
- Freshly cracked black pepper
- Ground coriander
- Chopped fresh parsley

Serves: 4
Preparation: 10 minutes

Salads

1 pound Great Northern beans

Dressing:
2 tablespoons sherry vinegar
Generous dash of fresh lemon juice
½ teaspoon salt
½ teaspoon freshly ground pepper
8 tablespoons virgin olive oil

2 bay leaves
½ pound fresh green beans; cut into 1-inch pieces
½ medium red onion, finely chopped
2 shallots, finely chopped
¼ cup finely chopped fresh parsley
½ teaspoon dried oregano
¼ teaspoon dried thyme
1 pound (more if desired) roast lamb, cut into julienne strips
1 pint cherry tomatoes
Boston lettuce

Serves: 6–8
Preparation: 20 minutes
Soaking: Overnight
Cooking: 1 hour
Chilling: 2 hours
Temperature: 350°

Lamb and Bean Salad

Great with iced tomato soup in summer or hot tomato soup in winter.

Place Great Northern beans in large kettle or Dutch oven. Cover with water and soak overnight.

Preheat oven to 350°.

Whisk together all dressing ingredients in small bowl.

Bring soaked beans to a boil. Add bay leaves; cover and simmer for 1 hour in the oven. Drain and place beans in large bowl. Remove bay leaves.

Cook green beans in medium-size saucepan until crisp tender. Drain. Add green beans, onion, shallots, parsley, oregano, thyme, lamb, tomatoes and dressing to beans in bowl; toss gently. Chill for at least 2 hours. (May marinate for up to 8 hours.) Serve on lettuce leaves.

Beef and Potato Salad in Sour Dough Round

Unique main dish salad—great for picnics.

Place mushrooms and vinaigrette in small bowl. Marinate for 1 hour.

Peel potatoes and cook in boiling salted water just until tender. Drain potatoes. Slice potatoes and place in large bowl.

Place mayonnaise in small bowl. Stir in mustard and vinegar. While potatoes are still hot, add enough mayonnaise mixture to coat. Add beef, mushrooms with vinaigrette, shallots, parsley, onion, salt and pepper. Toss gently, adding mayonnaise, as needed, to thoroughly coat.

Slice off top of bread and scoop out center, leaving shell about 1-inch thick for round and ½-inch thick for rolls.

Butter inside of shell generously and fill with salad. Chill at least 1 hour or until ready to serve.

Note: Potato preparation and marinating of mushrooms may be done ahead. Salad may be packed in bread shells several hours before serving. Actually better if made ahead.

½	pound mushrooms, thinly sliced
½	cup vinaigrette dressing (see page 307)
1	pound red potatoes
	Salt
1	cup mayonnaise
1	teaspoon Dijon mustard
1	tablespoon cider vinegar
1¼	pounds rare roast beef, thinly sliced and cut into strips
2	shallots, finely chopped
3	tablespoons finely chopped parsley
1	green onion, thinly sliced
	Salt
	Freshly ground pepper
1	(10-inch) round of unsliced sour dough bread (may substitute 4 large sour dough rolls)
	Butter, softened

Serves:	4–6
Preparation:	40 minutes
Marinating:	1 hour
Cooking:	30 minutes
Chilling:	1 hour

Salads

- 2 pounds red potatoes
- ½ cup olive oil
- 3–4 tablespoons white wine vinegar
- 2 tablespoons fresh lemon juice
- 1 teaspoon dried oregano
- 1 teaspoon salt
- ½ teaspoon pepper
- ¾ pound fresh mushrooms, sliced or quartered
- 4 ounces fresh snow peas, stems removed
- ¼ pound cooked ham, cut into julienne strips
- 1 medium green pepper, seeded and chopped
- ½ cup sliced celery
- 3 tablespoons chopped green onion
- 3 tablespoons chopped fresh parsley

Serves: 6
Preparation: 30 minutes
Cooking: 15 minutes
Chilling: 4–6 hours

Potato Salad Deluxe
Travel anywhere with this fabulous salad.

Cook whole unpeeled potatoes in water for 13–15 minutes or until barely tender. Drain and cool. Cut into quarters.

Whisk together oil, vinegar, lemon juice, oregano, salt and pepper. Pour over mushrooms.

Blanch snow peas for 1 minute. Drain. Pour mushrooms and all of the dressing over potatoes. Add snow peas and remaining ingredients. Toss gently.

Chill 4–6 hours but bring to room temperature to serve.

Greek Salad
Tangy and pretty—make ahead and serve.

Combine all salad ingredients in large bowl.

Whisk together dressing ingredients until well combined. Pour over salad; toss gently. Marinate in refrigerator for 4 hours before serving.

- 4 stalks celery, cut diagonally into ¼-inch slices
- 1 cucumber, cut diagonally into ¼-inch slices
- 2 green peppers, seeded and cut diagonally into ¼-inch slices
- 3–4 tomatoes, cut in wedges
- ½ cup sliced, pitted black olives
- ½ cup sliced pimiento-stuffed olives
- 1 medium onion, thinly sliced
- 1 cup cubed feta cheese (may substitute Swiss or Monterey Jack cheese)
- 1 (16-ounce) can artichoke hearts, drained and halved
- 1 cup halved fresh mushrooms

Dressing:
- 1½ cups oil
- ¾ cup red wine vinegar
- ¾ cup finely chopped onion
- 2 cloves garlic, minced
- 2 teaspoons crushed peppercorns
- 1 teaspoon dried rosemary
- 1 teaspoon dried basil
- 1 teaspoon dried oregano

Serves: 8
Preparation: 35 minutes
Chilling: 4 hours

Salads

Cheese and Wurst Salad
Distinguished flavors blend beautifully.

- 4 large knockwurst
- ½ cup thinly sliced celery
- ½ cup diced sweet pickles
- ½ cup seeded and diced green pepper
- ¼ pound natural Swiss cheese, diced
- 2 onions, thinly sliced
- 2 hard-cooked eggs, sliced

Mustard Dressing:
- ½ cup sour cream
- ½ cup mayonnaise
- 3 tablespoons Dijon mustard
- 1 tablespoon prepared horseradish
- 1 tablespoon white vinegar

Place knockwurst in large saucepan with enough water to cover. Bring to a boil; reduce heat and simmer for 10 minutes. Drain knockwurst and cool. Remove casings from meat and slice.

Combine celery, pickles and green pepper in small bowl.

Layer ingredients in large bowl in the following order: knockwurst, cheese, celery mixture, onions and eggs. Cover and chill.

Combine dressing ingredients. Pour over salad just before serving; toss gently.

Serves: 4
Preparation: 25 minutes
Cooking: 15 minutes
Chilling: 2–4 hours

Mandarin Chicken Salad
Light, savory combination.

- 3 cups diced cooked chicken
- 1 cup diced celery
- 2 tablespoons fresh lemon juice
- 1 tablespoon minced onion
- 1 teaspoon salt
- ⅓ cup mayonnaise
- 1 cup seedless green grapes, halved
- 1 (11-ounce) can mandarin oranges, drained
- ½ cup slivered almonds, toasted
- Leaf lettuce

Combine chicken, celery, lemon juice, onion and salt in large bowl. Chill thoroughly. Stir mayonnaise, grapes, mandarin oranges and almonds into chicken mixture. Toss well. Serve on lettuce.

Serving Suggestion: This salad would be lovely and delicious served in a brioche or Popover.

Serves: 6–8
Preparation: 25 minutes
Chilling: 1 hour

Chicken Cranberry Salad
The presentation is beautiful.

Grease 8-inch or 9-inch square pan with mayonnaise.

Combine chicken, celery, parsley, salt, pepper, cream, mayonnaise, lemon juice and almonds in large mixing bowl. Refrigerate for 1 hour.

Combine gelatin with cold water. Let stand for 5 minutes. Add hot water; stir to dissolve gelatin. Add to chicken mixture. Press into prepared pan. Refrigerate until set.

Beat cranberry sauce in small bowl with electric mixer at high speed until fluffy.

Dissolve lemon-flavored gelatin in boiling water in large bowl. Add orange juice and combine with cranberry sauce; mix well. Pour over chicken mixture. Refrigerate until set. Cut into squares and serve on lettuce leaves.

- 3 cups diced cooked chicken
- 1½ cups diced celery
- 2 tablespoons chopped fresh parsley
- 1 teaspoon salt
- ½ teaspoon freshly ground pepper
- ½ cup heavy (whipping) cream
- 1 cup mayonnaise
- 2 tablespoons fresh lemon juice
- ½ cup almonds, toasted
- 1 envelope unflavored gelatin
- ¼ cup cold water
- ¼ cup hot water

Topping:
- 1 (8-ounce) can jellied cranberry sauce
- 1 (3-ounce) package lemon-flavored gelatin
- ¾ cup boiling water
- 1 (6-ounce) can frozen orange juice concentrate, thawed
- Lettuce leaves

Serves: 6–8
Preparation: 25 minutes
Chilling: 6–8 hours, divided

Chicken Tostada Salad

A fun alternative to the typical taco salad.

2 cups shredded lettuce
2–3 cups diced cooked chicken
1 (4-ounce) can green chilies, undrained
½ teaspoon chili powder
¼ teaspoon ground cumin
½ teaspoon salt
¼ teaspoon garlic powder
1 (16-ounce) can kidney beans, drained
1 cup grated Cheddar cheese (may substitute Monterey Jack cheese)
1 large tomato, chopped
1 medium cucumber; peeled, seeded and chopped
⅓ cup ripe olives, sliced
½ cup sour cream
3 tablespoons taco sauce
8–12 tostada shells

Serves: 4–6
Preparation: 30 minutes
Chilling: Overnight

Place lettuce in bottom of deep 2½-quart bowl.

Combine chicken, chilies with liquid, chili powder, cumin, salt and garlic powder. Mix well to distribute spices. Spoon over lettuce. Layer beans, cheese, tomato, cucumber and olives on top.

Combine sour cream and taco sauce. Pour over layered mixture. Cover bowl with plastic wrap and refrigerate several hours or overnight.

When ready to serve, warm tostada shells in oven for 2–3 minutes or until just warm. Toss salad ingredients and serve on warm shells.

Chicken-Wild Rice Salad
Tangy, textured and terrific.

Combine chicken, pineapple and rice in large bowl. Whisk together vinegar, oil, salt and curry powder in small bowl. Combine with chicken mixture. Chill for 3 hours. Add remaining ingredients to chicken mixture. Toss gently. Serve on lettuce leaves.

- 4 whole chicken breasts, cooked and cubed
- 1 (8-ounce) can crushed pineapple, drained
- 1 (6-ounce) package long grain and wild rice, cooked according to package directions
- 1 tablespoon red wine vinegar
- 2 tablespoons oil
- 1 teaspoon salt
- ¾ teaspoon curry powder
- 1 cup diced celery
- ¼ cup seeded and chopped green pepper
- ½ cup chopped pecans
- 1½ cups mayonnaise
- 1–2 tablespoons dry sherry (optional)
- Lettuce leaves

Serves: 10–12
Preparation: 45 minutes
Chilling: 3 hours

Salads

Rice Salad
Festive and tasty.

5–6 cups cooked long grain rice, cooled completely
Carrots
Broccoli
Zucchini
Cherry tomatoes
Radishes
Green pepper
Green onions
Celery
Any other favorite fresh vegetable

Dressing:
4 ounces creamy Italian dressing (more if necessary)
½ cup mayonnaise
1 tablespoon Worcestershire sauce
Salt
Freshly ground pepper

Serves: 10–12
Preparation: 30 minutes
Marinating: Overnight

Chop a variety of fresh and colorful vegetables into bite-size pieces. Place in large bowl. Add rice.

Combine Italian dressing, mayonnaise and Worcestershire in small bowl. Add salt and pepper to taste; mix well. Pour over vegetables and toss gently. Place in refrigerator and marinate for several hours or overnight.

Note: The rice will absorb much of the dressing. Additional Italian dressing may need to be added before serving.

Shrimp-Filled Cucumber Boats
Elegant taste and appearance.

Place cucumbers close together in large skillet so they support each other while cooking. Pour broth and vermouth over cucumbers. Add bay leaf, thyme, salt and pepper. Simmer over low heat until tender but still firm, about 10 minutes. Cool in broth and refrigerate until well chilled. (Cucumbers may be prepared a day ahead.)

Prepare shrimp filling while cucumbers chill. Whisk together mayonnaise, parsley, oil, chives, capers, onion and anchovy paste. Fold in shrimp and artichokes. Refrigerate until ready to serve.

Remove yolk from egg and sieve. Slice egg white into strips. Combine parsley, basil and green onions.

Assemble just before serving. Make a bed of lettuce on individual plates or a platter, if for a buffet. Top with cucumber boats. Spoon shrimp mixture into cucumbers. Garnish by sprinkling tops with parsley mixture, sieved yolks and egg white strips. Crisscross pimiento strips on each cucumber.

- 4 (6-inch) cucumbers; peeled, halved lengthwise and seeded
- 2 cups rich chicken broth or stock
- ½ cup dry vermouth
- Bay leaf
- Dash of ground thyme
- Salt
- Freshly ground pepper

Filling:
- 1 cup mayonnaise
- 2 tablespoons chopped fresh parsley
- 2 tablespoons olive oil
- 2 tablespoons chopped fresh chives
- 1 tablespoon capers
- 1 tablespoon finely minced green onion
- 1 teaspoon anchovy paste
- 1 pound shrimp; cooked, peeled and coarsely chopped
- 4 large artichoke bottoms, cut into thin strips

Garnishes:
- 1 hard-cooked egg
- 2 tablespoons chopped fresh parsley
- 1 teaspoon dried basil
- 1 tablespoon chopped green onion
- Lettuce
- 2 whole pimientos, seeded and cut into thin strips

Serves: 8
Preparation: 30 minutes
Cooking: 10 minutes
Chilling: 2–6 hours

Crab Salad Printanier

Make ahead and assemble when ready to serve.

4 large fresh artichokes (may substitute 16-ounce can artichoke bottoms, drained)

Mayonnaise:
  2 egg yolks
  Salt
  Freshly ground pepper
  Pinch of dry mustard
  2 tablespoons oil
  2 teaspoons white wine vinegar

2 tablespoons vinaigrette dressing (see page 307)
Juice of ½ orange, reserve rind
4 large Bibb or Boston lettuce leaves
8 ounces cooked crab meat (may substitute frozen or canned crab meat)
2 ounces pitted black olives

Serves: 4
Preparation: 30 minutes
Marinating: 2 hours
Cooking: 50 minutes

Cook and prepare artichoke bottoms according to directions on page 205.

Prepare mayonnaise while artichokes cook. Beat egg yolks together in small bowl with salt, pepper and mustard until thick. Add oil, drop by drop, until mixture is very thick; beat constantly. Beat in vinegar. Add additional salt and pepper, if desired. Mayonnaise may be prepared in food processor or blender.

Spoon vinaigrette over artichoke bottoms and marinate in refrigerator until cold.

Remove a 3-inch strip of orange rind with peeler; cut into fine shreds. Place in small saucepan. Add ½ cup water and cook 2–3 minutes; drain well and reserve.

Arrange lettuce leaves on salad plates. Place artichoke bottom on lettuce and cover with crab meat. Flavor mayonnaise with small amount of orange juice to taste. Spoon mayonnaise over crab meat. Garnish with reserved shredded orange rind and olives.

Serving Suggestion: Brown bread with butter makes this a complete meal.

Shrimp Tomato Vinaigrette

Outstanding and only 210 calories per serving.

Combine tomatoes, shrimp, pea pods and onion in large bowl.

Whisk together remaining ingredients until well blended. Pour over shrimp mixture. Toss gently. Cover and refrigerate for several hours. Serve on lettuce leaves.

- 16 cherry tomatoes (may substitute 4 medium tomatoes, cut into wedges)
- 2 cups cooked jumbo or salad shrimp, cleaned
- 6–8 ounces fresh pea pods
- 2 tablespoons sliced green onion
- 2 tablespoons dry white wine
- 2 tablespoons white vinegar
- ¼ cup oil
- 1 package Italian salad dressing mix (may substitute your own seasoning selection)
- Freshly ground pepper
- 1–2 teaspoons drained capers (optional)
- Boston or leaf lettuce

Serves: 4
Preparation: 15 minutes
Chilling: 4–6 hours

Garden-Style Seafood Salad
Savor this inviting salad.

Prepare macaroni according to package directions. Drain well. Place in large bowl and add salad dressing. Toss gently. Add cucumber, tomatoes, onion, green pepper, celery, salt, pepper and drained seafood to macaroni.

Combine mayonnaise, mustard and dill weed in small bowl. Add to macaroni and toss gently. Cover and chill at least 4 hours before serving.

- 2½ cups macaroni, (seashell and wagon wheel make attractive salad)
- 1½ cups Italian salad dressing
- 2 cups peeled and sliced cucumber
- 1½ cups peeled and diced tomatoes
- ½ cup sliced green onion
- ⅓ cup seeded and chopped green pepper
- ⅓ cup chopped celery
- ¾ teaspoon salt
- ¼ teaspoon pepper
- 13 ounces seafood (solid white tuna, shrimp, crab or combination), drained if necessary
- 1 cup mayonnaise
- 1 tablespoon prepared mustard
- 1½ teaspoons dried dill weed

Yield: 12 (1 cup) servings
Preparation: 25 minutes
Chilling: 4 hours

Pesto and Pasta Salad
Personal taste and creativity make this masterpiece.

Combine pesto ingredients in blender or food processor and process thoroughly.

Cook desired amount of pasta, according to package directions. Cool.

Select any or all of the variations, using as much or as little as desired. A variety of colors looks the most appetizing.

Just before serving, combine variations, pasta and enough dressing to lightly cover ingredients. Add salt and pepper to taste. Serve immediately. Refrigerate leftovers. Bring to room temperature before serving again. Add more dressing, if needed.

Note: You are responsible for the quantity and combinations for this pasta salad. You can make no mistakes.

Pesto:
- ½ cup mayonnaise
- ½ cup freshly grated Parmesan cheese
- 1 cup finely chopped fresh parsley
- 1 clove garlic
- 2 teaspoons dried basil
- ½ teaspoon dried marjoram
- ½ cup olive oil
- ½ cup chopped walnuts

Pasta:
- Rotini (may substitute a combination of rotini and spinach tortellini filled with cheese)

Suggested Variations:
- Snow peas, blanched
- Broccoli, blanched
- Artichoke hearts
- Carrot rounds, lightly steamed
- Frozen peas, defrosted
- Zucchini rounds, sliced and quartered
- Cherry tomatoes
- Pimiento, cut into thin strips
- Black or green olives, sliced
- Red onion, thinly sliced
- Red or green peppers, seeded and sliced
- Chicken, cooked and cubed
- Pepperoni rounds
- Salami chunks
- Salt
- Freshly ground pepper

Yield: Your choice
Preparation: 30 minutes

Summer Pasta with Basil, Tomatoes and Cheese

Unique alliance of fresh tastes.

Toss together tomatoes, garlic, basil, mint, salt, black pepper, red pepper and oil in medium-size bowl. Let stand at room temperature, tossing occasionally, for 2–3 hours.

Cook pasta according to package directions until tender but still firm. Drain and transfer to large serving bowl. Measure ¼ cup of liquid from tomato mixture. Add to pasta; toss gently to coat.

Add cheeses to warm pasta and toss until cheese begins to melt. Add tomato mixture; toss until mixed.

Serve warm or at room temperature.

Ingredients

- 4 medium tomatoes; peeled, seeded and coarsely chopped
- 4 cloves garlic, minced
- ½ cup chopped fresh basil (may substitute ¼ cup chopped fresh parsley plus 2 tablespoons dried basil)
- 1 tablespoon chopped fresh mint
- 1 teaspoon salt
- ½ teaspoon freshly ground black pepper
- ¼ teaspoon crushed red pepper
- ½ cup virgin olive oil
- 1 pound small macaroni shells or rotini
- ½ cup freshly grated Parmesan cheese
- ½ pound Fontina cheese, finely diced (approximately 2 cups)

Serves: 8–10
Preparation: 30 minutes
Marinating: 3 hours

Crab Meat Mold

Cucumber sauce adds extra flavor to this attractive display.

Grease a 6-cup ring mold with mayonnaise.

Dissolve gelatin in water in large bowl. Stir in chili sauce and mayonnaise; mix well. Chill until slightly thickened, about 20 minutes.

Drain crab meat and remove any shells that may be present. Stir crab, relish and celery into gelatin mixture. Pour into prepared ring mold and chill until firm. Unmold on serving platter.

Combine ingredients for sauce in large bowl; mix well. Pour over mold. Garnish with cherry tomatoes, watercress and black olives.

- 2 (3-ounce) packages lemon-flavored gelatin
- 1½ cups boiling water
- 1 cup chili sauce
- 1 cup mayonnaise
- 2 (6½-ounce) cans crab meat
- 2 tablespoons pickle relish
- 1 cup chopped celery

Cucumber Sauce:
- 2 cups sour cream
- 2 cups seeded and grated cucumber, drained well
- 1 tablespoon fresh lemon juice
- ⅛ teaspoon granulated sugar
- Horseradish

Suggested Garnishes:
- Cherry tomatoes
- Watercress
- Black olives

Serves: 10–12
Preparation: 15 minutes
Chilling: 6–12 hours

Cucumber Aspic

Crunchy texture—refreshing flavor.

Grease a 1-quart mold or a 4-cup ring mold with mayonnaise.

Dissolve gelatin in water. Pour into blender or food processor. Add cream cheese, mayonnaise and onion. Process until well blended.

Stir in cucumber and nuts. Pour into prepared mold. Chill until firm. Unmold to serve.

- 1 (3-ounce) package lime-flavored gelatin
- ¾ cup boiling water
- 1 (3-ounce) package cream cheese, softened
- 1 cup mayonnaise
- 1 tablespoon grated onion
- ¾ cup peeled, seeded and grated cucumber
- ¾ cup slivered almonds (may substitute chopped pecans)

Serves: 6–8
Preparation: 20 minutes
Chilling: 4–6 hours

Blueberry Layer Mold

This lovely salad appeals to both men and women.

Grease a 2-quart mold, preferably a ring mold.

Dissolve lemon-flavored gelatin in boiling water. Place gelatin, half and half, vanilla, confectioners' sugar and cream cheese in blender. Process until well combined. Pour into mold and refrigerate until completely set.

Dissolve black-raspberry-flavored gelatin in boiling water. Stir in blueberries and pour over molded cream cheese mixture. Refrigerate until completely set. Unmold before serving.

First Layer:
- 1 (3-ounce) package lemon-flavored gelatin
- 1¼ cups boiling water
- 1 cup half and half
- 1 teaspoon vanilla
- 3 tablespoons confectioners' sugar
- 1 (8-ounce) package cream cheese, softened

Second Layer:
- 2 (3-ounce) packages black-raspberry-flavored gelatin
- 3 cups boiling water
- 2 (16-ounce) cans blueberries, well drained

Serves: 10–12
Preparation: 15 minutes
Chilling: 4–5 hours

Two-Layer Cranberry Salad
Color and taste complement fowl.

Lightly oil 6-cup ring mold.

Combine gelatin and sugar. Add boiling water and stir until completely dissolved. Blend in lemon juice and cranberry relish. Pour mixture into mold. Place mold in ice water and chill until set but not firm, about 15–20 minutes.

Boil cranberry juice and pour over gelatin. Stir until dissolved. Add remaining ingredients and stir until well mixed. Place bowl containing cottage cheese mixture in bowl of ice water and chill until mixture begins to set. Spoon over cranberry layer in mold. Chill until set. Unmold on a chilled plate.

First Layer:
- 1 (3-ounce) package orange-flavored gelatin
- 3 tablespoons granulated sugar
- 1 cup boiling water
- 2 teaspoons fresh lemon juice
- 1 (10-ounce) package frozen cranberry-orange relish

Second Layer:
- ½ cup cranberry juice
- 1 (3-ounce) package orange-flavored gelatin
- 1½ cups small curd, cream-style cottage cheese
- 1 cup sour cream
- 1 teaspoon fresh lemon juice
- ¼ teaspoon salt
- 1 cup diced celery
- ½ cup chopped walnuts

Serves:	16
Preparation:	15 minutes
Setting:	20 minutes
Chilling:	3 hours

Salads

- 1 (3-ounce) package lime-flavored gelatin
- 1 cup boiling water
- 1 (6-ounce) can crushed pineapple, drained (reserve juice)
- ½ cup granulated sugar
- 1 (3-ounce) package cream cheese, softened
- ½ cup chopped celery
- ½ cup chopped nuts

Serves: 6–8
Preparation: 15 minutes
Chilling: 4–5 hours

- 1 (16-ounce) can pitted dark cherries, drained (reserve juice)
- 1 (3-ounce) package black-cherry-flavored gelatin
- 1 cup port wine

Topping:
- 1 cup heavy (whipping) cream
- 1 cup miniature marshmallows
- 1 (3-ounce) package cream cheese, softened

Serves: 8
Preparation: 20 minutes
Chilling: 4–6 hours

Pineapple-Lime Mold
Refreshing color and flavor.

Grease a 5-cup mold with mayonnaise.

Dissolve gelatin in water.

Add enough water to the reserved pineapple juice to make 1 cup. Cook pineapple juice and sugar in medium-size saucepan over medium heat until clear, approximately 3–5 minutes. Cool slightly.

Blend gelatin, pineapple juice and cream cheese in blender. Stir in pineapple, celery and nuts. Pour into prepared mold and chill until thoroughly set.

Wine Cherry Supreme
No need to worry about unmolding this one.

Bring reserved cherry juice to a boil in small saucepan. Add gelatin and dissolve. Add port wine and cherries. Pour gelatin mixture into 6-cup serving bowl, preferably glass. Chill until set.

Soak marshmallows in whipping cream for 2 hours.

Add cream cheese to marshmallow mixture. Beat with electric mixer until whipped. Pour over gelatin and serve.

Note: Must be refrigerated.

Summertime Melon Salad
Light and tangy.

Combine lemonade, marmalade and Triple Sec in small bowl.

Combine melon balls, strawberries, pineapple and mandarin oranges in large bowl. Pour marinade over fruit mixture and stir gently. Cover and chill at least 2 hours. To serve, spoon fruit mixture into cantaloupe halves. Garnish each with a whole strawberry.

Marinade:
- 1 (6-ounce) can frozen lemonade concentrate, thawed
- ¼ cup orange marmalade
- 2 tablespoons Triple Sec, more if desired

- 3 cups assorted melon balls (honeydew, watermelon, cantaloupe)
- 1 cup hulled and halved, fresh strawberries
- 2 cups fresh pineapple chunks
- 1 (11-ounce) can mandarin oranges, drained (may substitute fresh orange sections)
- 4 cantaloupes, halved
- 8 whole strawberries

Serves: 8
Preparation: 20 minutes
Chilling: 2 hours

Orange and Avocado Salad
Delicate flavors unite in a lovely showpiece.

Pour lemon juice into shallow bowl. Peel avocados and cut lengthwise into ¼-inch slices. (While slicing, leave seed in avocado to prevent avocado from turning dark.) Immediately dip the slices into lemon juice.

Peel oranges and remove any remaining white skin. (The skin gives oranges a bitter taste.) Cut crosswise into ¼-inch slices; remove the seeds.

Mix mayonnaise, orange juice and paprika with wire whisk to make orange mayonnaise.

Line serving bowl with lettuce leaves. Place alternating layers of orange slices and avocado slices on lettuce, ending with avocado slices. *Do not toss.* Drizzle with a little of orange mayonnaise and serve remaining sauce at the table.

- ¼ cup fresh lemon juice
- 2 avocados
- 3 oranges
- ¾ cup mayonnaise
- ¼ cup fresh orange juice
- ½ teaspoon paprika
- Romaine or leaf lettuce

Serves: 4–6
Preparation: 30 minutes

Salads

2 (16-ounce) cans pear halves
2 (3-ounce) packages cream cheese, softened
1 tablespoon grated orange peel
2 tablespoons granulated sugar
¼ cup chopped pecans (may substitute walnuts)

Cranberry Dressing:
¾ cup whole berry cranberry sauce
¼ cup oil
1 tablespoon fresh lemon juice
1 tablespoon granulated sugar

Garnishes:
Salad greens
Whole cranberries

Serves: 6
Preparation: 20 minutes
Chilling: 6–8 hours

Pears with Cranberry Dressing
Dazzle your holiday company with this one.

Drain pears, reserving 2 tablespoons syrup.

Beat cream cheese, orange peel, sugar and enough reserved syrup to make mixture spreadable. Stir in pecans.

Spread cream cheese mixture over cut sides of 6 pear halves, covering entire surface. Top with pear half which has not been spread with mixture and press together. Chill thoroughly.

Combine cranberry sauce, oil, lemon juice and sugar in blender and blend until smooth.

Place stuffed pears upright on serving platter or individual salad plates lined with salad greens. Garnish with whole cranberries. Spoon dressing over pears.

Bananas, sliced
Fresh grapefruit sections
Orange sections
Avocado chunks
Bacon, fried crisp and crumbled
Cashews
Coconut (optional)
Celery Seed Dressing

Serves: 6
Preparation: 30 minutes

Fruit Salad Olé
Interesting mix of flavors and textures.

Combine equal amounts of each ingredient in large bowl. Toss with Celery Seed Dressing. Serve immediately.

Hint:
To section an orange or grapefruit, pare outer skin from fruit with serrated knife. Be sure to cut all white skin from fruit as skin causes bitter taste. Pull fruit to separate into halves. Holding fruit half in one hand, use knife to separate membrane from top section; remove seeds. Use knife to gently lift fruit section from bottom membrane. Repeat process for all remaining sections.

French Fruit Salad
Refreshing and elegant.

Place fruit in large bowl. Sprinkle with sugar and moisten with wine. Toss gently and refrigerate for 2–3 hours. Remove fruit from refrigerator just before serving. Add Cointreau and toss gently.

Note: Fruit begins to get soggy if allowed to sit longer than 3 hours.

Note: Seasonal fruits vary in natural sweetness. Sugar may be adjusted or omitted according to taste.

- 2 oranges, peeled and sectioned
- 2 bananas, peeled and sliced
- 2 pears, peeled and sliced
- 1 small pineapple; peeled, cored and cut into chunks
- ½ pint strawberries; washed, hulled and halved
- 3 tablespoons granulated sugar
- ¾ cup dry white wine
- 1–2 ounces Cointreau

Serves: 6–8
Preparation: 30 minutes
Chilling: 2 hours

Korean Salad Dressing
Delicious on any lettuce or spinach salad.

Combine all ingredients in medium-size saucepan. Place over medium heat; cook and stir until sugar dissolves. Cool.

- ½ cup granulated sugar
- ½ cup oil
- ¼ cup red wine vinegar
- 2 tablespoons Worcestershire sauce
- ¼ cup catsup

Yield: 1 cup
Preparation: 10 minutes

Poppy Seed Dressing
Keeps in refrigerator for weeks.

Chop onion in blender. Add sugar, salt, mustard and vinegar. Turn blender on high speed and slowly drizzle oil into onion mixture. Process until dressing is well mixed and thickened. Add poppy seed. Blend for 1 minute.

- 1 medium onion, quartered
- 1½ cups granulated sugar
- 2 teaspoons salt
- 2 teaspoons dry mustard
- ⅔ cup cider vinegar
- 2 cups oil
- 3 tablespoons poppy seed

Yield: 3–4 cups
Preparation: 10 minutes

 Dressings

- 1 green pepper, seeded and cut-up
- 4 stalks celery, cut-up
- 2 ripe avocados, peeled and cut-up
- ¾ cup safflower oil
- ¼ cup fresh lemon juice
- 2 tablespoons honey
- 2 cloves garlic
- Freshly ground pepper

Yield: 3 cups
Preparation: 15 minutes

- ¾ cup oil
- ½ cup red wine vinegar
- 5 tablespoons granulated sugar
- 1½ teaspoons salt
- 1 clove garlic, crushed
- ½ pound bacon, cooked and crumbled
- 2 tablespoons sesame seed, toasted
- 2 ounces blue cheese, crumbled

Yield: 1 cup
Preparation: 20 minutes

- ½ cup granulated sugar
- 1 teaspoon dry mustard
- 1 teaspoon salt
- ¼ medium onion, grated
- ⅓ cup cider vinegar
- 1 cup oil
- 1 tablespoon celery seed

Yield: 1½ cups
Preparation: 10 minutes

New Orleans Salad Dressing
Great on taco salad, sandwiches or as a dip.

Place green pepper, celery and avocados in blender or food processor. Add remaining ingredients. Blend until smooth. Refrigerate.

Note: The green pepper and celery give the dressing a wonderful texture.

Blue Cheese Salad Dressing
Ingredients with an affinity for one another.

Combine oil, vinegar, sugar, salt and garlic in large jar. Refrigerate until ready to serve. Add bacon, sesame seed and blue cheese to mixture just before serving. Shake jar until well combined. Serve over romaine lettuce or other salad greens.

Celery Seed Dressing
Wonderful for fruit salads.

Combine sugar, mustard, salt, onion and vinegar in blender or food processor. Blend until sugar is dissolved. While processor is running, add oil, 1 tablespoon at a time, until dressing is thick and creamy. Stir in celery seed.

Serving Suggestion: Place fresh grapefruit sections and avocado slices on bibb lettuce. Sprinkle with pomegranate seeds and spoon celery seed dressing on top.

Green Pepper Jelly
A Hoosier favorite.

Remove seeds from peppers. Process in blender or food processor until peppers are juice. (Peppers should yield 1 cup juice.) Strain through a sieve.

Combine strained juice, sugar and vinegar in large saucepan. Bring to a boil and add Certo and cayenne. Boil for 2 minutes more or until slightly thickened. Add a few drops of green food coloring, if desired. Pour hot mixture into hot sterilized jelly jars and seal.

3 large green peppers
6 cups granulated sugar
1½ cups cider vinegar
1 bottle Certo
1 teaspoon cayenne pepper
  Green food coloring
    (optional)

Yield: 7–8 cups
Preparation: 10 minutes
Cooking: 10 minutes

Indiana State Fair Peach Jam
A husband and wife team won a blue ribbon

Pit fruit but do not peel. Cut into small pieces or put into blender or food processor and mash coarsely.

Measure 8 cups mashed fruit into large saucepan. Add lemon juice and sugar. Mix well. Place over high heat. Bring to a full rolling boil and boil hard for 1½ minutes, stirring constantly.

Remove from heat and stir in pectin. Let cool slightly, then pour into hot sterilized jelly jars and seal.

6 pounds fully ripe peaches
1¼ cups fresh lemon juice
15 cups granulated sugar
1 (6-ounce) bottle fruit pectin

Yield: 17 cups
Preparation: 15 minutes
Cooking: 1½ minutes

Pickled Beets
So easy and so tasty.

Place beets in 1-quart jar.

Boil sugar, vinegar, water, salt and cloves for 1 minute. Pour liquid over beets. Cool and cover with lid. Refrigerate for at least 24 hours before serving.

2 (9½-ounce) cans small whole beets, drained
1 cup granulated sugar
¾ cup cider vinegar
¼ cup water
1 teaspoon salt
4–5 whole cloves

Yield: 1 quart
Preparation: 5 minutes
Chilling: 24 hours

Relishes

- 7 cups thinly sliced unpeeled cucumbers
- 1 cup thinly sliced onions, separated
- ½ cup seeded and sliced green peppers
- ½ cup seeded and sliced red peppers
- 1½ cups granulated sugar
- 1 cup white vinegar
- 1 teaspoon celery seed
- 1 teaspoon salt

Serves: 12
Preparation: 15 minutes
Chilling: Overnight

- 5 cups chopped, unpeeled apples (about 7–8 apples)
- 2 cups tomato sauce
- 1⅔ cups firmly packed brown sugar
- 1 cup cider vinegar
- 1 cup raisins
- 1 sweet red pepper, seeded and chopped
- 2 medium onions, chopped
- 1 tablespoon freshly grated ginger root
- 1 teaspoon salt

Yield: 4 pints
Preparation: 30 minutes
Cooking: 1 hour

Uncooked Cucumber Slices
A favorite standby.

Mix all ingredients; let stand in refrigerator overnight.

Note: Keeps for weeks in refrigerator.

Apple Chutney
Delicious flavor and easy to make.

Combine all ingredients in large heavy saucepan. Bring to a boil, stirring frequently. Reduce heat and simmer for 45–60 minutes or until thickened, stirring occasionally. Pour immediately into sterilized jelly jars and seal. (Chutney may be cooled, placed in sterilized jelly jars and stored in refrigerator.)

Note: Granny Smith apples or similar tart apples are best.

Eggs, Cheese and Pasta

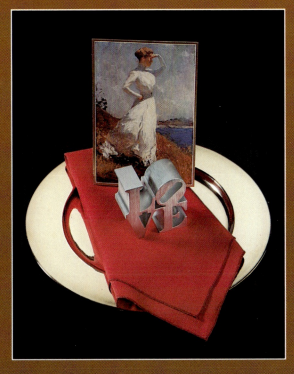

The Indianapolis Museum of Art

On a green rise overlooking the meandering passage of the White River, the Indianapolis Museum of Art commands the city's northwest horizon like the dominant jewel in a crown.

This magnificent modern facility, completed in 1970, houses a collection which spans 4,000 years of artistic creation and presents a kaleidoscopic assortment of art and art objects. Painting, sculpture, graphic and decorative arts are all exquisitely represented on the Museum's three handsome levels. Rubens and Rembrandt, Picasso and Monet are among the scores of Masters whose works are included in the permanent collection.

The Museum's setting, in the midst of 154 acres of lush botanical and natural gardens, encompasses a host of additional attractions. Oldfields Lilly Pavilion of Decorative Arts, once the home of Indianapolis pharmaceutical heir J. K. Lilly, showcases in period room settings, two centuries of English, Continental and American furniture, silver and ceramics. The lovely French Chateau mansion, built early in this century, houses a superlative porcelain gallery and one of the largest and most important textile exhibitions of its kind.

Showalter Pavilion, also on the Museum grounds, serves as a year-round stage for outstanding ballet and theater productions. In summer, the Museum's terrace becomes a setting for a variety of outdoor activities including a series of musical performances ranging in content from classics to jazz. Often guests bring picnic suppers and settle in at dusk to enjoy the acts and the ambience.

A late summer "Penrod Festival" is sponsored by an organization of businessmen/art lovers. Held on the Museum grounds, it presents a potpourri of buyable arts, crafts and edibles, features strolling performers, mimes and musicians, and attracts huge enthusiastic crowds to the site.

The Indianapolis Museum of Art unfailingly wins the unanimous admiration of visitors and of Indianapolis natives who count their art museum as a prime source of pride for their city.

EGGS, CHEESE AND PASTA

Eggs and Cheese
Brunch Eggs . . . 105
Cheese Soufflé with
 Seafood Sauce . . . 109
Chili Egg Puff . . . 108
Eggs Continental . . . 107
Ouefs avec Fruits de
 Mer . . . 106
Presnutz . . . 106
Soufflé Roll With
 Filling . . . 110
Three Cheese
 Casserole . . . 108

Quiche
Crustless Spinach
 Quiche . . . 111
Chicken-Broccoli
 Quiche . . . 112
Quiche Lorraine . . . 111
Seafood Quiche . . . 113

Brunch
Crab Meat Crêpes . . . 118
Curried Sausage
 Casserole . . . 117
E'Leis' Grit
 Casserole . . . 117
Gougère with Ham and
 Mushrooms . . . 116
Sausage en Croûte . . . 115
Spinach Frittata . . . 115
Torta Di Pasqua (Italian
 Easter Pie) . . . 114

Pasta
Country Noodles . . . 121
Lasagne Florentine . . . 120
Noodles and Swiss
 Cheese . . . 122
Noodle Kugel . . . 122
Spaghetti alla
 Carbonara . . . 120
Spaghetti and
 Meatballs . . . 119
Spinach Noodle
 Ring . . . 121

Brunch Eggs
Outstanding flavor.

Preheat oven to 350°.

Butter a 9-inch square baking dish.

Cook bacon until crisp; drain and crumble. Sauté onion in bacon drippings (may substitute butter).

Melt butter in large saucepan over medium heat. Add flour, stirring until mixture is smooth and bubbling. Remove from heat; stir in milk and cream gradually. Return to heat and bring to a boil over medium-high heat, stirring constantly. Boil for 1 minute. Reduce heat and add thyme, marjoram, basil and cheese. Stir until cheese is melted.

Layer in prepared baking dish as follows: ½ the sauce, ½ the eggs, ½ the spinach and ½ the onion. Reserve a few bacon bits. Sprinkle ½ the remaining bacon over onion. Repeat the layers. Sprinkle top with bread crumbs, then with reserved bacon and the parsley. Bake at 350° for about 40 minutes.

- ½ pound sliced bacon
- 2 medium onions, finely chopped
- 4 tablespoons (½ stick) butter
- ¼ cup all-purpose flour
- 1 cup milk
- 1 cup light (coffee) cream
- ¼ teaspoon dried thyme
- ¼ teaspoon dried marjoram
- ¼ teaspoon dried basil
- 1 pound Swiss, Gruyère or Cheddar cheese, grated
- 6 hard-cooked eggs; thinly sliced
- 1 pound fresh spinach; cooked, drained well and chopped (may substitute 10-ounce package frozen chopped spinach)
- Buttered fresh bread crumbs
- ¼ cup chopped fresh parsley

Serves: 6
Preparation: 30 minutes
Baking: 40 minutes
Temperature: 350°

Eggs and Cheese

Presnutz

Quick and unusual Serbian dish.

Preheat oven to 350°.

Melt butter in oven in 9x13-inch baking dish.

Squeeze spinach to remove excess moisture.

Combine all cheeses in large bowl. Add spinach, flour, eggs and milk to cheeses. Pour ½ of melted butter into cheese mixture. Return baking dish with remaining butter to oven. Stir cheese mixture until thoroughly combined; pour into heated baking dish. Bake at 350° for 45–60 minutes. Cut into squares to serve.

- ½ cup (1 stick) butter
- 2 (10-ounce) packages frozen chopped spinach, thawed
- 1 pound Monterey Jack cheese, cubed
- 1 pint large curd, cream-style cottage cheese
- ½ pint ricotta cheese
- ½ pound feta cheese
- ½ cup all-purpose flour
- 10 eggs, beaten
- 2 cups milk

Serves: 10–12
Preparation: 15 minutes
Baking: 1 hour
Temperature: 350°

Ouefs avec Fruits de Mer

Superior.

Preheat oven to 350°.

Grease 2 (9-inch) pie plates.

Melt 4 tablespoons butter in large skillet over medium heat. Sauté onions and mushrooms until most of mushroom juice has evaporated. Remove from heat; add remaining 2 tablespoons butter, stirring gently until melted. Stir in crab and shrimp; toss gently to cover with butter. Set aside to cool completely.

Beat eggs well in medium-size bowl. Add sour cream, wine, nutmeg, salt and pepper. Mix well. Pour into crab mixture in skillet; stir to combine. Divide mixture between 2 prepared pie plates. Sprinkle with paprika. Bake at 350° for 45–60 minutes or until toothpick inserted in center comes out clean. Let stand for 10 minutes before cutting into wedges and serve.

Note: To prepare ahead, bake pies then cover and refrigerate. Bring to room temperature before reheating at 350° for 20–30 minutes.

- 6 tablespoons butter, divided
- 1 medium onion, thinly sliced
- 1 pound fresh mushrooms, thinly sliced
- 2 (6½-ounce) cans crab meat, drained and picked clean
- 4 ounces cooked shrimp, chopped
- 8 eggs
- 1 cup sour cream
- ¼ cup dry white wine
- Dash of ground nutmeg
- Salt
- Freshly ground pepper
- Paprika

Serves: 8–10
Preparation: 15 minutes
Baking: 1 hour
Cooling: 10 minutes
Temperature: 350°

Eggs Continental
Fancy individual brunch fare.

Preheat oven to 400°.

Grease 4 (1¼-cup) casseroles or ramekins.

Combine bread, butter, Gruyère, garlic, ½ teaspoon salt and ¼ teaspoon paprika in small baking dish. Bake at 400° for 5 minutes; let cool. Transfer mixture to blender and process until well combined.

Combine sour cream, bacon, milk, onion, remaining ½ teaspoon salt, remaining ¼ teaspoon paprika and pepper in a bowl.

Divide baked crumb mixture equally among the prepared ramekins. Arrange 2 sliced eggs in each ramekin. Sprinkle eggs lightly with salt, if desired. Top each with ¼ of the sour cream mixture. Sprinkle each ramekin with ¼ cup Cheddar. Bake at 400° for 15 minutes or until cheese melts.

- 1 cup day-old, coarse white bread, cubed
- 2 tablespoons butter, melted
- 1 teaspoon grated Gruyère cheese (may substitute Parmesan cheese)
- 1 small clove garlic, crushed
- 1 teaspoon salt, divided
- ½ teaspoon sweet Hungarian paprika, divided
- 1 cup sour cream
- 3 slices bacon; cooked, drained and crumbled
- 1 tablespoon milk
- 1 tablespoon minced onion
- ⅛ teaspoon freshly ground pepper
- 8 hard-cooked eggs, sliced
  Salt
- 1 cup grated Cheddar cheese

Serves:	4
Preparation:	20 minutes
Baking:	15 minutes
Temperature:	400°

Eggs and Cheese

- 10 eggs
- ½ cup all-purpose flour
- 1 teaspoon baking powder
- ½ teaspoon salt
- 1 pint small curd, cream-style cottage cheese
- 1 pound Monterey Jack cheese, grated
- ½ cup (1 stick) margarine or butter, melted
- 1 (8-ounce) can large green chilies; rinsed, seeded and diced

Serves:	10–12
Preparation:	15 minutes
Baking:	30 minutes
Temperature:	350°

Chili Egg Puff

Unusual and spicy brunch or supper dish.

Preheat oven to 350°.

Butter well a 9x13-inch baking dish.

Beat eggs in large bowl with electric mixer until lemon colored. Stir in remaining ingredients and mix well. Pour into prepared baking dish. Bake at 350° for 30 minutes.

- 1 pint small curd, cream-style cottage cheese
- 1½ cups grated Cheddar cheese
- 1½ cups grated mozzarella cheese
- 3 eggs, lightly beaten
- 3 tablespoons all-purpose flour
- ¼ cup (½ stick) butter or margarine
- 1 (10-ounce) package frozen spinach, semi-thawed and cut into 1-inch cubes

Serves:	6
Preparation:	10 minutes
Baking:	1 hour
Standing:	15 minutes
Temperature:	350°

Three Cheese Casserole

Easy and hearty—perfect mid-day fare.

Preheat oven to 350°.

Butter an 8-inch square baking dish.

Combine all cheeses, eggs and flour in large bowl. Slice butter into small pieces; stir into mixture. Place in prepared baking dish. Arrange spinach cubes on top. Bake, uncovered, at 350° for 1 hour. Let stand for 15 minutes before serving.

Eggs and Cheese

Cheese Soufflé with Seafood Sauce

An elegant lunch or dinner for two.

Preheat oven to 350°.

Melt butter over low heat in heavy saucepan. Stir in flour, salt, peppers and mustard. Cook over low heat, stirring until mixture is smooth and bubbly. Remove from heat; stir in milk gradually. Return to heat and bring to a boil for 1 minute, stirring constantly. Stir in cheese. Remove from heat and stir in egg yolks.

Beat egg whites and cream of tartar until stiff. Fold in cheese mixture. Pour into ungreased 1-quart soufflé or baking dish. For high hat soufflé, make a groove in mixture 1 inch from edge of dish. Fill another slightly larger dish with 1 inch of hot water. Set baking dish in water. Bake at 350° for 50–55 minutes or until puffed and golden brown. Serve immediately with Seafood Sauce.

Melt butter over low heat in medium-size heavy saucepan. Stir in flour, salt and pepper. Cook over low heat until smooth and bubbly. Remove from heat and stir in milk gradually. Return to heat and bring to a boil. Boil for 1 minute, stirring constantly. Stir in cooked shrimp and Worcestershire. Season with sherry or lemon juice, if desired.

Soufflé:
- 2 tablespoons butter
- 2 tablespoons all-purpose flour
- ¼ teaspoon salt
- Freshly ground pepper
- Dash of cayenne pepper
- ¼ teaspoon dry mustard
- ⅔ cup milk
- ⅔ cup grated sharp Cheddar cheese
- 2 egg yolks, well beaten
- 2 egg whites
- ¼ teaspoon cream of tartar

Seafood Sauce: (makes 1 cup)
- 2 tablespoons butter
- 2 tablespoons all-purpose flour
- ¼ teaspoon salt
- ⅛ teaspoon pepper
- 1 cup milk
- 1 cup cooked shrimp (may substitute lobster, crab meat, salmon or tuna)
- Dash of Worcestershire sauce
- Sherry (optional)
- Fresh lemon juice (optional)

Serves:	2
Preparation:	30 minutes
Baking:	55 minutes
Temperature:	350°

Eggs and Cheese

Soufflé Roll With Filling

Unique and guaranteed to bring raves.

Soufflé Roll:
- 4 tablespoons (½ stick) butter or margarine
- ½ cup all-purpose flour
- 2 cups milk or half and half
- ¼ teaspoon salt
- ½ cup freshly grated Parmesan cheese
- ½ cup grated Cheddar cheese
- 4 egg yolks, slightly beaten
- 4 egg whites

Filling:
- 2 tablespoons butter or margarine
- ½ cup chopped onion
- ¼ pound fresh mushrooms, chopped
- 2 (10-ounce) packages frozen chopped spinach, thawed and drained
- 1 cup diced cooked chicken
- 1 (3-ounce) package cream cheese, softened
- ⅓ cup sour cream
- 2 teaspoons Dijon mustard
- Dash of ground nutmeg
- Salt
- Freshly ground pepper
- Cheddar cheese slices, cut into triangles (optional)

Serves: 8
Preparation: 1 hour
Baking: 65 minutes
Temperature: 325°

Preheat oven to 325°.

Grease and flour wax paper-lined 15x10-inch jelly roll pan.

Melt butter in large saucepan over low heat. Stir in flour. Cook and stir over medium heat until well blended, about 2 minutes. Add milk gradually. Stir constantly until mixture comes to a boil and thickens. Remove from heat; stir in salt and cheeses. Stir small amount of batter into yolks. (Mixture will be thick.) Add yolk mixture to batter and stir until well combined.

Beat egg whites in large bowl until stiff but not dry. Fold small amount of batter into whites; gently fold remaining batter into whites. Pour mixture into prepared pan. Bake at 325° for 40–45 minutes or until golden and surface springs back when lightly pressed. Cover with linen towel, invert onto another baking sheet and carefully remove wax paper. Roll up soufflé with the towel.

Melt butter over low heat in medium-size saucepan. Sauté onion and mushrooms over medium heat. Squeeze excess moisture from spinach. Stir in spinach, chicken, cream cheese and sour cream. Cook and stir until cheese is melted. Add mustard, nutmeg, salt and pepper.

Preheat oven to 375°.

Assemble by unrolling soufflé and spreading filling over the top. Beginning with long edge, roll up soufflé, using towel to help. Place, seam down, on serving platter. (Roll may be refrigerated overnight or frozen at this point. Bring to room temperature before reheating.) Cover soufflé with foil and reheat at 375° for 20 minutes or until heated through. Place Cheddar cheese triangles on top of soufflé and slide under broiler until cheese melts.

Variation: May substitute 1 cup diced ham for chicken. Increase Dijon mustard to 1 tablespoon. Increase nutmeg to ¼ teaspoon.

Quiche Lorraine
The best.

Preheat oven to 450°.

Prick holes in pastry shell and bake at 450° for 5 minutes. Remove from oven. Reduce heat to 350°.

Fry bacon in small skillet. Remove with slotted spoon and drain on paper towel. Place onion in skillet. Sauté in bacon grease over medium heat until golden. Drain grease. Spread onion, bacon and grated cheese in partially baked pastry shell.

Combine eggs, milk, cream, salt, cayenne, pepper and nutmeg in medium-size bowl; mix well. Pour into pastry shell. Place pie plate on a cookie sheet and bake at 350° for 30 minutes or until custard is golden brown and firm, and knife inserted in center comes out clean.

Variation: This is a basic recipe to which any of the following may be added: chopped vegetables such as spinach, broccoli, artichoke hearts or asparagus; chopped, cooked seafood or chicken; or well-drained cooked sausage.

- 1 (9-inch) pastry shell, unbaked
- 8–10 slices bacon, diced
- 1 onion, thinly sliced
- 1 cup grated natural Swiss cheese (may substitute Gruyère)
- 4 eggs, slightly beaten
- ¾ cup milk
- ¾ cup heavy (whipping) cream
- ½ teaspoon salt
- ⅛ teaspoon cayenne pepper
- Freshly ground pepper
- Freshly grated nutmeg

Serves: 6
Preparation: 30 minutes
Baking: 35 minutes
Temperature: 450°

Crustless Spinach Quiche
Just minutes to prepare this exceptional dish.

Preheat oven to 350°.

Butter a 9-inch pie plate or quiche dish.

Place oil in large skillet. Add onion and sauté over medium heat until onion is transparent. Add spinach and cook until excess moisture is evaporated. Cool.

Beat eggs in medium-size bowl. Add cheese. Stir into onion-spinach mixture and season with salt and pepper. Pour into prepared dish; spread evenly. Bake at 350° for 40–45 minutes or until nicely browned.

- 1 tablespoon oil
- 1 large onion, chopped
- 1 (10-ounce) package frozen chopped spinach, thawed and drained
- 5 eggs
- ¾ pound Muenster cheese, grated
- Salt
- Freshly ground pepper

Serves: 6–8
Preparation: 15 minutes
Baking: 45 minutes
Temperature: 350°

Quiche

Chicken-Broccoli Quiche

A complementary blend on a quickie crust.

- 1 pound fresh broccoli (may substitute 10-ounce package frozen chopped broccoli, drained)
- 1 (8-ounce) tube crescent rolls
- 1 whole chicken breast; cooked, skinned, boned and cut into 1-inch pieces
- 1 cup grated mozzarella cheese
- 3 eggs
- 1 cup heavy (whipping) cream
- 2 tablespoons fresh lemon juice
- 1 teaspoon salt
  Freshly ground pepper
  Minced green onion tops or chives

Serves:	6
Preparation:	20 minutes
Baking:	40 minutes
Standing:	10 minutes
Temperature:	375°

Preheat oven to 375°.

Remove woody stems from broccoli. Place in medium-size saucepan. Add 1 inch of water. Cook for 10–12 minutes or until crisp tender. Drain well and chop.

Spread out crescent rolls in 10-inch quiche pan or 10-inch pie plate to make smooth pastry shell. Be sure to seal perforations. Arrange broccoli, chicken and cheese in layers on shell.

Beat eggs, cream, lemon juice, salt and pepper until combined but not frothy. Pour over filling. Bake at 375° for 35–40 minutes or until center is set. Let stand for 10 minutes before cutting. Garnish with onions.

Note: This may be made a day ahead and reheated in the microwave. Freezes well.

Seafood Quiche
Seafood adds a richness to the quiche.

Preheat oven to 350°.

Prick pastry shell with fork. Brush shell with a bit of egg white. Bake at 350° for 5–7 minutes. Remove pastry shell from oven.

Preheat oven to 375°.

Beat together eggs, mayonnaise, sour cream, half and half, paprika and salt while pastry shell is baking. Set aside.

Layer shrimp, bacon, onion and cheese in partially baked pastry shell. Pour egg mixture over shrimp filling. Cover loosely with foil. Bake at 375° for 1 hour. Remove foil and bake an additional 15 minutes.

1	(9-inch) pastry shell, unbaked
	Egg white
3	eggs
⅓	cup mayonnaise
⅓	cup sour cream
⅓	cup half and half
¼	teaspoon paprika
¼	teaspoon seasoned salt
1	cup coarsely chopped, cooked shrimp or crab meat
6–8	strips bacon, cooked and crumbled
1	cup chopped onion
1½	cups grated Danish cheese (may substitute Swiss cheese)

Serves: 4–6
Preparation: 25 minutes
Baking: 1 hour, 15 minutes
Temperature: 350°

Brunch

Torta Di Pasqua (Italian Easter Pie)

Cut these hearty squares in smaller pieces and serve as hors d'oeuvres.

½ pound Italian sausage links, thinly sliced (may substitute either hot or mild bulk sausage)
3 eggs
1½ pounds ricotta cheese
8–10 slices prosciutto ham, coarsely chopped (may substitute chopped, baked or boiled ham)
½ pound mozzarella cheese, grated
1 cup freshly grated Parmesan cheese
2 tablespoons finely chopped fresh parsley
1 teaspoon dried oregano
Freshly ground pepper
Salt

Serves: 8–10
Preparation: 30 minutes
Baking: 45 minutes
Temperature: 350°

Preheat oven to 350°.

Butter a 7x11-inch baking dish, a 10-inch quiche dish or a 10-inch pie plate.

Brown sausage in medium-size skillet over medium heat; drain.

Beat eggs into ricotta cheese in large bowl. Add sausage, ham, mozzarella, Parmesan, parsley and oregano. Season with salt and pepper. Spread mixture in prepared baking dish. Bake at 350° for 40–45 minutes or until top is lightly browned. Cut into squares or wedges.

Spinach Frittata
Raves galore—from all ages.

Preheat oven to 350°.

Butter a 9-inch deep-dish pie plate.

Remove casings from sausage and crumble meat. Brown in large skillet over medium-high heat. Remove sausage from skillet and drain well. Set sausage aside. Add oil to skillet and heat until light haze forms. Add mushrooms and onions; sauté until onion is transparent. Remove from heat. Stir sausage into onion mixture. Squeeze spinach to remove all excess moisture and combine with sausage mixture; set aside.

Combine eggs, ¾ cup Parmesan, garlic, basil, marjoram, salt and pepper in a medium-size bowl; mix well. Stir in sausage mixture. Pour into prepared pie plate. Sprinkle with mozzarella and remaining Parmesan. Bake at 350° for 25 minutes or until golden brown.

Sausage en Croûte
Really attractive and hearty.

Preheat oven to 425°.

Line a baking sheet with brown paper cut from a paper bag.

Brown sausage in a large skillet over medium heat. Break up sausage into small bits as it cooks. Add onion and green peppers; cook for 5 minutes. Drain grease. Add tomato, cheese and parsley. Stir lightly.

Unfold and roll out pastry to a 10x14-inch rectangle. Transfer to prepared baking sheet. Spread sausage mixture to within ½ inch of the perimeter of the pastry. Roll up pastry, starting with long side. Pinch edges together to seal. Beginning at one end, cut ⅔ of the way through the roll at 1½-inch intervals. Turn pieces on a slant so that filling shows. Bake at 425° for 20 minutes or until golden brown.

- 3 Italian sausages
- ¼ cup oil
- ½ pound fresh mushrooms, sliced
- 1 medium onion, sliced
- 1 (10-ounce) package frozen spinach, thawed and drained
- 6 eggs, slightly beaten
- 1 cup freshly grated Parmesan cheese, divided
- 5 cloves garlic, minced
- ½ teaspoon dried basil
- ¼ teaspoon dried marjoram
- Salt
- Freshly ground pepper
- 1 cup grated mozzarella cheese

Serves: 6
Preparation: 20 minutes
Baking: 25 minutes
Temperature: 350°

- 1 sheet frozen puff pastry, thawed for 20 minutes
- 1 pound bulk pork sausage
- ½ cup chopped onion
- ⅓ cup seeded and chopped green pepper
- 1 large tomato, diced
- 1 cup grated Swiss cheese
- 3 tablespoons chopped fresh parsley

Serves: 6–8
Preparation: 45 minutes
Baking: 20 minutes
Temperature: 425°

Gougère with Ham and Mushrooms

Elegant meal for luncheon or dinner.

- 4 tablespoons (½ stick) butter
- 1 cup chopped onion
- ½ pound fresh mushrooms, sliced
- 1½ tablespoons flour
- 1 cup chicken broth
- 3 large tomatoes; peeled, seeded and cut into strips
- 3 cups julienne ham

Pâté Choux:
- ½ cup (1 stick) butter
- 1 cup water
- Pinch salt
- 1 cup all-purpose flour
- 4 eggs
- 1 cup grated Cheddar cheese, reserve 2 tablespoons for top

Serves:	6–8
Preparation:	30 minutes
Baking:	45 minutes
Temperature:	400°

Melt butter over low heat in large saucepan. Add onions; sauté over medium heat until soft and transparent. Add mushrooms; cook for 2 minutes. Stir in flour. Add broth gradually, stirring constantly. Simmer for 4 minutes. Add tomatoes and ham. Set aside.

Preheat oven to 400°.

Grease a 9x13-inch baking dish.

Combine butter, water and salt in 2-quart saucepan over medium heat. Heat until butter is melted and water is boiling. Remove pan from heat. Add flour and beat vigorously with a wooden spoon until well blended.

Place saucepan over medium heat and beat mixture with spoon for about 1 minute or until it forms a thick mass that clings to the spoon and comes away from the sides of the pan. Remove pan from heat; let stand for 5 minutes. Make a well in center of dough. Beat in eggs, 1 at a time, beating thoroughly after each addition. Beat until pastry is smooth and glossy. Add cheese. Spoon a narrow row of pastry around edge of prepared baking dish, leaving center open. Pour ham mixture in center; sprinkle with remaining 2 tablespoons cheese. Bake at 400° for 20 minutes. Reduce temperature to 350°; bake for 20–25 minutes or until gougère is puffed and brown and filling is bubbly. Serve at once.

Curried Sausage Casserole
Add fruit and salad to complete the meal.

Preheat oven to 350°.

Grease a 2-quart baking dish.

Brown sausage in large skillet over medium heat. Separate meat with fork. Add green peppers, onions and mushrooms. Cook until vegetables are tender. Drain fat.

Melt butter in medium-size saucepan over medium heat. Stir in flour and curry powder and cook until smooth and bubbly. Add milk gradually; stir until thickened. Add salt and pepper. Combine cream sauce with sausage mixture; mix carefully. Spoon mixture into prepared baking dish. Sprinkle top with bread crumbs and Parmesan. Bake at 350° for 30 minutes.

- 2 pounds bulk pork sausage
- 1 cup seeded and chopped green peppers (optional)
- ½ cup chopped onions
- 1 cup sliced fresh mushrooms
- 2 tablespoons butter
- 2 tablespoons all-purpose flour
- 2 teaspoons curry powder
- 1½ cups milk
- Salt
- Freshly ground pepper
- Dry bread crumbs
- Freshly grated Parmesan cheese

Serves: 6–8
Preparation: 30 minutes
Baking: 30 minutes
Temperature: 350°

E'Leis' Grit Casserole
Great alternative side dish.

Preheat oven to 350°.

Grease a 1½-quart or 2-quart baking dish.

Combine all ingredients in large bowl. Pour into prepared baking dish. Bake at 350° for 15–20 minutes.

Note: Add a little water if casserole appears too thick.

- 4 cups water
- 1 cup grits
- 1 (16-ounce) roll garlic cheese, softened and cut up
- 4 ounces sharp Cheddar cheese, grated
- Dash of Worcestershire sauce
- ½ cup (1 stick) butter, softened
- 1 teaspoon salt
- 1 teaspoon cayenne pepper

Serves: 10
Preparation: 5 minutes
Baking: 20 minutes
Temperature: 350°

16 crêpes (see page 305)

Sauce:
- ½ cup (1 stick) butter
- ½ cup all-purpose flour
- 1½ cups chicken stock or broth (may substitute 13½-ounce can chicken broth)
- ½ cup dry sherry
- 2 egg yolks
- ⅛ teaspoon pepper
- 2 cups light (coffee) cream

Crab Filling:
- ½ cup (1 stick) butter
- 1½ cups chopped fresh mushrooms
- ⅓ cup finely chopped green onions
- 1 tablespoon chopped fresh parsley
- 1½ pounds fresh crab meat
- ½ cup dry sherry
- ½ teaspoon salt
- ¼ teaspoon pepper
- ¼ teaspoon cayenne pepper
- 1 teaspoon Worcestershire sauce

Suggested Garnishes:
- ¼ cup freshly grated Parmesan or Swiss cheese
- 1 tablespoon chopped fresh parsley
- ⅛ teaspon paprika

Yield: 16–20 crêpes
Preparation: 20 minutes
Cooking: 20 minutes
Baking: 15 minutes
Temperature: 375°

Crab Meat Crêpes

Rich and delicate.

Butter 2 (9x13-inch) baking dishes.

Melt butter in medium-size saucepan over medium heat. Stir in flour until smooth and bubbly. Remove from heat and stir in broth and sherry. Return to heat and stir constantly until thickened. Beat together small amount of sauce and egg yolks; add to sauce. Stir in pepper. Continue stirring and gradually add cream. Simmer for about 2 minutes. (Sauce should be quite thick.)

Melt butter in medium-size saucepan over medium heat. Add mushrooms and onions. Cook, stirring until tender but not browned. Add remaining ingredients and stir gently until hot. Be careful not to break up the crab meat. Add ½ of the sauce and stir gently together.

Preheat oven to 375°.

Assemble by filling each crêpe with about 2 tablespoons of filling. Roll up each crêpe and place, seam down, in a single layer in prepared baking dishes. Top each dish with ½ of the remaining sauce. (Crêpes may be refrigerated or frozen at this point.) Bake at 375° until bubbly and hot, about 10–15 minutes. Garnish with cheese, parsley and paprika, if desired.

Spaghetti and Meatballs
Sauce can easily be doubled.

Preheat oven to 450°.

Beat eggs slightly in medium-size bowl. Add milk and bread crumbs; mix well. Let stand for 5 minutes. Add meat, onion, parsley, garlic, salt and pepper; mix until well combined. Shape into 24 meatballs, 1½ inches in diameter. Place in 9-inch square baking pan. Bake, uncovered, at 450° for 30 minutes.

Heat oil in 5-quart Dutch oven over medium heat. Add onion and garlic; sauté until golden. Add sugar, salt, basil, fennel, pepper, tomatoes, tomato paste and water. Bring to a boil; reduce heat and simmer, covered, for 30 minutes. Add meatballs and drippings. Simmer, covered, for 1 hour, stirring occasionally.

Cook spaghetti according to package directions; drain. Place spaghetti on serving dish. Top with meatballs and sauce. Sprinkle with cheese.

Meatballs:
- 2 eggs
- ½ cup milk
- 3 slices coarse white bread, crumbled
- 2 pounds lean ground chuck
- ½ cup finely chopped onion
- ½ cup finely chopped fresh parsley
- 1 clove garlic, crushed
- 1 teaspoon salt
- ½ teaspoon pepper

Sauce:
- ½ cup olive or salad oil
- ½ cup chopped onion
- 2 cloves garlic, crushed
- 2 tablespoons granulated sugar
- 1 tablespoon (3 teaspoons) salt
- 1½ teaspoons dried basil
- ½ teaspoon fennel seed
- ¼ teaspoon pepper
- 1 (2-pound, 3-ounce) can Italian-style tomatoes, cut up
- 2 (6-ounce) cans tomato paste
- ½ cup water

- 1 pound spaghetti
- ½ cup freshly grated Parmesan cheese

Serves: 6
Preparation: 30 minutes
Baking: 30 minutes
Cooking: 1 hour, 30 minutes
Temperature: 450°

Pasta

- ¼ pound bacon, diced
- 1 medium onion, chopped
- ⅓ cup dry white wine
- 3 eggs, slightly beaten
- 2 tablespoons chopped fresh parsley
- ¼ pound Parmesan cheese, freshly grated
- ¼ teaspoon pepper
- 1¼ pounds spaghetti

Serves:	6
Preparation:	45 minutes
Simmering:	15 minutes

- ½ pound lasagne noodles
- 1 tablespoon oil

Velouté Sauce:
- ½ cup (1 stick) unsalted butter
- ½ cup all-purpose flour
- 3 cups turkey stock or broth
- 1 cup heavy (whipping) cream
- 2 teaspoons salt
- ½ teaspoon freshly grated nutmeg
- Freshly ground pepper

- 2 (10-ounce) packages frozen chopped spinach
- 2 cups diced cooked turkey
- ¾ cup freshly grated Parmesan cheese

Serves:	8–10
Preparation:	45 minutes
Baking:	30 minutes
Standing:	15 minutes
Temperature:	350°

Spaghetti alla Carbonara

An authentic Italian recipe for pasta.

Cook bacon and onion in large skillet over medium heat. Add wine to undrained mixture and simmer for 15 minutes. Keep warm.

Combine eggs, parsley, Parmesan and pepper. Set aside.

Cook spaghetti according to package directions; drain. Place immediately in serving bowl and add egg mixture; toss until well combined. Pour hot bacon mixture over spaghetti; toss. Serve immediately.

Lasagne Florentine

Great way to use leftover Thanksgiving turkey.

Grease a 9x13-inch baking dish.

Cook noodles according to package directions. Place cold water and oil in large bowl. Drain cooked noodles and immediately place in bowl of cold water. Remove noodles and drain well.

Preheat oven to 350°.

Melt butter over low heat in medium-size saucepan; stir in flour until smooth and bubbly. Add turkey stock gradually. Cook over medium heat, stirring occasionally until mixture comes to a boil. Remove from heat and add cream, salt, nutmeg and pepper.

Cook spinach according to package directions; drain well. Combine ½ of the velouté sauce with the drained spinach.

Layer lasagne by spreading a thin layer of the spinach-velouté sauce over bottom of prepared baking dish. Cover with ½ of the lasagne noodles (about 4), ½ of the remaining spinach-velouté sauce, ½ of the turkey pieces, ½ of the plain velouté sauce and ½ of the Parmesan. Repeat layers, this time beginning with lasagne and ending with Parmesan. Bake at 350° for 30 minutes and let stand for 15 minutes before serving.

Country Noodles
Noodles with a zip.

Preheat oven to 350°.

Butter 3½-quart or 9x13-inch baking dish.

Cook noodles according to package directions; drain.

Combine cottage cheese, sour cream, garlic, onions, Worcestershire, Tabasco, salt and horseradish in large bowl. Add noodles and bacon; toss with 2 forks until well mixed. Place in prepared baking dish. Bake, covered, at 350° for 30–40 minutes. Remove cover and sprinkle with Parmesan. Broil until golden.

Variation: For a different taste, you may add 2 tablespoons poppy seed.

- 1 (16-ounce) package vermicelli noodles
- 3 cups small curd, cream-style cottage cheese
- 3 cups sour cream
- 2 cloves garlic, crushed
- 2 onions, minced
- 2 tablespoons Worcestershire sauce
- Dash of Tabasco sauce
- 4 teaspoons salt
- 2 tablespoons prepared horseradish
- ½ pound bacon, cooked and crumbled
- 1 cup freshly grated Parmesan cheese

Serves: 8–10
Preparation: 30 minutes
Baking: 40 minutes
Temperature: 350°

Spinach Noodle Ring
Colorful and filling dish for a crowd.

Preheat oven to 350°.

Grease well an 8-cup ring mold.

Cook noodles according to package directions; drain. Squeeze spinach to remove all excess moisture. Combine noodles and spinach in large bowl.

Melt butter in small skillet over medium heat. Add onions and sauté until tender. Add to noodle mixture.

Fold eggs into sour cream in small bowl. Add salt and pepper. Combine with noodle mixture and mix well. Pour into ring mold. Place mold in larger pan and add 1 inch of hot water. Bake at 350° for 45 minutes. Remove from oven and let mold sit for 10 minutes before running spatula around outside and inside edges of mold. Turn mold onto serving plate.

Serving Suggestions: Fill ring with Vegetable Delight.

- 8 ounces spinach noodles
- 2 (10-ounce) packages frozen chopped spinach, thawed (may substitute chopped cooked broccoli)
- ½ cup (1 stick) butter
- 1 onion, chopped
- 3 eggs, slightly beaten
- 1 cup sour cream
- 1 teaspoon salt
- ¼ teaspoon pepper

Serves: 8–10
Preparation: 35 minutes
Baking: 45 minutes
Cooling: 10 minutes
Temperature: 350°

Noodles and Swiss Cheese
Creamy smooth noodle casserole.

- 1 (8-ounce) package medium noodles
- ½ pound Swiss cheese, grated
- 1 tablespoon onion juice
- 1 teaspoon Worcestershire sauce
- ¼ cup (½ stick) butter, melted
- 2 cups sour cream
- ½ cup buttered dry bread crumbs

Serves: 8
Preparation: 30 minutes
Baking: 1 hour
Temperature: 350°

Preheat oven to 350°.

Butter 2-quart baking dish.

Cook noodles in large Dutch oven according to package directions; drain. Add cheese and toss gently. Add onion juice, Worcestershire and butter. Mix gently and cool. Add sour cream; toss lightly but thoroughly. Place in prepared baking dish and top with bread crumbs. Bake at 350° for 1 hour.

Noodle Kugel
This is sweet. Serve with a plain meatloaf or ham.

- 8 ounces broad noodles
- 1 (8-ounce) package cream cheese, softened
- ½ cup (1 stick) butter, melted
- ¼ cup granulated sugar
- 1 teaspoon vanilla
- 1½ cups milk
- 2 eggs, slightly beaten
- ½ cup crushed corn flakes
- 1 teaspoon ground cinnamon

Serves: 4–6
Preparation: 25 minutes
Chilling: 8 hours or overnight
Baking: 1 hour
Temperature: 350°

Prepare noodles according to package directions; drain.

Mix cream cheese, butter, sugar, vanilla, milk and eggs in large bowl. Add cooked noodles and refrigerate overnight.

Preheat oven to 350°.

Butter an 8-inch square baking dish.

Combine corn flakes and cinnamon. Sprinkle mixture over noodles. Bake at 350° for 1 hour.

Meats

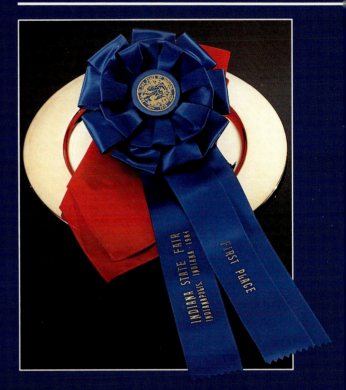

The State Fair

The Indiana State Fair is a celebration of the land and of its bounties—a mecca for visitors from around the state and throughout the world. More than a million fairgoers throng to the Indianapolis Fairground site each August to visit the displays, engage in the competitions, and sample the sights, sounds and savors.

From the bucolic atmosphere of its straw-littered animal barns to the raucous riotry of its neon-glittered midway, the Fair offers something for everyone. Crowds stand in line to feast on the barbecued pork chops and Hoosier rib-eye sandwiches, the giant confectionery "elephant ears" and the creamy thick milkshakes, all specialties of this annual extravaganza.

At the Women's Building, trophy-winning exhibits spotlight original art and photography, antiques and edibles, home-sewn fashions and intricately pieced patchwork quilts. In the gigantic Horse Barn, thoroughbred animals are viewed and judged, and riding competitions display the talented techniques of Hoosier equestrians.

Concerts featuring world-renowned "rock" groups and country and "pop" musicians attract overflow audiences to the huge outdoor arena, also the scene of unique contests ranging from hog-calling to tractor-pulling. Simultaneously, on a more modest scale, in a small rustic outbuilding, adults and toddlers clap hands and tap feet in time to bluegrass music played by a "down home" Indiana band on instruments including zithers and washboards, banjos and combs.

The blue ribbons adorning apple pies and hand-crocheted afghans, prize corn and prime steers, all testify to the nature of the Fair itself—evidence of a determination to be the best there is, a goal several million fairgoers will insist has long since been realized at the prize-winning Indiana State Fair.

MEATS

Beef
Barbecue Sauce . . . 137
Barbecued Beef
  Brisket . . . 128
Beef and Noodle
  Casserole . . . 136
Beef Curry . . . 132
Beef, Rice and Zucchini
  Skillet . . . 135
Cannelloni Crêpes . . . 134
Chinese Tenderloin . . . 123
Company Beef
  Tenderloin . . . 123
Continental
  Goulash . . . 133
Dressed-Up
  Hamburger . . . 136
Flank Steak . . . 127
Individual Beef Wellingtons
  with Horseradish
  Sauce . . . 131
J.B's Terrific
  Tenderloin . . . 124
Picnic Pot Roast . . . 129
Pizzaburger Meat
  Squares . . . 137
Pizza Fondue . . . 135
Sauerbraten with Ginger
  Snap Gravy . . . 130
Sherried Beef
  Tenderloin . . . 124
Smoked Beef
  Brisket . . . 128
Steak Roll . . . 125
Steak with Mustard
  Sauce . . . 125
Stuffed Flank Steak . . . 127
Sweet and Sour Pot
  Roast . . . 129
Yuji's Teriyaki
  Kabobs . . . 126

Veal
Braised Veal . . . 139
Veal à l'Orientale . . . 142
Veal Balls and Sour
  Cream . . . 143
Veal Blanchette . . . 139
Veal Forester . . . 141
Veal Tarragon . . . 140
Veal with Creole
  Sauce . . . 138

Lamb
Leg of Lamb
  Barbecue . . . 145
Leg of Lamb with Parsley
  Crust . . . 145
Marinated Butterflied Leg of
  Lamb . . . 144
Marinated Leg of
  Lamb . . . 146
Rack of Lamb
  Moutarde . . . 146

Pork
Barbecued Ribs . . . 154
Braised Pork Chops with
  Orange and
  Mustard . . . 153
Glazed Apple
  Halves . . . 151
Hungarian Pork
  Chops . . . 153
Loin of Pork with Garlic and
  Herbs . . . 151
Piquant Pork with Spiced
  Apple Rice . . . 147
Pork Loin with Orange
  Sauce . . . 149
Pork Tenderloin with Wine
  Sauce . . . 148
Real Italian Spaghetti
  Sauce . . . 152
Roast Pork with Plum
  Sauce . . . 152
Stuffed Crown Roast of
  Pork . . . 150

Ham
Ham and Artichoke
  Rolls . . . 155
Ham and Spinach
  Casserole . . . 156
Mommie Jewett's Ham
  Loaf . . . 156

Sausage
Sausage Bread . . . 154

Chinese Tenderloin
A delicious rich sauce enhances this stir-fry combination.

Melt butter in large skillet over medium-high heat. Add mushrooms and sauté for 2 minutes. Remove with slotted spoon and set aside.

Heat oil in Dutch oven over high heat until oil sizzles. Wipe meat with paper towels. Add tenderloin and cook for 2 minutes, turning frequently. Add onion, green pepper and mushrooms; stir-fry for 3 minutes. Combine cornstarch and water in small bowl. Add to meat mixture together with garlic, water chestnuts, beef broth, soy sauce and molasses. Lower heat and simmer for 5 minutes. Add pea pods and simmer for 5 more minutes. Do not overcook.

Serving Suggestion: Serve over wild rice prepared according to package directions.

- ½ cup (1 stick) butter, melted
- 1½ pounds fresh whole mushrooms, sliced
- 5 tablespoons oil
- 3 pounds beef tenderloin, thinly sliced and cut into strips
- 1 cup coarsely chopped onion
- 1 cup seeded and coarsely chopped green pepper
- 4 tablespoons cornstarch (optional)
- ½ cup water
- 2 cloves garlic, minced
- 1½ cups thinly sliced water chestnuts
- 1 quart beef broth or stock
- ½ cup soy sauce
- 2 tablespoons bead molasses
- 1 tablespoon monosodium glutamate (optional)
- 2 cups Chinese pea pods

Serves: 12–15
Preparation: 30 minutes
Cooking: 10 minutes

Company Beef Tenderloin
Tenderloin with a flair.

Preheat oven to 450°.

Fold in ends of tenderloin to make uniform thickness. Lay bacon strips side by side to equal the length of the tenderloin. Place tenderloin in middle and wrap bacon over tenderloin. Sprinkle with seasoned salt. Place in roasting pan. Place pan on second shelf of oven. Bake, uncovered, at 450° for 20 minutes for rare meat. Remove meat and sprinkle sparingly with dry mustard. Spread sour cream over beef. Return to oven and bake for 5 more minutes.

- 1 pound bacon
- 1 whole beef tenderloin, trimmed
- Seasoned salt
- Dry mustard
- 2 cups sour cream

Serves: 6
Preparation: 10 minutes
Baking: 25 minutes
Temperature: 450°

Beef

Sherried Beef Tenderloin
Small effort—large reward.

Preheat oven to 500°.

Season flour with salt, pepper and garlic salt. Dredge beef in flour mixture. Melt 4 tablespoons butter in small saucepan; add onion salt. Place beef in roasting pan. Pour butter over beef. Bake at 500° for 8 minutes; baste with drippings.

Melt remaining 2 tablespoons butter in medium skillet over medium-high heat. Sauté mushrooms until tender. Stir in sherry. Pour mushrooms over beef. Bake 15 minutes more. Serve with juices and mushrooms from pan.

- 1 (3-pound) beef tenderloin
- Flour
- Salt
- Freshly ground pepper
- Garlic salt
- 6 tablespoons butter, divided
- 1 teaspoon onion salt
- 8 ounces fresh mushrooms, sliced (may substitute 4-ounce can sliced mushrooms)
- ½ cup dry sherry

Serves: 6
Preparation: 10 minutes
Baking: 25 minutes
Temperature: 500°

J.B.'s Terrific Tenderloin
Great flavor—good company dish.

Preheat oven to broil.

Mix ginger, pineapple juice, soy sauce, red wine and garlic in large bowl. Add meat and marinate in refrigerator for 24 hours. Broil or grill about 4 inches from source of heat for approximately 3 minutes per side or until fillets are cooked to desired doneness.

- ¾ teaspoon ground ginger
- ⅔ cup unsweetened pineapple juice
- ⅓ cup soy sauce
- ⅓ cup red wine
- 1 clove garlic, minced
- 1 (3-pound) beef tenderloin, cut into 6 fillets

Serves: 6
Preparation: 5 minutes
Marinating: 24 hours
Broiling: 6–10 minutes
Temperature: Broil

Steak with Mustard Sauce

A dressed-up steak for something different.

Preheat oven to broil.

Sprinkle steaks with pepper. Spoon ½ teaspoon of lemon juice over each steak. Place on rack, about 4 inches from source of heat. Broil for 6 minutes or until steaks are cooked to desired doneness; turning once. Spoon ¼ of the sauce on each steak.

Make mustard sauce by placing all ingredients in small bowl. Stirring briskly. Divide evenly among 4 steaks.

- 4 (8-ounce) boneless strip or rib-eye steaks
- ½ teaspoon coarsely ground black pepper
- 2 teaspoons fresh lemon juice

Mustard Sauce:
- ¼ cup (½ stick) margarine, softened
- 2 tablespoons prepared brown mustard
- ⅛ teaspoon coarsely ground black pepper
- 2 teaspoons fresh lemon juice
- 1 tablespoon finely chopped fresh parsley

Serves: 4
Preparation: 15 minutes
Broiling: 10 minutes
Temperature: Broil

Steak Roll

Easy and juicy.

Preheat oven to 325°.

Spread steak with mustard. Lay bacon strips lengthwise on mustard. Cover with sliced onions. Roll up steak starting at bone and secure with toothpicks. Dredge steak roll in flour.

Heat oil in small roaster over medium heat. Brown steak roll for 5–8 minutes. Cover roaster and roast at 325° for 2 hours.

- 1 (1½ or 2-pound) round steak
- 2 tablespoons Dijon mustard
- 4 strips bacon
- 1 medium onion, thinly sliced and separated
- ¼ cup all-purpose flour
- 2 tablespoons oil

Serves: 4
Preparation: 15 minutes
Baking: 2 hours
Temperature: 325°

Yuji's Teriyaki Kabobs

An authentic Japenese Teriyaki.

Sauce: (about 3 cups)
- ½ cup dark soy sauce
- 1 cup sherry or sake
- ½ cup honey
- 5 cloves garlic, finely chopped
- 2 tablespoons finely grated fresh ginger root
- ¼ cup sesame oil (may substitute peanut or corn oil by adding 1 tablespoon sesame seed)
- ½ cup finely chopped green onions
- ¼ teaspoon cayenne pepper
- 1 tablespoon wine vinegar

Kabobs:
- 1 large top round steak
- 1 pound fresh mushrooms
- 1 medium zucchini, cut in ½-inch slices
- 1 green pepper, seeded and cut to make 12 pieces
- 1 large onion, cut into 12 wedges

Serves:	4–6
Preparation:	15 minutes
Marinating:	1 hour
Broiling:	10 minutes
Temperature:	Broil

Combine all sauce ingredients in large bowl; mix well.

Cut steak into thin slices on the diagonal and against the grain. Place meat and vegetables in large bowl. Pour sauce in bowl and toss meat and vegetables to thoroughly coat. Marinate for 1 hour at room temperature or overnight in refrigerator.

Preheat oven to broil.

Spear meat and vegetables on 6 to 8 skewers. Broil or grill to desired doneness.

Note: Meat and vegetables may also be stir-fried in wok or skillet.

Variation: Teriyaki sauce is excellent marinade for other cuts of beef, chicken, ribs, lamb and pork.

Stuffed Flank Steak
Easy and elegant looking.

Melt butter over medium-high heat in large saucepan. Add mushrooms and sauté until tender. Remove from heat. Add bread stuffing and cheese. Mix together and spread over flank steak. Roll up flank steak jelly-roll fashion, starting at narrow end. Fasten with skewers or string. Pour oil in slow-cooking pot. Roll steak in oil, coating all sides.

Prepare gravy mix according to package directions. Pour gravy, wine and onions over meat. Cover and cook on low for 8–10 hours. Remove meat from pot. Add jelly to sauce; stir until dissolved. Slice meat against the grain. Pour some sauce over meat. Serve remainder of sauce at the table.

Variation: May substitute seasoned or corn bread stuffing for bread stuffing.

- 4 tablespoons (½ stick) butter
- 8 ounces fresh mushrooms, diced
- 1 cup packaged bread stuffing
- 3 tablespoons freshly grated Parmesan cheese
- 1½ pounds flank steak (approximately 6x10 inches), scored on both sides
- 3 tablespoons oil

Sauce:
- 1 (¾-ounce) package brown gravy mix
- ¼ cup dry red wine
- 4 tablespoons minced green onions
- ⅓ cup currant jelly

Serves: 4–5
Preparation: 30 minutes
Cooking: 10 hours

Flank Steak
So easy.

Mix oil, parsley, garlic, salt, lemon juice and pepper in small bowl or jar. Pour mixture over meat and let stand at room temperature for at least 1 hour.

Grill about 4 inches from source of heat for 4–5 minutes per side or until cooked to desired doneness. Cut meat in thin slices across grain of meat.

- 1 tablespoon oil
- 2 teaspoons chopped fresh parsley
- 1 clove garlic, crushed
- 1 teaspoon salt
- 1 teaspoon fresh lemon juice
- ⅛ teaspoon pepper
- 1 (1-pound) flank steak

Serves: 4
Preparation: 10 minutes
Marinating: 1 hour
Grilling: 10 minutes

Beef

- 5–6 pound beef brisket
- 1 onion, sliced
- 1 bay leaf
- 16 whole cloves
- 1 clove garlic, minced

Sauce:
- 1 cup catsup
- ¼ cup Worcestershire sauce
- 2 teaspoons brown sugar
- 1 tablespoon dry mustard

Serves:	10–12
Preparation:	20 minutes
Cooking:	4 hours
Chilling:	8 hours or overnight
Baking:	30 minutes
Temperature:	350°

Barbecued Beef Brisket
Great to use for sandwiches.

Place brisket in pot large enough to hold roast. Cover with water. Add onion, bay leaf, cloves and garlic; bring to a boil. Cover and simmer over low heat for 4 hours. Remove from pan. Trim excess fat. Refrigerate overnight.

Preheat oven to 350°.

Combine catsup, Worcestershire, brown sugar and mustard in small bowl.

Slice meat very thin. Overlap slices in a 3-quart baking dish and cover with sauce. Bake at 350° for 30 minutes or until heated through.

- 1 (4-pound) boneless beef brisket
- 1 cup catsup
- ⅓ cup Worcestershire sauce
- 1 teaspoon chili powder
- 1 teaspoon salt
- 2 dashes Tabasco sauce
- 1 teaspoon liquid smoke
- 2 cups water

Serves:	6–8
Preparation:	10 minutes
Cooking:	4½ hours
Temperature:	350°

Smoked Beef Brisket
Simple and versatile.

Preheat oven to to 350°.

Place brisket in roasting pan and roast, covered, at 350° for 3 hours. Drain off fat from roasting pan. Remove excess fat from brisket, if necessary.

Mix catsup, Worcestershire, chili powder, salt, Tabasco, liquid smoke and water. Pour over brisket. Cover and cook an additional 1–1½ hours.

Note: Leftovers are great for making barbecue sandwiches.

Sweet and Sour Pot Roast
Outstanding—this one will catch your fancy.

Preheat oven to 350°.

Heat oil in Dutch oven and brown roast. Add bouillon, cranberry sauce and horseradish. Cover and bake at 350° for 1½ hours. Add carrots and onions to roast. Bake an additional 1½ hours.

Reserve pan juices and pour over meat. Serve with buttered noodles, if desired.

- 1 tablespoon oil
- 1 (4-pound) chuck roast
- 1 (10½-ounce) can beef bouillon
- 1 (16-ounce) can jellied cranberry sauce
- 1 (5-ounce) bottle prepared horseradish
- 8 carrots, peeled and cut into 2-inch pieces
- 2 onions, quartered

Serves: 6–8
Preparation: 15 minutes
Cooking: 3 hours
Temperature: 350°

Picnic Pot Roast
A "10" all the way.

Sprinkle meat tenderizer on both sides of pot roast. Let stand for 1 hour.

Mix soy sauce, lemon juice, bourbon and brown sugar; pour over meat. Marinate meat in refrigerator overnight, turning occasionally. Drain marinade from pot roast and charcoal broil to taste, as you would any tender cut of meat.

Variation: Round steak may be substituted for pot roast.

- 1 (5-pound) round bone pot roast, 2 inches thick
- Meat tenderizer
- ½ cup plus 2 tablespoons soy sauce
- 1 tablespoon fresh lemon juice
- ¼ cup bourbon
- ¼ cup firmly packed brown sugar

Serves: 6–8
Preparation: 5 minutes
Standing: 1 hour
Marinating: Overnight
Grilling: 10 minutes

Beef

- 1 (3 to 3½-pound) beef round roast or rolled rump roast
- 1 teaspoon salt
- ½ teaspoon pepper
- 4 bay leaves
- ½ teaspoon peppercorns
- 8 whole cloves
- 2 medium onions, sliced
- 1 small carrot, peeled and minced
- 1 stalk celery, chopped
- 1½ cups red wine vinegar
- 2½ cups water
- ¼ cup (½ stick) butter

Gravy:
- 2 tablespoons granulated sugar
- 1½ cups reserved hot marinade
- ½ cup water
- ⅔ cup gingersnap crumbs (about 8 gingersnaps)
- Salt

Serves: 6
Preparation: 20 minutes
Marinating: 48 hours
Cooking: 3 hours

Sauerbraten with Gingersnap Gravy
A traditional favorite.

Rub meat thoroughly with salt and pepper and place in a deep glass or earthenware bowl. Add bay leaves, peppercorns, cloves, onions, carrot and celery.

Combine vinegar and water in medium-size saucepan. Bring to a boil. Pour hot marinade over the meat. Let cool. Refrigerate in tightly covered bowl for at least 48 hours, turning meat twice a day.

Remove meat from marinade and dry with paper towels. Reserve marinade. Melt butter in Dutch oven and brown meat on all sides. Strain marinade and pour over the meat. Simmer meat slowly for 2½–3 hours or until tender when pierced with a fork. Remove meat to warmed serving platter and keep warm while making gravy. Reserve marinade and keep hot.

Melt sugar over low heat in large heavy skillet, stirring constantly until a nice golden brown. Stir in hot marinade and water gradually. Add gingersnap crumbs. Cook, stirring constantly until mixture thickens. (If mixture should become lumpy, place in blender to smooth, then reheat until thickened.) Salt to taste.

Individual Beef Wellingtons with Horseradish Sauce

Unusual recipe in constant demand.

Preheat oven to 425°.

Lightly grease a jelly roll pan.

Melt butter in large skillet over medium-high heat. Add mushrooms, shallot and parsley. Sauté for 3–4 minutes. Remove; drain well and cool.

Toss cheese, beef, horseradish and mushroom mixture in large bowl. Divide into 6 equal portions.

Place 1 puff pastry square on work surface and spoon 1 portion of filling mixture into center of pastry. Fold up corners of pastry, pinching to seal. Do not compress filling. Transfer to baking sheet, seam down. Repeat with remaining pastry and filling. Brush pastries with beaten egg mixture. Bake at 425° until puffed and golden, about 25–30 minutes.

Combine sour cream, horseradish and garlic; mix well. Serve Wellingtons hot, accompanied with sauce.

Note: May be made ahead. Refrigerate until ready to bake.

Variation: When time is short, deli roast beef may be substituted.

- 2 tablespoons butter
- 8 ounces fresh mushrooms, sliced
- 1 tablespoon minced shallot
- 1 teaspoon chopped fresh parsley
- 12 ounces Gruyère cheese, coarsely grated
- 8–12 ounces rare roast beef, cut into julienne strips
- 2 tablespoons prepared horseradish
- 6 puff pastry sheets, cut into 6-inch squares
- 1 egg, beaten with 1 teaspoon water

Horseradish Sauce:
- 1½ cups sour cream
- ¼ cup prepared horseradish
- ¼ teaspoon minced fresh garlic

Serves:	6
Preparation:	30 minutes
Baking:	30 minutes
Temperature:	425°

- 10 tablespoons butter, divided
- 3–4 pounds round steak, cut in cubes
- 2 medium onions, chopped
- 2 cloves garlic, minced
- 2 large stalks celery, diced
- 4 teaspoons all-purpose flour
- 1 quart beef broth or stock
- 1 bay leaf
- 1 teaspoon mace or ground nutmeg
- 2½ teaspoons curry powder
- ½ teaspoon dry mustard
- 2 green apples; peeled, cored and diced
- 1 (12-ounce) can tomato paste
- Long grain rice, prepared according to package directions

Condiments:
- Chopped peanuts
- Shredded coconut
- Raisins
- Chutney
- Hard-cooked egg yolks, sieved

Serves:	8
Preparation:	1 hour
Cooking:	3 hours

Beef Curry

A wonderful dish for entertaining and family alike.

Melt 2 tablespoons butter in large skillet over low heat. Add meat and brown over medium-high heat; drain grease. Transfer meat to large Dutch oven. Set aside.

Melt remaining 8 tablespoons butter in same skillet over low heat. Add onions, garlic and celery; sauté over medium-high heat until onions are transparent. Combine with meat. Stir flour into meat mixture; add beef broth, bay leaf, mace, curry powder, mustard, apples and tomato paste. Stir until well combined. Simmer, uncovered, for 2–3 hours. Serve over rice with condiments of choice.

Continental Goulash
Tender meat in a rich sauce.

Melt butter in Dutch oven over low heat. Add beef and brown.

Combine tomato sauce, Worcestershire, sugar, paprika, salt, pepper, caraway seed and garlic. Pour over meat. Cover and cook slowly over low heat for 2½ hours or until meat is tender. Stir occasionally. Just before serving, add sour cream to goulash. Stir until smooth and heated through. *Do not boil.* Serve over hot buttered noodles.

Note: *May also be cooked for 8–10 hours in a crock pot.*

- 2 tablespoons butter or margarine
- 2½ pounds beef chuck, cut into cubes (may substitute other beef suitable for stewing)
- 1 (8-ounce) can tomato sauce
- 2 teaspoons Worcestershire sauce
- 1 tablespoon granulated sugar
- 2 teaspoons paprika
- 2 teaspoons salt
- ⅛ teaspoon pepper
- 1½ teaspoons caraway seed
- 1 clove garlic, minced (optional)
- 1 cup sour cream
- 16 ounces noodles, prepared according to package directions
- **Butter**

Serves: 6
Preparation: 30 minutes
Cooking: 2½ hours

Cannelloni Crêpes

No leftovers on this one.

Preheat oven to 350°.

Place all crêpe ingredients in blender or food processor. Blend until smooth and well mixed. Let batter rest 2–3 hours at room temperature or up to 12 hours in refrigerator. Heat a 6-inch skillet and brush it with butter. Pour in 1 tablespoon batter and tilt the skillet immediately so that the batter will spread over the entire bottom of skillet. Cook the crêpe quickly on both sides over medium-high heat.

Brown ground beef in medium-size skillet over medium heat. Drain grease. Combine ground beef, cottage cheese, cream cheese, butter, parsley, egg, onion and salt; mix well. Spread 3 tablespoons of mixture over center of each crêpe. Roll up and place, seam down, in 8-inch square baking dish. Pour marinara sauce over crêpes and sprinkle with cheese. Bake at 350° for 20–30 minutes.

Variation: Cooked manicotti shells may be stuffed with beef mixture instead of using crêpes.

Crêpes:
- 2 eggs
- 2 egg yolks
- 1 cup all-purpose flour
- 1 cup milk
- 1 tablespoon oil
- Dash of salt
- Butter

- 1 pound lean ground beef
- 1 cup small curd, cream-style cottage cheese
- 1 (3-ounce) package cream cheese, softened
- 2 tablespoons margarine or butter, softened
- 2 tablespoons chopped fresh parsley
- 1 egg, beaten
- 1 tablespoon chopped green onion
- ⅛ teaspoon salt
- 1 (15-ounce) can Italian-style marinara sauce
- ¼ cup freshly grated Parmesan cheese

Serves:	4–6
Preparation:	1 hour
Standing:	3 hours
Baking:	30 minutes
Temperature:	350°

Pizza Fondue
Fun family dinner.

Preheat oven to 350°.

Brown beef and onion in large skillet over medium heat. Drain grease from meat. Set aside ½ cup pizza sauce; add remaining sauce to meat.

Mix fennel seed, oregano, garlic, cornstarch and reserved pizza sauce in small bowl. Add this mixture to the meat sauce and stir to combine. Add cheeses gradually and cook over low heat until cheese melts.

Toast French bread in oven at 350° for 3–5 minutes.

Place pizza mixture in fondue pot or chafing dish. Serve with toasted bread cubes.

Variation: This fondue makes a hearty hors d'oeuvres.

1	pound lean ground beef
1	onion, finely chopped
2	(10½-ounce) cans pizza sauce with cheese, divided
1½	teaspoons fennel seed
1½	teaspoons dried oregano
1	clove garlic, minced
1	tablespoon cornstarch
1¼	cups grated Cheddar cheese
1	cup grated mozzarella cheese
1	loaf French bread, cut into 1½-inch cubes

Serves: 4
Preparation: 30 minutes
Baking: 5 minutes
Temperature: 350°

Beef, Rice and Zucchini Skillet
Everyone loves this one.

Prepare rice according to package directions.

Brown meat and onion in a 10-inch skillet over medium-high heat; drain. Stir in zucchini, tomato sauce, tomato paste, water, sugar, salt, pepper and cooked rice. Bring to a boil. Reduce heat and simmer, uncovered, for 20 minutes or until zucchini is tender. Stir often. Sprinkle cheese over mixture in skillet; cover and cook about 3 minutes or until cheese is melted. Garnish with corn chips.

¾	cup long grain rice
1	pound lean ground beef
1	medium onion, chopped
2	medium-size zucchini (about 1 pound), cubed
1	(8-ounce) can tomato sauce
1	(6-ounce) can tomato paste
1	cup water
1¾	teaspoons granulated sugar
½	teaspoon salt
¼	teaspoon pepper
¼	pound Gruyère or Swiss cheese, grated
	Corn chips (optional)

Serves: 6
Preparation: 25 minutes
Cooking: 25 minutes

Beef

Beef and Noodle Casserole
Better than lasagne.

- 1½ pounds ground round beef
- 2 cloves garlic, minced
- 1 teaspoon salt
- ½ teaspoon pepper
- 1 teaspoon granulated sugar
- 1 (8-ounce) can tomato sauce
- 1 (8-ounce) package noodles
- 1 (8-ounce) package cream cheese, softened
- 1 cup sour cream
- 6 green onions, chopped
- ½ cup grated sharp Cheddar cheese
- 1 (3½-ounce) can onion rings (optional)

Brown meat and garlic in large skillet over medium heat; drain. Add salt, pepper, sugar and tomato sauce. Simmer, uncovered, for 15–20 minutes.

Cook noodles according to package directions and drain.

Preheat oven to 350°.

Combine cream cheese, sour cream and green onions. Layer in 9x13-inch baking dish as follows: ½ of the noodles, ½ of the meat mixture, ½ of the cream cheese mixture. Repeat layers. Top with grated cheese. Bake at 350° for 20–30 minutes. Place onion rings on top and bake 10 minutes more.

Serves: 8
Preparation: 35 minutes
Baking: 40 minutes
Temperature: 350°

Dressed-Up Hamburger
Fancy family hamburger.

- 1 pound lean ground beef
- 1 cup chili sauce
- 1 egg, slightly beaten
- 1 cup crushed corn flakes
- 3 tablespoons seeded and finely chopped green pepper
- 1 teaspoon salt
- ½ teaspoon pepper
- 4–6 strips bacon
- Catsup

Preheat oven to 350°.

Combine beef, chili sauce, egg, corn flakes, green pepper, salt and pepper; mix well. Shape into 4 individual serving size balls. Wrap 1 slice of bacon around each ball and secure with a toothpick. Flatten bottom slightly and decorate top of each ball with a crisscross of catsup.

Place on a rack in 8-inch square baking dish. Bake at 350° for 45 minutes.

Serves: 4
Preparation: 15 minutes
Baking: 45 minutes
Temperature: 350°

Pizzaburger Meat Squares
Great for kids—similar to meatloaf.

Preheat oven to 375°.

Combine tomato paste, water, onion, oregano, ½ teaspoon salt, basil, sugar, pepper and garlic in small saucepan. Bring to a boil; cover and simmer for 10 minutes. Remove garlic and discard. Measure 1 cup of sauce; reserve remainder.

Combine 1 cup of sauce, ground beef, cracker crumbs, egg and 1 teaspoon salt in large mixing bowl. Pack firmly into 8-inch square baking dish.

Bake at 375° for 40–45 minutes. Drain grease. Spread reserved sauce on top of meat. Arrange cheese over sauce. Bake at 375° for 15 more minutes or until cheese melts. Cool 10 minutes before cutting into serving pieces.

Variation: Cut meat into 2-inch squares and serve as hors d'oeuvres.

Barbecue Sauce
A tangy sauce good with pork, chicken or beef.

Heat oil in saucepan over medium heat. Add onions and cook until transparent. Add remaining ingredients. Simmer at least 30 minutes.

Beef | 137

- 1 (6-ounce) can tomato paste
- 1 cup water
- ½ cup chopped onion
- 1 teaspoon dried oregano
- 1½ teaspoons salt, divided
- ¼ teaspoon dried basil
- ¼ teaspoon granulated sugar
- Freshly ground pepper
- 1 clove garlic, halved
- 1½ pounds lean ground beef
- ¾ cup fine Ritz cracker crumbs
- 1 egg, slightly beaten
- 3–4 ounces sliced mozzarella cheese

Serves: 4–6
Preparation: 20 minutes
Baking: 1 hour
Cooling: 10 minutes
Temperature: 375°

- 2 tablespoons oil
- 1 onion, chopped
- 2 tablespoons cider vinegar
- 2 tablespoons brown sugar
- ¼ cup fresh lemon juice
- 1 cup catsup
- 3 tablespoons Worcestershire sauce
- ½ teaspoon prepared mustard
- ½ cup chopped celery
- Salt
- Freshly ground pepper (may substitute 3–4 drops Tabasco sauce)

Yield: 2 cups
Preparation: 10 minutes
Cooking: 30 minutes

Veal

¼ cup chopped fresh parsley
1 tablespoon chopped fresh chives
2 cloves garlic, chopped
1 (4-pound) boneless veal rump roast
½ cup all-purpose flour, approximately
Salt
Freshly ground pepper
3 tablespoons oil
4 slices bacon

Creole Sauce:
3 tablespoons drippings from roast
¼ cup finely chopped onion
½ cup green pepper strips
1 small clove garlic, minced
¾ pound fresh mushrooms, sliced
1 tablespoon all-purpose flour
5 large tomatoes; peeled, seeded and cut into small pieces (saving juices) (may substitute 16-ounce can tomatoes, undrained)
¼ cup dry red wine
⅛ teaspoon pepper
½ teaspoon salt
½ teaspoon granulated sugar
1 tablespoon chopped fresh parsley

Serves: 8
Preparation: 20 minutes
Roasting: 3½ hours
Temperature: 300°

Veal with Creole Sauce

A refreshing alternative for company dining.

Preheat oven to 300°.

Mince together parsley, chives and garlic. Stuff inside rolled roast. Season flour with salt and pepper. Dredge roast in seasoned flour. Heat oil in large heavy pot over medium-high heat; brown meat.

Place roast on rack in large open roasting pan. Place bacon slices on roast. Do not add water. Roast, uncovered, for 3–3½ hours or until meat thermometer registers 170° (about 45 minutes per pound). Let cool for 5 minutes. Slice and serve with Creole Sauce.

Thirty minutes before veal is finished, remove 3 tablespoons drippings from roasting pan and place in large heated skillet. Sauté onion, green pepper, garlic and mushrooms for about 5 minutes or until tender. Stir in flour. Add tomatoes, wine, pepper, salt and sugar. Cook until thickened. Add parsley.

Veal Blanchette
A gourmet delicacy well worth the effort.

Remove membrane and fat from veal. Cut into 1¼-inch pieces. Place veal in deep saucepan with lid. Add clove-studded onion, boiling water, carrots, bay leaf, thyme, parsley, celery, peppercorns and salt. Simmer, uncovered, for 1 hour or until tender. Strain stock, reserving 3 cups.

About 20 minutes before veal is done, melt 4 tablespoons butter in large skillet over medium heat. Add onions, cover tightly and cook for 3 minutes. Add mushrooms and sauté in same skillet for 15 minutes. Add to drained veal. Keep warm.

Melt remaining 2 tablespoons butter in saucepan over medium heat. Stir in flour until smooth. Stir in 3 cups reserved veal stock. Cook over medium heat until thick and boiling.

Beat egg yolks and lemon juice in small bowl with a wire whisk. Slowly whisk egg mixture to hot sauce, stirring constantly. Pour sauce over veal. Heat through. *Do not boil.*

- 2 pounds veal shoulder, boned
- 4 whole cloves
- 1 medium onion
- 1 quart boiling water
- 5 medium-size carrots, peeled and quartered
- 1 bay leaf
- ⅛ teaspoon dried thyme
- 2 sprigs parsley
- ½ cup thinly sliced celery
- 4 peppercorns
- 1 tablespoon (3 teaspoons) salt
- 6 tablespoons butter, divided
- 15 small white onions
- ½ pound small fresh mushrooms
- ¼ cup all-purpose flour
- 2 egg yolks
- 2 tablespoons fresh lemon juice

Serves: 4–6
Preparation: 25 minutes
Cooking: 65 minutes

Braised Veal
A low-calorie working woman's recipe.

Peel garlic and rub into iron or heavy skillet. Heat butter in skillet over medium-high until it begins to bubble. Brown both sides of veal quickly, about 3 minutes per side. Add wine and cover pan. Cook meat for 2 minutes and turn; cover again and cook 2 minutes longer. Serve immediately.

- 1 clove garlic
- 3 tablespoons butter
- 1 pound veal sirloin, boned and pounded to ⅛-inch thickness
- ¼ cup sweet white wine

Serves: 4
Preparation: 2 minutes
Cooking: 10 minutes

Veal

2½ pounds veal cutlets
Salt
Freshly ground pepper
All-purpose flour
¼ cup (½ stick) butter or margarine
¼ cup olive oil
½ teaspoon dried tarragon
¼ cup fresh lemon juice
¼ cup dry sherry
1 cup sour cream

Suggested Garnish:
Lemon slices

Serves: 6
Preparation: 10 minutes
Cooking: 10 minutes

Veal Tarragon

A splendid veal dish.

Pound cutlets to ⅛-inch thickness. Sprinkle meat with salt and pepper; coat lightly with flour. Heat butter and oil in large skillet until bubbly. Cook veal over medium-high heat until browned, about 2–3 minutes on each side. Remove meat and keep warm.

Stir tarragon, lemon juice and sherry into skillet, scraping bottom of skillet to loosen cooked particles. Cook over medium-high heat until liquid is reduced by half. Reduce heat to low; stir in sour cream. Cook over low heat until sour cream is hot, about 2 minutes. *Do not boil.* Return veal to skillet; cook for 2 minutes, turning veal to coat both sides with sauce. Arrange veal on serving platter, spoon remaining sauce over veal. Garnish with lemon slices.

Note: *Veal may be browned 2 hours in advance. Serve by cooking in sour cream sauce until hot, about 4 minutes.*

Variation: Skinned and boned chicken breasts may be substituted for veal to make dish less expensive.

Veal Forester

Light and colorful.

Pound cutlets to ⅛-inch thickness. Dust lightly with flour.

Melt butter in large skillet. Cook meat over medium-high heat until light brown, about 2–3 minutes per side. Add more butter, if necessary. Remove meat from skillet.

Combine mushrooms, vermouth, water, salt and pepper in same skillet. Heat to boiling. Reduce heat to low, simmer for 5 minutes. Return meat to skillet and heat through. Stir in chopped parsley.

Melt butter in small skillet over medium heat and briefly sauté cherry tomatoes. Arrange veal on platter. Garnish with tomatoes and parsley sprigs.

- 1 pound veal cutlets
- ¼ cup all-purpose flour
- 4 tablespoons (½ stick) butter or margarine
- ½ pound fresh mushrooms, sliced
- ½ cup dry vermouth
- 2 tablespoons water
- ¾ teaspoon salt
- Freshly ground pepper
- 1 tablespoon chopped fresh parsley

Garnish:
- 2 tablespoons butter or margarine
- 8–10 cherry tomatoes, stems removed
- Parsley sprigs

Serves: 4
Preparation: 15 minutes
Cooking: 25 minutes

Veal à l'Orientale

A touch of zest.

- 2½ pounds veal cutlets, ¼-inch thick
- Salt
- Freshly ground pepper
- 2 tablespoons all-purpose flour
- ¼ cup (½ stick) butter
- 1½ teaspoons freshly grated ginger
- ½ cup dry white wine
- 2 small lemons (extract juice from one and thinly slice other)
- 1 clove garlic, minced
- ¾ teaspoon dried tarragon
- ⅓ cup finely chopped fresh parsley, divided

Serves: 6
Preparation: 10 minutes
Cooking: 15 minutes

Pound cutlets to flatten. Sprinkle lightly with salt and pepper. Dust with flour. Melt butter in large skillet over medium-high heat. Sauté veal in butter until browned, about 2 minutes per side. Cook a few at a time. Keep browned veal warm until all are finished.

Combine ginger, wine, juice from 1 lemon and garlic.

Return all meat to skillet. Sprinkle with tarragon and about ½ of the parsley. Arrange lemon slices on top of veal. Pour ginger-wine mixture over veal and simmer for 5 minutes.

Remove meat to serving platter. Pour sauce from skillet over veal and sprinkle with remaining parsley.

Note: The whole cooking process should take only 15 minutes. Veal will be tough if overcooked.

Veal Balls and Sour Cream
Delicate and delectable.

Place veal, salt, pepper, egg, milk, onion, parsley, bread crumbs and flour in large bowl. Work mixture with hands until well combined. Roll into 24 balls.

Heat ¼ cup butter in 10-inch skillet. Brown veal balls on all sides. Continue cooking for 20 minutes. Remove veal balls from skillet with slotted spoon. Keep warm.

Scrape pan juices to one side of the skillet; add 1 tablespoon butter. Sauté mushrooms over medium heat until tender and remove from pan with slotted spoon. Pour sour cream into skillet. Mix sour cream with pan scrapings. Stir in mushrooms. Add veal balls and gently coat with sauce. *Do not overcook sour cream or it will curdle.*

Note: Veal balls may be prepared a day in advance. Reserve pan scrapings and prepare sauce just before serving.

Serving Suggestion: Veal balls are excellent with green noodles or a mixed grain rice. Serve with dark rye rolls as well.

Veal Balls:
- 1 pound ground veal
- 1 teaspoon salt
- ¼ teaspoon pepper
- 1 egg, slightly beaten
- ¼ cup milk
- 1 medium onion, chopped
- 2 tablespoons chopped fresh parsley
- ½ cup dry bread crumbs
- 2 tablespoons all-purpose flour
- ¼ cup (½ stick) butter

Sauce:
- 1 tablespoon butter
- ½ pound fresh mushrooms, sliced
- 1½ cups sour cream

Serves: 4–6
Preparation: 15 minutes
Cooking: 30 minutes

Lamb

1 (7-pound) leg of lamb; boned, butterflied and pounded to an even thickness

Marinade:
- 3 cups dry red wine
- ½ cup olive oil
- 1 tablespoon dried thyme
- 6 sprigs parsley
- 2 bay leaves, crumbled
- 2 cloves garlic, crushed
- ½ teaspoon pepper
- 2 teaspoons salt
- 2 onions, thinly sliced

Suggested Garnish: Watercress

Serves:	8–10
Preparation:	10 minutes
Marinating:	At least 24 hours
Broiling:	20 minutes
Cooling:	10 minutes
Temperature:	Broil

Marinated Butterflied Leg of Lamb

This lamb is not only good but versatile.

Place lamb in 9x13-inch glass dish.

Combine all marinade ingredients, except for onions, in large bowl. Whisk together until well blended. Stir in onions. Pour over lamb and marinate in refrigerator for 1 or 2 days, turning several times.

Preheat oven to broil.

Drain lamb; pat dry with paper towels. Place lamb on broiler pan, arranging lamb to maintain even thickness. Broil lamb 4 inches from heat for 12 minutes on each side for medium-rare meat.

Simmer drained marinade while lamb is cooking. Transfer cooked lamb to cutting board. Let stand for 10 minutes, then cut meat diagonally into ½-inch slices. Arrange slices on heated platter. Strain marinade and pour some over meat. Serve remainder of sauce at table. Garnish with watercress, if desired.

Note: May be cooked on outdoor grill. Reduce cooking time to 5 minutes per side for a gas grill; increase to 15 minutes per side for conventional grill.

Leg of Lamb with Parsley Crust
Simple elegance.

Rub oil, garlic and rosemary to paste in a mortar. Season paste generously with salt and pepper. Wipe lamb with a damp cloth. Spread garlic mixture over lamb and allow lamb to absorb mixture for 3 hours.

Preheat oven to 300°.

Place roast in roasting pan and roast lamb at 300° for 23 minutes per pound for pink or 28 minutes per pound for medium-well meat.

Mix bread crumbs and parsley in a bowl. Spoon off enough pan juices to make a paste of the parsley mixture; add butter if necessary.

Thirty minutes before lamb is finished, remove it from oven. Pack parsley mixture over top of lamb. Return lamb to oven and complete cooking.

Remove lamb to serving platter and keep warm. Add wine and water to pan juices. Stir over medium heat until well combined and thoroughly heated. Serve warm over lamb.

- 3 tablespoons olive oil
- 2–3 large cloves garlic
- ½ teaspoon dried rosemary, crushed
- Salt
- Freshly ground pepper
- 1 (3½-pound) leg of lamb, boned and rolled
- ½ cup fine dry bread crumbs
- ⅓ cup finely chopped fresh parsley
- 2 tablespoons butter, melted

Gravy:
- Pan juices
- ½ cup dry red wine
- ¾ cup water

Serves: 6
Preparation: 20 minutes
Marinating: 3 hours
Roasting: 1 hour, 20 minutes
Temperature: 300°

Leg of Lamb Barbecue
A favorite summer entrée.

Combine mustard, soy sauce, garlic, rosemary and ginger in small bowl. Whisk olive oil into mixture, 1 teaspoon at a time, to make a thick, creamy dressing.

Place lamb in large glass dish. Paint top of lamb with ⅔ of marinade. Let stand at room temperature for 1 hour. Turn lamb, paint other side with remaining marinade and let stand for 30 minutes.

Place lamb, fat side up, over medium-hot coals for 30–40 minutes. Turn and baste periodically.

Note: Marinade may be prepared several days in advance and refrigerated.

- 1 (6-pound) leg of lamb, boned and flattened

Marinade:
- ½ cup Dijon mustard
- 2 tablespoons soy sauce
- 1 clove garlic, crushed
- 1 teaspoon dried rosemary or thyme, crushed
- ¼ teaspoon ground ginger
- 2 tablespoons olive oil

Serves: 8
Preparation: 10 minutes
Marinating: 1½ hours
Grilling: 40 minutes

Lamb

Marinated Leg of Lamb
Fresh lemon juice and olive oil make this a winner.

1 (6–7 pound) leg of lamb

Marinade:
- 2 cloves garlic, crushed
- 2 teaspoons salt
- 1 teaspoon dried oregano
- 1 teaspoon dried thyme
- 1 teaspoon paprika
- 1 teaspoon pepper
- 1/3 cup olive oil
- 2 teaspoons fresh lemon juice

Whisk together all marinade ingredients until creamy. Place lamb in plastic bag. Pour marinade over lamb and seal bag. Let stand at room temperature for 2 hours; turn occasionally.

Preheat oven to 325°.

Remove lamb from marinade bag and place in roasting pan. Roast, uncovered, at 325° for 20–25 minutes per pound. Meat should be pink to enjoy the natural juices.

Serves: 8–10
Preparation: 10 minutes
Marinating: 2 hours
Roasting: About 2 hours
Temperature: 325°

Rack of Lamb Moutarde
Superb—a touch of class.

- 2 (6 to 8-rib) racks of lamb
- 1 cup fresh bread crumbs
- 1/4 cup chopped fresh parsley
- 2 cloves garlic, crushed
- 1 teaspoon salt
- 1/4–1/2 teaspoon cracked pepper
- 2 1/2 tablespoons Dijon mustard
- 1/4 cup (1/2 stick) butter, melted
- Chopped fresh parsley

Preheat oven to 450°.

Wipe lamb with damp paper towels. Trim off all fat. Place lamb, bone side up, in shallow roasting pan. Roast, uncovered, at 450° for 15 minutes. Remove roast from oven; let cool for 15 minutes.

Combine crumbs, parsley, garlic, salt and pepper. Spread mustard over top of lamb. Firmly press crumb mixture into mustard; drizzle with butter. Roast an additional 5–8 minutes depending on desired doneness. Meat thermometer should register 145° for rare to 165° for well done. Garnish with parsley.

Serving Suggestion: Stuffed Tomatoes with Zucchini Filling and oven-browned potatoes are good accompaniments.

Serves: 4–6
Preparation: 20 minutes
Roasting: 20–30 minutes
Temperature: 450°

Piquant Pork with Spiced Apple Rice

This unique recipe comes from Australia.

Butterfly pork tenderloins by slicing horizontally almost all the way through and laying open. Pound tenderloins to flatten.

Melt butter in small saucepan. Add onion and cook until transparent. Place onion in medium-size bowl with sausage, parsley, sage, bread crumbs, eggs, salt and pepper. Mix well.

Cover 1 tenderloin with the sausage filling. Top with the other tenderloin. Tie securely with string. (This can be prepared several hours ahead.)

Heat butter and oil in Dutch oven. Brown tenderloin on all sides over medium-high heat. Remove pork. Sauté onion and apple in drippings until softened. Stir in curry and cook for 1 minute; then stir in chicken stock. Return tenderloin to pan; cover and cook on low for approximately 1 hour.

Prepare rice while pork is cooking. Melt butter in large saucepan. Sauté onion, apple and celery in butter until tender. Stir in rice and cook for 1–2 minutes. Add apple juice and bring to a boil. Cover and cook over low heat until liquid is absorbed, about 20–25 minutes. Add cinnamon, cloves and parsley. Stir in brandy, if desired.

Remove pork from Dutch oven. Remove strings and slice tenderloin. Strain the sauce. Place Spiced Apple Rice on warm serving platter and top with tenderloin slices. Pour sauce over it.

- 2 pork tenderloins (approximately 2½ pounds total)

Filling:
- 2 tablespoons butter
- 1 small onion, finely diced
- ¼ pound bulk pork sausage
- 2 tablespoons finely chopped fresh parsley
- Pinch of dried sage
- 1 cup dry bread crumbs
- 2 large eggs, slightly beaten
- ½ teaspoon salt
- Freshly ground pepper

- 1 tablespoon butter
- 1 tablespoon oil
- 1 small onion, finely diced
- 1 small cooking apple, chopped
- 1 teaspoon curry powder
- 1 cup chicken stock or broth

Spiced Apple Rice:
- 3 tablespoons butter
- 1 onion, grated
- 1 cooking apple, finely chopped
- 1 cup chopped celery
- 1 cup long grain rice
- 2 cups apple juice
- Pinch of ground cinnamon
- Pinch of ground cloves
- 2 tablespoons chopped fresh parsley
- 1 tablespoon brandy (optional)

Serves: 6
Preparation: 30 minutes
Cooking: 1 hour

Pork

1 pork tenderloin
  (approximately 1 pound)
  Bacon to wrap tenderloin

Sauce:
  2 tablespoons butter or
    margarine
  2 tablespoons oil
  1 medium onion, chopped
  1 tablespoon finely chopped
    fresh parsley (optional)
  2 cups sliced fresh
    mushrooms (about ½
    pound)
  1½ cups rich beef stock (may
    substitute 10½-ounce
    can beef bouillon plus
    enough water to equal
    1½ cups)
  4 ounces dry white wine or
    dry vermouth
    Dash of cayenne pepper
  1 teaspoon fresh lemon juice
  2 teaspoons all-purpose flour

Serves: 3–4
Preparation: 5 minutes
Broiling: 40 minutes
Temperature: Broil

Pork Tenderloin with Wine Sauce

Classic in its simplicity.

Preheat oven to broil.

Wrap tenderloin completely in bacon. Broil or grill 6–8 inches from source of heat for 40 minutes, turning meat every 10 minutes.

Prepare sauce while cooking tenderloin. Place butter and oil in large skillet over low heat; add onion, parsley and mushrooms. Sauté over medium heat until tender. Add stock, wine, cayenne and lemon juice. Bring to a boil. Whisk in flour and cook until thickened. Pour sauce over tenderloin and serve.

Pork Loin with Orange Glaze
Magical blend of flavors.

Preheat oven to 325°.

Make slits in meat and insert garlic slivers. Rub meat all over with generous mixture of rosemary, salt and pepper. Place meat in roasting pan, fat side up. Roast pork, uncovered, at 325° for 35 minutes per pound or until meat thermometer registers 170°. (Juices should run clear when meat is tested with fork.)

Prepare glaze about 30 minutes before roast is done. Mix together mustard, marmalade, brown sugar and ¼ cup orange juice. Pour over meat and continue roasting until done. Baste 2 or 3 times.

Place cooked roast on heated platter and remove strings, if any. Keep warm. Skim all excess fat from pan juices. Add wine, remaining orange juice and Curaçao to pan. Bring sauce to boil over medium-high heat. Add orange slices and heat through. Spoon some sauce over loin. Arrange orange slices around loin and sprinkle meat lightly with parsley. Serve remainder of sauce at the table.

1 (4–5 pound) boneless pork roast
1 clove garlic, slivered
Rosemary, crumbled or ground
Salt
Freshly ground pepper

Glaze:
2 tablespoons Dijon or French mustard
2 heaping tablespoons orange marmalade
1 tablespoon brown sugar
½ cup fresh orange juice (about 2 oranges), divided

Sauce:
¼ cup dry white wine
1–2 tablespoons Curaçao (orange liqueur)
2 oranges, thinly sliced
Finely chopped fresh parsley

Serves:	8–10
Preparation:	10 minutes
Roasting:	2½ hours
Temperature:	325°

Pork

1 crown roast of pork (about 16 ribs)
Salt
Pepper
Thyme

Sausage Stuffing:
2 cups fresh bread crumbs
⅓ cup milk
½ cup minced onion
2 tablespoons butter
½ pound bulk pork sausage
¾ cup chopped celery
¼ cup raisins
¼ cup chopped cranberries
2 tart apples; peeled, cored and diced
Salt
Pepper
Thyme
Sage

Mustard Sauce:
2 tablespoons reserved drippings
2 tablespoons all-purpose flour
½ cup dry white wine
½ cup hot chicken broth
1 cup heavy (whipping) cream
1 tablespoon Dijon mustard
Salt
Pepper

Serves: 12–16
Preparation: 20 minutes
Roasting: 2 hours, 10 minutes
Temperature: 400°

Stuffed Crown Roast of Pork
Festive Christmas feast.

Have butcher prepare a 16-chop crown roast of pork, leaving a 2½-inch cavity.

Preheat oven to 400°.

Sprinkle pork with salt, pepper and thyme. Fit an empty tin can, top and bottom lids removed, into hollow center. (This helps to brown inner part of roast.)

Cover ends of chops with foil. Put roast in pan just large enough to hold it. Roast pork at 400° for 20 minutes. Reduce heat to 325° and roast for 40 minutes more. Prepare sausage stuffing while meat is roasting.

Soak bread crumbs in milk in small bowl. Squeeze crumbs dry. Set aside.

Sauté onions in butter in large skillet until soft. Add sausage. Brown slightly, breaking up meat with fork. Drain excess grease. Add celery, raisins, cranberries and apples. Cook mixture for 5 minutes. Transfer mixture to large bowl. Add bread crumbs and stir until well combined. Season stuffing to taste with salt, pepper, thyme and sage.

Remove pork from oven after 1 hour. Discard tin can. Fill cavity with stuffing, mounding it. Return roast to oven for 1 hour and 10 minutes or until meat thermometer registers 170°. Reserve 2 tablespoons fat in roasting pan. Place roast on serving platter. Remove foil from chops and replace with paper frills. Serve with Mustard Sauce.

Add flour to reserved fat in roasting pan. Cook, stirring over low heat, for 2 minutes. Pour in wine and scrape all brown bits clinging to the bottom of pan. Reduce wine to 2 tablespoons over high heat. Add broth and cream. Stir and cook sauce for about 5 minutes or until thickened. Stir 2 tablespoons of sauce into mustard and add mustard to sauce. Season to taste with salt and pepper.

Note: Sausage stuffing may be made ahead and brought to room temperature before stuffing center of roast.

Serving Suggestion: Glazed Apple Halves are a savory garnish for this feast.

Glazed Apple Halves
A nice complement to any pork dish.

Preheat oven to broil.

Bring water, sugar and lemon juice to boil in medium-size saucepan. Cook syrup over medium heat for 5 minutes. Poach apples in syrup until tender. Remove apples with slotted spoon. Arrange on baking sheet. Sprinkle with confectioners' sugar. Broil for 2–3 minutes until sugar is melted and apples are glazed. (If apples are made ahead, wait until serving time before sprinkling with sugar and broiling to glaze.) Fill centers with cranberry sauce made by bringing cranberries, sugar and water to boil in small saucepan. Simmer mixture for 5 minutes, stirring occasionally.

Note: Apples may be made ahead and kept in refrigerator. Sauce may be made ahead, refrigerated and reheated.

- 2 cups water
- ¾ cup granulated sugar
- 3 tablespoons fresh lemon juice
- 4–6 apples; peeled, cored and halved
- Confectioners' sugar

Sauce:
- 1 cup fresh cranberries
- ½ cup granulated sugar
- 2 tablespoons water

Serves: 4–6
Preparation: 15 minutes
Broiling: 3 minutes
Temperature: Broil

Loin of Pork with Garlic and Herbs
An original French recipe.

Cut skin off loin of pork; leave fat unless it is very thick. Slash the meat deeply and insert slivers of garlic to the bone. Rub salt and pepper into the pork. Place pork in roasting pan, fat side up. Combine thyme and wine; pour over pork. Marinate for 2–3 hours at room temperature, basting occasionally.

Preheat oven to 350°.

Cover undrained pork with aluminum foil and roast at 350° for 1 hour and 15 minutes. Reduce heat to 300°. Remove aluminum foil. Cut off pork fat.

Combine bread crumbs, parsley and mustard; spread on pork. Baste with the cooking liquid and continue cooking at 300° for 45 minutes, basting occasionally. Serve on heated plate and cut into chops. Strain pan juices and serve with chops.

- 1 (3-pound) loin of pork
- 1–2 cloves garlic, slivered
- Salt
- Freshly ground pepper
- ½ teaspoon dried thyme, crushed
- ¾ cup dry red wine
- 3 tablespoons soft bread crumbs
- 3 tablespoons finely chopped fresh parsley
- 3–4 tablespoons Dijon mustard

Serves: 4–6
Preparation: 10 minutes
Marinating: 3 hours
Baking: 2 hours
Temperature: 350°

Pork

Real Italian Spaghetti Sauce

The best ever with a bonus of a succulent pork roast.

½ cup olive oil
¼ cup corn oil
3 medium onions, chopped
1 (2½ to 3-pound) pork roast
2 (28-ounce) cans whole tomatoes, cut into small pieces
2 (12-ounce) cans tomato paste
2 (15-ounce) cans tomato sauce with tomato bits
1 tablespoon Italian seasoning
¾ teaspoon oregano
6 cloves garlic, crushed
Salt
Freshly ground pepper

Heat oils in 6-quart heavy pot over medium-high heat. Cook onion in oil until lightly browned. Add pork and brown on all sides. Add remaining ingredients and simmer, uncovered, over low heat for at least 5 hours. (Sauce is ready when oil rises to top.) Remove pork roast.

Note: Pork roast is to be eaten later either hot or cold.

Serving Suggestion: This sauce is the perfect companion to Spaghetti and Meatballs.

Serves: 12
Preparation: 25 minutes
Cooking: 5 hours

Roast Pork with Plum Sauce

The unique sauce makes this one different.

1 (2½–3 pound) boneless pork loin roast
2 cloves garlic, minced
1 teaspoon ground sage
½ teaspoon pepper

Plum Sauce:
½ cup plum jam
1½ tablespoons red wine vinegar
2 tablespoons soy sauce
½ teaspoon dry mustard
⅛ teaspoon ground allspice

Preheat oven to 325°.

Combine garlic, sage and pepper; rub mixture over entire roast. Place roast on rack in roasting pan. Insert meat thermometer into thickest part of roast and bake, uncovered, at 325° for approximately 2 hours or until the meat thermometer registers 170°.

Combine all ingredients for sauce in small saucepan and bring to a boil. Reduce heat and cook for 2 minutes, stirring constantly. Spread a portion of sauce over roast during last ½ hour of cooking. Serve remainder of sauce at the table.

Note: Sauce may be doubled, if desired.

Serves: 4–6
Preparation: 10 minutes
Baking: 2 hours
Temperature: 325°

Hungarian Pork Chops

Wonderful sauce elevates the basic pork chop.

Trim fat from chops. Sprinkle meat with salt and pepper. Heat butter in large skillet. Add chops and sauté over medium-high heat until browned. Turn chops; add onion, garlic, thyme and bay leaf. Sauté until chops are browned. Lower heat; add stock or wine. Cover and cook for 30 minutes. Remove chops to warm serving platter. Keep warm.

Reduce pan liquid to ½ the amount by boiling rapidly. Discard bay leaf. Add sour cream and paprika to liquid. Heat through but *do not boil.* Pour sauce over meat. Serve hot.

- 6 (1½-inch thick) pork chops
- Salt
- Freshly ground pepper
- 3 tablespoons butter
- ½ cup chopped onion
- 1 clove garlic, minced
- Pinch of dried thyme
- 1 bay leaf
- ¾ cup chicken stock or dry white wine
- 1 cup sour cream
- 1 tablespoon Hungarian paprika

Serves: 6
Preparation: 10 minutes
Cooking: 45 minutes

Braised Pork Chops with Orange and Mustard

Spicy, refreshing sauce.

Sprinkle pork chops with salt and pepper. Brown in oil in large skillet over medium-high heat, about 5 minutes per side.

Combine orange juice, soy sauce, mustard, honey, ginger and garlic and pour evenly over pork chops. Cover and simmer over low heat for 30 minutes or until pork chops are fork tender and cooked through. Place meat on platter and drizzle sauce over pork chops. Garnish with orange slices and watercress, if desired.

- 6 (1-inch thick) pork chops
- Salt
- Freshly ground pepper
- 2 tablespoons oil
- ½ cup fresh orange juice
- 3 tablespoons soy sauce
- 1 tablespoon Dijon mustard
- 3 teaspoons honey
- 2–3 teaspoons freshly minced ginger
- 2 cloves garlic, crushed

Suggested Garnishes:
Orange slices
Watercress

Serves: 4–6
Preparation: 10 minutes
Cooking: 30 minutes

Pork

3–4 pounds country-style pork ribs, cut in pieces
1 large onion, thinly sliced
1 cup catsup
⅓ cup Worcestershire sauce
1 teaspoon chili powder
1 teaspoon salt
2 dashes Tabasco sauce
2 cups water

Serves: 4
Preparation: 25 minutes
Baking: 1½ hours
Temperature: 450°

---

1 (16-ounce) package hot roll mix
1 pound mild fresh bulk pork sausage
½ cup finely chopped onion
8 ounces fresh mushrooms, chopped (may substitute 4-ounce can mushroom pieces, drained)
2 tablespoons chopped fresh parsley
2 eggs, slightly beaten
¼ cup grated Romano cheese
½ cup grated Swiss cheese
½ teaspoon salt

Serves: 8
Preparation: 30 minutes
Baking: 40 minutes
Cooling: 10 minutes
Temperature: 400°

Barbecued Ribs
Finger-licking good!

Preheat oven to 450°.

Place ribs in large shallow roasting pan, meaty side up. Place a thin slice of onion on each piece. Bake, uncovered, at 450° for 30 minutes. Reduce heat to 350°. Drain excess grease from pan.

Combine remaining ingredients in medium-size saucepan. Bring to a boil. Pour over ribs; continue baking at 350° for 1 hour. Baste ribs with the sauce every 15 minutes. Add more water if sauce gets too thick.

Note: The ribs may be made in a crock pot. Brown ribs under broiler for 20 minutes to remove excess fat. Layer ribs and onions in crock pot. Add barbecue sauce. Cover and cook on low setting for 6–8 hours or high setting for 3–4 hours.

Sausage Bread
May be main dish for brunch or supper.

Preheat oven to 400°.

Grease a cookie sheet.

Prepare hot roll mix according to package instructions.

Prepare sausage mixture while dough is rising. Place sausage, onion, mushrooms and parsley in large skillet. Cook over medium heat until sausage is brown and onion is tender. Drain. Combine sausage mixture with remaining ingredients.

Divide dough into two equal parts. Roll dough into two 12x18-inch rectangles. Spread each rectangle with sausage mixture to within ½ inch of each edge. Start with 12-inch side and roll up each rectangle jelly-roll fashion. Place on prepared cookie sheet, seam down, tucking ends under.

Bake at 400° for 30–40 minutes. Cool for 10 minutes before cutting into 1½-inch slices to serve.

Ham and Artichoke Rolls
Good for luncheon or dinner.

Preheat oven to 350°.

Butter a 9x9-inch baking dish.

Melt butter in medium-size saucepan over medium heat. Stir in flour until smooth. Remove from heat and stir in milk. Return to heat, stirring constantly until thickened. Add salt, pepper, nutmeg and paprika. Add cheeses and stir until melted. Remove from heat and stir in sherry.

Cut artichoke hearts in half. Wrap 2 halves, end to end, in a slice of ham. Arrange, seam down with sides touching, in prepared dish. Pour sauce over ham. Combine bread crumbs and cheeses; sprinkle over top. Bake at 350° for 25–30 minutes.

- 4 tablespoons butter
- 4 tablespoons all-purpose flour
- 2 cups milk, warmed
- Dash seasoned salt
- Dash cayenne pepper
- ¼ teaspoon ground nutmeg
- Pinch paprika
- ⅔ cup shredded Swiss cheese
- ⅔ cup freshly grated Parmesan cheese
- 4 tablespoons dry sherry
- 2 (8½-ounce) cans artichoke hearts, drained
- 12 thick slices baked or boiled ham

Topping:
- ⅔ cup buttered fresh bread crumbs
- ⅔ cup freshly grated Parmesan cheese
- ⅓ cup grated Swiss cheese

Serves: 6–8
Preparation: 35 minutes
Baking: 30 minutes
Temperature: 350°

Ham

- 6 eggs, beaten
- ½ cup (1 stick) margarine, cubed
- 8 ounces sharp Cheddar cheese, cubed
- 24 ounces cream-style, small curd cottage cheese
- 2 (10-ounce) packages frozen chopped spinach, thawed and well drained
- 2 tablespoons all-purpose flour
- 2 cups chopped baked or boiled ham

Serves: 6–8
Preparation: 20 minutes
Baking: 30 minutes
Temperature: 350°

- 1½ pounds lean ham
- 1½ pounds lean pork (have butcher grind ham and pork together)
- 4 eggs, beaten
- 3 cups milk
- 12 whole graham crackers, crushed

Topping:
- 1 cup firmly packed brown sugar
- 1½ teaspoons dry mustard
- ¼ cup vinegar

Serves: 10
Preparation: 15 minutes
Baking: 1½ hours
Temperature: 350°

Ham and Spinach Casserole

Terrific family meal, even with the spinach.

Preheat oven to 350°.

Grease 9x13-inch baking dish.

Combine all ingredients and pour into baking dish. Bake at 350° for 30 minutes.

Mommie Jewett's Ham Loaf

Graham crackers make this a winner.

Preheat oven to 350°.

Combine ham and pork mixture with eggs and milk in large bowl. Add graham cracker crumbs and mix well with hands. Divide into 2 (9x5-inch) loaf pans, filling each ¾ full.

Combine topping ingredients. Pour ½ of mixture over top of each ham loaf. Bake at 350° for 1½ hours. Let stand a few minutes before slicing.

Note: Loaves may be frozen before baking. Thaw before cooking. Bake at 350° for 1½ hours.

Poultry and Game

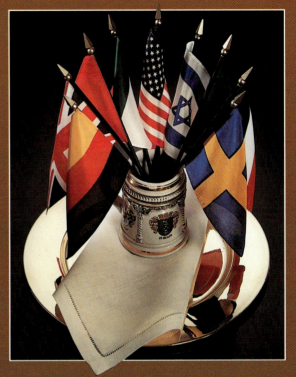

Ethnic Heritage

Indianapolis a melting pot? Surprisingly, yes.

Indianapolis's ethnic settlement has arrived primarily in successive waves of immigrants. The first influx of German and English population in the early years of the nineteenth century was augmented by a number of Irish who came to help build the Central Canal and the railroads. Gradually, as the twentieth century unfolded, people of varying origins began to make their way west from the East Coast debarkation points.

Before World War I, Italians, Greeks and Slavs seeking seasonal agricultural work added to the Indianapolis cultural mix, increased by a smattering of peoples from Poland, Russia and the Scandinavian countries. After World War II, Hispanics and Eastern Europeans began arriving here in significant numbers. The aftermath of the Vietnam conflict resulted in an influx of Orientals.

Today in Indianapolis, eleven separate ethnic groups are represented by significant population segments, each numbering in the thousands. People of several other national origins also constitute sizable elements of the Indianapolis population. Although, true to the American tradition, most of these ethnic groups have assimilated into the local society, the richness of their cultural heritage is not lost here.

A thriving Indianapolis International Center now serves as a rallying point for a number of ethnic groups. The Center-sponsored annual International Festival attracts vast and varied crowds, who come to sample the cuisine, music and crafts of a score of nationalities.

Most importantly, our newcomers have traditionally found a warm welcome here. One recent immigrant said it all: "You are not a stranger in this city. People are friendly and open here." This warmth and this attitude have enriched our lives, our city, and made winners of us all.

POULTRY AND GAME

Chicken
Baked Chicken Reuben . . . 177
Barbecued Chicken Broilers . . . 171
B'Stilla (Moroccan Chicken Pie) . . . 168
Chicken and Ham Bake . . . 180
Chicken and Hearts of Palm . . . 173
Chicken Artichoke Élégante . . . 164
Chicken Bombay . . . 176
Chicken Breast and Egg White . . . 169
Chicken Ceci . . . 167
Chicken Chaud-Froid . . . 157
Chicken Crescents . . . 177
Chicken Curry . . . 178
Chicken Cynthia à la Champagne . . . 159
Chicken Dijonnaise . . . 171
Chicken Enchiladas . . . 161
Chicken Piccata . . . 167
Chicken San Marino . . . 166
Chicken Sausage and Wild Rice . . . 165
Chinese Walnut Chicken . . . 174
Crab Stuffed Chicken . . . 158
Crispiest Fried Chicken . . . 175
Country Chicken Kiev . . . 173
Hot and Sour Chicken . . . 163
Lemon Coriander Chicken Pot-au-Feu . . . 172
Lemon-Herb Chicken Breasts . . . 179
Marinated Chicken . . . 166
Mexican Kiev . . . 181
Mozzarella Chicken . . . 170
"Oven Easy" Fried Chicken . . . 172
Pecan Chicken with Mustard Sauce . . . 162
Suprême de Volaille en Croûte . . . 160
Sweet and Sour Chicken . . . 175
Swiss Chicken Extraordinaire . . . 179
Texas-Style Barbecue Chicken . . . 170

Turkey
Mock Vitello Tonnato . . . 182

Game
Quail in Casserole . . . 184
Roast Wild Duck . . . 185
Tarragon Baked Cornish Hens . . . 184
Wine Basted Cornish Hens . . . 183

Stuffings
Chestnut Dressing . . . 186
Mom's Wild Rice Stuffing . . . 186

Chicken Chaud-Froid
Summer luncheon par excellence.

Simmer chicken breasts for 30 minutes or until tender. Cool in broth. Skin, bone and pound to flatten.

Mix cream cheese and mayonnaise until smooth. Add dill weed, lemon juice, lemon rind and salt. Mix to form smooth paste.

Spread topping on chicken breasts and chill, covered, overnight.

Assemble by placing each breast on a bed of lettuce leaves. Top each with slivered almonds and surround with avocado slices and mandarin oranges.

8 chicken breast halves

Topping:
- 2 (3-ounce) packages cream cheese, softened
- ½ cup mayonnaise
- 1 tablespoon dried dill weed (2 tablespoons snipped fresh dill, if available)
- 3 tablespoons fresh lemon juice
- 1 teaspoon freshly grated lemon rind
- ½ teaspoon salt
- Bibb or red-tip lettuce leaves
- ½ cup slivered almonds, toasted
- Avocado slices
- Mandarin oranges

Serves: 8
Preparation: 15 minutes
Cooking: 30 minutes
Chilling: Overnight

Hint:
Poaching chicken with the skin on, in a rich chicken stock, enhances the chicken flavor.

Chicken

- 2 tablespoons butter or margarine
- ¼ cup finely chopped green onion
- ½ pound fresh mushrooms, chopped (may substitute 4-ounce can mushrooms, drained)
- 1 cup cooked crab meat
- ½ cup coarsely crushed saltine cracker crumbs
- 2 tablespoons snipped fresh parsley
- 2 tablespoons dry white wine
- Dash salt
- 4 (5-ounce) whole chicken breasts, skinned and boned
- Oil

Shrimp Newburg Sauce: (1¾ cups)
- 2 tablespoons butter or margarine
- 2 tablespoons all-purpose flour
- ¼ teaspoon salt
- ¼ teaspoon paprika
- 1½ cups half and half
- 1 cup cooked and shelled shrimp
- 2 tablespoons dry sherry

Long grain rice (prepared according to package directions)
Chopped fresh parsley
Paprika

Serves: 4
Preparation: 45 minutes
Baking: 30 minutes
Temperature: 375°

Crab Stuffed Chicken
Elegant and rich.

Preheat oven to 375°.

Pound chicken breasts to flatten.

Melt butter in medium-size skillet. Add green onion and mushrooms. Cook over medium-high heat until tender, stirring occasionally. Stir in crab meat, cracker crumbs, parsley, wine and salt; mix well. Spoon about ⅓ cup stuffing mixture down center of each chicken breast. Roll loosely, tucking in edges, and tie with string. Place in 8-inch square baking dish. Brush chicken with oil. Cover and bake at 375° for 30 minutes or until tender.

Prepare Shrimp Newburg Sauce while chicken is cooking. Melt butter in medium-size saucepan over low heat. Stir in flour, salt and paprika; cook until smooth and bubbly. Add half and half. Stir constantly over medium-high heat until mixture thickens and bubbles. Stir in shrimp and sherry. Keep warm.

Remove string from cooked chicken breasts. Place chicken breasts on top of rice on individual plates. Spoon about ½ cup Shrimp Newburg Sauce over each chicken breast. Sprinkle with parsley and paprika.

Chicken Cynthia à la Champagne
Très bonne!

Preheat oven to 350°.

Combine flour and salt. Coat chicken pieces with flour mixture. Heat 1 tablespoon butter and the oil in large skillet. Add chicken and cook over medium-high heat for 5 minutes on each side. Place chicken in 9-inch square baking dish. Bake, uncovered, for 20 minutes.

Pour fat from skillet; add Curaçao, champagne and broth. Bring to a simmer. Add chicken. Simmer, uncovered, for 20 minutes or until tender.

Sauté mushrooms in remaining 1 tablespoon butter in small skillet over medium heat. Add to chicken along with cream. Spoon into chafing dish and garnish with orange wedges and grapes.

Note: Fruit may be served separately in compotes.

- 3 tablespoons all-purpose flour
- 1 teaspoon salt
- 4 chicken breast halves, skinned and boned
- 4 chicken thighs, skinned and boned
- 2 tablespoons butter or margarine, divided
- 1 tablespoon oil
- 2 tablespoons Curaçao (orange liqueur)
- ¾ cup dry champagne
- 1 cup chicken stock or broth
- 1 cup sliced fresh mushrooms
- ½ cup heavy (whipping) cream

Garnishes:
    Orange wedges
    Seedless grapes

Serves:	4–6
Preparation:	25 minutes
Baking:	20 minutes
Cooking:	20 minutes
Temperature:	350°

Chicken

8 chicken breast halves

Stuffing:
- ½ pound bulk sausage, uncooked
- ½ cup finely chopped onion
- 1 small clove garlic, crushed
- ¼ pound raw chicken livers, chopped
- 1 cup ground ham
- 1 slice fresh coarse white bread, crumbled
- ⅓ cup pistachios, shelled and coarsely chopped
- 2 tablespoons chopped fresh parsley
- 1 egg, beaten
- 1 tablespoon cognac
- Salt
- Freshly ground pepper

- 8 frozen patty shells, thawed for 20 minutes
- 1 egg white, beaten with 1 tablespoon water

Sauce:
- 1 (10-ounce) jar currant jelly
- 1½ teaspoons prepared mustard
- 1½ tablespoons port wine
- 2 tablespoons fresh lemon juice

Serves: 8
Preparation: 1½ hours
Baking: 30 minutes
Temperature: 425°

Suprêmes de Volaille en Croûte
(Chicken Breasts in Pastry)

This can be assembled in stages to relieve preparation time.

Simmer chicken in water in large saucepan for 30 minutes or until tender. Cool broth. Skin and bone, keeping breast intact. Set aside.

Combine sausage, onion and garlic in large skillet while chicken is simmering. Cook sausage over medium heat until it loses its pink color; drain grease. Add livers and cook briefly. Remove from heat. Stir in remaining ingredients. Set aside to cool. (These two steps may be refrigerated at this point and assembled at a later time.)

Preheat oven to 425°.

Roll each patty shell into an 8-inch circle on a lightly floured board. Place 4–5 tablespoons stuffing in the center of each circle; top with a cooked chicken breast. Moisten the two opposite edges of the pastry. Bring to top, overlap and pinch to seal. Fold up moistened ends of pastry toward center. Pinch to seal. Place bundles, seam down, 2 inches apart on ungreased cookie sheet. Brush with beaten egg white. Bake at 425° for 30 minutes or until lightly browned.

Heat currant jelly in small saucepan over low heat. Stir in remaining ingredients. Serve warm sauce over chicken. (May be prepared ahead and reheated.)

Note: Chicken in pastry may be prepared ahead and frozen. Bake for 15 minutes before freezing. To serve, defrost completely and bake at 425° for 15–20 minutes.

Variation: A mushroom sauce may be substituted for the currant sauce.

Hint:
Chicken breasts may be poached, skinned and boned and then frozen for up to 6 months. The cooked breasts give you a head start in your recipe preparation.

Chicken Enchiladas
Consistently rated excellent.

Preheat oven to 350°.

Combine tomato sauce, oil, cumin, chili powder and pepper in medium-size saucepan. Simmer for 30 minutes.

Combine 1½ cups Enchilada Sauce, tomatoes and chilies to make Smothering Sauce.

Combine chicken, onion, tomatoes, chilies, olives, chili powder, cumin and pepper in large saucepan or Dutch oven. Simmer for 15 minutes.

Assemble by brushing inside of tortillas with 2 tablespoons Enchilada Sauce. Top each tortilla with 3–4 tablespoons of chicken mixture.

Mix grated cheeses. Place 2–3 tablespoons cheese on each tortilla and roll.

Place rolls, seam down, in 9x13-inch baking dish. Add remaining Enchilada Sauce to Smothering Sauce and pour over enchiladas. Top with remaining cheese. Bake at 350° for 20–25 minutes. Garnish with parsley. Serve with sour cream and guacamole as toppings.

Enchilada Sauce: (makes 2½ cups)
- 2½ cups tomato sauce
- 2 tablespoons oil
- 1 tablespoon ground cumin
- ¾ teaspoon chili powder
- ¼ teaspoon pepper

Smothering Sauce:
- 1½ cups Enchilada Sauce
- 1¼ cups stewed tomatoes
- ¼ cup chopped green chilies, drained

Chicken Filling:
- 3 cups shredded cooked chicken
- 1 medium onion, chopped
- 1½ cups drained stewed tomatoes
- ¾ cup chopped green chilies, drained
- ¾ cup sliced black olives
- 1 teaspoon chili powder
- 1 teaspoon ground cumin
- ½ teaspoon pepper
- 10 (8-inch) flour tortillas
- 1 pound Cheddar cheese, grated
- 1 pound Monterey Jack cheese, grated

Condiment Suggestions:
- Chopped fresh parsley (optional)
- Sour cream
- Guacamole

Serves: 8
Preparation: 35 minutes
Cooking: 30 minutes
Baking: 25 minutes
Temperature: 350°

Chicken

4 chicken breast halves, skinned and boned
Salt
Freshly ground pepper
10 tablespoons butter or margarine, divided
3 tablespoons Dijon mustard, divided
6 ounces pecans, ground
2 tablespoons safflower or vegetable oil
⅔ cup sour cream

Serves: 4
Preparation: 30 minutes
Cooking: 10 minutes
Temperature: 200°

Pecan Chicken with Mustard Sauce
Very rich but so delicious.

Pound chicken breasts to flatten. Sprinkle with salt and pepper.

Melt 6 tablespoons butter in small saucepan over medium heat. Remove from heat and whisk in 2 tablespoons of the mustard. Dip each piece of chicken into mustard mixture. Coat each with ground pecans.

Preheat oven to 200°.

Melt remaining 4 tablespoons butter in large skillet. Stir in oil. Sauté chicken about 3 minutes per side or until fully cooked. Remove to a 9x13-inch baking dish. Discard butter and oil. Spoon any remaining pecans from the skillet onto the chicken, unless they are too burned. If so, discard them. Keep chicken warm in oven.

Deglaze skillet with sour cream, scraping up all browned bits. Whisk the remaining tablespoon of mustard and dash of freshly ground pepper into the sauce. Remove from heat.

Place a dollop of sour cream sauce in the middle of warmed dinner plates. Cover with piece of chicken. Use remaining sauce as gravy for noodles or rice.

Hot and Sour Chicken
Arouse your sense of taste.

Mix cornstarch, sherry, salt, pepper and peanut oil in medium-size bowl. Place chicken in mixture and marinate for 15 minutes at room temperature.

Prepare sauce by mixing cornstarch, red pepper, peanut oil, soy sauce, rice vinegar and chicken broth. Set aside.

Heat peanut oil in wok or large skillet. Add garlic, ginger and black beans. Stir-fry briefly. Add chicken and stir-fry until white, about 3–5 minutes. Remove chicken and vegetables from wok. Place green pepper, carrots and bamboo shoots in wok and stir-fry very briefly. Return chicken to wok or skillet. Add sauce and cook until clear and thickened. Serve with rice.

3 chicken breast halves; skinned, boned and cut into bite-size pieces

Marinade:
- 2 teaspoons cornstarch
- 2 teaspoons dry sherry
- ¼ teaspoon salt
- ¼ teaspoon pepper
- 1½ teaspoons peanut oil

Sauce:
- 2 teaspoons cornstarch
- ½ teaspoon red pepper
- 1½ tablespoons peanut oil
- 2 tablespoons soy sauce
- 2½ tablespoons rice vinegar
- ½ cup chicken broth or stock

- 1 tablespoon peanut oil
- 2 large cloves garlic, crushed
- 1–2 teaspoons freshly grated ginger
- 2 teaspoons fermented black beans, rinsed and chopped
- 1 green pepper, chopped
- 1 large carrot, peeled and sliced
- 1 (8-ounce) can bamboo shoots, drained (may substitute 6-ounces fresh bamboo shoots)
- Rice, prepared according to package directions

Serves: 3–4
Preparation: 30 minutes
Marinating: 15 minutes
Cooking: 15 minutes

Chicken Artichoke Élégante

The combination of flavors and textures is a winner.

- 1 (10-ounce) package frozen chopped spinach, cooked and drained
- 2 cups cooked, long grain white rice (may substitute brown rice)
- 1 egg, slightly beaten
- 4 tablespoons (½ stick) butter or margarine, softened (divided)
- 1 (14½-ounce) can artichoke hearts
- 1½ cups diced cooked chicken
- 1½ cups grated Monterey Jack cheese
- ½ pound fresh mushrooms, sliced
- ½ medium onion, chopped (optional)
- 2 tablespoons all-purpose flour
- 1 clove garlic, crushed
- 1 teaspoon prepared mustard
- Salt
- Freshly ground pepper
- 1 cup milk

Grease a 9-inch pie plate.

Squeeze spinach to remove all excess moisture. Combine spinach, rice and egg in medium-size bowl. Add 2 tablespoons butter and mix well. Press into prepared pie plate, covering bottom and sides. Cover and chill for 30–60 minutes.

Drain artichokes and blot dry. Cut each into 2 or 3 pieces. Arrange over rice and spinach crust. Arrange chicken and cheese over artichokes.

Preheat oven to 350°.

Melt remaining 2 tablespoons butter in medium-size skillet over low heat. Add mushrooms and onions; sauté over medium heat until tender. Stir in flour, garlic, mustard and salt and pepper to taste. Add milk gradually. Cook until mixture thickens. Pour over pie. (At this point dish may be refrigerated.) Bake, uncovered, at 350° for 45 minutes.

Note: Bake for 1 hour if pie is chilled. Recipe may be doubled and placed in 9x13-inch casserole.

Serving Suggestion: A tomato aspic goes well with this dish.

Serves:	6
Preparation:	35 minutes
Chilling:	30 minutes
Baking:	45 minutes
Temperature:	350°

Chicken, Sausage and Wild Rice
Good for luncheon or dinner party.

Preheat oven to 350°.

Cook rice according to package directions.

Brown sausage in large skillet over medium heat. Remove sausage with slotted spoon. Sauté mushrooms and onions in sausage fat until onion is transparent. Drain and stir in chicken. Set aside.

Mix flour with cream in medium-size saucepan; whisk until smooth. Add broth and cook over medium heat until mixture resembles a thick white sauce. Pour into large bowl. Add seasonings, rice, sausage and chicken mixture. Mix thoroughly. Place in 9x13-inch baking dish and bake at 350° for 25–30 minutes.

Note: May be made ahead and refrigerated or frozen. Bring to room temperature before baking. May substitute 6-ounce box long grain and wild rice for wild rice, oregano, thyme and marjoram.

- 2 cups wild rice
- 1 pound bulk pork sausage, uncooked
- 1 pound fresh mushrooms, sliced
- 2 medium onions, chopped
- 2½–3 pounds cooked chicken; skinned, boned and cut into chunks
- ¼ cup all-purpose flour
- ½ cup heavy (whipping) cream
- 2½ cups chicken stock or broth
- Pinch of dried oregano
- Pinch of dried thyme
- Pinch of dried marjoram
- 1 teaspoon salt
- ⅛ teaspoon pepper

Serves: 10–12
Preparation: 45 minutes
Baking: 30 minutes
Temperature: 350°

Chicken

12 chicken breast halves, skinned and boned
12 (¼-inch thick) slices Gruyère or Fontina cheese, cut into 1x2½-inch rectangles
12 thin slices prosciutto or Westphalian ham
    Salt
    All-purpose flour
2 eggs, well beaten
    Fine dry bread crumbs
4–6 tablespoons butter
3 tablespoons cognac
½ cup heavy (whipping) cream

Serves:	12
Preparation:	30 minutes
Chilling:	At least 4 hours
Cooking:	15 minutes
Baking:	25 minutes
Temperature:	350°

Chicken San Marino

The cognac sauce makes the difference.

Pound chicken breasts to flatten. Roll each rectangle of cheese in a ham slice. Wrap a chicken breast around each ham log, enclosing completely. Sprinkle rolls with salt, then coat with flour. Shake off excess. Dip each roll in egg, then roll in bread crumbs. Place rolls, side by side without touching, on a baking sheet. Cover and refrigerate for several hours or overnight.

Preheat oven to 350°.

Melt 4 tablespoons butter in large skillet. Add rolls and cook over moderate heat to brown evenly on all sides, about 15 minutes. Add butter as needed to keep rolls moist. Set skillet aside for later use. Transfer rolls to 9x13-inch baking dish. Bake at 350° for 20–25 minutes.

Add cognac to pan in which the chicken was browned. Set aflame at once. Shake pan to burn off alcohol. Pour in cream. Boil until slightly thickened and large shiny bubbles form. Pour sauce over baked chicken and serve.

½ cup honey
½ cup Dijon mustard
1 tablespoon curry powder
2 tablespoons soy sauce
4–6 chicken breast halves

Serves:	4
Preparation:	10 minutes
Marinating:	6 hours
Baking:	1 hour
Temperature:	350°

Marinated Chicken

A fantastic no-work chicken.

Mix honey, mustard, curry powder and soy sauce in 9x13-inch baking dish. Place chicken in sauce, coat thoroughly and marinate in refrigerator for 6 hours.

Preheat oven to 350°.

Bake, uncovered, at 350° for 1 hour. Baste often.

Chicken Piccata
Elegant dining in just minutes.

Pound chicken breasts to flatten. Mix flour, salt and pepper in plastic bag. Dip chicken in mixture to coat. Shake off excess flour. Chill. (Chicken may be cooked without chilling, but chilling seems to retard burning when sautéing.)

Heat butter and oil in large skillet over medium heat until it sizzles. Sauté chicken breasts, 3 at a time, for 2–3 minutes per side. Drain on paper towels. Keep warm until all are cooked.

Stir wine and lemon juice into drippings and scrape bottom of skillet to deglaze. Heat, but do not boil. Return chicken to pan and turn to coat. Remove from pan. Pour pan juices over chicken. Sprinkle with parsley and capers, if desired.

- 6 chicken breast halves, skinned and boned
- ½ cup all-purpose flour
- 1½ teaspoons salt
- ¼ teaspoon pepper
- ¼ cup (½ stick) butter or margarine
- ¼ cup olive oil
- ¼ cup dry white wine
- Juice of ½ lemon
- ¼ cup chopped fresh parsley
- Capers (optional)

Serves: 6
Preparation: 20 minutes
Chilling: 30 minutes
Cooking: 4–6 minutes

Chicken Ceci
Be daring—a pleasant surprise.

Mix together onion, peas, ham, pepperoni, oil, vinegar and Italian seasoning. Place chicken in 9x13-inch glass baking dish, meat side down. Pour chick pea mixture over chicken. Cover and marinate overnight in refrigerator.

Preheat oven to 350°.

Bake, uncovered, at 350° for 50–55 minutes.

Note: Chick peas are marketed as garbanzo beans in some areas.

- 1 large onion, chopped
- 1 (16-ounce) can chick peas, drained (optional)
- ¼ pound boiled or baked ham, diced
- 1 (3½ to 4-ounce) package pepperoni, diced
- ½ cup oil
- 3 tablespoons red wine vinegar
- 1 tablespoon Italian seasoning
- 8 chicken breast halves, skinned

Serves: 6–8
Preparation: 20 minutes
Marinating: Overnight
Baking: 55 minutes
Temperature: 350°

Chicken

- 4 pounds chicken, legs and thighs
- 3 cups water
- 1½ cups (3 sticks) unsalted butter, divided
- 1 cup chopped fresh parsley
- 1 large onion, grated
- 1 (3-inch) stick cinnamon
- 1 teaspoon pepper
- ¾ teaspoon ground ginger
- ¼ teaspoon ground turmeric
- ¼ teaspoon saffron
- Pinch of salt
- ¼ cup oil
- 1 pound blanched whole almonds
- ½ cup confectioners' sugar
- 2 teaspoons ground cinnamon
- ¼ cup fresh lemon juice
- 10 eggs, well-beaten
- 1 (1-pound) box phyllo pastry

Suggested Garnishes:
Confectioners' sugar
Ground cinnamon

Serves: 12
Preparation: 2 hours
Baking: 30 minutes
Temperature: 425°

B'stilla (Moroccan Chicken Pie)
This exotic taste experience is a must.

Combine chicken, water, ½ cup butter, parsley, onion, cinnamon stick, pepper, ginger, turmeric, saffron and salt in a soup kettle. Cover and bring to a boil over high heat. Reduce heat; simmer 1 hour. Stir occasionally.

Heat oil in large skillet. Add almonds and brown lightly. Remove and drain on paper towel. Transfer almonds to food processor and process until almonds are coarsely chopped. Add ¼ cup butter, sugar and cinnamon and process with almonds. Set mixture aside.

Remove chicken from broth; cool slightly. Skin and bone chicken. Shred into 1½-inch pieces. Set aside.

Discard cinnamon stick from broth. Reduce liquid to 1¾ cups by boiling rapidly. Reduce heat to simmer. Add lemon juice and continue to simmer. (At this point you may freeze chicken, almond mixture and broth, keeping each separate.) Pour eggs into hot liquid, stirring constantly until eggs are cooked and slightly congealed. Transfer eggs to a baking sheet with a slotted spoon. Refrigerate until cool.

Preheat oven to 425°.

Melt the remaining ¾ cup butter. Brush a 10x14-inch baking pan with butter. Cover pan with 1 sheet of phyllo, keeping unused sheets covered with damp towel. Drape ½ the remaining sheets onto pan, 1 at a time, allowing ½ of each sheet to extend beyond the edge of pan. Drizzle or brush a little butter on each sheet. Spread chicken evenly on bottom of pan. Cover with well-drained egg mixture. Sprinkle with almond mixture. Cover quickly with all but 4 sheets of phyllo, buttering each sheet. Fold extended sheets over top of pie to cover and enclose. Place remaining 4 sheets on top, buttering each lightly. Tuck ends of phyllo into pan around outer edge of pie. Pour remaining butter over the top of pie.

Bake at 425° for 10 minutes. Remove pan from oven. Shake pan or loosen edges of pie with spatula. Invert pie into larger casserole. Return to oven and continue to bake for 15–20 minutes or until crisp and golden brown. Dust lightly with confectioners' sugar and cinnamon. Serve immediately.

Chicken Breast and Egg White
A memorable taste experience.

Cut chicken into thin slices 1 inch long. Place chicken in large bowl. Add salt, egg whites and cornstarch. Stir gently and marinate for 10 minutes.

Heat 4 tablespoons oil in wok or skillet and stir-fry chicken for 1 minute. Remove with slotted spoon and set aside.

Stir-fry lettuce until warm but still crisp. Sprinkle with salt. Remove and place on serving dish.

Wipe out wok and add remaining 2 tablespoons oil; briefly stir-fry ginger root and onion. Add peas, chicken, sherry and salt. Stir until hot, about 2 minutes; place on top of lettuce. Splash sesame oil over all and toss lightly. Serve immediately.

Note: Do not let chicken brown. Chicken and egg white should be pure white. Serve at room temperature if not served immediately. Do not reheat.

Variation: Cut ¼ sweet red pepper in long thin strips and sauté along with onions and ginger.

Variation: Beat the 2 reserved egg yolks. Heat 1 tablespoon butter in small skillet; add yolks and cook until firmly set. Remove from pan and cool slightly. Slice into long slivers and add to chicken along with peas.

- 1 whole breast, skinned and boned
- ½ teaspoon salt
- 2 egg whites
- 1 tablespoon cornstarch
- 6 tablespoons oil, divided
- 1 head iceberg lettuce, shredded or slivered
- Salt
- 1 teaspoon freshly grated ginger root (more if desired)
- 1 large green onion, chopped
- 8 ounces (½ cup hulled) fresh green peas, (may substitute frozen peas)
- 1 tablespoon sherry
- 1 teaspoon salt
- 1 teaspoon sesame oil

Serves: 4
Preparation: 25 minutes
Cooking: 5 minutes

Chicken

6–7 pounds chicken pieces
Juice of 1 large lemon
4 cloves garlic, minced
2 tablespoons (6 teaspoons) coarse salt
2 tablespoons sweet Hungarian paprika
2 teaspoons cayenne pepper

Serves:	8–10
Preparation:	15 minutes
Marinating:	8 hours
Baking:	45 minutes
Temperature:	350°

4 chicken breast halves, skinned and boned
2 heaping tablespoons all-purpose flour
¼ teaspoon pepper
¼ cup oil
2 medium-size zucchini
1 medium-size green pepper, chopped
1 small onion, sliced
1 clove garlic, minced
1–1½ cups spaghetti sauce
½ teaspoon granulated sugar
1 teaspoon Italian seasoning
4 ounces sliced mozzarella cheese (may substitute 1 cup grated mozzarella cheese)

Serves:	4
Preparation:	30 minutes
Cooking:	15 minutes

Texas-Style Barbecue Chicken
Different—paprika is a winner.

Brush chicken with lemon juice; rub with garlic. Combine salt, paprika and pepper; sprinkle on chicken pieces. Place chicken, skin side up, in roasting pan. Refrigerate, uncovered, for 8 hours or overnight.

Preheat oven to 350°.

Bake chicken, covered, at 350° for 30 minutes. Turn heat to broil. Remove cover and broil chicken 6 inches from heat for 15 minutes or until chicken is cooked and browned.

Variation: Chicken may also be cooked on a grill for 30–40 minutes or until done.

Mozzarella Chicken
Great family fare.

Pound chicken breasts to ½-inch thickness. Mix flour and pepper; coat chicken with mixture.

Heat oil in 10-inch skillet over medium-high heat. Add chicken and cook until browned. Remove chicken.

Quarter zucchini lengthwise, then cut into ¾-inch chunks. Place in skillet with green pepper, onion and garlic. Cook vegetables in drippings, stirring frequently, until crisp tender. Return chicken to skillet. Add spaghetti sauce, sugar and Italian seasoning. Cook over low heat for 15 minutes or until chicken and vegetables are tender. Place cheese over chicken; cover and simmer until melted.

Note: May be prepared ahead. Heat and add cheese just prior to serving.

Chicken Dijonnaise
Easy and delicious.

Coat chicken with mustard. Arrange chicken, skin side up, in 8x12-inch roasting pan. Cover and marinate at room temperature for 2 hours.

Preheat oven to 350°.

Season lightly with pepper. Pour vermouth or wine around the chicken. Place roasting pan on center rack of oven and bake at 350°, basting occasionally, for 30–40 minutes or until chicken is done. (Dark meat may require 5–10 more minutes.)

Scrape mustard off chicken and return to roasting pan. Transfer chicken to a serving platter. Cover and keep warm.

Skim off as much fat as possible from the cooking juices. Place roasting pan over medium heat. Bring to a boil. Whisk in heavy cream. Reduce heat. Simmer sauce for 5–10 minutes or until reduced by about ⅓. Season lightly with salt and pepper to taste. Spoon sauce over the chicken. Serve hot or at room temperature.

2½–3 pounds chicken pieces
⅓ cup Dijon mustard
Freshly ground black pepper
⅓ cup vermouth or dry white wine
½ cup heavy (whipping) cream
Salt
Pepper

Serves: 2–4
Preparation: 30 minutes
Marinating: 2 hours
Baking: 40 minutes
Temperature: 350°

Barbecued Chicken Broilers
Wonderful flavor.

Clean and dry broilers. Place in 9x13-inch pan. Combine remaining ingredients and purée in blender. Pour over chicken. Marinate in refrigerator for 3–4 hours, turning once. Place chicken on grill, skin side up. Reserve marinade. Grill until done, about 30 minutes. Baste frequently with marinade.

2 (2-pound) broiler chickens, halved
2 teaspoons fresh lime juice
¼ cup oil
2 tablespoons vinegar
1 tablespoon Worcestershire sauce
⅛ teaspoon Tabasco sauce
1 teaspoon salt
1 teaspoon granulated sugar
1 clove garlic
½ teaspoon paprika

Serves: 8
Preparation: 10 minutes
Marinating: 3–4 hours
Grilling: 30 minutes

Chicken

Lemon Coriander Chicken Pot-au-Feu

A wonderful aroma and combination of flavors.

- ⅓ cup olive oil
- 1 large onion, thinly sliced
- 1 clove garlic, minced or mashed (optional)
- 1 tablespoon chopped fresh parsley
- 1 tablespoon freshly ground coriander seeds
- 1 teaspoon salt
- ½ teaspoon coarse pepper
- 1–2 pinches of powdered saffron
- 1 (2½-pound) chicken (may substitute 1 broiler-fryer or assorted pieces)
- ½ lemon, cut into wedges
- ⅓ cup chopped green olives

Heat oil in large Dutch oven over medium heat. Stir in onion, garlic, parsley, coriander, salt, pepper and saffron. Add chicken; turn and coat with onion mixture. Place lemon wedges on top. Cover and simmer 1½–2 hours. Place chicken on platter and keep warm.

Reduce remaining liquid to a thick sauce by boiling rapidly. Add olives and heat through. Pour over chicken.

Serves: 6
Preparation: 20 minutes
Cooking: 2 hours

"Oven Easy" Fried Chicken

A no-fuss family favorite.

- ¼ cup (½ stick) butter
- ¼ cup all-purpose flour
- 1½ teaspoons paprika
- 1 teaspoon salt
- ½ teaspoon pepper
- 2 pounds chicken pieces

Preheat oven to 400°.

Place butter in a shallow roasting pan or 9x13-inch baking dish and melt in oven.

Mix flour, paprika, salt and pepper in a paper or plastic bag.

Shake 1 or 2 pieces of chicken at a time in bag until all chicken pieces are coated. Arrange chicken, skin side down, in single layer in baking dish. Bake, uncovered, at 400° for 30 minutes. Turn chicken and bake 25 minutes more.

Variation: Substitute ½ cup biscuit mix, 1 tablespoon curry powder, ¾ teaspoon salt and ¼ teapoon pepper for flour mixture.

Serves: 4
Preparation: 10 minutes
Baking: 1 hour
Temperature: 400°

Country Chicken Kiev
An attractive dish guaranteed to bring raves.

Preheat oven to 350°.

Melt butter in saucepan.

Combine bread crumbs, Parmesan, basil, oregano, garlic salt and salt in pie plate.

Dip chicken breasts in butter, then roll in crumb mixture. Place in ungreased 9-inch square baking dish. Bake at 350° for 50–60 minutes.

Prepare sauce while chicken is baking. Add enough butter to what is left in saucepan to make ½ cup. Add wine, onions and parsley. Simmer until onions are tender. When chicken is done, pour mixture over chicken. Bake 5 minutes longer.

- ⅔ cup butter (more, if needed)
- ½ cup fine dry bread crumbs
- 2 tablespoons freshly grated Parmesan cheese
- 1 teaspoon dried basil
- 1 teaspoon dried oregano
- ½ teaspoon garlic salt
- ½ teaspoon salt
- 4 chicken breast halves, skinned and boned
- ¼ cup apple wine
- ¼ cup chopped green onions
- ¼ cup chopped fresh parsley

Serves: 4
Preparation: 20 minutes
Baking: 1 hour
Temperature: 350°

Chicken and Hearts of Palm
Delightfully different.

Preheat oven to 400°.

Pound chicken breasts to flatten. Wrap each breast around a heart of palm. Secure with toothpick. Arrange in 9x13-inch glass baking dish, leaving space between breasts. Brush with melted butter. Sprinkle with salt and white pepper. Bake at 400° for 20–25 minutes. Baste with melted butter after 12–15 minutes.

Place egg whites, salt, white pepper and lemon juice in blender. Heat butter to bubbling point. Turn blender on medium speed and slowly drizzle hot butter into mixture. Pour over chicken just before serving.

Note: Chicken may be prepared one day ahead, covered and refrigerated. Sauce must be made just before serving.

- 8 chicken breast halves, skinned and boned
- 1 (14-ounce) can hearts of palm
- Salt
- White pepper
- 3 tablespoons butter, melted

Sauce:
- 3 egg whites
- ¼ teaspoon salt
- ⅛ teaspoon white pepper
- 1 tablespoon fresh lemon juice
- 1 cup (2 sticks) butter

Serves: 4–6
Preparation: 15 minutes
Baking: 25 minutes
Temperature: 400°

Chicken

- 1 cup coarsely broken walnuts
- ¼ cup oil
- 4 chicken breast halves; skinned, boned and cut lengthwise into thin strips
- ¼ teaspoon salt
- 1 cup sliced onion
- 1½ cups diagonally sliced celery
- 1¼ cups chicken broth, divided
- 1 teaspoon granulated sugar
- 1 tablespoon cornstarch
- ¼ cup soy sauce
- 2 tablespoons dry sherry
- 1 (5-ounce) can bamboo shoots, drained
- 1 (5-ounce) can water chestnuts, drained and sliced

Serves: 4
Preparation: 35 minutes
Cooking: 20 minutes

Chinese Walnut Chicken

Crisp and crunchy.

Toast walnuts in hot oil in large skillet or wok, stirring constantly. Remove nuts and drain on paper towels. Place chicken in skillet. Sprinkle with salt. Cook 5–10 minutes or until tender, stirring constantly. Remove chicken.

Place onion, celery and ½ cup chicken broth in skillet. Cook, uncovered, for 5 minutes or until vegetables are crisp tender.

Combine sugar, cornstarch, soy sauce and sherry. Add remaining ¾ cup chicken broth. Pour over vegetables in skillet. Cook and stir until sauce thickens.

Add chicken, bamboo shoots, water chestnuts and walnuts. Heat through.

Variation: Fresh pea pods may be added during last step.

Sweet and Sour Chicken
This one hit the top of the scale.

Heat oil in deep fryer or large heavy saucepan to 375°.

Mix eggs, cornstarch, flour and water. Coat chicken with paste and deep fry in oil 6–8 minutes. (Do not overcook the chicken or it will dry out.) Set aside on paper towels.

Combine sauce ingredients in small saucepan; bring to a boil. (If thicker sauce is desired, add 1 tablespoon cornstarch to small amount of sauce. Return to saucepan and stir until thickened.) Pour sauce over chicken to serve.

Note: *If using heavy saucepan for deep frying, add enough oil to cover chicken, approximately 3 inches. Heat oil to 375°.*

Variation: The sauce makes a tasty dip for chicken nuggets.

Oil for frying chicken
4 chicken breast halves; skinned, boned and cut into bite-size pieces
2 eggs, beaten
½ cup cornstarch
½ cup all-purpose flour
½ cup water

Sauce:
1 tablespoon oil
½ cup water
2 tablespoons white vinegar
½–1 cup granulated sugar
½ cup catsup
1 clove garlic, minced

Serves: 4
Preparation: 20 minutes
Cooking: 10 minutes

Crispiest Fried Chicken
The peanuts make this recipe very unique.

Preheat oven to 400°.

Mix eggs and milk in pie plate.

Mix cereal and peanuts in another pie plate. Dip chicken pieces into egg mixture. Coat with flour. Dip into egg again, then roll in cereal mixture.

Melt ½ cup butter in each of 2 (9x13-inch) baking dishes in 400° oven.

Place chicken, skin down, in butter. Turn skin side up. Bake at 400° for 45–60 minutes or until tender. Serve warm or cold.

Note: *Recipe may be cut in half.*

4 eggs, beaten
¼ cup milk
2 cups finely crushed wheat cereal flakes
1¼ cups finely chopped cocktail peanuts
6 pounds chicken pieces
Flour
1 cup (2 sticks) butter, divided

Serves: 12
Preparation: 30 minutes
Baking: 1 hour
Temperature: 400°

Chicken

- 2 cups stewed tomatoes with liquid
- 1/3 cup currants
- 1 cup diced green pepper
- 1 clove garlic, minced
- 1/4 teaspoon dried oregano
- 1/4 teaspoon Tabasco sauce
- 1 tablespoon finely chopped fresh parsley
- 2 teaspoons salt
- 1 teaspoon pepper
- 1/4 teaspoon curry powder
- 1/2 cup (1 stick) butter, divided
- 1 medium yellow onion, thinly sliced
- 1 pound fresh mushrooms, sliced
- 6 chicken breast halves; skinned, boned and diced

Serves: 6
Preparation: 30 minutes
Cooking: 1 hour

Chicken Bombay
East meets West.

Place tomatoes, currants, green pepper, garlic, oregano, Tabasco, parsley, salt, pepper and curry powder in 4-quart saucepan. Cover and simmer over low heat for 30 minutes.

Melt 4 tablespoons butter in large skillet over low heat. Add onion and mushrooms; sauté over medium heat until tender. Remove with slotted spoon and set aside. Melt remaining 4 tablespoons butter in skillet over low heat. Add diced chicken and brown over medium-high heat.

Transfer chicken, onion and mushrooms with slotted spoon to saucepan; continue to simmer, covered, for 30 minutes.

Note: If prepared ahead, just reheat. May be refrigerated up to 2 days.

Chicken Crescents
A delicious package.

Preheat oven to 350°.

Beat together cream cheese and softened butter in large bowl. Add chicken, salt, pepper, milk, onion and pimiento. Mix well.

Unroll crescent rolls and divide dough into 4 squares. Pinch perforations together. Place ¼ chicken mixture in center of each square. Fold 4 corners together. Pinch dough so that it encloses chicken mixture. Brush pastry with melted butter. Sprinkle with crouton crumbs. Place on ungreased cookie sheet. Bake at 350° for 20 minutes.

- 1 (3-ounce) package cream cheese, softened
- 2 tablespoons butter, softened
- 2 cups cubed cooked chicken
- ¼ teaspoon salt
- Freshly ground pepper
- 2 tablespoons milk
- 1 tablespoon chopped onion
- 1 tablespoon chopped pimiento
- 1 (8-roll) package crescent rolls
- 2 tablespoons butter, melted
- ½ cup crushed cheese croutons

Serves: 4
Preparation: 30 minutes
Baking: 20 minutes
Temperature: 350°

Baked Chicken Reuben
A breeze to make.

Preheat oven to 325°.

Grease a 9x13-inch baking dish.

Place chicken in prepared baking dish. Sprinkle with salt and pepper.

Press excess liquid out of sauerkraut. Place sauerkraut over chicken. Top with Swiss cheese. Pour dressing evenly over cheese.

Cover with foil. Bake at 325° for 1 hour and 15 minutes or until fork can be inserted into chicken with ease.

Sprinkle with parsley and serve.

- 8 chicken breast halves, skinned and boned
- ¼ teaspoon salt
- ¼ teaspoon pepper
- 1 (16-ounce) can sauerkraut, drained
- 4 (4x6-inch) slices Swiss cheese
- 1¼ cups Thousand Island salad dressing
- 1 tablespoon chopped fresh parsley

Serves: 4
Preparation: 10 minutes
Baking: 1 hour, 15 minutes
Temperature: 325°

- 3 pounds boneless chicken, cut into 1-inch cubes
- ¼ cup oil
- 2 medium onions, chopped
- 1 tablespoon curry powder
- 1 teaspoon salt
- ¼ teaspoon pepper
- 2 cups beef stock or broth
- 1 apple; peeled, cored and chopped
- 3 tablespoons all-purpose flour
- 2 tablespoons cold water
- 1 cup sour cream

Condiment Suggestions:
   Chutney
   Salted peanuts
   Raisins
   Flaked coconut

Serves: 6
Preparation: 30 minutes
Cooking: 1 hour, 15 minutes

Chicken Curry
A savory blend of ingredients.

Pat chicken dry with paper towels. Brown chicken thoroughly in oil in large skillet. Remove chicken. Sauté onions in same skillet. Add curry powder, salt and pepper. Return chicken to skillet. Add broth. Cover and simmer slowly for 1 hour.

Add chopped apple. Cook 10 minutes longer.

Mix flour and water; blend into chicken. Stir until hot, bubbly and slightly thickened. Remove from heat; stir in sour cream.

Serve over hot rice with condiments.

Note: *If prepared ahead, add sour cream just before serving.*

Swiss Chicken Extraordinaire

Great for family or company.

Preheat oven to 200°.

Mix flour and salt. Roll chicken breasts in mixture. Heat oil over medium-high heat in large skillet. Add chicken and brown. Reduce heat. Cover and cook for 15 minutes.

While chicken is cooking, top each bread slice with slice of cheese. Place in oven for 12 minutes or until cheese begins to melt.

Remove chicken from skillet and set aside. Melt butter in skillet. Add mushrooms and sauté for 3 minutes. Push mushrooms to side of skillet. Add wine, salt and pepper. Return chicken to pan and cook until sauce thickens. Remove bread from oven. Place chicken on bread. Pour sauce over breasts. Serve immediately.

Note: May add 1 teaspoon all-purpose flour to sautéed mushrooms, if thicker sauce is desired.

- 6 chicken breast halves, skinned and boned
- ½ cup all-purpose flour
- 1 teaspoon seasoned salt
- ¼ cup oil
- 6 slices French bread, ½-inch thick
- 6 slices Swiss cheese, ⅛-inch thick
- 1–2 tablespoons butter
- ½ pound fresh mushrooms, sliced
- ⅔ cup white wine
- ½ teaspoon salt
- ¼ teaspoon pepper

Serves: 6
Preparation: 25 minutes
Cooking: 25 minutes
Baking: 12 minutes
Temperature: 200°

Lemon-Herb Chicken Breasts

Easy is the word for this colorful gem.

Pound chicken breasts to flatten slightly. Sprinkle with salt and pepper. Coat lightly with flour. Shake off excess.

Heat butter and oil over medium heat in large skillet. Add chicken breasts and sauté without crowding for 4–6 minutes. Turn and sauté for 4–6 minutes more or until golden. Add tomatoes and cook until heated through. Make sure breasts are done by cutting a slit in thick part of one to see that meat has lost pink color. *Do not overcook.* Transfer chicken and tomatoes to warm plates or place in warm oven.

Add tarragon, parsley and lemon juice to skillet and deglaze. Heat for a few seconds and pour a little over each breast.

- 4 chicken breast halves, skinned and boned
- Salt
- Pepper
- All-purpose flour
- 4 tablespoons (½ stick) butter
- 1 tablespoon oil
- 8–12 small whole cherry tomatoes
- ¼ teaspoon crushed dried tarragon
- 2 tablespoons chopped fresh parsley
- 2 teaspoons fresh lemon juice

Serves: 4
Preparation: 20 minutes

Chicken

¼ cup chopped onion
½ pound fresh mushrooms, sliced
6 tablespoons butter or margarine, divided
3 tablespoons all-purpose flour
½ teaspoon salt
¼ teaspoon pepper
1 cup light (coffee) cream
2 tablespoons dry sherry (optional)
2 cups cubed cooked chicken or turkey
1 cup cubed cooked ham
1 (5-ounce) can water chestnuts, drained and sliced
½ cup grated Swiss cheese
1½ cups soft fresh bread crumbs

Serves: 6
Preparation: 30 minutes
Baking: 25 minutes
Temperature: 375°

Chicken and Ham Bake

Great for casual entertaining.

Preheat oven to 375°.

Grease a 1½-quart baking dish.

Sauté onion and mushrooms in 3 tablespoons butter in large skillet over medium heat. Stir in flour, salt and pepper. Add cream and sherry. Cook and stir until thickened. Add chicken, ham and water chestnuts. Mix well and pour into prepared baking dish. Top with cheese. Melt remaining 3 tablespoons butter in small skillet. Toss bread crumbs in butter. Sprinkle on top of casserole. Bake at 375° for 25 minutes.

Mexican Kiev
A south-of-the-border favorite designed for a microwave.

Pound chicken breasts to flatten. Combine 4 tablespoons butter and cheese spread. Add onion, salt and chilies. Divide mixture equally among the chicken pieces. Spread each chicken breast half with mixture to within ½ inch of edge. Start with narrow end and roll each piece, tucking in ends. Fasten with toothpicks.

Melt remaining 4 tablespoons butter in small skillet. Combine cracker crumbs and taco seasoning mix in medium-size bowl. Dip each roll in melted butter, then coat with cracker crumb mixture.

Arrange rolls, seam down, in 8x12-inch microwave-safe baking dish. Cover and place in microwave. Cook on High for 10–12 minutes. Serve on a bed of lettuce and tomatoes. Top with sliced olives, sour cream and taco sauce.

- 8 chicken breast halves, skinned and boned
- ½ cup (1 stick) butter or margarine, softened (divided)
- 3 tablespoons Old English cheese spread
- 1 tablespoon finely chopped green onion
- 1 teaspoon salt
- 2 tablespoons chopped green chilies
- 1 cup crushed Cheddar cheese crackers
- 1½ tablespoons taco seasoning mix

Suggested Garnishes:
Shredded lettuce
Chopped tomatoes
Sliced olives
Sour cream
Taco sauce

Serves: 6–8
Preparation: 45 minutes
Microwave: 12 minutes

Turkey

- 1 (4–5 pound) turkey breast*
- 3 cups chicken stock or broth
- 3 cups dry white wine
- 2 ribs celery, sliced
- 2 carrots, sliced
- 1 large onion, sliced
- 2 cloves garlic, halved
- 1 (6½-ounce) can tuna, drained
- 1 (2-ounce) can anchovies, chopped
- 1½ cups mayonnaise
- Juice of 1 large lemon
- 3 tablespoons capers, divided
- ½ cup finely chopped fresh parsley
- 2 lemons, sliced (optional)

Serves:	10–12
Preparation:	30 minutes
Cooking:	1 hour, 20 minutes
Chilling:	At least 36 hours

Mock Vitello Tonnato

A classic Italian summer party dish worth the preparation.

Bone turkey by cracking along breastbone. Loosen meat from bones along rib cage. Bone with knife, leaving breast in one piece. Place, skin side down, on work surface. Roll, wrapping skin around meat. Tie with string in several places. Wrap in several thicknesses of cheesecloth. Secure ends with string. Place in 12-quart saucepan. Add stock, wine, celery, carrots, onion and garlic. Bring to a boil. Reduce heat. Cover and simmer until meat reaches 165° on meat thermometer, about 1 hour and 15 minutes. Chill in broth overnight.

Remove turkey from broth. Reduce broth over high heat to ½ its original volume. Reserve ⅓ cup for dressing.

Stir together tuna, anchovies, mayonnaise, lemon juice, 1 tablespoon capers and reserved broth.

Unwrap turkey. Slice across breast into medallions. Place turkey medallions, overlapping, on serving platter. Spoon sauce over turkey. Cover and refrigerate at least 12 hours.

Garnish with parsley, remaining 2 tablespoons capers and lemon slices, if desired.

*Note: Turkey breast may be boned and wrapped by butcher.

Wine Basted Cornish Hens
The easy preparation makes this one popular.

Preheat oven to 450°.

Remove giblets from hens. Place giblets in medium-size saucepan with a stalk of celery and ½ small onion. Add enough salted water to cover giblets. Cook, covered, until tender, about 1 hour. Remove giblets and chop. Strain broth and reserve. Discard celery and onion.

Sprinkle inside cavity of each bird with seasoned salt and pepper. Place piece of celery and onion halves inside each hen. Pull skin over cavity opening and tie legs together with string. Place birds in small shallow pan. Pour butter over birds. Sprinkle with seasoned salt and pepper. Roast at 450° for 20 minutes.

Mix wine, orange juice, lemon juice and soy sauce. Spoon over birds. Continue roasting, basting often with pan sauces until birds are tender and nicely browned, about 40 minutes. Remove birds to hot plate and keep warm.

Make pan sauce by skimming off excess fat from juices in pan. Stir ½ cup giblet broth into pan. Bring to a boil, loosening all brown particles. Taste and correct seasonings if necessary. Add chopped giblets. Spoon pan sauce over hens when served.

Variation: Sauce may be used as marinade for chicken pieces or for basting grilled chicken.

2–4	Cornish game hens
	Celery
3–5	small onions, halved
	Seasoned salt
	Pepper
⅓	cup butter, melted

Sauce:
- ½ cup sauterne
- ⅓ cup fresh orange juice
- 1 tablespoon fresh lemon juice
- 1 tablespoon soy sauce

Serves:	2–4
Preparation:	20 minutes
Baking:	1 hour
Temperature:	450°

Game

2 (1½-pound) Cornish game hens
¼ cup dry white wine
2 tablespoons fresh lemon juice
2 teaspoons oil
¼ teaspoon minced fresh garlic
2 teaspoons dried tarragon leaves
1¼ teaspoons salt
¼ teaspoon pepper

Serves: 4
Preparation: 15 minutes
Marinating: 1 hour
Baking: 1 hour
Temperature: 350°

8–12 quail (allow about 2 per person)
½ cup all-purpose flour
1 teaspoon salt
1 teaspoon lemon pepper
½ cup (1 stick) butter or margarine
1 medium onion, chopped
2 cups beef bouillon
¼ cup currant jelly

Serves: 4–6
Preparation: 10 minutes
Cooking: 1 hour, 10 minutes

Tarragon Baked Cornish Hens
Light, tender and juicy.

Remove giblets from hens. (Reserve for soup stock.) Rinse hens with cold water. Pat dry with towels. Split each hen in half lengthwise with knife or shears.

Combine wine, lemon juice, oil, garlic, tarragon, salt and pepper in a 9x13-inch glass baking dish. Turn hens in marinade to coat thoroughly, leaving hens skin side up. Cover and marinate in refrigerator for 1 hour.

Preheat oven to 350°.

Turn hens over. Bake, uncovered, for 30 minutes. Turn hens again. Baste with pan juices. Bake 30 minutes more, basting every 10–15 minutes. Brown hens by broiling 6 inches from heat for 2–3 minutes. Serve pan juices with hens.

Note: Cooked hens may be frozen. Do not thaw before baking. Cover with foil and bake at 350° for 35–40 minutes.

Quail in Casserole
A delectable blend of flavors.

Quarter each quail. Combine flour, salt and lemon pepper in pie pan or plastic bag. Roll each quail quarter lightly in flour mixture.

Heat butter in heavy skillet (electric skillet is preferable) over medium-high. Brown quail quickly on all sides. Add onion and cook until transparent. Add bouillon and jelly. Cover and simmer for 1 hour. Remove quail to serving platter.

Place liquid and brown scrapings from pan in blender. Blend until smooth. Return to skillet. (Thicken, if necessary, with 1 tablespoon cornstarch dissolved in water.) Add additional salt and pepper, if desired. Pour sauce over quails. (May be refrigerated at this point. Warm at 350° for 30 minutes to serve.) Serve with currant jelly on the side.

Variation: This recipe is terrific for any white meat bird, pheasant or Cornish hen.

Roast Wild Duck
The hunter's reward.

Preheat oven to 450°.

Clean ducks with heads removed and tail section cut off. Make sure cavity is cleaned out. Soak clean ducks in lightly salted water for 3 hours.

Stuff cavity of duck with quartered pieces of apple or orange and onion. Stuff as much as possible. Arrange ducks in a roasting pan. Place bacon strips over tops of ducks. (Additional bacon may be used; grease coats the ducks.)

Brown ducks at 450° for 20 minutes. Pour lots of cream sherry over ducks and cover. Reduce heat to 300° and bake for 2 hours or until ducks are done. Baste ducks constantly, adding more sherry if necessary. Remove ducks from oven and empty fruit cavity. Reserve fruit. Do not remove bacon. Arrange ducks on platter. Garnish with reserved fruit or substitute fresh orange sections and apple slices. Serve au jus.

Note: Temperature may be turned down from 300° to extend serving time.

Serving Suggestion: A wild rice casserole and glazed carrots complement the duck nicely.

- 4 wild ducks
- 2 apples or oranges, quartered
- 1 large onion, peeled and quartered
- 16 strips bacon
- 1⅓ (750-milliliter) bottles cream sherry

Serves:	4
Preparation:	30 minutes
Soaking:	3 hours
Roasting:	2 hours, 20 minutes
Temperature:	450°

Stuffings

- ½ cup (1 stick) butter or margarine
- ¼ cup finely chopped onion
- 1–2 cloves garlic, finely chopped
- ½ pound mushrooms, chopped
- 2–3 teaspoons salt
- 1 pound wild rice, washed and drained well
- 4 cups boiling water
- ¾ cup chopped pimiento
- ½ cup chopped fresh parsley
- 2 ounces slivered almonds
- 1 cup beef salami, chopped into tiny cubes

Yield:	15-pound turkey
Preparation:	15 minutes
Cooking:	1 hour
Standing:	15 minutes

- 30 chestnuts
- 6 tablespoons butter, divided
- 1 pound fresh mushrooms, chopped
- 4 onions, finely chopped
- ¼ pound bulk pork sausage
- 2 teaspoons fresh lemon juice
- ½ teaspoon tarragon vinegar
- Salt
- Freshly ground pepper
- ⅓ cup vermouth
- ⅓ cup dry sherry or cognac
- 2 tablespoons chopped fresh parsley
- 2½ cups Grapenuts

Yield:	12-pound turkey
Preparation:	20 minutes
Cooking:	30 minutes

Mom's Wild Rice Stuffing
The salami imparts a wonderful flavor.

Melt butter in large skillet over medium heat. Add onion and garlic; sauté for 2 minutes. Add mushrooms and sauté until all moisture is absorbed. Do not brown mushrooms. Add salt, rice and water. Cover skillet. Reduce heat to low and simmer about 1 hour. *Do not boil.* Remove from heat and let rice sit for 15 minutes. (Stuffing may be made ahead up to this point.)

Add pimiento, parsley, almonds and salami on the day turkey is to be stuffed. Fill cavity of turkey. Lace to enclose turkey cavity.

Note: A cheesecloth bag may be made by hand or on a sewing machine. Fill bag with stuffing and place inside turkey. The stuffing can easily be removed for serving. The turkey still needs to be laced when using the bag.

Variation: Rice stuffing may be placed in greased 2-quart baking dish. Bake, covered, at 350° for 30 minutes.

Chestnut Dressing
A delightful variation for traditional dressing.

Make a crosscut incision on the flat side of each chestnut with a sharp pointed knife. Place chestnuts in large saucepan. Cover with boiling water and simmer for 20 minutes. Drain chestnuts and remove the shells and skins. (The meat of the nut should be tender enough to break into pieces. If not, boil chestnuts in salted water until tender.) Drain and break into pieces.

Simmer mushrooms in covered skillet in 4 tablespoons butter for 15 minutes. Remove lid and cook until dry.

Cook onions and sausage in remaining 2 tablespoons butter until slightly brown. Add mushrooms, lemon juice, vinegar, salt, pepper, vermouth, cognac, parsley, Grapenuts and chestnut pieces. Mix well and stuff turkey.

Fish and Seafood

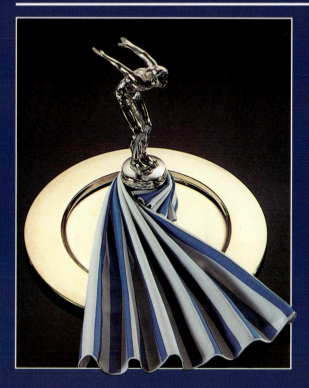

The Sports Scene

Indianapolis—"a city on a fast track," as described by the Indiana Sports Corporation, a unique organization committed to the promotion of amateur sports. Almost daily, a major sporting event, amateur or professional, is held in one of Indianapolis's championship facilities.

When, in 1982, Indianapolis played host to almost 3,000 of America's finest amateur athletes competing in the National Sports Festival, 6,700 enthusiastic community volunteers turned out to help. In 1984, when the officials of the international Pan American Games were scouting American cities for a site for their 1987 events, the unanimous choice was Indianapolis—a city within a day's drive of half of America.

Why Indianapolis? The answers are multifold. This city of dedicated sports lovers has poured over $180 million, secured from grants, endowments, public and private funds, into world-class sports facilities. The stunning 4,700-seat Indiana University Natatorium is, quite simply, the world's fastest pool. Olympic trials, national swimming, diving and water polo championships and the World Cup Synchronized Swimming Championships have all been held here.

Our Major Taylor Velodrome, one of the world's finest in its class and one of only 13 in the country, has drawn numerous national and international championship bicycle racing competitions to this city. Market Square Arena, with its 17,000 seats in downtown Indianapolis, is the home of our National Basketball Association team, and has played host to a number of other sporting and entertainment events, including the National Figure Skating Championships.

The completion of our $80 million Hoosier Dome in 1984 has assured this city's ability to host NFL football, track or virtually any sport in an indoor facility. More than 67,000 ardent fans watched the 1984 summer exhibition game of the Men's and Women's Olympic Basketball teams.

And there is much more, from prime professional tennis and track facilities to a major annual amateur "State Games" sports festival. Indianapolis "on a fast track"—concerned with the context and content of winning.

FISH AND SEAFOOD

Fish
Australian Fish . . . 188
Cold Sole with Mustard Fruits . . . 187
Fillet of Sole Meunière . . . 192
Greek Fish with Lemon and Tomato Sauce . . . 190
Heavenly Sole . . . 191
Redfish Antibes . . . 191
Salmon Loaf with Cucumber Sauce . . . 193
Sole Fillets with Asparagus . . . 190
Stuffed Sole Fillets . . . 189

Seafood
Broiled Scallops . . . 201
Coquille St. Jacques . . . 202
Crab Meat Mornay . . . 200
Crab-Shrimp Bake . . . 198
Crab Thermidor . . . 199
Lobster in Champagne Sauce . . . 200
Portia's Bay Scallops . . . 203
Sautéed Scallops Provençale . . . 201
Savory Frogs' Legs . . . 203
Seafood Ensemble . . . 204
Scampi Delectable . . . 194
Shrimp and Pesto "en Papillote . . . 197
Shrimp Jambalaya . . . 196
Southern Barbecued Shrimp . . . 195

Cold Sole with Mustard Fruits
Tasty, tangy summer dish.

Lightly butter an 8x12-inch flame-proof baking dish.

Place fillets in prepared baking dish. Combine wine, lemon juice, garlic, monosodium glutamate, Maggi and Tabasco in medium-size bowl; pour over fillets. Cover with piece of wax paper. Bring to a boil over medium heat; reduce heat and simmer for 10 minutes or until fish is white and firm. Remove from heat. Transfer fillets with a spatula to a serving platter. Cool in refrigerator.

Arrange crab meat, grapes, shrimp and orange sections over cooled fillets.

Combine all Mustard Mayonnaise ingredients; spread over fish and fruits. Decorate edges of serving platter with quartered tomatoes, cold white asparagus and lemon slices. Garnish with parsley and watercress.

Note: May be assembled several hours before serving, if desired.

Serving Suggestion: Accompany sole with cold soup, crusty bread and a favorite dessert.

- 6 fillets of Dover sole
- 2 cups dry white wine
- Juice of 2 lemons
- 1 clove garlic, minced
- 1 teaspoon monosodium glutamate (optional)
- 1 teaspoon Maggi seasoning
- 1 drop Tabasco sauce
- 1 cup lump crab meat
- 1 cup seedless grapes
- 1 pound cooked shrimp
- 1 cup mandarin orange sections

Mustard Mayonnaise:
- 2 cups mayonnaise
- 1 teaspoon garlic salt
- 1 teaspoon monosodium glutamate (optional)
- 1 teaspoon Maggi seasoning
- 1 drop Tabasco sauce
- 3 tablespoons finely chopped onion
- 3 tablespoons Dijon mustard
- Juice of 1 lemon
- 3 tablespoons finely chopped fresh parsley
- Freshly ground black pepper

Suggested Garnishes:
- Tomatoes
- White asparagus
- Lemon slices
- Parsley sprigs
- Watercress

Serves:	6
Preparation:	25 minutes
Cooking:	10 minutes
Chilling:	2–4 hours

- ½ pound fresh mushrooms, sliced (may substitute 4½-ounce can sliced mushrooms, drained)
- 2 tablespoons butter
- 1 tablespoon oil
- ½ cup freshly grated Parmesan, Cheddar or Cheshire cheese
- 1½ pounds fillet of sole (or any white fish)
- ¼ teaspoon salt
- ¼ teaspoon pepper
- 4 tablespoons chopped green onions
- 6 tablespoons white wine or vermouth
- 2 teaspoons fresh lemon juice
- 1 tablespoon chopped fresh parsley

Serves: 4
Preparation: 30 minutes
Baking: 20 minutes
Temperature: 450°

Australian Fish

Deliciously light entrée.

Preheat oven to 450°.

Melt butter in medium-size skillet over low heat. Add mushrooms and sauté over medium heat until tender.

Rub oil over shallow 4-quart baking dish. Sprinkle with grated cheese.

Place fish on cheese. Sprinkle fish with salt and pepper. Add onions. Top with mushrooms. Pour wine over fillets. Bake at 450° for 20 minutes or until fish flakes. Sprinkle with lemon juice and parsley.

Variation: This recipe is also recommended for flounder, whiting and orange roughey.

Stuffed Sole Fillets

Can be prepared in the morning and baked at the last minute.

Preheat oven to 375°.

Butter lightly an 8x12-inch glass baking dish.

Combine bread crumbs, egg, parsley, onion, shrimp and crab in medium-size bowl. Add salt and pepper; mix well. Add wine as needed to make proper consistency for stuffing.

Place ⅛ of stuffing on larger end of fillet and roll up. Repeat for remaining fillets. Place rolls, seam down, in single layer in prepared baking dish.

Wash lemon. Cut in half and remove seeds. Squeeze juice into small saucepan and place lemon halves in pan with juice. Add butter, water, sugar and parsley. Cook over medium heat until butter has melted. Remove lemon halves. Pour sauce over fillets.

Bake at 375° for 30 minutes, basting fillets with sauce 2 or 3 times during the baking.

Note: If using fresh shrimp and crab, cook before stuffing the sole fillets.

- 1 cup soft bread crumbs
- 1 egg, beaten
- 1 teaspoon chopped fresh parsley
- 1 tablespoon chopped onion
- 1 (6-ounce) package frozen shrimp and crab combination, drained [may substitute 1 (6-ounce) package of either one]
- ½ teaspoon salt
- ⅛ teaspoon pepper
- ¼ cup dry white wine
- 8 fresh fillets of sole

Lemon Butter Sauce:
- 1 lemon
- ½ cup (1 stick) butter
- ½ cup water
- 1 tablespoon granulated sugar
- 2 tablespoons chopped fresh parsley

Serves:	6–8
Preparation:	20 minutes
Baking:	30 minutes
Temperature:	375°

Fish

Sole Fillets with Asparagus

Good spring entrée when fresh asparagus is reasonably priced and plentiful.

- 1 pound asparagus spears
- 4 fillets of sole (about 1 pound)
- Salt
- 1/8 teaspoon freshly ground pepper
- 1/2 teaspoon freshly grated lemon rind
- 3 tablespoons butter, melted
- 1 tablespoon finely chopped shallots
- 1 teaspoon Dijon mustard

Serves: 4
Preparation: 25 minutes
Baking: 20 minutes
Temperature: 400°

Preheat oven to 400°.

Butter well an 8-inch square baking dish.

Cut asparagus into 2-inch lengths. Cook in salted boiling water for 5 minutes and drain.

Season skin side of fillets with salt, pepper and lemon rind. Divide asparagus spears into four equal parts. Place 1/4 of the spears at narrow end of each fillet. Start at narrow end and roll fillet. Secure with toothpicks. Repeat process with remaining 3 fillets. Place fillets in prepared baking dish, seam down. Combine butter, shallots and mustard; pour over fish. Bake at 400° for 15–20 minutes or until fish flakes easily. Baste twice.

Greek Fish with Lemon and Tomato Sauce

Excellent low calorie meal.

- 1 1/2 pounds fresh fish (sole, turbot, scrod or trout)
- 1 lemon, cut in half
- 2 tomatoes, peeled and diced
- 1/2 cup olive oil (less if desired)
- 1/3 cup dry white wine
- 1/2 cup chopped fresh parsley
- 1 clove garlic, minced
- Salt
- Freshly ground pepper
- Lemon slices

Serves: 4
Preparation: 15 minutes
Baking: 30 minutes
Temperature: 350°

Preheat oven to 350°.

Grease a 9x13-inch baking dish.

Salt cavity of fish, if whole fish is used. Place fish in prepared baking dish. Squeeze juice from 1/2 of lemon on fish. Remove seeds and chop remaining 1/2 of lemon. Arrange evenly over fish.

Combine tomatoes, olive oil, wine, parsley, garlic, salt and pepper. Pour tomato mixture over fish and spread to cover thoroughly. Bake at 350° for 25–30 minutes; baste frequently. Garnish with lemon slices.

Serving Suggestion: Serve with Greek salad and bread sticks.

Heavenly Sole
Heavenly, indeed.

Grease well a bake-and-serve platter. Place fillets in single layer on prepared platter. Brush fillets with lemon juice and let stand for 8–10 minutes.

Preheat oven to broil.

Combine remaining ingredients in small bowl. Stir until cheese mixture is well blended.

Broil fillets 4 inches from heat for 5–7 minutes or until fish flakes. Remove from heat and spread cheese mixture on fillets. Broil 1–2 minutes longer or until lightly browned.

- 1 pound fillets of sole, skinned and boned
- 1 tablespoon fresh lemon juice
- ¼ cup freshly grated Parmesan cheese
- 2 tablespoons butter, softened
- 1½ tablespoons mayonnaise
- 1½ tablespoons chopped green onion
- Salt

Serves:	3
Preparation:	15 minutes
Marinating:	10 minutes
Broiling:	8 minutes
Temperature:	Broil

Redfish Antibes
Fish with perfect taste and texture.

Preheat oven to 350°.

Grease well an 8x12-inch baking dish.

Thaw fillets if frozen. Skin fillets and place in a single layer in prepared baking dish. Sprinkle first with lemon juice, then with salt and lemon pepper. Bake at 350° for 15–20 minutes or until fish flakes easily when tested with a fork.

Melt margarine in medium-size saucepan over low heat. Add mushrooms, parsley and almonds and sauté until mushrooms are tender.

Remove fish to a heated platter. Spoon sautéed mixture over fish and serve immediately.

- 2 pounds fillets of redfish or red snapper, fresh or frozen
- 1 tablespoon fresh lemon juice
- 1 teaspoon salt
- ¼ teaspoon lemon pepper
- 3 tablespoons margarine
- 1½ cups sliced fresh mushrooms
- 2 tablespoons chopped fresh parsley
- ½ cup chopped hickory flavored almonds, roasted and salted

Serves:	6
Preparation:	15 minutes
Baking:	20 minutes
Temperature:	350°

Fish

Fillet of Sole Meunière

Delightfully delicate.

- 8 small fillets of Dover sole (about 2 pounds), skinned (may substitute similar white fish, turbot or scrod)
- 2 tablespoons all-purpose flour
- ½ teaspoon salt
- ½ teaspoon paprika
- Freshly ground pepper
- 6 tablespoons unsalted butter, divided
- 4 large strips lean bacon
- Juice of ½ small lemon
- Salt
- Freshly ground pepper
- ½ teaspoon dried tarragon (may substitute 1½ teaspoons chopped fresh tarragon)
- 1 teaspoon chopped fresh parsley
- ½ teaspoon dried basil (may substitute 1½ teaspoons chopped fresh basil)

Wash and dry fillets. Season flour with salt, paprika and pepper. Coat fillets with flour. Heat 2 tablespoons butter in large skillet over medium-high heat until butter foams. Sauté fillets in butter until golden brown on both sides, about 8–10 minutes.

Cook bacon until crisp while fillets are browning. Drain bacon and set aside.

Arrange cooked fillets on pre-warmed serving platter with a strip of bacon between each 2 fillets. Wipe out skillet. Add remaining 4 tablespoons butter and cook over medium heat until butter turns nut-brown. Add lemon juice, salt, pepper and herbs. Lift skillet and swirl to blend liquid and herbs. Cook until butter begins to foam; pour over fish and serve immediately.

Serving Suggestion: A Greek salad is a nice complement to the sole.

Serves: 4
Preparation: 5 minutes
Cooking: 15 minutes

Salmon Loaf with Cucumber Sauce

Assemble in the morning and serve for dinner.

Preheat oven to 350°.

Grease a 9x5-inch loaf pan.

Combine salmon, crumbs, mayonnaise, onion, celery, green pepper, egg, salt and pepper. Mix with hands until well combined. Place in prepared pan. Bake at 350° for 40 minutes. Cool and refrigerate for 2 or more hours. Serve with Cucumber Sauce.

Combine sauce ingredients and chill until ready to serve.

- 1 (16-ounce) can salmon, flaked and drained
- ½ cup dry bread crumbs
- ½ cup mayonnaise
- ½ cup finely chopped onion
- ¼ cup finely chopped celery
- ¼ cup finely chopped green pepper
- 1 egg, beaten
- ½ teaspoon salt
- ⅛ teaspoon white pepper

Cucumber Sauce:
- ½ cup mayonnaise
- ½ cup sour cream
- ½ cup chopped cucumber
- 2 teaspoons chopped onion
- ½ teaspoon dried dill weed

Serves:	4
Preparation:	30 minutes
Baking	40 minutes
Chilling:	2–4 hours
Temperature:	350°

Seafood

- 2 pounds fresh jumbo shrimp; cleaned, deveined and butterflied
- 4 cloves garlic, minced
- ¼ teaspoon salt
- ¼ cup olive oil
- ¼ cup (½ stick) butter, melted
- ½ cup dry white wine
- 3 tablespoons fresh lemon juice
- ⅛ teaspoon freshly ground pepper

Serves:	4
Preparation:	15 minutes
Marinating:	3 hours
Broiling:	6–8 minutes
Temperature:	Broil

Scampi Delectable

Superb! A great first course, too.

Whisk together garlic, salt, oil, butter, wine, lemon juice and pepper. Add shrimp and toss. Marinate at room temperature for 3–4 hours.

Preheat oven to broil.

Arrange shrimp in a single layer in a shallow pan. Pour marinade over shrimp. Broil about 4 inches from heat for 6–8 minutes. *Do not overcook.*

Variation: Shrimp may be charcoal grilled. Grill for approximately 5 minutes. Baste constantly with sauce and watch carefully.

Serving Suggestion: Curried rice or Almond Rice Pilaf provide a nice complement to the shrimp.

Hint:
To butterfly shrimp, peel the shrimp down to the tail, leaving tail intact. Devein. Hold so that underside is up. Slice down length of underside, almost to the vein, to form the hinge. Spread and flatten shrimp to form the butterfly shape.

Southern Barbecued Shrimp

Very hot! An exciting eating experience.

Preheat oven to 450°.

Heat butter and oil in 2-quart saucepan. Add Worcestershire, pepper, lemons, Tabasco, Italian seasoning, garlic, paprika and salt. Mix thoroughly and simmer for 5–7 minutes until well blended and heated through.

Place shrimp in large Dutch oven. Pour heated sauce over shrimp. Cook over medium heat for 6–8 minutes or until shrimp begins to turn pink. Place uncovered Dutch oven in the oven and bake at 450° for 10 minutes, turning shrimp once.

Serving Suggestion: Add boiled new potatoes to the shrimp and hot sauce and serve in soup bowls. Accompany with French bread and fresh green salad.

Serving Suggestion: Peel shrimp and chill. Serve over shredded lettuce as first course.

- 1 cup (2 sticks) butter
- 1 cup olive oil
- ¼ cup plus 2 tablespoons Worcestershire sauce
- 1½ tablespoons pepper (more, if desired)
- 2 lemons, sliced
- ½ teaspoon Tabasco sauce (more, if desired)
- 1½ teaspoons Italian seasoning
- 2 cloves garlic, minced
- ½ teaspoon paprika
- 2 teaspoons salt
- 4 pounds raw jumbo shrimp, unpeeled and deveined
- Boiled new potatoes (optional)

Serves: 4–6
Preparation: 20 minutes
Baking: 10 minutes
Temperature: 450°

Seafood

- 6 strips bacon, diced
- 1 bunch green onions
- 1 (10-ounce) package frozen okra, thawed and chopped
- 1½ quarts rich chicken broth (may substitute 46-ounce can chicken broth)
- 1 (29-ounce) can tomato sauce
- 2 teaspoons dried thyme
- 1 teaspoon pepper
- 2 teaspoons Worcestershire sauce
- 1 teaspoon paprika
- 1 tablespoon chopped fresh parsley
- 1 (10-ounce) package frozen small shrimp
- 3–4 cups chopped baked or boiled ham
- 1 (29-ounce) can tomatoes
- Salt, if desired
- All-purpose flour, if necessary
- Long grain rice, cooked according to package directions (optional)

Serves: 8–10
Preparation: 30 minutes
Cooking: 2 hours

Shrimp Jambalaya

The flavor develops with each reheating.

Cook bacon until crisp in large soup kettle or Dutch oven. Chop white portion of green onions and add to pot. Add okra. Chop green part of onion; add to pot and continue to sauté. Add broth, tomato sauce, thyme, pepper, Worcestershire, paprika, parsley, shrimp, ham and tomatoes. Stir to combine. Add salt, if necessary. Simmer for 1½–2 hours. Thicken with flour, if necessary. Serve over rice.

Variation: May add crushed garlic.

Shrimp and Pesto "en Papillote"
Easy to do and voilà!

Recipe requires cooking parchment, available at culinary stores.

Blend together in food processor or blender, the herbs, Parmesan, oil and lemon juice until finely chopped and saucelike.

Cut or tear 4 sheets of cooking parchment, each about 24 inches long (width is generally 15 inches). Start about 2 to 3 inches in from the middle of long side of paper and brush melted butter in a circle, approximately 4 inches in diameter (large enough to group 6 shrimp together). Center 6 shrimp on the buttered section. Top with ¼ of Pesto Sauce and 1 lemon slice. Sprinkle lightly with salt and pepper. Fold narrow strip of long side of parchment over the shrimp; fold remaining parchment over the top and continue folding until all of parchment has been used and shrimp is enclosed. Double tuck open ends and fold under packet to seal. Repeat process with next 3 servings. (Packets may be assembled a day ahead and refrigerated.)

Preheat oven to 500°.

Set packets, folded ends down, on baking sheet. Brush tops of packets with oil. Place baking sheet at least 8 inches from top heat source and bake at 500° for 7–10 minutes. Transfer packets at once to dinner plates. Cut packets down center with sharp knife. Tear sides back to expose contents, but do not allow juices to run out.

Note: Individual ramekins with lids may be substituted for the parchment.

Pesto Sauce:
- ¾ cup lightly packed fresh basil leaves (may substitute 2 tablespoons dry basil leaves and ¾ cup lightly packed fresh parsley)
- ⅓ cup freshly grated Parmesan cheese
- 3 tablespoons olive oil
- 3 tablespoons fresh lemon juice

- 2–3 tablespoons butter, melted
- 24 jumbo shrimp; cooked, peeled and deveined
- 4 thin lemon slices
- Salt
- White pepper
- Oil

Serves:	4
Preparation:	30 minutes
Baking:	10 minutes
Temperature:	500°

Seafood

Crab-Shrimp Bake
So rich—so good.

Preheat oven to 350°.

Have ready 6 scallop shells or 1-quart baking dish.

Combine filling ingredients in large bowl.

Melt butter in small skillet over medium heat. Add flour and stir until smooth and bubbly. Remove from heat and add milk, stirring constantly. Return to heat and stir until thickened. Add white sauce to filling mixture and stir until well combined. Divide mixture evenly among the 6 scallop shells. Sprinkle bread crumbs on top. Bake at 350° for 20–30 minutes.

Filling:
- 1 (7½-ounce) can crab meat
- ¾ pound large shrimp; cooked, peeled and deveined (may substitute frozen ready-to-eat shrimp)
- 1 medium onion, chopped
- 1 medium green pepper, chopped
- 1 cup chopped celery
- 1 teaspoon Worcestershire sauce
- 3 hard-cooked eggs, chopped
- ½ cup mayonnaise
- ¼ cup sliced water chestnuts, drained (optional)
- 1 (4-ounce) can button mushrooms (optional)

Medium White Sauce:
- 3 tablespoons butter
- 3 tablespoons all-purpose flour
- 1½ cups milk

Dry bread crumbs

Serves: 6
Preparation: 30 minutes
Baking: 30 minutes
Temperature: 350°

Crab Thermidor
Splurge and enjoy.

Preheat oven to 350°.

Have ready 4 scallop shells or individual baking dishes.

Melt 2 tablespoons butter in medium skillet over medium heat. Sauté mushrooms until tender but not browned. Set aside.

Melt remaining 2 tablespoons butter in medium-size saucepan over medium heat. Stir in flour and cook until bubbly. Remove from heat and gradually stir in cream. Return to heat; continue stirring until sauce thickens. Add sauterne, salt, cayenne and mustard. Stir in crab meat, mushrooms and 1 tablespoon Parmesan. Heat through.

Pour equal amounts into shells. Sprinkle with remaining Parmesan. Drizzle lightly with butter. Bake at 350° for 10 minutes or until bubbly.

Note: *Use smaller shells and serve this as first course.*

Variation: Crab Thermidor makes a wonderful filling for crêpes.

- 4 tablespoons (½ stick) butter, divided
- ¾ pound fresh mushrooms, sliced (may substitute 4-ounce jar sliced mushrooms, drained)
- 3 tablespoons sifted all-purpose flour
- 1 cup warmed light (coffee) cream
- 1 tablespoon sauterne
- ½ teaspoon salt
- Pinch of cayenne pepper
- ⅛ teaspoon dry mustard
- 1 cup flaked, snow white crab meat
- 2 tablespoons freshly grated Parmesan cheese, divided
- 1–2 tablespoons butter, melted

Serves: 4
Preparation: 10 minutes
Cooking: 10 minutes
Baking: 10 minutes
Temperature: 350°

Crab Meat Mornay
Little effort—big treat.

Bake pastry shells while preparing Mornay sauce.

Melt butter in large skillet over medium heat. Add onions and sauté until onions are transparent. Stir in flour; cook until smooth and bubbly. Pour cream in slowly, stirring constantly. Stir in sherry. Add cheese and stir until melted. Gently fold in crab meat and continue cooking for about 5 minutes. Pour into baked pastry shells. Garnish with fresh parsley sprigs.

- 1 (10-ounce) package frozen pastry shells, baked according to package directions
- ½ cup (1 stick) butter
- 4 small green onions, chopped
- 2 tablespoons all-purpose flour
- 1 pint light (coffee) cream
- 2 tablespoons dry sherry
- ½ pound Swiss cheese, grated
- 1 pound frozen or canned crab meat
- Fresh parsley sprigs (optional)

Serves: 6
Preparation: 15 minutes
Cooking: 5 minutes

Lobster in Champagne Sauce
An expensive dish, but worth it for a special occasion.

Rinse and drain lobster tails. Combine lobster (in shell), champagne, the 2 minced green onions and salt in Dutch oven or large skillet. Heat to boiling. Reduce heat to low. Cover and simmer for 15 minutes. Remove lobster. Add cream to sauce in skillet. Boil sauce quickly until reduced to ⅓ cup. Whisk in butter, 1 tablespoon at a time, until smooth. Keep warm.

Remove lobster from shells. Slice into medallions and arrange on serving platter. Spoon sauce over each medallion. Sprinkle with green onion strips.

Variation: One pound large shrimp may be used instead of lobster.

- 3 frozen lobster tails, thawed and drained
- ⅔ cup champagne or sparkling white wine
- 4 green onions, 2 minced and 2 cut into thin lengthwise strips
- ¼ teaspoon salt
- ¼ cup heavy (whipping) cream
- 4 tablespoons (½ stick) unsalted butter

Serves: 2–3
Preparation: 10 minutes
Cooking: 30 minutes

Broiled Scallops
Simplicity at its best.

Preheat oven to broil.

Melt butter in small saucepan over low heat. Sauté garlic for a few minutes. *Do not brown.* Add lemon juice, Worcestershire and parsley.

Rinse and thoroughly dry scallops with a paper towel. Toss scallops in butter mixture. Remove scallops with slotted spoon and place on broiling pan. Sprinkle with ⅛ teaspoon paprika and ¼ teaspoon onion powder. Add remaining paprika and onion powder to butter mixture.

Broil scallops 4 inches from heat until light brown, about 4–6 minutes on each side. After scallops have been turned, baste with butter mixture. Use lemon slices as garnish.

- 4 tablespoons (½ stick) butter or margarine
- 2 small cloves garlic, minced
- 2 tablespoons fresh lemon juice
- 1 teaspoon Worcestershire sauce
- 1 tablespoon chopped fresh parsley
- 1 pound scallops
- ¼ teaspoon paprika, divided
- ½ teaspoon onion powder, divided
- 4 lemon slices (optional)

Serves: 3–4
Preparation: 10 minutes
Broiling: 12 minutes
Temperature: Broil

Sautéed Scallops Provençale
Fast, easy and elegant.

Heat oil in large heavy skillet. Sauté garlic and shallot over low heat until tender but not browned. Increase heat and add scallops. Sauté until scallops are lightly browned and opaque, about 5 minutes. Add lemon juice, tomato, salt, pepper and parsley. Cook just long enough to heat through. Serve over rice, if desired.

Note: Amount of olive oil may be decreased for the diet conscious.

Variation: Use this dish as first course and serve in shells.

- 5 tablespoons olive oil
- 2 cloves garlic, minced
- 1 shallot, finely chopped
- 1½ pounds bay or sea scallops (quartered if large); rinsed, drained and patted dry
- 1 tablespoon fresh lemon juice
- 1 large ripe tomato; peeled, chopped and seeded (more, if desired)
- Salt
- Freshly ground pepper
- ¼ cup finely chopped fresh parsley
- Cooked rice (optional)

Serves: 4–6
Preparation: 20 minutes

Seafood

Coquille St. Jacques*
The St. Jacques makes a wonderful first course, too.

- 1 cup dry white wine
- ½ teaspoon salt
- 1 bay leaf
- 2 tablespoons minced onion
- 1 parsley sprig
- 2 tablespoons minced celery
- 1½ pounds bay scallops (halve if using sea scallops)
- ½ pound fresh mushrooms, sliced
- ¼ cup fresh lemon juice
- 3 tablespoons butter
- 4 tablespoons all-purpose flour
- ½ cup milk
- 2 egg yolks, beaten
- ¾ cup heavy (whipping) cream
- Dry white wine (as needed)
- ½ cup buttered soft bread crumbs
- ¾ cup finely grated Gruyère or Swiss cheese

Serves:	6
Preparation:	15 minutes
Cooking:	40 minutes
Broiling:	5 minutes
Temperature:	Broil

Recipe calls for 6 scallop shells but small ramekins or a 2-quart baking dish may be substituted.

Simmer wine, salt, bay leaf, onion, parsley and celery for 5 minutes in stainless steel or enamel saucepan. Remove bay leaf and parsley.

Wash scallops. Add scallops to liquid in saucepan. Add water, if necessary, to cover. Simmer until tender, about 5 minutes. Remove scallops from liquid and boil rapidly to reduce to 1 cup.

Preheat oven to broil.

Pour lemon juice over mushrooms in large skillet. Cook over medium heat until tender.

Melt butter in medium-size saucepan over medium heat; stir in flour until smooth and bubbly. Remove from heat and whisk in milk, egg yolks, cream and liquid from scallops. Return to heat to thicken. Thin sauce with wine if it is too thick. Add scallops and mushrooms to sauce. Divide mixture evenly into the scallop shells or pour into baking dish. Sprinkle with buttered bread crumbs and cheese. Brown gently under broiler. (When preparing in advance, reheat in a 350° oven until bubbling and then brown under broiler, if necessary.)

Note: Do not freeze in metal pan. Use glass or china and wrap tightly in plastic.

Variation: Recipe will serve 10–12 as a first course.

*Monastery St. Jacques, located on the northern coast of Spain, is the purported birthplace of the Apostle James. The recipe is the authentic scallop dish brought from St. James in Europe to St. James, Long Island and thence westward.

Seafood

Portia's Bay Scallops
A pleasing combination.

Preheat oven to 350°.

Butter a 1-quart baking dish.

Wash and drain scallops. Sauté in butter over medium heat. Add flour and stir until smooth and bubbly. Add cream slowly, stirring continuously until thickened. Add dill, mustard, salt and pepper. Cook over low heat for 5 minutes, stirring occasionally.

Pour into prepared baking dish and sprinkle crumbs over top. Bake at 350° for 15 minutes.

Note: If sea scallops are used, cut into small pieces before sautéing.

- 1 pound fresh bay scallops (may substitute frozen)
- 2 teaspoons butter
- 3 tablespoons all-purpose flour
- ½ pint heavy (whipping) cream
- 1 teaspoon dill weed (may substitute 1 tablespoon snipped fresh dill)
- 1 teaspoon Dijon mustard
- Salt
- Freshly ground pepper
- ½ cup buttered bread or cracker crumbs

Serves: 4
Preparation: 20 minutes
Baking: 15 minutes
Temperature: 350°

Savory Frogs' Legs
Outstanding flavor and appearance with simple preparation.

Split each pair of frog's legs into 2 legs, if using large legs.

Prepare small legs by slipping one leg in between the two muscles of the lower part of the other leg. (This keeps frog's legs flat so they brown easily.)

Soak legs briefly in milk. Drain but do not dry. Dredge each pair in flour seasoned with salt and pepper.

Heat oil and ½ cup butter in a large skillet. Cook legs until golden on one side, then turn and cook other side until golden, about 10 minutes total cooking time. (Legs become tough when overcooked.)

Remove legs to heat-proof serving dish. Squeeze juice from 2 lemon quarters over frogs' legs. Keep warm.

Melt remaining ¾ cup of butter in small saucepan and add garlic. Cook over low heat until butter is hot and foamy. Pour over frogs' legs. Sprinkle legs with parsley and serve with remaining lemon quarters.

- 12 large pairs or 24 small pairs frogs' legs
- 1 cup milk
- 1 cup all-purpose flour, approximately
- Salt
- Freshly ground pepper
- ¼ cup oil
- 1¼ cups (2½ sticks) butter, divided
- 2 lemons, quartered
- 1 tablespoon minced garlic
- ¼ cup finely chopped fresh parsley

Serves: 6
Preparation: 15 minutes
Cooking: 15 minutes

Seafood

Seafood Ensemble
Good through and through.

- 2 slices coarse white bread
- ¾ cup water
- 2 tablespoons butter
- ½ cup chopped celery
- ½ cup chopped green pepper
- ½ cup chopped onion
- 2 cups crab meat
- 2 cups cooked and peeled medium shrimp
- 1 (7½-ounce) can sliced water chestnuts, drained
- ½ cup mayonnaise
- 1 egg, beaten
- ½ pound sharp Cheddar cheese, grated
- Dash of Tabasco sauce
- 1 tablespoon Worcestershire sauce
- 1 (13¾-ounce) can artichoke hearts, drained well and quartered

Serves: 6–8
Preparation: 25 minutes
Baking: 30 minutes
Temperature: 350°

Preheat oven to 350°.

Butter a 2-quart baking dish.

Soak bread in water until liquid is absorbed. Pinch bread into small pieces. Set aside.

Melt butter in small skillet over medium heat. Sauté celery, green pepper and onion in butter until tender.

Combine bread, sautéed vegetables and remaining ingredients in large bowl. Stir until well blended. Pour into prepared baking dish. Bake at 350° for 30 minutes.

Note: This dish is better if made a day ahead, refrigerated and reheated before serving.

Vegetables

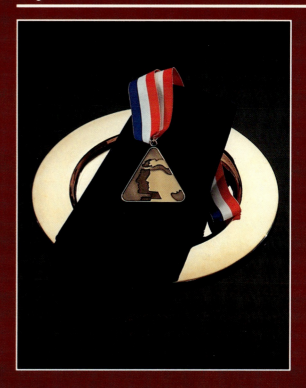

White River State Park

A stellar state park is unfolding in the unexpected confines of the urban core of a major metropolis. White River State Park—an idea whose time has come and an Indianapolis dream soon to be realized.

By the mid 1990's a world-class park, constructed in the environs of downtown Indianapolis, will reach completion. Now in the advanced planning stages, this spectacular new activity will be set on the restructured and landscaped banks of the White River.

The unique new showplace, with its picturesque riverside setting, will enclose a 74-acre zoo, complete with safari adventure area accessible by mini-trains; a complex family entertainment center with an aerial tramway, theater and a variety of rides; and a massive glass "palace" covering extensive underroof botanical displays, restaurant and party areas. A replica of Pisa's "leaning tower," with ramps leading to its turret, will dominate the site and offer visitors a 30-40 mile panoramic view.

Reinforcing the history of this area, a three-level pedestrian bridge will span the river in the exact location of an original covered bridge crossed by emigrants in their westward journey over the Old National Road. More than 250 acres of parkland, paved with secluded walkways and pastoral paths, will invite quiet strolls and simple pleasures in the surroundings and in the view. It will be as planned, "a park for every season and every mood."

One White River event has been underway since 1983, in advance of the completion of the Park. The White River State Games offer competition in 14 categories from basketball to wrestling. They annually attract thousands of gifted amateur athletes from all parts of Indiana, and serve as a "grass roots" stepping stone on the road to the Olympics.

White River State Park . . . a winning Indianapolis adventure.

VEGETABLES

Almond Rice Pilaf . . . 222
Artichoke Bottoms with
 Creamed Spinach . . . 206
Asparagus à la Anne . . . 207
Asparagus Polonaise . . . 208
Barbecued Green
 Beans . . . 209
Broccoli Ring . . . 209
Carciofi Ripieni (Stuffed
 Artichokes) . . . 207
Carrots in Horseradish
 Sauce . . . 214
Carrot Puff . . . 212
Carrot Purée in Mushroom
 Caps . . . 212
Cauliflower with
 Hazelnuts . . . 215
Chinese Peas . . . 220
Company Cabbage . . . 211
Coppelini Con
 Broccoli . . . 211
Corn Pudding . . . 216
Crab Stuffed
 Potatoes . . . 225
Cucumbers with
 Bacon . . . 217
Eggplant Pie . . . 218
Feta Cheese and Broccoli
 Pie . . . 210
Fresh Corn Sauté . . . 217
Fresh Pumpkin Bake . . . 221
Fresh Tomato Pie . . . 226
Glazed Radishes . . . 220
Ginger Candied
 Carrots . . . 214
Gourmet Potatoes . . . 225
Great Onion Rings . . . 218
Green Beans with Water
 Chestnuts . . . 208
Grilled Corn in
 Husks . . . 217
Hearty Vegetable
 Stew . . . 232
Hot Bacon Potato
 Salad . . . 223
How to Prepare Artichokes
 and Bottoms . . . 205
Italian-Style
 Cauliflower . . . 215
Mexican Corn
 Casserole . . . 216
Never Fail
 Asparagus . . . 208
Peas with Bacon and
 Mushrooms . . . 219
Perfect Rice . . . 222
Potato Dumplings . . . 224
Ranch Potatoes . . . 224
Ratatouille
 Monterey . . . 228
Scott's Parmesan
 Spinach . . . 229
Sformata Di Verdura . . . 213
Spinach in Onion
 Shells . . . 219
Squash Soufflé . . . 229
Stuffed Tomatoes with Two
 Fillings . . . 227
Stuffed Zucchini . . . 231
Sweet Potatoes with
 Topping . . . 226
Vegetable Delight . . . 231
Vegetables 3-Way . . . 232
Wild Rice-Vegetable
 Medley . . . 223
Zucchini Alfredo . . . 230
Zucchini Creole . . . 230

How to Prepare Artichokes and Bottoms

Cut off artichoke stems at base to make smooth bottom. Remove any tough or discolored leaves from bottom. Cut off about 1 inch of top leaves. Trim remaining tips from leaves using kitchen shears. Rub base and all cut portions with a lemon half to prevent discoloration.

Combine all ingredients except artichokes in 5-quart Dutch oven or saucepan; bring to boil. Add artichokes, partially cover with lid and return to boil. Cook until stem end is easily pierced with fork, about 25–30 minutes. (It will take about 40–50 minutes for large artichokes.) Remove from liquid. Drain upside down. Serve hot or cold, stuffed or marinated, or by dipping leaves into sauce. (May be cooked and stored, covered, in refrigerator for several days. If serving warm, return to simmering liquid for 5–10 minutes or until heated through.)

Prepare bottoms using cooled, cooked artichokes. Remove all leaves and scrape off fuzzy choke from bottom. (The bottoms may be refrigerated for several days or wrapped in foil and frozen.) The leaves may be saved and used as hors d'oeuvres with a mustard sauce. The leaves may also be scraped. These scrapings may be used instead of canned hearts in cooking. The scrapings freeze well.

Note: Artichokes will discolor and take on a metallic taste if cooked in cast iron or if carbon steel or aluminum utensils are used.

6–8 medium artichokes (may substitute 4 large artichokes)
4 quarts water
2 teaspoons salt
6 tablespoons fresh lemon juice
1 tablespoon olive oil
12 whole peppercorns

Serves: 6–8
Preparation: 10 minutes
Cooking: 30 minutes

Artichoke Bottoms with Creamed Spinach

Elegant appearance, elegant taste.

Béchamel Sauce: (about 2 cups)
- ¼ cup (½ stick) butter
- ¼ cup all-purpose flour
- 2 cups milk, at room temperature
- 2 tablespoons freshly grated Parmesan cheese

- 1 pound fresh spinach; washed, stem and roots discarded
- 2 cups boiling water
- ½ teaspoon salt
- 1 tablespoon butter
- Salt
- Freshly ground pepper
- ⅛ teaspoon freshly grated nutmeg
- 1 egg yolk, beaten
- 1 tablespoon heavy (whipping) cream
- 6 cooked artichoke bottoms
- 6 teaspoons freshly grated Parmesan cheese

Serves: 6
Preparation: 40 minutes
Baking: 10 minutes
Temperature: 400°

Melt butter for Béchamel Sauce in 2-quart saucepan until butter foams. Add flour and mix well. Cook over medium heat until lightly browned, stirring frequently. Remove from heat; slowly add milk and whisk until smooth. Return to heat and simmer for 5 minutes, stirring constantly. Remove from heat; stir in Parmesan. (This sauce freezes well.)

Preheat oven to 400°.

Cook spinach in boiling salted water in medium-size saucepan for about 1 minute, stirring several times. Drain well. Squeeze spinach to remove all excess moisture. Chop finely. (Chopping may be done in food processor.)

Melt butter in small skillet. Add spinach, salt, pepper and nutmeg. Cook over medium-low heat until thoroughly heated. Combine ½ cup Béchamel Sauce (freeze remaining sauce for another use), egg yolk and cream; stir into spinach. Continue cooking until just simmering; stir constantly. *Do not boil.*

Arrange artichoke bottoms in 9-inch square baking dish. Fill with spinach mixture. Sprinkle with Parmesan. Bake at 400° for 10 minutes or until slightly glazed. (May brown lightly under broiler, if desired.)

Note: These may be assembled 1 day ahead.

Carciofi Ripieni (Stuffed Artichokes)
Unique and absolutely wonderful.

Wash each artichoke, remove damaged outer leaves. Cut off stem. With knife or scissors cut 1 inch off top of artichoke and cut off tips of large outer leaves. Remove choke by gently prying artichoke open and scraping out sharp inner leaves and fuzz.

Mix garlic, parsley, salt, pepper and bread crumbs in small bowl. Place ¼ cup of mixture into center of each artichoke. Place wedge of cheese in center of each artichoke. Place artichokes close together in upright position in pan with tight fitting lid. Pour 1 tablespoon of olive oil over each artichoke. Pour water around artichokes. Cover and steam over medium heat for 25 minutes or until tender. Check to make sure there is always liquid in bottom of pan. Serve hot.

- 4 large firm artichokes
- 1–2 large cloves garlic, minced
- ½ cup chopped fresh parsley
- ½ teaspoon salt
- ⅛ teaspoon pepper
- ⅓ cup dry bread crumbs
- 4 (2x3½-inch) wedges white cheese (Swiss, Monterey Jack or Muenster)
- 4 tablespoons olive oil
- 2 cups water

Serves: 4
Preparation: 15 minutes
Cooking: 25 minutes

Asparagus à la Anne
Embellished with simple elegance.

Preheat oven to 350°.

Grease a 7x11-inch baking dish.

Clean and snap off lower ends of asparagus. Place in large saucepan with small amount of water. Cook over medium heat until crisp tender, about 8 minutes. Drain.

Melt butter in top of double boiler over medium heat. Stir in flour and salt. Slowly add half and half; stir until thick.

Cut asparagus spears in half crosswise. Place layer of asparagus on bottom of prepared baking dish. Pour a layer of sauce over asparagus. Sprinkle some cashews and cheese on top. Lightly season with salt and pepper. Repeat layers until dish is full, ending with cheese. Bake at 350° for 30 minutes.

- 60 asparagus spears
- 6 tablespoons butter
- 6 tablespoons all-purpose flour
- 1 teaspoon salt
- 3 cups half and half
- 1 cup split cashews
- 1 cup freshly grated Parmesan cheese
- Salt
- Freshly ground pepper

Serves: 10–12
Preparation: 1 hour
Baking: 30 minutes
Temperature: 350°

Vegetables

Never Fail Asparagus

Keeps asparagus green and crisp—great when entertaining.

Asparagus
½ teaspoon granulated sugar (optional)
½ teaspoon salt

Preparation: 5 minutes
Cooking: 3 minutes
Standing: 30 minutes

Prepare asparagus for cooking by snapping off lower part of asparagus stalks. Place asparagus in large skillet and cover with cold water. Stir in sugar and salt. Bring to a full boil and cook for 1–3 minutes, depending on freshness and size of stalks. Remove from heat and let stand, uncovered, at least 30 minutes. Asparagus may remain in water for hours. When ready to serve, reheat just to a boil; drain and serve.

Asparagus Polonaise

Fresh, subtle topping.

4 pounds fresh asparagus
1 teaspoon salt
¾ cup (1½ sticks) butter
3 hard-cooked eggs, sieved
3 tablespoons fresh lemon juice
Salt
Freshly ground pepper

Serves: 8
Preparation: 10 minutes
Cooking: 10 minutes

Rinse asparagus and snap off the lower woody part of the stalk. Trim ends so stalks are even. Tie in serving bunches with string. Place upright in deep cooking-pot with 1 inch water. Add salt and cook, covered, over medium-high heat for 10 minutes or until crisp tender. Drain.

Melt butter in small saucepan. Remove from heat and add eggs, lemon juice, salt and pepper. Arrange asparagus on serving dish. Pour butter mixture over asparagus.

Green Beans with Water Chestnuts

Clean combination of ingredients that blend naturally.

1–2 cups water
2 pounds green beans, washed and snipped
2 teaspoons salt
5 slices bacon
1 (8-ounce) can water chestnuts, drained and thinly sliced

Serves: 8
Preparation: 30 minutes

Bring water to a boil in large saucepan. Add green beans and salt. Cover and simmer over low heat until crisp tender. (Beans may be steamed.) Plunge immediately into cold water to arrest cooking.

Cook bacon until crisp in large skillet. Drain bacon thoroughly and crumble. Discard fat from skillet leaving scrapings in bottom. Place bacon, water chestnuts and cooked green beans in skillet. Toss together and heat thoroughly. Serve immediately.

Barbecued Green Beans
A real crowd pleaser.

Preheat oven to 250°.

Cook bacon and onion together in medium-size skillet over medium heat until bacon is crisp. Remove with slotted spoon and place in ungreased 2-quart baking dish. Add green beans.

Mix brown sugar and catsup in medium-size bowl. Fold into green beans. Bake, covered, at 250° for 3 hours.

- 6 slices bacon, diced
- 1 onion, chopped
- 4 (1-pound) cans cut green beans, drained (fresh do not work as well)
- 1 cup firmly packed brown sugar
- 1 cup catsup

Serves: 6–8
Preparation: 15 minutes
Baking: 3 hours
Temperature: 250°

Broccoli Ring
A great dish for entertaining.

Preheat oven to 350°.

Grease a 10-cup ring mold and line with dry bread crumbs.

Combine broccoli, onion and water in large saucepan. Cook over medium heat for 10 minutes or until vegetables are crisp tender. Drain well. Add remaining ingredients and pour into prepared ring mold. Place mold in larger pan. Add 1 inch of boiling hot water to larger pan. Bake at 350° for 45–55 minutes or until a knife inserted in center comes out clean. Unmold and serve.

- Dry bread crumbs
- 3 cups chopped broccoli [may substitute 3 (10-ounce) packages frozen broccoli, thawed]
- 2 tablespoons chopped onion
- 1 cup water
- 6 eggs, slightly beaten
- 2 cups half and half
- 2 teaspoons salt
- ¼ teaspoon pepper
- ¼ teaspoon ground nutmeg

Serves: 8
Preparation: 15 minutes
Baking: 45 minutes
Temperature: 350°

Feta Cheese and Broccoli Pie
Unique presentation and unusual taste.

Preheat oven to 350°.

Wash broccoli; trim leaves and stem ends. Split heavy stalks with sharp knife and coarsely chop stems and flowerets. Place in large skillet; add water and cook, covered, over medium heat for 5 minutes. Remove from skillet and drain well.

Melt ¼ cup butter in large skillet over low heat. Add onion and sauté over medium heat until onion is golden, about 3 minutes; stir occasionally. Add chopped broccoli; sauté for 1 minute. Remove from heat.

Beat eggs slightly in large bowl. Add feta cheese, parsley, dill, salt, pepper and broccoli mixture. Mix well.

Center 1 sheet of phyllo across bottom of 9-inch springform pan. Center another sheet of phyllo perpendicular to the first sheet. Brush with butter. Diagonally layer 4 more sheets of phyllo, brushing butter on each sheet after it is placed. Pour filling into prepared pan. Fold overlapping edges of pastry leaves over top of filling. Cut 4 (9-inch) circles from 2 remaining phyllo leaves with scissors. Brush each circle with melted butter. Stack the phyllo circles and place on top of pie. Cut through leaves with knife to make 8 sections. Pour any remaining butter over top. Place springform pan on jelly roll pan to catch drippings. Bake at 350° for 40–45 minutes or until crust is puffy and golden brown. Remove to rack; cool 10 minutes. Remove sides of pan and cut into wedges. Use pie server to remove wedges. Serve warm.

Note: To keep phyllo sheets from drying out, cover with damp towel.

Ingredients

- 2 pounds fresh broccoli [may substitute 3 (10-ounce) packages frozen chopped broccoli, thawed and drained]
- ½ cup boiling water
- ¼ cup (½ stick) butter
- ½ cup finely chopped onion
- 3 eggs
- ½ pound feta cheese, crumbled
- ¼ cup chopped fresh parsley
- 2 tablespoons chopped fresh dill (may substitute 1 tablespoon dried dill weed)
- ½ teaspoon salt
- Freshly ground pepper
- 8 phyllo dough sheets, at room temperature
- ½ cup (1 stick) butter, melted

Serves: 8
Preparation: 30 minutes
Baking: 45 minutes
Cooling: 10 minutes
Temperature: 350°

Coppelini Con Broccoli
An interesting side dish for both family and company.

Trim woody stems from broccoli. Place in Dutch oven with water and salt. Bring to a boil and cook until crisp tender. Transfer broccoli with slotted spoon to large bowl. Reserve water.

Melt 3 tablespoons butter in medium-size skillet over low heat. Add mushrooms and sauté over medium heat until tender. Add to broccoli.

Cook egg noodles in the reserved water until barely tender. Drain and add to broccoli mixture.

Melt remaining 5 tablespoons butter. Pour over broccoli mixture. Add Parmesan and toss gently. Serve immediately.

Company Cabbage
Unique combination carries cabbage beyond family dining.

Heat water in wok or 3-quart saucepan over medium heat. Add bouillon granules and stir until dissolved. Add cabbage, carrots, onions and salt. Cook, covered, over medium heat for 5–10 minutes or until tender, stirring once. Drain, if necessary.

Combine butter, pecans and mustard in small bowl. Pour mixture over vegetables. Toss to mix. Place in serving dish and sprinkle with paprika.

1 bunch fresh broccoli (may substitute 10-ounce package of frozen broccoli spears)
3 cups water
1 teaspoon salt
8 tablespoons (1 stick) butter, divided
½ pound fresh mushrooms, sliced
5 ounces very thin egg noodles
1 cup freshly grated Parmesan cheese

Serves: 4–6
Preparation 30 minutes

¼ cup water
1 teaspoon instant beef bouillon granules
5 cups coarsely shredded cabbage
1 cup coarsely shredded carrots
½ cup sliced green onions (including tops)
½ teaspoon salt
2 tablespoons butter, melted
⅓ cup chopped pecans
1 teaspoon prepared mustard
Paprika

Serves: 6
Preparation: 20 minutes
Cooking: 5 minutes

Vegetables

- 8 large fresh mushrooms
- 6 tablespoons butter, divided
- 1 tablespoon fresh lemon juice
- 6 medium-size carrots, peeled and quartered
- Salt
- Freshly ground pepper
- ¼–½ teaspoon granulated sugar
- 2 tablespoons heavy (whipping) cream

Serves: 8
Preparation: 10 minutes
Cooking: 10 minutes
Baking: 15 minutes
Temperature: 350°

- 1 pound carrots, peeled and cut into 1-inch pieces
- ½ cup (1 stick) margarine, melted
- 3 eggs
- 1 cup granulated sugar (less, if desired)
- 3 tablespoons all-purpose flour
- 1 teaspoon baking powder
- 1 teaspoon vanilla

Serves: 6
Preparation: 10 minutes
Cooking: 20 minutes
Baking: 45 minutes
Temperature: 350°

Carrot Purée in Mushroom Caps

Taste and eye-appeal are both winners.

Preheat oven to 350°.

Remove stems from cleaned mushrooms and reserve for another use. Melt 4 tablespoons butter in small skillet; stir in lemon juice. Sauté mushrooms over medium-high heat until just tender, about 3–5 minutes.

Place carrots in large saucepan. Add salted water to cover. Bring to a boil and simmer until crisp tender, about 8 minutes. (Length of time varies with size and age of carrots.) Drain. Stir in remaining 2 tablespoons butter, salt, pepper and sugar. Place carrots in blender or food processor with cream. Purée until smooth. Pipe purée through a pastry bag into mushroom caps. Place on cookie sheet and bake at 350° for 10–15 minutes.

Variations: For a sweet fruit flavor, add 1–2 tablespoons orange marmalade and ¼ teaspoon ground ginger to drained carrots and omit salt, pepper, sugar and cream. Purée as instructed above. Potato-Cauliflower Purée also makes a delicious filling.

Carrot Puff

Sweet and smooth.

Preheat oven to 350°.

Grease an 8-inch square baking dish.

Place carrots in medium-size saucepan and cover with salted water. Bring to a boil; reduce heat and simmer, uncovered, for 20 minutes or until carrots are tender. Drain.

Place margarine, eggs, sugar, flour, baking powder and vanilla in blender. Add carrots a little at a time and purée the mixture. Pour into prepared baking dish. Bake at 350° for 45 minutes or until firm. Let stand for 5 minutes before serving.

Note: This may be made a day ahead and refrigerated. Bring to room temperature before cooking.

Sformata Di Verdura

An elegant and delicious carrot loaf.

Place carrots in medium-size saucepan. Cover with water and boil for 10 minutes. Drain and let cool. Cut into small pieces.

Melt 4 tablespoons butter in large saucepan over medium heat. Sauté carrots gently for 15 minutes. Season with salt and pepper. Cool completely, about 30 minutes.

Make Béchamel Sauce while carrots are cooling. Heat milk in small saucepan. *Do not boil.* Melt 6 tablespoons butter in large saucepan over medium heat. Add flour. Cook and stir until well combined and golden brown. (This roux may be made ahead and returned to heat later. Warm roux over low heat before making sauce.) Add hot milk all at once. Stir briskly to prevent lumps. Bring to boiling point. Add salt to taste and continue to stir and cook slowly for 12–14 minutes. Remove from heat; cover and cool for 30 minutes.

Preheat oven to 400°.

Butter a 9x5-inch loaf pan. Line with dry bread crumbs.

Transfer béchamel to large bowl and add egg yolks and cheese. Mix well. Fold in carrots; correct seasonings, if necessary.

Add nutmeg and mix gently. Pour mixture into prepared loaf pan. Place loaf pan inside a 9x13-inch baking pan; fill larger pan with 1 inch of water. Bake at 400° for 1 hour and 30 minutes. If Sformata begins to darken too much during baking, cover with sheet of foil. Remove from oven and cool for 20 minutes. Carefully invert onto serving dish and serve immediately.

Variation: Use other vegetables and omit nutmeg.

- 1 pound carrots, peeled
- 4 tablespoons butter
- Salt
- Freshly ground pepper

Béchamel Sauce:
- 2 cups milk
- 6 tablespoons butter
- ½ cup all-purpose flour
- Salt

- ¼ cup dry bread crumbs
- 4 egg yolks
- 3 tablespoons freshly grated Parmesan cheese
- Freshly grated nutmeg

Serves: 6
Preparation: 50 minutes
Cooling: 30
Baking: 1 hour, 30 minutes
Standing: 20 minutes
Temperature: 400°

Ginger Candied Carrots
Caraway adds unique twist to carrots.

12 medium-size carrots, peeled and cut into 1-inch pieces [may substitute 2 (10½-ounce) packages frozen carrots]
4 tablespoons (½ stick) unsalted butter
¼ cup firmly packed brown sugar
1½ teaspoons ground ginger
½ teaspoon caraway seed

Serves: 4–6
Preparation: 15 minutes
Cooking: 20 minutes

Place carrots with small amount of water in medium-size saucepan. Steam over medium-high heat until carrots are tender, about 15 minutes. Melt butter in another medium-size saucepan while carrots are cooking. Add brown sugar, ginger and caraway seed. Stir until ingredients are mixed. Set aside. Drain cooked carrots and place in saucepan with sugar mixture. Cook over low heat for 5 minutes, stirring occasionally. Serve immediately.

Carrots in Horseradish Sauce
Tangy—a different taste for carrots.

6–8 carrots, peeled and cut into 3-inch strips
½ cup mayonnaise
2 tablespoons prepared horseradish
2 tablespoons water
Chopped fresh parsley

Serves: 4
Preparation: 10 minutes
Cooking: 15 minutes
Baking: 8 minutes
Temperature: 350°

Preheat oven to 350°.

Place carrots and ½ cup water in medium-size saucepan. Boil until tender. Drain carrots and place in 1-quart baking dish.

Mix together mayonnaise, horseradish and water in small bowl. Pour mixture over carrots. Bake, uncovered, at 350° for 5–8 minutes until sauce is bubbly. *Do not overbake.* Sprinkle with parsley and serve.

Serving Suggestion: Serve with roast pork or baked chicken.

Italian-Style Cauliflower
Just the right blend of spices in this dish.

Place cauliflower and small amount of water in medium-size saucepan. Steam for 7–8 minutes. Remove from heat and set aside.

Slowly heat oil in large heavy skillet over medium heat. Add garlic; sauté until golden but not brown, about 3 minutes. Remove garlic and discard. Combine cauliflower, salt, tomato, parsley and basil in same skillet. Cook about 3 minutes, stirring constantly. Place in serving dish and sprinkle with Parmesan.

- 1 head cauliflower, broken into flowerets
- 3 tablespoons oil
- 3 cloves garlic
- ½ teaspoon salt
- 1 cup chopped fresh tomato
- 3 tablespoons chopped fresh parsley
- 3 tablespoons chopped fresh basil (may substitute 1 teaspoon dried basil)
- ¼ cup freshly grated Parmesan cheese

Serves: 6
Preparation: 15 minutes
Cooking: 6 minutes

Cauliflower with Hazelnuts
The nut topping would be great on any vegetable.

Remove leaves and stalk from cauliflower. Soak, head down, in cold salted water for 5 minutes. Drain cauliflower and discard water. Place cauliflower in uncovered kettle. Add milk to keep cauliflower white. Add salt to boiling water and pour over cauliflower. Cook until tender, about 20 minutes. Drain cauliflower and place in oven-proof serving dish. Cover with nut topping and keep in warm oven until serving time.

Prepare nut topping while cauliflower is cooking. Melt butter in small saucepan. Add bread crumbs and nuts. Stir and cook until crumbs are brown. Add pepper. Spread over top of cauliflower.

Microwave: Cauliflower may be steamed in microwave. Place prepared head in 1½-quart glass bowl with 2 tablespoons water. Cover with lid or plastic wrap. Microwave on High for 8–10 minutes until tender.

Variation: Experiment with different types of nuts and different types of crumbs such as whole wheat bread or corn bread.

- 1 whole fresh cauliflower
- ½ cup milk
- 2 quarts boiling water
- ¼ teaspoon salt

Nut Topping:
- ⅓ cup butter
- ⅓ cup soft bread crumbs
- ¼ cup chopped hazelnuts
- Freshly ground pepper

Serves: 6
Preparation: 15 minutes
Cooking: 20 minutes

Mexican Corn Casserole

Spicy but blends with many entrées.

Preheat oven to 350°.

Grease well a 7x11-inch baking dish.

Cut corn from cobs. Purée ½ of corn, butter and eggs in blender or food processor.

Mix remaining ½ of corn, sour cream, cheese, corn meal, green chilies and salt in medium-size bowl. Add puréed mixture and mix well. Pour into prepared baking dish. Bake, uncovered, at 350° for 50–60 minutes.

- 9 ears yellow corn, husked [may substitute 2 (10-ounce) packages frozen corn, thawed]
- ½ cup (1 stick) butter, melted
- 2 eggs
- 1 cup jalepeño sour cream (may substitute plain sour cream)
- 10 ounces Monterey Jack cheese, grated
- ½ cup yellow corn meal
- 1 (4-ounce) can diced green chilies, drained
- 1½ teaspoons salt

Serves: 8
Preparation: 15 minutes
Baking: 1 hour
Temperature: 350°

Corn Pudding

A different way to serve good old corn.

Preheat oven to 350°.

Grease a 1½-quart baking dish.

Cut corn from ears. (If using frozen corn, thaw and drain in colander.) Purée ½ of corn in blender for 4 seconds. Combine puréed corn with whole corn in large bowl. Add flour, sugar, salt, pepper and cayenne. Mix in cream, butter and eggs. Pour into prepared baking dish. Set dish into another pan; fill larger pan with hot water to a depth of 1 inch. Bake, uncovered, at 350° for about 1 hour and 10 minutes or until toothpick inserted in center comes out clean. Serve hot.

- 10–12 ears white corn [may substitute 2 (10-ounce) packages frozen white corn]
- ¼ cup all-purpose flour
- 1 tablespoon sugar
- 1 teaspoon salt
- ¼ teaspoon pepper
- 3 dashes cayenne pepper
- 2 cups light (coffee) cream
- 4 tablespoons (½ stick) butter, melted
- 3 eggs, well beaten

Serves: 6–8
Preparation: 15 minutes
Baking: 1 hour, 10 minutes
Temperature: 350°

Fresh Corn Sauté
Mouth-watering freshness.

Husk and clean corn, carefully removing the silk. Cut or scrape kernels from the cob into a large skillet. (Be sure to get the milk from the corn.) Add butter. Cover and cook slowly over medium heat until corn is still crisp but no longer starchy tasting. Turn frequently with spatula. Season with salt and pepper. Add cream, if desired, and stir until heated thorough.

Note: Two medium-size ears corn yields about ½ cup kernels. Allow at least ½ cup corn per person.

8	medium-size ears fresh corn
2–3	tablespoons unsalted butter
	Salt
	Freshly ground pepper
2	tablespoons heavy (whipping) cream (if desired)

Serves: 4
Preparation: 25 minutes

Grilled Corn in Husks
Terrific for camping or cookouts.

Dip unhusked corn into ice water for 2 minutes. Place corn 4 to 5 inches from hot coals and grill until husks blacken, about 10–20 minutes. Turn corn frequently to cook evenly. Using gloves, remove husks with quick, pulling motion. Serve immediately with butter, salt and pepper.

Fresh corn on the cob
Butter
Salt
Freshly ground pepper

Serves: As many as you want
Preparation: 5 minutes
Cooking: 20 minutes

Cucumbers with Bacon
A different vegetable—light and refreshing.

Peel cucumbers and cut in half lengthwise. Remove pulp and seeds. Cut cucumbers into sticks about 2½–3 inches long.

Melt butter in skillet over medium heat. Sauté cucumbers until they turn transparent, about 4–5 minutes. Add chicken broth; cover and cook until tender, about 5 minutes. Remove cucumber sticks with slotted spoon. Place in serving dish and garnish with bacon.

2	large cucumbers
¼	cup (½ stick) butter
⅓–½	cup rich chicken broth
3	slices bacon, cooked and crumbled

Serves: 4–6
Preparation: 5 minutes
Cooking: 10 minutes

Vegetables

- ½ cup (1 stick) unsalted butter
- 1 medium eggplant, unpeeled and cubed (about 4 cups)
- 2 cups coarsely chopped fresh mushrooms
- 2 cloves garlic, minced
- 4 tablespoons chopped fresh parsley
- 1 teaspoon salt
- ½ cup tomato paste
- 1 (9-inch) pastry shell, unbaked
- ¼ cup freshly grated Parmesan cheese

Serves:	4
Preparation:	20 minutes
Cooking:	20 minutes
Baking:	45 minutes
Temperature:	350°

- 12 ounces beer
- 1 tablespoon baking powder
- 1 teaspoon seasoned salt
- 1 egg, slightly beaten
- 1½ cups all-purpose flour
- Oil for deep frying
- 3 large Spanish onions, cut into ¼ to ½-inch slices and separated into rings

Serves:	4–6
Preparation:	10 minutes
Cooking:	15 minutes
Temperature:	275°

Eggplant Pie

Eggplant merges with other flavors to create new taste that even children enjoy.

Preheat oven to 350°.

Melt butter in large skillet and sauté eggplant over medium-high heat. Cover and cook for 10 minutes over low heat. Add mushrooms and garlic to eggplant and cook, stirring constantly until mushrooms begin to wilt. Add parsley, salt and tomato paste. Stir until blended. Spoon into pastry shell. Bake at 350° for 45 minutes. Cool slightly. Sprinkle with Parmesan cheese before serving.

Great Onion Rings

Steak or hamburgers—these add the perfect touch.

Preheat oven to 275°.

Combine beer, baking powder, salt and egg in large bowl; mix well. Gradually add flour, stirring to form loose paste.

Place enough oil in electric skillet or deep heavy skillet to allow the onions to float freely. (May use deep fat fryer.) Heat oil to 375°.

Dip onion rings into batter; coat well. Fry in batches until golden brown, turning once. Remove with slotted spoon and drain on paper towel. Keep onion rings hot in 275° oven while cooking other rings.

Spinach in Onion Shells

A savory blend of ingredients.

Preheat oven to 350°.

Squeeze spinach to remove all excess moisture.

Beat cream cheese and egg in medium-size bowl until light. Add bread crumbs, cheese, milk, salt and pepper. Mix well. Stir in spinach.

Cut onion in half from top to bottom. Separate layers to form shells. Place in 9-inch square baking dish. Spoon spinach mixture into shells. Cover baking dish with foil. Bake at 350° for 35–40 minutes or until onions are tender and filling is set.

Variation: Finely chopped broccoli may be substituted for the spinach. Add 1 tablespoon lemon juice, if desired.

Peas with Bacon and Mushrooms

Wine adds delightful touch.

Melt butter in large skillet over medium-high heat. Add onion and mushrooms; cook until soft. Add peas, bacon, wine, salt and pepper. Simmer, covered, until peas are crisp tender, about 4 minutes. Remove with a slotted spoon to a serving dish or serve in a small pastry shell.

Vegetables

- 1 (10-ounce) package frozen chopped spinach; cooked and drained
- 1 (3-ounce) package cream cheese, softened
- 1 egg, slightly beaten
- ½ cup soft bread crumbs
- ¼ cup freshly grated Parmesan cheese (may substitute freshly grated Romano cheese)
- ¼ cup milk
- ¼ teaspoon salt
- Freshly ground pepper
- 1 large flat onion

Serves: 6
Preparation: 25 minutes
Baking: 35 minutes
Temperature: 350°

- 6 tablespoons butter
- ½ cup diced onion
- ¼ pound fresh mushrooms, sliced
- 2½ pounds fresh peas, hulled (may substitute 1 pound frozen peas, thawed)
- 3–6 strips bacon, cooked
- ½ cup white wine
- Salt
- Freshly ground pepper

Serves: 8 minutes
Preparation: 15 minutes

Vegetables

- 2 (10-ounce) packages frozen peas
- 2 green onions, (including tops), chopped
- 1 teaspoon granulated sugar
- 6 tablespoons butter, divided
- 1 teaspoon monosodium glutamate (optional)
- 2 tablespoons chopped fresh parsley
- 2 tablespoons chopped fresh chives
- ⅛ teaspoon cracked pepper
- 1 bay leaf
- Lettuce leaves

Serves: 6–8
Preparation: 15 minutes

Chinese Peas
Uncomplicated and pleasing.

Separate peas and place in large skillet. Add green onions, sugar, 2 tablespoons butter, monosodium glutamate (if desired), parsley, chives, pepper and bay leaf. Cover mixture with very wet lettuce leaves. Cover tightly and bring to a boil over medium-high heat. Turn off heat and steam for 3 minutes. Remove lettuce leaves and bay leaf. Slice remaining 4 tablespoons butter into peas. Stir until melted. Serve immediately.

- 3 bunches radishes; unpeeled, washed and trimmed at both ends
- ½–¾ cup chicken broth or stock
- 3 tablespoons butter

Serves: 6–8
Preparation: 15 minutes

Glazed Radishes
A must—cooking removes the sting and creates a delicate and tender radish.

Place radishes and chicken broth in medium-size saucepan. Cook, covered, over high heat until crisp tender, about 10 minutes. Remove radishes, reduce liquid to about ¼ cup by boiling rapidly. Add butter and stir until butter is melted. Return radishes to saucepan to coat with liquid. Heat through.

Variation: Two tablespoons of heavy cream and ¼ teaspoon of white pepper may be added to the glaze if a richer glaze is desired.

Fresh Pumpkin Bake

An exciting feast for vegetarians and meat-lovers, too.

Melt 5 tablespoons of the butter in large skillet. Sauté onion until transparent over medium heat. Add rice to skillet and stir until coated with butter. Add apple juice, hot vegetable broth, garlic and salt and pepper. Add saffron; continue stirring. Cover and cook mixture over low heat for 20 minutes. Set aside.

Preheat oven to 425°.

Cut a 7-inch-round top from the pumpkin. Remove seeds and strings. Sprinkle inside of pumpkin with Worcestershire, salt and pepper. Let pumpkin stand for 10 minutes.

Heat remaining 1 tablespoon butter and olive oil (enough to cover bottom of skillet) in large skillet. Sauté green onions over medium heat for about 2 minutes. Add eggplant and stir to coat. Sauté for 10 minutes, stirring constantly. Season with salt and pepper and a splash of Worcestershire. Steam carrots until just tender, about 5–7 minutes.

Combine rice mixture, eggplant mixture, carrots, beans and seeds in large bowl. Fill pumpkin with mixture. Replace pumpkin top. Place pumpkin in oven-proof serving dish to fit. Bake at 425° for 1 hour. Serve hot from pumpkin.

Note: May be made ahead and refrigerated. Bring pumpkin to room temperature and bake as above or bake chilled pumpkin for 1 hour and 15 minutes or until hot.

- 6 tablespoons butter, divided
- 1 medium onion, chopped
- 2 cups long grain rice
- ½ cup apple juice
- 5 cups hot vegetable broth
- 1–2 cloves garlic, minced
- Salt
- Freshly ground pepper
- ¼ teaspoon saffron
- 1 medium-size pumpkin (about 10–12 inches in diameter)
- 3 tablespoons olive oil
- 6 green onions (including tops), chopped
- 1 large eggplant; washed, peeled, sliced and cubed
- Worcestershire sauce
- 3 carrots, thickly chopped
- 1⅓ cups cooked kidney beans
- ½ cup pumpkin seeds, roasted
- ⅓ cup sunflower seeds or kernels, roasted

Serves: 8
Preparation: 35 minutes
Cooking: 25 minutes
Baking: 1 hour
Temperature: 425°

Vegetables

Perfect Rice

A dish to accompany just about any menu.

Spray vegetable oil
3 tablespoons butter or margarine
½ cup finely chopped onion
2 cups long grain rice
3 cups chicken stock or broth (may substitute beef broth or consommé)
Bouquet garni
½ teaspoon Tabasco sauce
Salt
Freshly ground pepper

Spray a large skillet with vegetable oil.

Melt butter in skillet over medium heat. Add onions and cook until onions are transparent, about 5 minutes. Add rice and stir until grains are coated. Add chicken broth and bouquet garni. Stir in Tabasco. Bring mixture to a boil. Cover tightly. Reduce heat to low and simmer for exactly 17 minutes. Remove from heat and uncover. Stir rice. Add salt and pepper. Place in serving dish and serve.

Serves: 10
Preparation: 10 minutes
Cooking: 20 minutes

Almond Rice Pilaf

Interesting flavors and crunchy texture.

½ cup (1 stick) butter or margarine
1 cup long grain rice
1 cup sliced fresh mushrooms
1 teaspoon Italian seasoning (may substitute ¼ teaspoon each basil, oregano, thyme and marjoram)
¾ cup chopped green onions
2⅔ cups chicken broth or stock
¾ cup slivered or sliced almonds

Preheat oven to 325°.

Grease lightly a shallow 2-quart baking dish.

Melt butter in medium-size skillet over medium heat. Stir in rice, mushrooms, Italian seasoning and green onions. Cook, stirring constantly, until onions and mushrooms are tender, about 5 minutes.

Spoon mixture into prepared baking dish. (At this point the mixture may be covered and refrigerated.) Stir in broth and almonds. Bake, covered, at 325° for 1 hour. (If mixture was refrigerated, allow 1 hour and 10 minutes for baking.) Let stand for 10 minutes before serving.

Serves: 6
Preparation: 15 minutes
Baking: 1 hour
Temperature: 325°

Wild Rice-Vegetable Medley
Lovely, tasty and a wonderful company dish.

Preheat oven to 350°.

Cook rice according to package directions.

Cook each vegetable separately in lightly salted water until crisp tender. (Vegetables may be steamed or cooked in microwave according to manufacturer's directions.) Drain.

Combine vegetables and rice in 9x13-inch baking dish. Bake at 350° until heated through, about 20–25 minutes. Just before serving, remove casserole from oven and sprinkle top with cheese and almonds. Return to oven and heat until cheese melts.

- 1 (6-ounce) package long grain and wild rice
- 4 large carrots, peeled and cut into 1½-inch julienne strips
- 2 medium zucchini, cut into ¼-inch slices
- 1 stalk fresh broccoli, cut into bite-size pieces
- 1½ cups bite-size pieces fresh cauliflower
- 2 cups grated Monterey Jack cheese (may substitute Co-Jack)
- ½ cup slivered almonds, toasted

Serves: 8–10
Preparation: 20 minutes
Baking: 25 minutes
Temperature: 350°

Hot Bacon Potato Salad
Unique and distinctive taste.

Scrub potatoes and place in large saucepan. Fill pan ½ full with water. Add salt and bring water to a boil over high heat. Reduce heat to medium-low and simmer for 40 minutes or until tender. Drain and cool.

Preheat oven to 350°.

Grease a 9x13-inch baking dish.

Peel and dice potatoes. Combine potatoes, cheese, onions and mayonnaise in large bowl; mix well. Place in prepared baking dish. Top with bacon and green olives. Bake, uncovered, at 350° for 1 hour.

- 8 medium red potatoes
- 1 teaspoon salt
- 1 pound American cheese, diced
- ½ cup chopped onion
- 1 cup mayonnaise
- ½ pound bacon, cooked and crumbled
- ¼ cup sliced green olives

Serves: 8
Preparation: 30 minutes
Cooking: 40 minutes
Baking: 1 hour
Temperature: 350°

Vegetables

Potato Dumplings

You will be glad you invested the extra minutes.

- 10 medium-size Idaho potatoes
- ½ pound bacon, diced
- 1 medium onion, chopped
- 1 cup seasoned croutons
- 1 large egg, beaten
- 1 clove garlic, minced
- ½ cup chopped fresh parsley
- 1 tablespoon all-purpose flour
- Salt
- Freshly ground pepper
- 2 tablespoons very fine dry bread crumbs
- 1 cup (2 sticks) butter, melted
- Chopped fresh parsley (optional)

Serves:	12–14
Preparation:	45 minutes
Cooking:	45 minutes
Baking:	40 minutes
Temperature:	350°

Place potatoes in large saucepan. Cover with water and boil until tender, about 45 minutes. Drain and cool. Peel and grate potatoes. *Do not mash.* Place in large mixing bowl.

Place bacon and onion in large skillet. Cook over medium-high heat until bacon is crisp and onion becomes transparent. Pour off excess fat. Add croutons to skillet and mix. Pour over potatoes. Fold egg, garlic, parsley, flour, salt and pepper in mixture.

Preheat oven to 350°.

Grease a 9x13-inch baking dish.

Run hands under cold water, dry and dust with flour. Form golf-ball-size dumplings. Place dumplings in prepared baking dish. Do not stack dumplings. Dust with fine bread crumbs. Drizzle with butter. Bake at 350° for 30–40 minutes. Garnish with parsley, if desired.

Note: May make a day ahead, but do not dust with bread crumbs or drizzle with butter until day of cooking. Bring potatoes to room temperature before baking.

Ranch Potatoes

Great taste and super easy.

- 8 potatoes
- ½ cup (1 stick) butter or margarine, melted
- 2 tablespoons freshly grated Parmesan cheese
- 1 teaspoon salt
- 1 teaspoon garlic powder
- 1 teaspoon paprika

Serves:	8
Preparation:	10 minutes
Baking:	40 minutes
Temperature:	375°

Preheat oven to 375°.

Cut each unpeeled potato into 8 pieces.

Combine butter, Parmesan, salt, garlic powder and paprika in large mixing bowl. Add potatoes and toss until potatoes are coated with mixture. Place potatoes on ungreased cookie sheet and bake at 375° for 40 minutes.

Crab Stuffed Potatoes
Rich and wonderful.

Preheat oven to 425°.

Scrub potatoes and poke with a fork. Bake at 425° for 1 hour. Remove potatoes. Reduce oven temperature to 400°.

Cut potatoes in half lengthwise. Scoop out potato pulp taking care not to damage shells. Place pulp in large mixing bowl. Add butter, cream, salt, pepper, onion and cheese. Whip until smooth. Fold in crab meat. Fill potato shells with mixture. Sprinkle paprika on top. Bake at 400° for 15 minutes.

Variation: May omit crab meat and cream and add 1 (10-ounce) package frozen chopped spinach (thawed and squeezed dry), ¼ teaspoon dried dill weed and 1 cup sour cream.

Serving Suggestion: Serve with steak for dinner party or use as a luncheon entrée with salad.

- 3 large baking potatoes
- ½ cup (1 stick) butter
- ½ cup light (coffee) cream
- 1 teaspoon salt
- ½ teaspoon pepper
- 4 teaspoons grated onion
- 1 cup grated sharp Cheddar cheese
- 1 (6½-ounce) can crab meat, drained
- ½ teaspoon paprika

Serves: 6
Preparation: 15 minutes
Baking: 1 hour, 15 minutes
Temperature: 425°

Gourmet Potatoes
Easy and impressive.

Preheat oven to 350°.

Grease a 2-quart baking dish.

Peel and coarsely shred potatoes.

Combine cheese and 8 tablespoons butter in a large saucepan. Cook over low heat, stirring occasionally, until almost melted. Remove from heat and stir in sour cream, onions, salt and pepper. Fold in potatoes and pour mixture into prepared baking dish. Dot with remaining butter. (At this point, dish can be frozen for later use.)

Bake at 350° for 25 minutes or until heated through.

Microwave: Prepared dish may be cooked, covered, in microwave for 12 minutes.

- 8 medium potatoes, boiled with skins and cooled completely
- 2 cups grated Cheddar cheese
- 10 tablespoons butter, divided
- 1½ cups sour cream, at room temperature
- ½ cup chopped green onions (including tops)
- 1 teaspoon salt
- ½ teaspoon pepper

Serves: 8
Preparation: 15 minutes
Cooking: 40 minutes
Baking: 25 minutes
Temperature: 350°

Vegetables

Sweet Potatoes with Topping

A family favorite.

3 cups mashed cooked sweet potatoes
½ cup granulated sugar
1 teaspoon vanilla
½ cup milk

Topping:
⅓ cup all-purpose flour
⅔ cup firmly packed brown sugar
⅓ cup margarine
1 cup chopped nuts

Serves:	4–6
Preparation:	30 minutes
Baking:	30 minutes
Temperature:	350°

Preheat oven to 350°.

Butter a 2-quart baking dish.

Combine potatoes, sugar, vanilla and milk. Pour mixture into prepared baking dish.

Mix together flour and brown sugar. Cut in margarine until mixture resembles coarse crumbs. Stir in nuts. Sprinkle topping over sweet potatoes. Bake, uncovered, at 350° for 30 minutes.

Fresh Tomato Pie

Even winter tomatoes are good when cooked this way.

2 tablespoons butter
2 large onions, thinly sliced
12 slices bacon, divided
2 cups fresh soft bread crumbs, divided
3–4 fresh ripe tomatoes, thinly sliced
2 cups grated sharp Cheddar cheese
3 eggs
½ teaspoon salt
⅛ teaspoon freshly ground pepper
Chopped fresh parsley

Serves:	6
Preparation:	20 minutes
Baking:	40 minutes
Temperature:	350°

Preheat oven to 350°.

Butter a 9-inch pie plate.

Melt butter in medium-size skillet over medium heat. Sauté onions for 3–5 minutes. Set aside.

Cook 9 slices of the bacon. Drain and crumble. Reserve remaining 3 slices.

Place 1 cup bread crumbs in prepared pie plate. Place ingredients in layers as follows: tomatoes, onions, cheese and bacon. Repeat layers until all ingredients are used. The pie will be mounded but cooks down.

Beat eggs well; add salt and pepper. Pour over pie. Sprinkle with remaining 1 cup bread crumbs. Drape remaining bacon slices over top of pie. Bake at 350° for 35–40 minutes. Garnish with parsley and slice to serve.

Stuffed Tomatoes with Two Fillings

Two different stuffings—both extremely good.

Preheat oven to 350°.

Slice tops from tomatoes. Scoop out pulp and reserve for Walnut Rice Stuffing or for another use. Sprinkle cavities with salt, if desired. Turn tomatoes upside down and drain for 15 minutes. Set aside.

Walnut Rice Stuffing: Heat olive oil in large skillet over low heat. Add onion and sauté until transparent. Stir in rice, parsley, water, lemon juice, salt, oregano, thyme and pepper. Bring to a boil over medium-high heat. Cover, turn heat to medium-low and simmer for 15–20 minutes. Stir in walnuts, wheat germ and reserved tomato pulp. Fill tomato cavitites with stuffing. Top with cheese. Bake at 350° for 30 minutes.

Zucchini Stuffing: Heat butter and oil in large saucepan over low heat. Add onions and sauté until transparent. Add zucchini, garlic, monosodium glutamate (if desired), Maggi, Tabasco and chicken base. Cook 6–8 minutes. Fill tomato cavities with mixture. Top with bread crumbs and cheese. Bake at 350° for 30 minutes.

Note: May be prepared ahead and heated before serving. If refrigerated, add a few minutes to the cooking time.

---

8 medium tomatoes
Salt (optional)

Walnut Rice Stuffing:
- 4½ teaspoons olive oil
- ¾ cup chopped onion
- ¾ cup long grain rice
- 3 tablespoons chopped fresh parsley
- 1⅓ cups water
- 2 tablespoons fresh lemon juice
- 1¼ teaspoons salt
- ½ teaspoon dried oregano
- ½ teaspoon dried thyme
- Freshly ground pepper
- ¾ cup chopped walnuts
- ¼ cup wheat germ
- Reserved tomato pulp
- ¾–1 cup grated Swiss cheese

Zucchini Stuffing:
- 2 tablespoons butter
- 2 tablespoons oil
- 1 small bunch green onions (including tops), chopped
- 6 small zucchini; trimmed, washed and thinly sliced
- 1 clove garlic, minced
- 1 teaspoon monosodium glutamate (optional)
- 1 teaspoon Maggi seasoning
- 1 drop Tabasco sauce
- 1 tablespoon chicken base
- Dry bread crumbs
- Freshly grated Parmesan cheese

Serves: 8
Preparation: 30 minutes
Cooking: 15 minutes
Baking: 30 minutes
Temperature: 350°

Vegetables

- 6 slices bacon, cut into 1-inch pieces
- 1 large onion, sliced
- 1 (6-ounce) can tomato paste
- 1½ teaspoons salt
- 1 teaspoon dried thyme
- 1 large clove garlic, minced
- 2 tablespoons all-purpose flour
- 1½ pounds garden fresh tomatoes and their juices (may substitute 28-ounce can whole peeled tomatoes, cut up and juice reserved)
- 1 eggplant (about 1¼ pounds), peeled and cut into ½-inch slices
- ½ pound zucchini, cut into ½-inch slices
- 1 green pepper, cut into strips
- 1 pound Monterey Jack cheese, sliced

Serves: 6–8
Preparation: 30 minutes
Baking: 50 minutes
Temperature: 400°

Ratatouille Monterey
A meal in itself.

Preheat oven to 400°.

Fry bacon and onion in large skillet over medium heat, stirring often until cooked. Stir in tomato paste, salt, thyme, garlic and flour. Add tomatoes and their juice. Simmer tomato mixture until thickened. Lightly cover bottom of 9x13-inch baking dish with ½ cup of tomato mixture. Layer eggplant, zucchini and green pepper in dish. Spread tomato mixture on top. Cover with cheese. Bake at 400° for 50 minutes.

Scott's Parmesan Spinach
Rich but simple—good for brunch or dinner.

Preheat oven to 350°.

Squeeze spinach to remove all excess moisture. Place in large bowl; add remaining ingredients and mix thoroughly. Pour mixture into ungreased 9x13-inch baking dish. Bake at 350° for 15–20 minutes. Garnish with lemon twists.

Note: May be made a day in advance and baked prior to serving. Freezes well.

8	(10-ounce) packages frozen chopped spinach, cooked and drained
1	cup freshly grated Parmesan cheese
1	cup freshly grated Romano cheese
⅔	cup chopped onion
⅔	cup heavy (whipping) cream
½	cup (1 stick) butter, melted
½	teaspoon salt
	Lemon twists (optional)

Serves:	12–14
Preparation:	20 minutes
Baking:	20 minutes
Temperature:	350°

Squash Soufflé
The combination complements the squash nicely.

Preheat oven to 350°.

Place squash and onion in medium-size saucepan. Add salt and enough water to partially cover vegetables. Bring to a boil and cook until tender, about 15 minutes. Drain and cool. Place in large mixing bowl. Add eggs and pimiento. Mix well. Pour into ungreased 1½-quart baking dish. Sprinkle with cheese. Top with cracker crumbs. Dot with butter and sprinkle with paprika and pepper. Bake at 350° for 20 minutes or until heated.

2	pounds small yellow squash, peeled and sliced
3	tablespoons chopped onion
½	teaspoon salt
2	eggs, beaten
2	tablespoons chopped pimiento (optional)
¼	pound sharp Cheddar cheese, grated
¾	cup Ritz cracker crumbs
2	tablespoons butter
	Paprika
	Freshly ground pepper

Serves:	6–8
Preparation:	20 minutes
Baking:	20 minutes
Temperature:	350°

Vegetables

- 2 medium-size zucchini, cut into ½-inch thick rounds
- 3 tablespoons butter
- 3 tablespoons all-purpose flour
- 3 large tomatoes, chopped
- 1 small green pepper, seeded and chopped
- 1 small onion, chopped
- 1 teaspoon salt
- 1 tablespoon firmly packed brown sugar
- ½ bay leaf
- 2 cloves
- ½ cup dry bread crumbs
- ¼ cup freshly grated Parmesan cheese

Serves: 6
Preparation: 10 minutes
Cooking: 15 minutes
Baking: 30 minutes
Temperature: 350°

- 2½ pounds zucchini
- Salt
- ½ cup (1 stick) butter, softened
- ½ cup heavy (whipping) cream, barely warmed
- Freshly ground pepper
- Freshly grated nutmeg
- 1¼ cups freshly grated Parmesan cheese

Serves: 8
Preparation: 20 minutes

Zucchini Creole

A delicious way to prepare garden produce.

Preheat oven to 350°.

Grease a 2-quart baking dish.

Place zucchini in medium-size saucepan. Add water to partially cover zucchini. Bring to a boil and cook until tender, about 6–8 minutes. Drain and place in prepared baking dish.

Melt butter over medium heat in medium-size saucepan. Add flour; stir until smooth and bubbly. Add tomatoes, green pepper, onion, salt, brown sugar, bay leaf and cloves. Cook for 5 minutes. Remove cloves and bay leaf. Pour mixture on top of zucchini. Top with bread crumbs and cheese. Bake, uncovered, at 350° for 30 minutes.

Zucchini Alfredo

Like fettucini—more delicate and equally spectacular.

Cut zucchini lengthwise into ⅛-inch wide slices. Cut each slice into long spaghetti-like strands, about ⅛-inch wide. (At this point zucchini may be covered with plastic wrap and refrigerated. Bring to room temperature 1–2 hours before cooking.)

Bring 8–10 quarts water to a boil in a large kettle or Dutch oven; add dash of salt. Add zucchini slowly to water so water continues to boil. Cook until crisp tender, about 2 minutes. Drain well in colander. Place in serving bowl and toss immediately with butter. Sprinkle pepper and nutmeg into the cream; add cream to hot zucchini. Toss lightly. Add cheese and toss gently to coat. Serve immediately.

Stuffed Zucchini
Unique taste and look as though you spent hours preparing them.

Preheat oven to 350°.

Trim ends from zucchini; cut in half lengthwise. Place in large saucepan. Cover with water. Add 1 teaspoon salt and bring to a boil. Boil for 5 minutes. Drain. Hollow out inside of each zucchini half and discard pulp.

Beat egg in medium-size mixing bowl. Stir in feta, garlic, pepper, nutmeg and spinach. Fill zucchini halves with mixture. Place in shallow baking dish. Sprinkle with Parmesan. Cover with foil. Bake at 350° for 20 minutes. Remove foil and bake another 10–15 minutes.

- 3 medium-size zucchini
- 1 teaspoon salt
- 1 egg
- ½ cup crumbled feta cheese
- 1 clove garlic, minced
- ⅛ teaspoon ground pepper
- ⅛ teaspoon ground nutmeg
- 1 pound fresh spinach, chopped
- ½ cup freshly grated Parmesan cheese

Serves: 6
Preparation: 15 minutes
Cooking: 10 minutes
Baking: 30 minutes
Temperature: 350°

Vegetable Delight
Rich flavor and texture enhance this interesting combination.

Melt butter over low heat in a heavy saucepan. Stir in flour, salt and pepper. Cook over low heat, stirring until mixture is smooth and bubbly. Remove from heat. Stir in milk. Return to heat and slowly bring to a boil; stir constantly. Boil for 1 minute. Add mustard and cheese. Stir until cheese is melted. Add artichoke hearts, peas and water chestnuts. Cook until mixture is heated, about 5 minutes.

Note: Other vegetable combinations may be used.

Serving Suggestion: Use to fill the center of Spinach Noodle Ring and serve with pork tenderloin.

- 2 tablespoons butter
- 2 tablespoons all-purpose flour
- ¼ teaspoon salt
- ⅛ teaspoon pepper
- 1 cup milk
- ¼ teaspoon dry mustard (optional)
- ½ cup grated Cheddar cheese (more, if desired)
- 1 (14-ounce) can artichoke hearts, drained and quartered
- 1 (10-ounce) package frozen peas, thawed
- 1 (8-ounce) can water chestnuts, sliced

Serves: 4–6
Preparation: 15 minutes
Cooking: 5 minutes

Vegetables

Hearty Vegetable Stew
Nutritious vegetarian main dish.

Combine all ingredients except nuts in large saucepan or Dutch oven. Bring to a boil over high heat. Reduce heat, cover and simmer for 1 hour. Sprinkle with nuts and serve.

- 2 (16-ounce) cans tomatoes, cut-up
- 1 (15½-ounce) can red kidney beans
- 1 (15-ounce) can Great Northern beans
- 1 (15-ounce) can garbanzo beans
- 3 medium onions, chopped (about 1½ cups)
- 1 medium zucchini, halved lengthwise and sliced
- ½ cup water
- 2 cloves garlic, minced
- 2 teaspoons chili powder
- ½ teaspoons dried basil, crushed
- ¼ teaspoon pepper
- 1 bay leaf
- 1 cup cashews (optional)

Serves: 8
Preparation: 10 minutes
Cooking: 1 hour

Vegetables 3-Way
Quick and especially tasty.

Cut zucchini in half lengthwise. Cut each half into 1-inch slices.

Melt butter in large skillet over medium-high heat. Add mushrooms, onion and zucchini; sauté until tender. Drain excess liquid. Reduce heat to low. Add sour cream and pepper. Heat until warm. *Do not boil.*

- 1 medium-size zucchini
- 3 tablespoons butter
- 1 pound fresh mushrooms, quartered
- 1 medium onion, sliced
- 1 cup sour cream
- Freshly ground pepper

Serves: 6
Preparation: 15 minutes

Breads

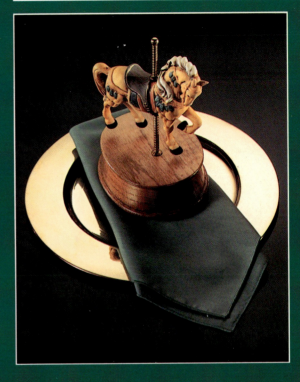

The Children's Museum of Indianapolis

Imagine a three-ring circus with no admission charges, open on an almost daily basis, 52 weeks of every year. Indianapolis's magical and magnificent Children's Museum, the largest facility of its type in the world, attracts more than a million delighted visitors annually.

Both the young and the young-at-heart find fulfillment for their childhood fancies in this unique collection of entrancing treasures. Museum visitors can ride the vividly painted, handcarved horses decorating a turn-of-the-century carousel or view firsthand, the rustic interior of an authentic pioneer log cabin. They can explore the twisting passageways of an Indiana limestone cave or clamber aboard a nineteenth-century railroad locomotive. A whole new world of scientific fact and enchanting fantasy is there for the taking.

The Museum's exhibits invite "hands-on" participation. In its Physical Science Gallery, both children and adults enjoy activating pulleys, lights, buzzers and bells, experiencing for themselves the marvels and realities of science. In the Natural Science Hall, fascinated youngsters may hold and stroke live animals from the Museum's diverse menagerie. The Playscape Gallery offers a tactile introduction to exhibits for preschoolers. Tots may try on nineteenth-century clothing, make brass rubbings from objects in the Museum's collection, or play happily and messily at sand and water tables.

Museum visitors can look up to the 9½-foot height of a 12,500-year-old mastodon skeleton or look down to live stage performances in the tiered Lilly Theater. They may delve into the world of American Indians by examining a variety of intricate Indian crafts or shiver deliciously over the wrapped remains of an ancient Egyptian mummy.

An award winner from the day it opened, the Indianapolis Children's Museum cites as its only admission costs, "an interest in the past, an enjoyment of the present, and a curiosity about the future."

BREADS

Yeast Breads
Dilly Casserole Bread . . . 239
Elephant Ears . . . 238
Fennel Breadsticks . . . 239
French Baguettes . . . 235
Honey Whole Wheat Bread . . . 234
Hoosier Fried Biscuits . . . 238
J.B.'s Famous Butterhorns . . . 236
Medieval Parsley Bread . . . 233
Petal Bread . . . 237
Quick Yeast Muffins . . . 237

Toasts
Celery Rolls in a Loaf . . . 240
Herbed Toasted Pita Bread . . . 240
Sesame Herb Toast . . . 241

Quick Breads
Almond Crumb Loaf . . . 244
Apple Butter Bread . . . 244
Banana Bread . . . 245
Basic Popovers . . . 242
Best Ever Corn Bread . . . 242
Blueberry Bread . . . 243
Grandma's Bread and Butter Pudding . . . 241
Lemon Bread . . . 245
Orange and Date Bread . . . 246
Pumpkin Tea Muffins . . . 246

Breakfast Breads
Apple Cream Coffee Cake . . . 250
Blueberry Coffee Cake . . . 252
Cherry Coffee Cake . . . 254
Coffee Cake Supreme . . . 253
Cupfins . . . 248
Little Apple Sauce Muffins . . . 248
Monkey Bread . . . 250
Heath Coffee Cake . . . 253
Orange Crunch Muffins . . . 247
Ring-a-Lings . . . 249
Zuchinni Coffee Cake . . . 251

Pancakes
Batter Fried French Toast . . . 256
French Toast Pockets . . . 256
Grandma's Buttermilk Pancakes . . . 255
Great Day Pancakes . . . 255
Hard Scramble Pancakes . . . 254

Medieval Parsley Bread
Delightfully subtle herb flavor.

Sprinkle yeast on ½ cup of the warm water. Mix in honey. Let stand for 5 minutes. Add remaining warm water. Beat in about 2½–3 cups of flour. Beat with wooden spoon for about 200 strokes. Cover with a damp towel and put in warm place. Allow this mixture to rise for 30–40 minutes or until doubled.

Stir down.

Beat 5 of the whole eggs plus the yolk. Stir in currants. Beat in salt and butter. Mix into batter.

Crush rosemary, basil and chopped parsley to a paste. Mix in cinnamon. Add to batter and beat well. Add remaining flour, first with spoon, then with hands until dough comes away from sides of bowl. Turn out onto lightly floured board or marble and knead until smooth, shiny and elastic, about 10–12 minutes. Add small amounts of flour, if necessary.

Place dough in buttered bowl. Turn to coat all sides with butter. Cover with damp towel. Let rise in warm place until doubled in bulk, about 1 hour. Punch down. Cover and let rise again until doubled in bulk, about 30 minutes. Punch down again. Turn out onto floured surface. Let rest for 5 minutes.

Preheat oven to 375°.

Butter a cookie sheet. Shape dough into 2 free-form curls or twists. Place on prepared cookie sheet. Cover lightly with damp towel and let rise in warm place to double, about 25 minutes. Beat remaining whole egg and brush tops of loaves.

Bake for 50 minutes or until nicely browned and loaves sound hollow when tapped on top and bottom. Cool on rack.

Serving Suggestion: Serve with hard cheese, butter and white wine.

- 2 packages active dry yeast
- 1¾ cups warm water, divided
- 6 tablespoons honey
- 7–8 cups (or more) unbleached flour, divided
- 6 small whole eggs
- 1 egg yolk
- ⅔ cup currants, softened in warm water and drained
- 1⅔ tablespoons coarse salt (may substitute table salt)
- 6 tablespoons butter, melted (may substitute vegetable shortening)
- 1½ teaspoons dried rosemary
- 1½ teaspoons dried basil
- ⅔ cup finely chopped fresh parsley
- 1½ teaspoons ground cinnamon

Yield:	2 loaves
Preparation:	40 minutes
Rising:	2 hours, 40 minutes
Baking:	50 minutes
Temperature:	375°

Honey Whole Wheat Bread
Nourishing and flavorful.

- 1 cup milk
- ¾ cup vegetable shortening
- ½ cup honey
- 2 teaspoons salt
- 2 packages dry yeast
- ¾ cup warm water
- 3 eggs, slightly beaten
- 4½ cups all-purpose flour (approximately)
- 1½ cups whole wheat flour
- Butter

Yield: 2 loaves
Preparation: 25 minutes
Rising: 2 hours
Baking: 40 minutes
Temperature: 375°

This recipe requires the use of a stationary electric mixer.

Scald milk in small saucepan. Remove from heat. Add shortening, honey and salt. Stir until shortening is melted. Cool to lukewarm.

Sprinkle yeast over warm water in large bowl. Stir until yeast is dissolved. Add milk mixture and eggs.

Combine all-purpose and whole wheat flour. Add ⅔ of flour mixture to yeast mixture and beat with an electric mixer at low speed for 2 minutes or until smooth. Add remaining flour gradually, using greased hands to work it in after mixture is too thick for mixer. Knead on floured surface until dough is smooth and elastic. Add more flour in small amounts, if needed. Place dough in greased bowl. Turn to coat all sides of dough with grease. Cover loosely with plastic wrap. Let rise in warm place until double, about 1 hour.

Grease 2 (9x5-inch) loaf pans.

Punch down dough. Shape dough into 2 loaves, folding ends under. Place in prepared loaf pans. Cover each loaf pan loosely with plastic wrap. Let rise in warm place until double, about 1 hour. Dough should rise above rim of pans.

Preheat oven to 375°.

Bake at 375° for 30–40 minutes or until bottoms sound hollow when thumped. Remove loaves from pans. Let cool on rack. Brush tops with butter while warm. Allow to cool before slicing.

French Baguettes

A recipe designed for experienced breadmakers.

This recipe requires the use of a large stationary mixer or food processsor.

Sprinkle yeast over water in medium-size mixing bowl. Stir to dissolve. Let stand 5 minutes. Add 1–2 cups flour. Beat with electric mixer at high speed for 10 minutes. Dough will thicken and be smooth. Beat in dissolved salt. Add remaining flour, ¼ cup at a time if using a dough hook, or ½ cup at a time if mixing by hand. Knead 5 minutes with dough hook or 8 minutes by hand, occasionally throwing down against kneading surface. Dough will be velvety and soft. Place in large, greased bowl. Turn to coat all sides of dough with grease. Cover loosely with plastic wrap and let rise at room temperature for 2 hours. Dough will double and may triple in volume.

Punch down dough. Knead 2–3 minutes and return to bowl. Cover and let rise at room temperature for 1 hour and 30 minutes. Dough will again double or triple in volume.

Grease 2 baguette pans or 1 baking sheet.

Divide dough into 2 equal pieces. Let rest for 5 minutes. Roll each piece under palms into loaves 15–20 inches long. Place in prepared pans or on baking sheet. Use patience while shaping as this dough is resilient and requires gentle persuasion. Cover and let rise at room temperature 1 hour.

Place broiler pan on lowest rack of oven. Preheat oven to 450°. Pour 1 cup of water into broiler pan after oven is preheated. Take care to avoid hot steam. Let stand 5 minutes. Make shallow diagonal cuts down length of each loaf with razor blade or sharp knife. Place loaves on top shelf of oven. Bake at 450° for 25–30 minutes or until bread is golden and bottoms of loaves sound hollow when thumped. Remove from pans and cool on rack.

1 package dry yeast
1¼ cups cool water (70°–75°)
3 cups bread flour (approximately), divided
1 teaspoon salt, dissolved in 1 teaspoon water

Yield:	2 loaves
Preparation:	15 minutes
Rising:	4 hours, 30 minutes
Baking:	30 minutes
Temperature:	450°

J.B.'s Famous Butterhorns

These award-winners become even flakier after freezing.

- 1 cake yeast (do not substitute dry)
- 2 teaspoons granulated sugar
- 1½ cups milk
- 1 cup (2 sticks) butter (do not substitute margarine)
- ½ cup granulated sugar
- 1 teaspoon salt
- 3 eggs
- 5½ cups all-purpose flour, sifted
- 8 tablespoons (1 stick) butter, softened

Yield:	32 rolls
Preparation:	20 minutes
Rising:	Overnight plus 2 hours
Baking:	15 minutes
Temperature:	375°

Crumble yeast cake. Mix with 2 teaspoons sugar and set aside.

Scald milk.

Place 1 cup butter, ½ cup sugar and salt in large bowl. Add hot milk and stir until butter is melted. Add eggs, 1 at a time, beating well after each addition. Add yeast mixture. Add 3 cups flour and mix well. Add remaining flour gradually, beating well after each addition. Dough will be sticky. Cover bowl with plastic wrap and let rise in warm place until double in bulk. Punch down. Cover and refrigerate overnight.

Grease a baking sheet.

Punch down dough and divide into 4 equal parts. Work with one part at a time, refrigerating remaining parts until ready for use. Roll into 12-inch circle on floured surface. Spread with 2 tablespoons softened butter. Cut into 8 wedges as though a pie. Roll each wedge from wide end to point. Curve into crescent shape and place on prepared baking sheet. Cover loosely with plastic wrap and let rise at room temperature for 2 hours.

Preheat oven to 375°.

Bake at 375° for about 15 minutes or until golden.

Note: Dough will keep in refrigerator for 2 weeks. Make fresh batches of butterhorns, as desired.

Variation: For Cloverleaf Rolls, make 1-inch balls of dough. Drop 3 balls into greased muffin tin cups. Let dough rise until double. Bake at 375° for 10–15 minutes.

Petal Bread
Great for fondue dipping.

Sprinkle yeast over warm water in large bowl. Let stand 5 minutes. Stir. Add egg, butter, sugar, salt and 1 cup flour. Beat with electric mixer at medium speed for 2 minutes. Stir in remaining flour with spoon. Cover with damp towel and let rise in a warm place for 45 minutes or until double.

Punch down and roll out on floured surface until dough is ¼ inch thick. Cut pieces with a diamond shape cookie cutter and dip in melted butter. Use all the dough by re-rolling scraps. Layer diamonds in bundt or tube pan, arranging in various directions to form the "petals." Cover and let rise in warm place for 30 minutes.

Preheat oven to 400°.

Bake at 400° for 25 minutes or until light brown. Cool slightly. Invert pan to remove bread. Individual pieces can be pulled off.

- 1 package dry yeast
- 1 cup warm water
- 1 egg
- 2 tablespoons butter, softened
- 2 tablespoons granulated sugar
- 1 teaspoon salt
- 3¼ cups all-purpose flour, divided
- 4 tablespoons (½ stick) butter, melted

Yield:	1 loaf
Preparation:	30 minutes
Rising:	1 hour, 15 minutes
Baking:	25 minutes
Temperature:	400°

Quick Yeast Muffins
The yeast does not require time to rise.

Preheat oven to 350°.

Grease a muffin pan or pans.

Dissolve yeast in warm water and set aside.

Combine butter, sugar and egg. Beat well. Stir in yeast mixture. Gradually add flour, mixing well after each addition. (Mixture may be used immediately or stored in the refrigerator for up to 2 days in an airtight container.)

Fill muffin cups ⅔ full. Bake at 350° for 30 minutes.

- 1 package dry yeast
- 2 cups warm water
- ¾ cup butter, melted
- ¼ cup granulated sugar
- 1 egg
- 4 cups self-rising flour

Yield:	24 muffins
Preparation:	10 minutes
Baking:	30 minutes
Temperature:	350°

Breads

1 package dry yeast
3 tablespoons warm water
3 tablespoons vegetable shortening, melted
1 cup lukewarm milk
3 tablespoons granulated sugar
2 teaspoons salt
3¼ cups all-purpose flour (approximately)
1 quart vegetable oil, for frying

Yield: 24 biscuits
Preparation: 10 minutes
Rising: 1 hour
Frying: 10–15 minutes

Hoosier Fried Biscuits
Heavenly with butter and apple butter.

Dissolve yeast in warm water in large bowl. Stir in shortening. Add milk, sugar and salt. Add flour gradually to make a stiff dough. Knead on floured surface until dough is mixed and smooth. Place in a greased bowl. Turn to coat all sides of dough with grease. Cover with damp towel and let rise until double, about 1 hour.

Punch down. Flour hands. Pinch off walnut-size pieces of dough. Stretch and pat into a biscuit shape.

Heat oil in 2-quart saucepan or deep fat fryer to 375°. Drop into hot oil and fry until golden on one side. Turn and fry on other side. Drain on paper towels. Serve hot.

Note: Dough keeps well in refrigerator for 3–4 days.

---

1 cup milk
1 cup water
3 tablespoons granulated sugar
3 tablespoons vegetable shortening
1 tablespoon (3 teaspoons) salt
1 package dry yeast
6 cups all-purpose flour
1 quart vegetable oil, for frying
½ cup granulated sugar
1 teaspoon ground cinnamon

Yield: 24 pieces
Preparation: 30 minutes
Rising: 1 hour
Frying: 45 minutes

Elephant Ears
A State Fair classic.

Combine milk, water, sugar, shortening and salt in a small saucepan. Heat, but do not boil. Cool to lukewarm. Pour into large mixing bowl. Add yeast; stir to dissolve. Stir in flour (2 cups at a time), beating until smooth after each addition. Knead dough 8–10 minutes or until smooth and elastic. Place in greased bowl. Turn to coat all sides of dough with grease. Cover with damp towel and let rise in a warm place until double, about 1 hour.

Combine sugar and cinnamon; set aside.

Pinch off golf-ball-size pieces of dough and roll out into 6–8 inch circles. Heat oil in large skillet to 375°. Fry 3–5 minutes per side. Drain on paper towels. Sprinkle with reserved sugar mixture while still warm.

Dilly Casserole Bread
Easy bread with a delicate flavor.

Grease 2-quart baking dish.

Sprinkle yeast over warm water and let stand for 5 minutes.

Heat cottage cheese to lukewarm. Combine yeast, cottage cheese, sugar, onion, dill seed, salt, egg, baking soda and butter; mix well. Gradually add enough flour to form a stiff dough which is no longer sticky. Place in prepared baking dish. Cover loosely with plastic wrap and let rise in a warm place until double in bulk, about 1 hour.

Preheat oven to 350°.

Bake at 350° for 50–60 minutes. Slice in wedges to serve.

- 1 package dry yeast
- ¼ cup warm water
- 1 cup small curd, cream-style cottage cheese
- 2 tablespoons granulated sugar
- 1 tablespoon instant minced onion
- 2 teaspoons dill seed
- 1 teaspoon salt
- 1 egg, slightly beaten
- ¼ teaspoon baking soda
- 1 tablespoon butter, softened
- 2½ cups all-purpose flour, unsifted

Serves:	6–8
Preparation:	10 minutes
Rising:	1 hour
Baking:	1 hour
Temperature:	350°

Fennel Breadsticks
Nice accompaniment to soups and pasta.

Sprinkle yeast over water in large bowl. Let stand for about 5 minutes. Add beer, oil, fennel seed and salt; mix well. Beat in 2 cups flour. Turn out dough onto a floured surface and knead until smooth and elastic, about 7 minutes. Add more flour while kneading if dough is sticky. Place dough in greased bowl. Turn to coat all sides of dough with grease. Cover with plastic wrap. Let rise in warm place until double in bulk, about 30–45 minutes.

Preheat oven to 325°

Line a baking sheet with foil. Generously butter foil.

Punch down dough. Knead 4–5 times. Divide dough into 12 equal pieces. Roll each piece into a 9-inch long stick or snake. Arrange on prepared baking sheet. Brush each stick with egg mixture. Sprinkle with coarse salt, if desired.

Bake at 325° for 35 minutes or until evenly brown. Serve warm or at room temperature.

- 1 teaspoon dry yeast
- ¼ cup warm water
- ½ cup beer, at room temperature
- 6 tablespoons olive oil
- 2 teaspoons fennel seed
- ¾ teaspoon salt
- 2–2½ cups all-purpose flour
- 1 egg beaten with 1 tablespoon water
- Coarse salt (optional)

Yield:	12 breadsticks
Preparation:	25 minutes
Rising:	30 minutes
Baking:	35 minutes
Temperature:	325°

Celery Rolls in a Loaf
Pluck and enjoy!

1 small loaf unsliced white bread
½ cup (1 stick) butter, softened (do not substitute margarine)
1 teaspoon celery seed
¼ teaspoon salt
¼ teaspoon paprika
Dash cayenne pepper

Serves: 6
Preparation: 5 minutes
Chilling: 24 hours
Baking: 15 minutes
Temperature: 400°

Trim crust from all sides of loaf. Slice center of loaf lengthwise, almost to bottom crust. Make 5 cuts across width and almost to bottom crust so that loaf is divided into 6 equal widths, creating 12 equal sections.

Combine butter, celery seed, salt, paprika and cayenne in small bowl. Spread butter mixture on all inside cut surfaces. Seal in a plastic bag or wrap airtight in foil and refrigerate for at least 24 hours.

Preheat oven to 400°.

Remove loaf from bag or foil and place on baking sheet. Bake at 400° for 15 minutes or until brown. Serve hot.

Herbed Toasted Pita Bread
Casual or elegant—pita is perfect.

4–6 pita flat breads
2 tablespoons unsalted butter, softened
½ teaspoon dried basil
½ teaspoon dried thyme or rosemary
Juice of 1 lemon

Serves: 8
Preparation: 10 minutes
Baking: 5–7 minutes
Temperature: 400°

Preheat oven to 400°.

Split pitas in half carefully. Cut into quarters with sharp knife. Spread inside surface of each quarter with butter. Place on baking sheet, butter side up.

Crush basil and thyme in small bowl. Add lemon juice. Stir until combined. Drizzle over pita pieces. Toast at 400° until crisp on edges and bubbling, about 5 minutes. Serve hot.

Serving Suggestion: Good accompaniment to salad or soup.

Sesame Herb Toast
Versatile bread noon or night.

Preheat oven to 325°.

Slice loaf of bread into thin diagonal slices.

Combine remaining ingredients in small bowl. Spread butter mixture on each slice of bread. Place on cookie sheet, butter side up. Bake at 325° for 15 minutes or until crisp.

- 1 small loaf French bread
- ½ cup (1 stick) butter, softened
- 1 tablespoon chopped fresh chives
- ¼ teaspoon dried basil
- ¼ teaspoon dried rosemary
- 1 tablespoon sesame seed

Serves: 6–8
Preparation: 10 minutes
Baking: 15 minutes
Temperature: 325°

Grandma's Bread and Butter Pudding
The best survive generations.

Preheat oven to 350°.

Generously grease an 8-inch square glass baking dish.

Spread each slice of bread with butter. Cut each slice into quarters. Arrange in staggered layers in prepared pan. Sprinkle lightly with paprika.

Combine eggs, milk, salt, mustard and pepper in large bowl. Mix thoroughly. Stir in cheese. Pour over bread.

Bake at 350° for 30 minutes or until knife inserted in center comes out clean. Serve hot.

- 6 slices white bread, crusts removed (may substitute whole wheat bread)
- 2½ tablespoons butter, softened
- Paprika
- 4 eggs, slightly beaten
- 2½ cups milk
- 1 teaspoon salt
- 1 teaspoon dry mustard
- ¾ teaspoon white pepper
- 1¼ cups grated extra sharp Cheddar cheese

Serves: 6–8
Preparation: 15 minutes
Baking: 30 minutes
Temperature: 350°

Best Ever Corn Bread
Basic and wonderful companion to meals.

Shortening
- ⅓ cup all-purpose flour
- 1 tablespoon granulated sugar
- 1 teaspoon baking powder
- ½ teaspoon baking soda
- ½ teaspoon salt
- 1⅓ cups corn meal
- 1 egg, slightly beaten
- 1 cup sour cream
- 2 tablespoons oil

Serves: 6–8
Preparation: 15 minutes
Baking: 25 minutes
Temperature: 400°

Preheat oven to 400°.

Place 8-inch square baking pan in oven and when heated, grease generously with shortening.

Sift together flour, sugar, baking powder, baking soda and salt in medium-size bowl. Stir in corn meal.

Combine egg, sour cream and oil in small bowl. Add to dry ingredients, mixing just until moistened. Pour into prepared pan.

Bake at 400° for 20–25 minutes or until bread springs back when lightly touched. Serve hot with butter.

Basic Popovers
These are good filled with creamed chicken.

- 1 cup all-purpose flour
- ¼ teaspoon salt
- 1 cup skim or 2% milk
- 3 large eggs
- 6 tablespoons shortening, divided
- Butter

Yield: 12 popovers
Preparation: 8 minutes
Baking: 45 minutes
Temperature: 375°

Preheat oven to 375°.

Combine flour and salt in medium-size bowl. Stir in milk. Beat in eggs until batter is completely blended.

Place 1½ teaspoons shortening in bottom of each of 12 custard cups or large muffin tins. Place in oven and heat until shortening is melted and cups are hot. Fill each cup ⅔ full with batter.

Bake at 375° for 45 minutes. *Do not open oven door while popovers are baking.* To do so will prevent them from "popping."

Serve hot with butter.

Blueberry Bread
Moist and yummy.

Preheat oven to 325°.

Grease 2 (9x5-inch) loaf pans.

Sprinkle blueberries with 2 tablespoons flour. Toss gently; set aside.

Place boiling water in large bowl. Add butter; stir until melted. Add orange juice, eggs and sugar. Mix well. Stir in remaining flour, baking powder, baking soda and salt. Fold in blueberries. Pour into prepared loaf pans.

Combine sugar, flour and cinnamon. Cut in butter until mixture is crumbly. Sprinkle over batter in loaf pan.

Bake at 325° for 1 hour or until pick inserted in center comes out clean. Cool for 10 minutes, then remove from pan.

Bread:
- 2 cups blueberries, drained well (may substitute frozen blueberries, unthawed)
- 4 cups all-purpose flour, divided
- ½ cup boiling water
- 4 tablespoons (½ stick) butter
- 1 cup fresh orange juice
- 2 eggs, slightly beaten
- 2 cups granulated sugar
- 2 teaspoons baking powder
- ½ teaspoon baking soda
- ½ teaspoon salt

Topping:
- 4 tablespoons granulated sugar
- 4 tablespoons all-purpose flour
- 2 teaspoons ground cinnamon
- 4 tablespoons (½ stick) butter, chilled

Yield:	2 loaves
Preparation:	20 minutes
Baking:	1 hour
Cooling:	10 minutes
Temperature:	325°

Apple Butter Bread
Rich and moist.

Preheat oven to 350°.

Grease and flour a 9x5-inch loaf pan.

Combine flour, sugar and cinnamon in medium-size bowl. Set aside.

Combine eggs, butter, apple butter and milk in large bowl. Beat well. Stir in pecans and raisins. Add flour mixture. Stir just to moisten. Pour batter into loaf pan. Bake at 350° for 1 hour and 5 minutes or until pick inserted in center comes out clean. Cool in pan 10 minutes. Remove from pan and place on rack. Cool completely before slicing.

- 2 cups self-rising flour
- 1 cup granulated sugar
- 1½ teaspoons ground cinnamon
- 2 eggs
- 1 cup (2 sticks) butter, melted
- ¾ cup apple butter
- 2 tablespoons milk
- ½ cup chopped pecans
- ½ cup golden raisins

Yield:	1 loaf
Preparation:	10 minutes
Baking:	1 hour, 5 minutes
Cooling:	10 minutes
Temperature:	350°

Almond Crumb Loaf
Crunchy and spicy.

Preheat oven to 350°.

Generously grease a 9x5-inch loaf pan. Line bottom and sides of pan with a single piece of wax paper, allowing 2 inch overhang of paper at top.

Sift flour, sugar, baking powder and salt into large bowl. Cut in butter until mixture resembles coarse meal.

Transfer ½ cup of flour mixture to medium-size bowl. Add almonds, cinnamon and allspice. Mix until well combined.

Stir eggs, milk, vanilla and almond extract into remaining mixture. Beat until well combined.

Pour about 1 cup of batter into prepared pan. Sprinkle with ⅓ of nut mixture. Repeat twice, ending with nut mixture. Bake at 350° until pick inserted in center comes out clean, about 1 hour and 15–20 minutes. Let cool in pan on rack for 15 minutes.

Loosen loaf from sides of pan with wide spatula. Grasp wax paper and carefully lift loaf from pan. Transfer to rack, discard wax paper and cool.

- 2 cups all-purpose flour
- 1¼ cups granulated sugar
- 2 teaspoons baking powder
- ¼ teaspoon salt
- ⅔ cup butter
- ½ cup chopped, slivered almonds
- ¾ teaspoon ground cinnamon
- ¼ teaspoon ground allspice
- 2 eggs
- ¾ cup milk
- 1 teaspoon vanilla
- 1 teaspoon almond extract

Serves:	8–12
Preparation:	15 minutes
Baking:	1 hour, 20 minutes
Cooling:	15 minutes
Temperature:	350°

Banana Bread
Tried and true.

Preheat oven to 350°.

Grease 9x5-inch loaf pan.

Beat together butter and sugar. Add eggs; mix well. Add sour cream, flour, baking soda, vanilla and bananas; mix well. Pour into prepared loaf pan. Bake at 350° for 45 minutes or until toothpick inserted in center comes out clean.

- ½ cup (1 stick) butter, softened
- 1¼ cups granulated sugar
- 2 eggs, beaten
- 4 tablespoons sour cream
- 1½ cups all-purpose flour, unsifted
- 1 teaspoon baking soda
- 1 teaspoon vanilla
- 1 cup mashed bananas (about 2 medium bananas)

Yield:	1 loaf
Preparation:	10 minutes
Baking:	45 minutes
Temperature:	350°

Lemon Bread
Light and delicious.

Preheat oven to 300°.

Grease 2 (9x5-inch) loaf pans.

Squeeze juice from lemons and set aside for use in making icing.

Grate lemon rind into large bowl. Add sugar and oil, mixing well. Add eggs, 1 at a time, beating well after each addition. Add flour (1⅔ cups less 2 tablespoons), salt and baking powder; mix well. Toss nuts with reserved flour and add to mixture. Pour into prepared loaf pans. Bake at 300° for 1 hour.

Combine confectioners' sugar and reserved juice to make icing. Mixture will be very thin.

Poke several holes in bread with ice pick or similar utensil. Pour icing over loaves while they are still warm.

- 2 lemons
- 1½ cups granulated sugar
- 1 cup salad oil
- 6 eggs
- 1⅔ cups all-purpose flour, reserve 2 tablespoons
- Pinch salt
- 2 teaspoons baking powder
- 1 cup chopped nuts

Icing:
- 2 cups confectioners' sugar
- Reserved lemon juice

Yield:	2 loaves
Preparation:	15 minutes
Baking:	1 hour
Temperature:	300°

Orange and Date Bread

Wrapped in foil, this will keep in refrigerator for several weeks.

Preheat oven to 375°.

Grease and flour a 9x5-inch loaf pan.

Beat together butter and sugar in large bowl. Add eggs, orange rind and dates. Sift together flour and baking soda. Add to butter mixture alternately with buttermilk. Pour into prepared loaf pan. Bake at 375° for 45 minutes.

Combine orange juice, sugar and orange rind in small saucepan. Heat just to boiling point. Pour over bread. Leave in pan until cool.

Bread:
- ½ cup (1 stick) butter, softened
- 1 cup granulated sugar
- 2 eggs
- 1 tablespoon freshly grated orange rind
- 1 cup chopped dates
- 2 cups all-purpose flour
- 1 teaspoon baking soda
- ⅔ cup buttermilk

Glaze:
- ½ cup fresh orange juice
- ½ cup granulated sugar
- 1 tablespoon freshly grated orange rind

Yield:	1 loaf
Preparation:	20 minutes
Baking:	45 minutes
Temperature:	375°

Pumpkin Tea Muffins

A different luncheon bread.

Preheat oven to 350°.

Combine oil and sugar in a large bowl. Add pumpkin and eggs; mix well. Combine dry ingredients and sift into pumpkin mixture; mix well. Fill muffin tins ½ full. Bake at 350° for 15 minutes.

- 1 cup oil
- 3 cups granulated sugar
- 2 cups cooked pumpkin (do not use pie filling)
- 3 eggs, slightly beaten
- 3 cups all-purpose flour
- 1 teaspoon ground cinnamon
- 1 teaspoon ground nutmeg
- 1 teaspoon ground cloves
- 1 teaspoon baking powder
- 1 teaspoon baking soda
- 1 teaspoon salt

Yield:	24 muffins
Preparation:	10 minutes
Baking:	15 minutes
Temperature:	350°

Orange Crunch Muffins
You'll love these!

Preheat oven to 400°.

Grease muffin tin or use paper cupcake liners.

Stir together flour, granulated sugar, brown sugar, baking powder, salt and cinnamon in large bowl. Set aside.

Combine egg, oil, milk and orange rind in small bowl; mix well. Add all at once to dry ingredients, stirring just to moisten. Fill muffin tins ⅔ full with batter.

Mix topping ingredients until crumbly. Sprinkle over batter in tins. Bake at 400° for 20 minutes. Remove from pan. Combine icing ingredients. Drizzle over muffins.

Muffins:
- 1½ cups sifted all-purpose flour
- ¼ cup granulated sugar
- ¼ cup firmly packed brown sugar
- 2 teaspoons baking powder
- ½ teaspoon salt
- ½ teaspoon ground cinnamon
- 1 egg, slightly beaten
- ½ cup oil
- ½ cup milk
- 1 teaspoon freshly grated orange rind

Topping:
- ½ cup chopped nuts
- ½ cup firmly packed brown sugar
- ¼ cup all-purpose flour
- ¼ teaspoon ground cinnamon
- 2 tablespoons butter, at room temperature

Icing:
- ¾ cup sifted confectioners' sugar
- 1 tablespoon fresh orange juice
- ½ teaspoon vanilla

Yield:	12 muffins
Preparation:	20 minutes
Baking:	20 minutes
Temperature:	400°

Little Applesauce Muffins

You can't eat just one!

Preheat oven to 425°.

Grease 1 or more mini-muffin tins.

Beat together ½ cup butter and ½ cup sugar in large bowl. Beat in eggs, 1 at a time, until light and fluffy. Beat in applesauce.

Stir together flour, baking powder and salt. Add to butter mixture. Stir just to moisten. Fill prepared muffin tins ⅔ full. Bake at 425° for 15 minutes or until golden.

Combine remaining ½ cup sugar and cinnamon. Dip tops of warm muffins into melted butter and then into the cinnamon-sugar. Serve warm.

- ½ cup (1 stick) butter, softened
- 1 cup granulated sugar, divided
- 2 eggs
- ¾ cup applesauce
- 1¾ cups all-purpose flour
- 1 tablespoon baking powder
- ½ teaspoon salt
- ¼ teaspoon ground cinnamon
- 4 tablespoons (½ stick) butter, melted

Yield:	36 muffins
Preparation:	10 minutes
Baking:	15 minutes
Temperature:	425°

Cupfins

Spicy cupcakes.

Preheat oven to 350°.

Grease muffin tins.

Combine butter, nuts, applesauce and raisins in medium-size bowl. Stir in eggs. Set aside.

Combine flour, sugar, baking soda, cinnamon and nutmeg in large bowl. Add applesauce mixture. Stir just to moisten. Fill prepared muffin tins ½ full. Bake at 350° for 20 minutes.

- ½ cup (1 stick) butter, melted
- ½ cup chopped nuts
- 1½ cups applesauce
- ½ cup raisins
- 2 eggs, slightly beaten
- 2½ cups all-purpose flour
- 2 cups granulated sugar
- 1½ teaspoons baking soda
- 1 teaspoon ground cinnamon
- ½ teaspoon ground nutmeg

Yield:	24 muffins
Preparation:	10 minutes
Baking:	20 minutes
Temperature:	350°

Ring-a-Lings
Festive and so tasty.

Use 1 or 2 baking sheets.

Soften yeast in warm water; set aside.

Combine butter and scalded milk in large bowl. Stir until butter melts. Cool to lukewarm. Add sugar, salt, orange rind, eggs and the yeast mixture. Gradually add enough sifted flour to form a stiff dough. Mix thoroughly. Cover and let stand for 30 minutes.

Combine confectioners' sugar and filberts. Cut in butter.

Roll dough into a 22x12-inch rectangle. Spread nut filling on half of dough along 22-inch side. Fold uncovered dough over filling. Cut into 1-inch strips, starting at narrow end. Twist each strip 4 or 5 times. Hold one end down on baking sheet (for center of roll). Curl strip around center, tucking end under. Cover with a towel and let rise in a warm place for 45 minutes or until double in size.

Preheat oven to 375°.

Bake at 375° for 15 minutes.

Prepare glaze while rolls are baking. Combine orange juice and sugar. Brush tops of baked rolls with glaze and continue baking 5 minutes longer. Remove from baking sheet immediately.

Dough:
- 2 packages dry yeast
- ¼ cup warm water
- ⅓ cup butter
- ¾ cup scalded milk
- ⅓ cup granulated sugar
- 2 teaspoons salt
- 2 teaspoons freshly grated orange rind
- 2 eggs, slightly beaten
- 4–5 cups sifted all-purpose flour

Nut Filling:
- 1 cup sifted confectioners' sugar
- 1 cup finely chopped filberts
- ⅓ cup butter

Glaze:
- ¼ cup fresh orange juice
- 3 tablespoons granulated sugar

Yield:	12–18 rolls
Preparation:	45 minutes
Rising:	1 hour, 15 minutes
Baking:	20 minutes
Temperature:	375°

HINT:
Filberts are also known as hazelnuts.

250 Breads

- ½ cup coarsely chopped walnuts
- 2 teaspoons ground cinnamon
- 1½ cups granulated sugar, divided
- ½ cup (1 stick) margarine, softened
- 2 eggs
- 1 teaspoon vanilla
- 2 cups all-purpose flour
- 1 teaspoon baking soda
- ½ teaspoon salt
- 1 teaspoon baking powder
- 1 cup (8 ounces) sour cream
- 1 medium apple; pared, cored and thinly sliced

Serves:	10–12
Preparation:	20 minutes
Baking:	40 minutes
Cooling:	30 minutes
Temperature:	375°

Apple Cream Coffee Cake
Moist and delicious.

Preheat oven to 375°.

Grease a 9-inch tube pan with removable bottom.

Mix walnuts, cinnamon and ½ cup sugar in a small bowl. Set aside.

Beat margarine in large bowl until creamy. Add remaining 1 cup sugar gradually, beating until light and fluffy. Beat in eggs, 1 at a time, mixing well after each. Add vanilla.

Sift together flour, baking soda, salt and baking powder. Add sifted ingredients alternately with sour cream to butter mixture, beating after each addition. Spread ½ of batter in the pan. Top with apple slices. Sprinkle ½ of walnut mixture over apples. Spread remaining batter over all and top with remaining walnut mixture. Bake at 375° for 40 minutes.

Remove from oven and let stand in pan for 30 minutes. Remove from pan.

- 4 tubes refrigerator biscuits (10 biscuits per tube)
- 1¾ cups granulated sugar, divided
- 1 teaspoon ground cinnamon
- ½ cup chopped pecans (optional)
- ¾ cup (1½ sticks) butter
- 1½ teaspoons ground cinnamon

Serves:	12–16
Preparation:	20 minutes
Baking:	45 minutes
Temperature:	350°

Monkey Bread
Kids love to help make this.

Preheat oven to 350°.

Quarter each biscuit.

Combine ¾ cup sugar and cinnamon in a bag. Shake several biscuit pieces at a time in the sugar mixture. Distribute coated pieces evenly in a 12-cup bundt or angel food cake pan. Sprinkle with nuts, if desired.

Combine remaining 1 cup sugar, butter and cinnamon in a small saucepan. Bring to a boil. Pour syrup over biscuit pieces. Bake at 350° for 40–45 minutes. Turn out onto a plate. Serve warm.

Note: Recipe can be cut in half. Reduce baking time to about 30 minutes if using 12-cup pan.

Zucchini Coffee Cake
A great use for plentiful zucchini.

Preheat oven to 350°.

Lightly grease 1 (9x13-inch) or 2 (8-inch) square baking pans.

Combine flour, granulated sugar, brown sugar, baking soda, baking powder, salt, nutmeg, cinnamon and pecans in large bowl. Combine eggs, oil, vanilla and zucchini in another large bowl. Add to dry ingredients; mix well. Pour into prepared pan or pans.

Combine all topping ingredients in a small bowl. Sprinkle over batter in pan. Bake at 350° for 40 minutes.

- 2 cups all-purpose flour
- ¾ cup granulated sugar
- ¾ cup firmly packed brown sugar
- 2 teaspoons baking soda
- ½ teaspoon baking powder
- 1 teaspoon salt
- ¼ teaspoon ground nutmeg
- ¼ teaspoon ground cinnamon
- ¾ cup chopped pecans (use more or less, as desired)
- 3 eggs, slightly beaten
- 1 cup oil
- 1 tablespoon (3 teaspoons) vanilla
- 2 cups shredded zucchini (about 1 large)

Topping:
- ¼ cup firmly packed brown sugar
- ¼ cup chopped pecans
- ¼ teaspoon ground nutmeg
- ¼ teaspoon ground cinnamon

Serves: 18
Preparation: 10 minutes
Baking: 40 minutes
Temperature: 350°

Breads

Topping:
- ½ cup granulated sugar
- 1 teaspoon ground cinnamon
- 4 tablespoons (½ stick) butter
- ¼ cup chopped pecans (optional)

Cake:
- 2 cups all-purpose flour
- 1 teaspoon baking powder
- 1 teaspoon baking soda
- Dash of salt
- ½ cup (1 stick) margarine
- 1 cup granulated sugar
- 2 eggs
- 1 cup sour cream
- 1 teaspoon vanilla
- 2 cups fresh blueberries (may substitute frozen blueberries)

Serves:	8–10
Preparation:	40 minutes
Chilling:	30 minutes
Baking:	40 minutes
Temperature:	350°

Blueberry Coffee Cake

Prepare for the raves.

Combine sugar and cinnamon in small bowl. Cut in butter until mixture is crumbly. Refrigerate topping for 30 minutes.

Preheat oven to 350°.

Grease a 9x13-inch baking pan.

Sift together flour, baking powder, baking soda and salt. Set aside.

Beat together margarine and sugar in large bowl. Add eggs, sour cream and vanilla. Mix well. Add dry ingredients; mix well. Fold in blueberries. Pour into prepared pan. Sprinkle topping mixture over batter. Bake at 350° for 40–45 minutes.

Coffee Cake Supreme
A winner, indeed!

Preheat oven to 350°.

Extend height of center of large bundt pan or tube cake pan 2 to 3 inches with foil. Grease pan.

Combine butter and sugar in large bowl. Beat until creamy. Add eggs, 1 at a time, beating well after each addition. Add vanilla.

Sift together flour, baking powder and salt. Beat dry ingredients alternately with cream into butter mixture. Begin and end with dry ingredients.

Combine ingredients for filling in medium-size bowl.

Scatter ½ of the filling on bottom and sides of pan. Pour ½ the batter over filling. Sprinkle remaining filling over batter. Pour in remaining batter. Bake at 350° for 1 hour and 15 minutes or until pick inserted in cake comes out clean. Let stand 15 minutes before removing from pan. Remove from pan and place on rack to cool.

Heath Coffee Cake
A real taste treat.

Preheat oven to 350°.

Grease 2 (8-inch) round baking pans.

Mix together sugar, brown sugar, butter and flour in large bowl. Reserve ½ cup of mixture for topping.

Dissolve baking soda in buttermilk. Add buttermilk, egg and vanilla to sugar/flour mixture; mix well. Pour into prepared pans. Sprinkle first with reserved topping, then with crushed Heath candy bars. Sprinkle nuts over candy. Bake at 350° for 30–35 minutes.

Breads | 253

- 1 cup (2 sticks) butter, softened
- 1½ cups granulated sugar
- 6 extra large eggs
- 2 teaspoons vanilla
- 5 cups all-purpose flour
- 4½ teaspoons baking powder
- 1 teaspoon salt
- 1 pint heavy (whipping) cream

Filling:
- 2 cups confectioners' sugar, sifted
- 1½ cups chopped nuts
- 2 tablespoons ground cinnamon

Serves: 10–12
Preparation: 20 minutes
Baking: 1 hour, 15 minutes
Cooling: 15 minutes
Temperature: 350°

- 1 cup granulated sugar
- 1 cup firmly packed brown sugar
- ½ cup (1 stick) butter, softened
- 2 cups all-purpose flour
- 1 teaspoon baking soda
- 1 cup buttermilk
- 1 egg, slightly beaten
- 1 teaspoon vanilla
- 3 Heath candy bars, crushed
- ½ cup chopped nuts

Serves: 16
Preparation: 10 minutes
Baking: 35 minutes
Temperature: 350°

- ½ cup (1 stick) margarine, softened
- 1 cup granulated sugar
- 2 eggs
- 1 cup sour cream
- 2 cups all-purpose flour
- ½ teaspoon salt
- 1½ teaspoons baking powder
- ½ teaspoon baking soda
- 1 teaspoon vanilla
- 1 (21-ounce) can cherry-pie filling

Topping:
- ½ cup granulated sugar
- 1 teaspoon ground cinnamon
- ½ cup all-purpose flour
- ½ cup chopped pecans
- 2 tablespoons margarine

Serves:	12–16
Preparation:	20 minutes
Baking:	50 minutes
Temperature:	350°

- ¾ cup rolled oats
- 1½ cups buttermilk
- 1 extra large egg
- ½ cup all-purpose flour
- ¾ teaspoon salt
- ½ teaspoon baking soda
- 1 tablespoon granulated sugar
- Unsalted butter
- Syrup

Yield:	10–12 pancakes
Preparation:	25 minutes
Cooking:	5 minutes

Cherry Coffee Cake
Consistently rated as excellent.

Preheat oven to 350°.

Grease and flour a 9x13-inch baking pan.

Combine margarine and sugar in large bowl. Beat until creamy. Beat in eggs and sour cream.

Sift together flour, salt, baking powder and baking soda. Add gradually the sifted dry ingredients to creamed mixture. Beat after each addition. Add vanilla. Pour ½ of this mixture into the prepared pan. Spread with cherry-pie filling. Pour remaining ½ of mixture over pie filling.

Mix sugar, cinnamon, flour and pecans in a small bowl. Cut in margarine with two knives. Sprinkle over batter. Bake at 350° for 50 minutes or until toothpick inserted in center comes out clean.

Variation: May substitute other ready-made fruit pie fillings or an equal amount of homemade fruit pie filling.

Hard Scramble Pancakes
Deliciously different!

Soak oats in buttermilk in large bowl for 15–20 minutes. Add egg, flour, salt, baking soda and sugar to oats and beat with fork until blended.

Melt butter in large skillet or on griddle over medium-high heat. Spoon mixture onto hot skillet. Cook until bubbles form on top of pancake. Turn once and cook 60 seconds longer or until golden. Serve with syrup.

Variation: One cup chopped raw apple may be added to the batter before frying.

Great Day Pancakes
A great way to start the day.

Heat lightly greased griddle or skillet to medium-high.

Mix flour, cornmeal, bran flakes, salt, sugar and baking powder in large bowl. Set aside.

Stir baking soda into buttermilk in small bowl. Add eggs and butter. Add to dry mixture and mix well.

Pour 4-inch circles of batter into skillet. Turn when bubbles form on top. Fry for 2 more minutes or until golden. Serve with honey butter.

Blend confectioners' sugar, butter and honey using blender or food processor to make honey butter.

Pancakes:
- 1 cup all-purpose flour
- ½ cup corn meal
- 1 cup bran flakes
- ½ teaspoon salt
- 2 tablespoons granulated sugar
- 2½ teaspoons baking powder
- ½ teaspoon baking soda
- 1 cup buttermilk
- 4 eggs, well beaten
- 3 tablespoons butter, melted

Honey Butter:
- 1¼ cups confectioners' sugar
- ½ cup (1 stick) butter
- ½ cup honey

Serves: 6
Preparation: 5 minutes
Cooking: 15 minutes

Grandma's Buttermilk Pancakes
You will never use box mix again!

Beat egg slightly in medium-size bowl. Add salt and sugar. Stir in buttermilk.

Combine baking soda, baking powder and flour in small bowl. Add to buttermilk mixture. Stir in butter.

Heat griddle to medium-high. Grease lightly. Pour 4-inch circles of batter on griddle. When bubbles rise to surface and break, turn and continue cooking until golden brown.

Serve with favorite toppings.

Variation: Add anything that strikes your fancy to this basic batter: blueberries, chocolate chips, chopped nuts.

- 1 egg
- ½ teaspoon salt
- 1 tablespoon granulated sugar
- 1 cup buttermilk
- ½ teaspoon baking soda
- ½ rounded teaspoon baking powder
- 1 cup sifted all-purpose flour
- 3 tablespoons butter, melted

Serves: 2
Preparation: 5 minutes
Cooking: 15 minutes

Breads

- 1 (8-ounce) package cream cheese, softened
- 1½ teaspoons vanilla, divided
- ½ cup chopped walnuts (optional)
- 1 (16-ounce) loaf French bread
- 4 eggs
- 1 cup heavy (whipping) cream
- ¼ teaspoon ground nutmeg

Sauce:
- 1 (12-ounce) jar apricot preserves
- 2 tablespoons butter
- ½ cup fresh orange juice
- 1 tablespoon fresh lemon juice

Serves: 8–10
Preparation: 25 minutes
Cooking: 20 minutes

French Toast Pockets
What a treat!

Beat together cream cheese and 1 teaspoon vanilla. Stir in nuts and set aside.

Cut bread into 10–12 slices, 1½ inches thick. Using a sharp serrated knife, make a 2-inch deep cut across top crust of bread to form a pocket. Fill each pocket with 1½ tablespoons of the cream cheese mixture.

Preheat griddle or large skillet to medium high.

Beat together eggs, cream, ½ teaspoon vanilla and nutmeg in a large bowl. Dip the filled bread slices into the egg mixture. Remove with tongs and place on lightly greased, medium-hot griddle. Cook until golden brown on both sides.

Heat together preserves, butter, orange juice and lemon juice in a small saucepan. Drizzle sauce over the hot French toast to serve.

- 1 tablespoon butter, melted
- ¼ cup milk
- ¼ cup all-purpose flour
- 2 eggs, slightly beaten
- 1 teaspoon brandy
- ¼ teaspoon ground cinnamon
- ⅛ teaspoon salt
- ⅔ cup light (coffee) cream
- ⅓ cup oil
- 4 slices white bread, ¾ inch thick
- Maple syrup
- Confectioners' sugar

Serves: 2
Preparation: 5 minutes
Cooking: 10 minutes

Batter-Fried French Toast
A hint of brandy makes all the difference.

Mix together butter, milk, flour, eggs, brandy, cinnamon and salt in large bowl.

Pour light cream in another large bowl.

Heat oil in large skillet over medium-high heat.

Dip bread slices into cream, then into egg mixture. Place bread in skillet and fry on both sides until golden brown. Pour syrup over toast and sprinkle with confectioners' sugar.

Desserts

The Indianapolis Motor Speedway

"Gentlemen, start your engines!" With that time-honored command, an official of the Indianapolis Motor Speedway annually signals the opening of competition in the world's oldest and most celebrated automobile race.

Famous drivers from all parts of the globe vie intensely for entry to the Indianapolis 500, considered the most prestigious single contest of its type. Speedway enthusiasts proudly point out the race's excellent overall safety record and its significant contribution to the development of both technology and safety in the automobile industry.

A record-breaker in every sense of the word, the Indy 500 has achieved international recognition as the most-attended one-day sporting event held anywhere. Some 250,000 avid race fans attend the two weekends of preliminary qualifications, and 300,000 or more jam the track's infield and surrounding 559 acres on the day of the race, the May Sunday preceding Memorial Day.

An additional attraction for race fans is available on a twelve-month basis. The Hall of Fame Museum at the Indianapolis Motor Speedway presents one of the world's largest and most varied collections of racing, classic and antique passenger cars, including more than 25 Indianapolis 500 winning cars.

In early May of every year, "500 Fever" overtakes Indianapolis. The city erupts in a spate of black and white checkered regalia and on-and-off the media commentary. Banners fly from lightposts around Monument Circle and along our major avenues, visibly announcing the forthcoming race. Lavish dinners, parties and balls herald the occasion, and the spectacular 500 Festival Parade is broadcast on national television.

More than any other event or institution, the Indianapolis 500—"the greatest spectacle in racing"—symbolizes Indianapolis for both racing buffs and the uninitiated. Winning is the hub of this suspense-charged event, and winning becomes a palpable portion of the Indianapolis air in our very merry month of May.

DESSERTS

Cakes
Black Bottom Cupcakes . . . 264
Black Forest Cherry Torte . . . 262
Blitz Torte . . . 263
Gâteau Bête Noire (Black Beast Cake) . . . 260
L.S. Ayres Buttermilk Cake . . . 258
One Hundred Dollar Chocolate Cake . . . 259
Perfect Chocolate Cake . . . 257
Pumpkin Roll . . . 261
Raw Apple Cake . . . 264

Candy
Apricot Fingers . . . 265
Butterscotch Bon Bons . . . 265
English Butter Toffee . . . 266
Grandmother's Caramels . . . 266

Cheesecake
Bavarian Cheesecake . . . 267
Grasshopper Cheesecake . . . 269
Old Fashioned Cheesecake . . . 268
Pumpkin Cheesecake . . . 270

Cookies and Bars
A NO Chocolate Brownie . . . 276
Almond Butter Cookies . . . 271
Apricot Spice Bars . . . 280
Butter Pecan Turtle Cookies . . . 274
Chinese Chews . . . 274
Chocolate Pralines . . . 271
Chocolate Rum Brownies . . . 277
Cookie Chip Chocolates . . . 276
Crunch Rich Chocolate Chips . . . 275
Date Cookies . . . 273
Kahlúa Party Bars . . . 278
Peanut Butter Oatmeal Cookies . . . 275
Peppermint Cookies . . . 272
Refrigerator Mint Bars . . . 279
Russian Tea Cakes . . . 273

Desserts
Brandied Strawberry Fondue . . . 283
Champagne Sabayon . . . 280
Cherry Berry Delight . . . 287
Chocolate Dipped Strawberries . . . 281
Chocolate Mousse Cups . . . 282
Cinnamon Pudding . . . 289
Cranberry Pudding . . . 289
Crème Brulée (Burnt Cream) . . . 288
Cuban Blueberry Pudding . . . 288
Gateau Rolla (Layered Chocolate Meringue Cake) . . . 286
Kiwi Mousse . . . 283
Lemon Cups . . . 290
Poires au Cointreau . . . 282
Strawberry Meringue Croquembouche . . . 284
Strawberry Trifle . . . 285
Viennese Torte . . . 281

Frozen Desserts
Fresh Peach Ice Cream . . . 292
Fresh Peach Spectacular . . . 291
Frozen Caramel Dessert . . . 290
Luscious Lemon Mousse Freeze . . . 294
Profiteroles with Chocolate Cognac Sauce . . . 295
Spumoni . . . 293
Tortoni . . . 292

Pies
Black Bottom Pie . . . 297
Crumb Apple Pie . . . 301
French Silk Pie . . . 299
Mother's Fruit Pies . . . 298
Never Fail Pie Crust . . . 296
Paté Brisée . . . 301
Peach Pie . . . 299
Pumpkin Chiffon Pie . . . 298
Sour Cream Apple Pie . . . 296
Swiss Apple Tart . . . 300

Sauces
Chocolate Butternut Sauce . . . 302
German Pudding Sauce . . . 302
Lemon Sauce . . . 302

Perfect Chocolate Cake
Cake is even better the second day.

Preheat oven to 350°.

Grease and flour 3 (9-inch) round cake pans.

Combine cocoa with boiling water in medium-size bowl; mix with wire whisk until smooth. Set aside to cool completely.

Sift flour with soda, salt and baking powder in another bowl and set aside.

Use electric mixer set at high speed and beat butter, sugar, eggs and vanilla in large bowl until light, about 5 minutes. Beat in flour mixture (in fourths) alternately with cocoa mixture (in thirds), on low speed of mixer. Begin and end with flour mixture. *Do not overbeat.*

Divide evenly into pans, smooth tops. Bake at 350° for 25–30 minutes or until surface springs back when gently pressed with fingertip. Cool in pans for 10 minutes. Carefully loosen sides with spatula and remove from pans; cool on racks.

Combine chocolate, cream and butter in medium-size saucepan. Stir over low heat until smooth. Remove from heat. Add confectioners' sugar and mix with wire whisk. Set bowl in larger bowl filled with ice. Beat until frosting holds shape. Prepare filling.

Combine cream, sugar and vanilla in medium-size bowl. Whip with electric mixer. Refrigerate.

To assemble cake, place first layer, top side down, on a plate. Spread with ½ of filling. Place second layer, top side down, on top of first. Spread with remaining filling. Place third layer, top side up, on top of second layer. Spread frosting on sides of cake with a spatula, taking care to cover filling. Spread remaining frosting on top. Refrigerate at least 4 hours before serving.

Note: Must be stored in refrigerator.

HINT:
To fill baking pans evenly, use a scoop and add one scoop at a time to each pan until you have used up the mixture.

Cake:
- 1 cup unsweetened cocoa
- 2 cups boiling water
- 2¾ cups sifted all-purpose flour
- 2 teaspoons baking soda
- ½ teaspoon salt
- ½ teaspoon baking powder
- 1 cup (2 sticks) butter, softened
- 2½ cups granulated sugar
- 4 eggs
- 1½ teaspoons vanilla

Frosting:
- 6 (1-ounce) squares semi-sweet baking chocolate
- ½ cup light (coffee) cream
- 1 cup (2 sticks) butter
- 2½ cups confectioners' sugar

Filling:
- 1 cup heavy (whipping) cream, chilled
- ¼ cup confectioners' sugar
- 1 teaspoon vanilla

Serves:	12
Preparation:	45 minutes
Baking:	30 minutes
Cooling:	45 minutes
Chilling:	4 hours
Temperature:	350°

Cakes

L. S. Ayres Buttermilk Cake
Absolutely mouth-watering.

Preheat oven to 350°.

Grease and flour angel food cake pan.

Beat together shortening and sugar in large bowl with electric mixer at medium speed. Add salt, vanilla, lemon juice and lemon rind. Beat until fluffy. Add egg yolks and beat well. Set aside.

Place flour in large bowl. Add cornstarch. Set aside.

Combine baking soda and buttermilk in small bowl; mix well. Add flour and buttermilk alternately to sugar mixture; mix well. Beat egg whites until stiff and fold into sugar mixture. Pour mixture into prepared pan. Bake at 350° for 1 hour and 15 minutes. Invert over plate and cool. Remove tube pan when cool.

Combine sauce ingredients in medium-size saucepan. Cook over medium heat, stirring constantly until mixture comes to a boil. Remove from heat. Cut cake into serving pieces and pour warm lemon sauce over cut cake slices.

Note: Cake is best when sauce is warm.

Cake:
- 1 cup solid shortening
- 3 cups granulated sugar
- 1 teaspoon salt
- 1 teaspoon vanilla
- 2 teaspoons fresh lemon juice
- 1 tablespoon freshly grated lemon rind
- 6 eggs, separated
- 2½ cups plus 2 tablespoons all-purpose flour, sifted
- 6 tablespoons cornstarch
- ½ teaspoon baking soda
- 1 cup buttermilk

Old-fashioned Lemon Sauce:
- 1 cup (2 sticks) butter
- 1 cup granulated sugar
- ¼ cup water
- 1 egg, well beaten
- 3 tablespoons fresh lemon juice
- 1 tablespoon freshly grated lemon rind

Serves: 20
Preparation: 30 minutes
Baking: 1 hour, 15 minutes
Temperature: 350°

One Hundred Dollar Chocolate Cake

Excellent texture—be prepared for seconds.

Preheat oven to 350°.

Grease and flour 2 (8-inch) cake pans.

Melt chocolate in top of double boiler over low heat; cool. Beat together butter and sugar. Add eggs, vanilla, chocolate and baking powder. Mix well. Add milk and flour alternately in ½ cup quantities. Pour into prepared cake pans. Bake at 350° for 30 minutes. Cool cakes in pans for 10 minutes. Remove from pans and cool on rack.

Melt chocolate in top of double boiler over low heat; cool. Beat together butter and confectioners' sugar. Add egg, lemon juice, vanilla and chocolate. Spread icing between layers, then on sides and top of cake.

Cake:
- 4 (1-ounce) squares unsweetened chocolate
- ½ cup (1 stick) butter, softened (no substitution)
- 2 cups sugar
- 2 eggs
- 2 teaspoons vanilla
- 2 teaspoons baking powder
- 1½ cups milk
- 2 cups cake flour

Icing:
- 2 (1-ounce) squares unsweetened chocolate
- ½ cup (1 stick) butter, softened
- 1 pound (3½ cups) confectioners' sugar
- 1 egg, beaten
- 1 teaspoon fresh lemon juice
- ½ teaspoon vanilla

Serves:	8–10
Preparation:	1 hour
Baking:	30 minutes
Temperature:	350°

HINT:
One cup sifted cake flour can be substituted with ⅞ cup (1 cup less 2 tablespoons) sifted all-purpose flour.

Gâteau Bête Noire (Black Beast Cake)

Rich, versatile and easy despite the lengthy directions.

Preheat oven to 350°.

Butter a 9-inch round cake pan. Cut a 9-inch circle of wax paper and place on bottom of pan. Butter wax paper.

Combine water with 1 cup sugar in heavy 2-quart saucepan. Bring to a boil and cook for 4 minutes or until candy thermometer registers 220°. Remove saucepan from heat and quickly add unsweetened and semi-sweet chocolate pieces, stirring until they are melted and smooth. Add butter immediately, 1 piece at a time, stirring until mixture is smooth and blended.

Beat eggs and remaining ⅓ cup sugar in large bowl with electric mixer at high speed for about 15 minutes or until mixture is thick, pale yellow and tripled in volume. Beat in chocolate mixture gradually with mixer at low speed. Mix only until chocolate mixture is fully incorporated. (Overbeating results in air bubbles.) Spoon mixture into prepared pan. Set cake pan in larger pan. Pour boiling water around cake pan to a depth of ¾ inch. Bake at 350° for 25 minutes or until knife inserted in center of cake comes out clean. Do not bake longer than a total of 35 minutes. Cool in pan for 10 minutes; run sharp knife around edge of cake. Unmold on a cookie sheet. Place serving plate over cake and turn right side up. Serve cake warm with German Pudding Sauce.

Note: The texture of the cake changes if refrigerated; it is still delicious but firmer.

Variation: Cake may also be served at room temperature or cold. Serve with whipped cream flavored with a mint liqueur.

- ½ cup water
- 1⅓ cups granulated sugar, divided
- 8 (1-ounce) squares unsweetened chocolate, chopped
- 4 (1-ounce) squares semi-sweet chocolate, chopped
- 1 cup (2 sticks) unsalted butter, cut into small pieces and at room temperature
- 5 extra large eggs, at room temperature

Serves: 8
Preparation: 30 minutes
Baking: 35 minutes
Cooling: 10 minutes
Temperature: 350°

Pumpkin Roll
A unique alternative for holiday meals.

Preheat oven to 375°.

Grease jelly roll pan and line with wax paper. Grease and flour wax paper.

Beat eggs with electric mixer at high speed for 5 minutes. Add sugar, lemon juice and pumpkin.

Sift together flour, baking powder, cinnamon, ginger, nutmeg and salt. Fold into egg mixture. Pour batter into prepared pan. Top with nuts. Bake at 375° for 15 minutes. Turn immediately onto a clean linen towel that has been sprinkled lightly with confectioners' sugar. Roll lengthwise in the towel and cool.

Beat together filling ingredients. Unroll cake and spread with filling. Reroll (without towel) and chill. Store in refrigerator. Slice to serve.

Cake:
- 3 eggs
- 1 cup granulated sugar
- 1 teaspoon fresh lemon juice
- ⅔ cup pumpkin
- ¾ cup all-purpose flour
- 1 teaspoon baking powder
- 2 teaspoons ground cinnamon
- 1 teaspoon ground ginger
- ½ teaspoon ground nutmeg
- ½ teaspoon salt
- 1 cup chopped walnuts or pecans
- Confectioners' sugar

Filling:
- 1 cup confectioners' sugar
- 2 (3-ounce) packages cream cheese, softened
- 4 tablespoons (½ stick) butter, softened
- ½ teaspoon vanilla

Serves:	8–12
Preparation:	30 minutes
Baking:	15 minutes
Cooling:	30 minutes
Temperature:	375°

Black Forest Cherry Torte

A wonderful creation worth the effort.

Cherry Filling:
- 2½ cups sour red cherries
- ½ cup port wine
- 1 tablespoon kirsch
- 3 drops almond extract
- 2 tablespoons cornstarch

Chocolate Mousse:
- 3 (1-ounce) squares semi-sweet chocolate
- 3 tablespoons kirsch
- 1 egg, beaten
- 1 cup heavy (whipping) cream
- 2 tablespoons granulated sugar

Cake:
- 2 eggs, separated
- 1½ cups granulated sugar, divided
- 1¾ cups cake flour
- ¾ teaspoon baking soda
- 1 teaspoon salt
- ⅓ cup oil
- 1 cup milk, divided
- 2 (1-ounce) squares unsweetened chocolate, melted

Butter Frosting:
- ⅓ cup butter
- 4 cups sifted confectioners' sugar, divided
- 2 egg yolks
- 1 teaspoon vanilla
- 1½ teaspoons light (coffee) cream
- 2 cups heavy (whipping) cream
- 2 tablespoons granulated sugar
- 1 teaspoon vanilla
- Confectioners' sugar
- Long stemmed cherries
- Chocolate curls

Combine cherries, wine and kirsch. Add almond extract. Chill overnight.

Drain cherries; reserve juice. Combine reserved juice with cornstarch in medium-size saucepan. Cook over medium heat until thickened. Cool. Add cherries to thickened juice.

Combine chocolate and kirsch in top of double boiler. Stir until chocolate melts and mixture is smooth. Slowly stir into beaten egg. Whip cream with sugar. Fold into chocolate. Chill 2 hours.

Preheat oven to 350°.

Grease 2 (9-inch) round cake pans. Line with wax paper. Grease wax paper. Flour bottom and sides of pans.

Beat 2 egg whites to soft peaks. Add ½ cup sugar, beating until stiff peaks form. Set aside.

Sift together remaining 1 cup sugar, flour, baking soda and salt in large bowl. Add oil and ½ cup milk. Beat 1 minute. Add remaining ½ cup milk, 2 egg yolks and melted chocolate. Beat 1 minute. Fold in egg whites. Pour into prepared pans. Bake at 350° for 30–35 minutes. Cool cake completely. Split each layer, making 4 thin layers.

Beat together butter and 2 cups sifted confectioners' sugar. Beat in egg yolks and vanilla. Beat in remaining 2 cups confectioners' sugar. Beat in light cream to make mixture of spreading consistency. Chill 30 minutes.

Place 1 cake layer on serving plate, cut side up. Spread ½ cup Butter Frosting on layer. Form a ridge ½-inch wide and ¾-inch high around outside edge of layer with the remaining frosting. Chill 30 minutes. Fill space inside ridge with cherry filling. Place another cake layer on top. Spread second layer with chocolate mousse. Place another cake layer on top. Chill 30 minutes. Whip heavy cream with sugar and vanilla. Spread third layer with 1½ cups whipped cream and place last layer of cake on top. Chill 30 minutes. Reserve about ½ cup whipped cream. Frost sides of torte with remaining whipped cream. Sift confectioners' sugar over top. Place dollops of reserved whipped cream on top. Center each dollop with a long stemmed cherry. Garnish with chocolate curls.

Note: May be assembled 24 hours in advance. Flavor improves with age.

Serves:	12
Preparation:	3 hours over 2-day period
Chilling:	Overnight
Baking:	35 minutes
Temperature:	350°

Blitz Torte
Your efforts will be rewarded.

Preheat oven to 350°.

Grease and flour 2 (9-inch) cake pans.

Beat sugar and butter in large bowl. Add egg yolks; mix well.

Sift together flour and baking powder. Add flour and milk alternately to batter. Pour batter into prepared pans.

Beat egg whites until soft peaks form. Add sugar gradually, beating constantly. Add vanilla. Beat until stiff peaks form. Spread meringue on top of batter in pans. Sprinkle almonds on top. Bake at 350° for 30 minutes. Cool. Remove from pans.

Combine sugar, salt and flour in medium-size saucepan. Stir in milk. Bring to a boil over low heat. Boil for 1 minute. Remove from heat. Stir 1 cup of hot mixture into egg yolks and return to hot mixture in saucepan. Bring to a boil. Cool slightly and stir in vanilla. Cool completely.

Place 1 cake layer on serving plate, meringue side down. Spread with filling. Place second layer on top, meringue side up. Serve by slicing into small wedges. Refrigerate if not serving within 2 hours.

Note: Leftover torte must be refrigerated.

Cake:
- ¾ cup granulated sugar
- ¾ cup (1½ sticks) butter, softened
- 6 egg yolks, beaten
- 1½ cups all-purpose flour
- 1½ teaspoons baking powder
- ½ cup milk

Meringue:
- 6 egg whites, at room temperature
- 1½ cups granulated sugar
- 1 teaspoon vanilla
- ½ cup sliced almonds

Filling:
- ½ cup granulated sugar
- ½ teaspoon salt
- 6 tablespoons all-purpose flour
- 2 cups milk
- 4 egg yolks, beaten
- 2 teaspoons vanilla

Serves:	12–14
Preparation:	1 hour
Baking:	30 minutes
Temperature:	350°

Cakes

Topping:
- 1 (8-ounce) package cream cheese, softened
- 1 egg
- ⅓ cup granulated sugar
- Pinch of salt
- 6 ounces semi-sweet chocolate chips

Cupcake:
- 1½ cups sifted all-purpose flour
- 1 cup granulated sugar
- 1 teaspoon baking soda
- ½ teaspoon salt
- 1 cup water
- ⅓ cup oil
- 1 tablespoon vinegar
- 1 teaspoon vanilla
- ¼ cup cocoa

Yield:	24
Preparation:	20 minutes
Baking:	30 minutes
Temperature:	350°

- 1 cup granulated sugar
- 4 baking apples, peeled and finely chopped
- ¼ cup (½ stick) butter, softened
- 1 egg, slightly beaten
- 1 cup all-purpose flour, sifted
- 1 teaspoon baking soda
- 1 teaspoon ground nutmeg
- 1 teaspoon ground cinnamon
- ¼ teaspoon salt

Serves:	12
Preparation:	25 minutes
Baking:	40 minutes
Temperature:	350°

Black Bottom Cupcakes
The best.

Preheat oven to 350°.

Fill cupcake forms with paper cupcake liners.

Mix cream cheese with egg, sugar and pinch of salt in medium-size bowl. Beat well. Stir in chocolate chips; set aside.

Beat all cupcake ingredients until well combined. Fill cupcake liners ½ full. Top each cupcake with 1 tablespoon of the cream cheese mixture. Bake at 350° for 25–30 minutes.

Variation: These cupcakes can be made in miniature cupcake pans and baked at 350° for 20–25 minutes.

Raw Apple Cake
Moist and light texture.

Preheat oven to 350°.

Grease a 9x13-inch baking pan.

Combine sugar, apples, butter and egg in large bowl. Mix well and set aside.

Combine remaining ingredients and add to apple mixture. Mix well. Pour into prepared baking pan and bake at 350° for 30–40 minutes.

Serving Suggestion: Great served warm with dollop of vanilla ice cream.

Apricot Fingers
Nutritious and lightly sweet.

Wash orange, cut in fourths and remove seeds. *Do not peel.* Place in food processor or blender with apricots and process until mixture is finely chopped. Place orange mixture, including all juices, in heavy 2-quart saucepan. Add 1½ cups sugar; mix until well combined. Mixture will be stiff. Bring to a boil over low heat. Boil for 8 minutes, stirring constantly. Remove from heat, cool slightly.

Place remaining 1 cup sugar in small bowl. Drop a scant tablespoon of orange mixture into sugar; coat evenly. Form into a 2-inch roll, ¾-inch in diameter. (It may be necessary to dip roll in sugar again to shape.) Place on wax paper. Repeat process for remaining orange mixture. Allow to dry thoroughly, about 12 hours. Store in airtight container.

Variation: Dip finished candy in melted semi-sweet chocolate to cover ½ of the roll.

- 1 medium-large orange
- 12 ounces (2¼ cups) dried apricots, washed and drained
- 2½ cups granulated sugar, divided

Yield: 50 pieces
Preparation: 1 hour
Drying: 12 hours

Butterscotch Bon Bons
Do not be put off by unlikely combination—these are delicious.

Melt butterscotch chips and peanut butter in double boiler or in medium-size dish in microwave. Stir until well blended. Remove from heat and add remaining ingredients. Stir well. Drop in bite-size pieces on ungreased cookie sheet. Chill until firm, approximately 15–20 minutes.

Note: Leftovers should be stored in refrigerator.

- 6 ounces butterscotch chips
- ½ cup smooth peanut butter
- 1½ cups Special K cereal
- 1 cup miniature marshmallows
- ½ cup raisins

Yield: 2 dozen
Preparation: 20 minutes
Chilling: 20 minutes

Candy

1 cup finely chopped pecans, divided
24 ounces milk chocolate, divided
1 cup (2 sticks) unsalted butter
4 tablespoons water
1 cup granulated sugar

Yield: 2 pounds
Preparation: 45 minutes

English Butter Toffee
Delicious holiday gifts.

Recipe requires use of candy thermometer.

Butter an 7x11-inch or 8-inch square pan. Sprinkle with ½ cup pecans.

Melt 12 ounces of the chocolate in top of double boiler over boiling water. Spread over the nuts in pan.

Melt butter in a small heavy saucepan over low heat. Add water and sugar, stirring to blend well. Cook over medium heat, stirring occasionally, until mixture registers 290° on a candy thermometer. Continue to cook and stir for about 3 minutes or until mixture turns golden brown. Pour immediately into pan. Spread to cover chocolate.

Melt remaining 12 ounces of chocolate in top of double boiler over boiling water and spread over toffee mixture. Sprinkle with remaining ½ cup pecans. Cool completely. Break into pieces to serve. Store in airtight container in a cool place.

1⅓ cups dark corn syrup
3½ cups granulated sugar
1 pound (4 sticks) butter
1 (14-ounce) can sweetened condensed milk

Yield: About 100 pieces
Preparation: 45 minutes
Cooking: 18 minutes

Grandmother's Caramels
A favorite and a classic.

Butter lightly a 9x13-inch pan.

Place syrup in heavy saucepan and bring to a boil. Add sugar and stir slightly. Add butter when mixture comes to a boil. Bring mixture back to a boil and add milk. Cook over medium heat until mixture registers 245° on a candy thermometer or turns a caramel color, approximately 18 minutes. Pour in prepared pan. Cool and cut into 1-inch squares. Wrap each piece in wax paper.

Cheesecakes

Bavarian Cheesecake
A classic.

Grease an 8-inch springform pan.

Combine crust ingredients in food processsor or medium-size bowl. Press mixture evenly into bottom and up sides of springform pan. Refrigerate for 30 minutes.

Preheat oven to 375°.

Beat together cream cheese and sugar until light and fluffy. Add eggs, 1 at a time, beating well after each addition. Add lemon juice, lemon rind and vanilla; mix well. Pour into chilled crust. Bake at 375° for 45 minutes. Remove from oven and let cool for 30 minutes.

Preheat oven to 400°.

Combine sour cream, sugar and vanilla. Carefully spread mixture over baked cake. Bake at 400° for 10 minutes. Cool. Refrigerate overnight before serving.

Crust:
- 2 cups finely crushed vanilla wafers
- 2 tablespoons granulated sugar
- 1 teaspoon ground cinnamon
- ¼ teaspoon ground nutmeg
- ⅓ cup butter, melted

Filling:
- 3 (8-ounce) packages cream cheese
- 1 cup granulated sugar
- 3 eggs
- 1 tablespoon fresh lemon juice
- 1 teaspoon grated lemon rind
- ½ teaspoon vanilla

Topping:
- 2 cups sour cream
- 3 tablespoons granulated sugar
- 1 teaspoon vanilla

Suggested Garnishes:
- Kiwi fruit
- Strawberries
- Orange sections

Serves:	12
Preparation:	35 minutes
Baking:	55 minutes
Cooling:	30 minutes
Chilling:	Overnight
Temperature:	375°

Cheesecakes

Crust:
- 1½ cups zwieback crumbs
- 2 tablespoons butter, melted
- 2 tablespoons granulated sugar

Cake:
- ½ cup granulated sugar
- 2 tablespoons all-purpose flour
- ¼ teaspoon salt
- 2 (8-ounce) packages cream cheese, softened
- 1 teaspoon vanilla
- 4 egg yolks
- 1 cup light (coffee) cream
- 4 egg whites, at room temperature

Suggested Garnishes:
- Whipped cream
- Fruit
- Confectioners' sugar

Serves: 8–10
Preparation: 30 minutes
Baking: 1 hour, 15 minutes
Temperature: 325°

Old-Fashioned Cheesecake

A superb light cheesecake.

Preheat oven to 325°.

Mix zwieback crumbs, butter and sugar. Press into bottom of 9-inch springform pan; set aside.

Combine sugar, flour and salt.

Beat cream cheese in large bowl until smooth. Add sugar mixture and vanilla; beat until fluffy. Add egg yolks, 1 at a time, mixing well after each addition. Add cream, mixing thoroughly. Beat egg whites until stiff. Fold into cheese mixture. Pour mixture on top of crust. Bake at 325° for 1 hour and 15 minutes or until set. (Center may crack.) Cool. May be garnished with whipped cream and fruit or simply sprinkled with confectioners' sugar.

Grasshopper Cheesecake
Refreshing variation.

Preheat oven to 350°.

Combine crust ingredients and press into the bottom and up sides of 9-inch springform pan.

Beat cream cheese and sugar together in medium-size bowl. Add eggs, beating until smooth. Stir in creme de menthe and creme de cacao. Pour filling into crust. Bake at 350° for 55–60 minutes. Cool.

Combine topping ingredients; spread over cooled cake. Refrigerate for 8 hours or overnight.

Crust:
- 2 cups chocolate wafer crumbs
- 1 tablespoon granulated sugar
- 3 tablespoons butter, melted

Filling:
- 3 (8-ounce) packages cream cheese, softened
- 1½ cups granulated sugar
- 4 eggs
- ¼ cup creme de menthe
- ½ cup white creme de cacao

Topping:
- 5 ounces sweet chocolate, melted
- ¾ cup sour cream

Serves:	12–16
Preparation:	20 minutes
Baking:	1 hour
Cooling:	1 hour
Chilling:	8 hours
Temperature:	350°

HINT:
Baking results will be far better if all ingredients are at room temperature, unless otherwise specified, before beginning recipe preparation.

Cheesecakes

Crust:
- 1½ cups graham cracker crumbs
- ⅓ cup ground almonds
- ½ teaspoon ground ginger
- ½ teaspoon ground cinnamon
- 2 tablespoons granulated sugar (optional)
- ⅓ cup butter, melted

Filling:
- 4 (8-ounce) packages cream cheese, softened
- 1¼ cups granulated sugar
- 3 tablespoons maple syrup
- 3 tablespoons cognac
- 1 teaspoon ground ginger
- 1 teaspoon ground cinnamon
- ½ teaspoon ground nutmeg
- 4 eggs, at room temperature
- ¼ cup heavy (whipping) cream
- 1 cup pumpkin

Topping:
- 2 cups sour cream
- ¼ cup granulated sugar
- 1 tablespoon maple syrup
- 1 tablespoon cognac
- ¼ cup blanched whole almonds, sautéed in butter (optional)

Serves:	12–16
Preparation:	25 minutes
Baking:	2 hours, 20 minutes
Cooling:	1 hour
Chilling:	3 hours
Temperature:	425°

Pumpkin Cheesecake

Outstanding for Thanksgiving or anytime.

Preheat oven to 425°.

Combine crust ingredients and press evenly into bottom of 10-inch springform pan. Bake at 425° for 10 minutes. Remove pan from oven and reduce temperature to 325°.

Beat cream cheese in large bowl until smooth. Add sugar gradually, beating until fluffy and light. Add maple syrup, cognac, ginger, cinnamon and nutmeg. Add eggs, 1 at a time, beating thoroughly after each addition. Add cream and pumpkin; mix well.

Pour filling mixture into crust. Bake at 325° for 45–60 minutes until center is set. Turn off oven. Do not open oven door. One hour after oven is turned off, remove cake.

Preheat oven to 425°.

Stir together sour cream, sugar, syrup and cognac until well blended; spread over cake. Bake at 425° for 10 minutes. Allow cheesecake to cool at room temperature for about 1 hour.

Arrange almonds in a ring around perimeter of cake. Chill at least 3 hours before removing sides of pan.

Note: Must be refrigerated.

Chocolate Pralines
Easy and delicious. Fun to do with children.

Preheat oven to 400°.

Line 10x15-inch jelly roll pan with foil.

Cover bottom of pan with whole graham crackers.

Bring sugar and butter to a boil in a medium-size saucepan. Boil for 3 minutes. Pour mixture over crackers. Bake at 400° for 5 minutes. Remove from oven and sprinkle with chocolate chips. Spread chocolate over mixture as chips melt. Sprinkle pecans over chocolate before chocolate sets. Cut into squares while still warm. Freeze. Remove from freezer 30 minutes before serving.

Variation: Crust is also delicious when made with 48–60 individual saltine crackers.

- 24 whole graham crackers
- 1 cup firmly packed brown sugar
- 1 cup (2 sticks) butter
- 12 ounces semi-sweet chocolate chips
- 1 cup finely chopped pecans

Yield: 3 dozen
Preparation: 20 minutes
Baking: 5 minutes
Temperature: 400°

Almond Butter Cookies
You are never too full for this cookie.

Preheat oven to 350°.

Beat together butter and sugar until creamy in large bowl. Add flour, salt and almond extract; stir well. Chill dough for 1 hour.

Remove dough from refrigerator. Pinch about 1 tablespoon of dough and roll into 1-inch ball. Flatten in crisscross pattern using tines of fork dipped in sugar. Press almond half into center. Repeat process until all dough has been used. Bake on ungreased cookie sheet at 350° for 12–15 minutes. Remove cookies from cookie sheet and while still warm, dip top into granulated sugar. Cool on racks.

- 1 cup (2 sticks) butter, softened
- ½ cup granulated sugar
- 2 cups all-purpose flour
- ¼ teaspoon salt
- 1 teaspoon almond extract
- 36 almond halves
- Granulated sugar

Yield: 3 dozen
Preparation: 20 minutes
Chilling: 1 hour
Baking: 15 minutes
Temperature: 350°

Peppermint Cookies

1984 Indiana State Fair "Archway Cookie Contest" winner.

- 2 cups sifted all-purpose flour
- 1 teaspoon baking soda
- ½ teaspoon salt
- 1 cup (2 sticks) margarine, softened
- 1 cup firmly packed brown sugar
- 1 egg
- 2 cups quick oats
- ½ cup crushed peppermint candy (approximately 20 round mints)

Glaze:
- 1½ cups sifted confectioners' sugar
- 3 tablespoons milk
- 3 tablespoons crushed peppermint candy (approximately 4 round mints)

Yield:	3–3½ dozen
Preparation:	20 minutes
Baking:	10 minutes
Cooling:	15 minutes
Temperature:	375°

Preheat oven to 375°.

Sift together flour, soda and salt in medium-size bowl. Set aside.

Place margarine and brown sugar in large bowl. Beat together until light and fluffy. Beat in egg. Add flour mixture and mix well. Stir in oats and peppermint; mix well.

Drop by teaspoonfuls on ungreased cookie sheet. Bake at 375° for 8–10 minutes. Cool for 1 minute; remove from cookie sheet. Cool completely.

Combine all glaze ingredients in medium-size bowl. Mix well. Drizzle glaze over cooled cookies.

Note: Allow glaze to cool completely before storing cookies. Place wax paper between cookies when stacking so that glaze will not stick.

Date Cookies
A family Christmas tradition.

Grease cookie sheets.

Stuff each date with a nut half (or a portion of a pecan). Set aside.

Preheat oven to 400°.

Beat together butter and brown sugar until creamy. Add egg and mix well.

Sift flour, baking powder, baking soda and salt together. Add alternately with sour cream to sugar mixture. Stir in dates. Drop onto prepared cookie sheet 1 date per cookie. Bake at 400° for 8–10 minutes. Cool. Frost with Golden Frosting.

Melt butter in medium-size saucepan over medium heat until lightly browned. Remove from heat. Gradually beat in confectioners' sugar and vanilla. Add milk slowly until frosting is of spreading consistency. Spread on cooled cookies.

- 1 pound pitted dates, approximately 70
- 1 (3-ounce) package pecan halves
- ¼ cup (½ stick) butter, softened
- ¾ cup firmly packed brown sugar
- 1 egg, slightly beaten
- 1¼ cups all-purpose flour
- ½ teaspoon baking powder
- ½ teaspoon baking soda
- ¼ teaspoon salt
- ½ cup sour cream

Golden Frosting:
- ½ cup (1 stick) butter
- 3 cups sifted confectioners' sugar
- 1 teaspoon vanilla
- 3 tablespoons milk

Yield: 6 dozen
Preparation: 1 hour, 30 minutes
Baking: 10 minutes
Temperature: 400°

Russian Tea Cakes
Cookie flavor enhances with age.

Preheat oven to 300°.

Beat together butter and sugar until creamy in medium-size bowl. Add vanilla, flour and pecans; stir well. Pinch about 1 tablespoon of dough and roll into 1-inch ball. Place on ungreased cookie sheet. Repeat until all dough has been used. Bake at 300° for 30 minutes.

Remove from oven and while still warm, roll in confectioners' sugar.

- ½ cup (1 stick) butter, softened
- 2 tablespoons granulated sugar
- 1 teaspoon vanilla
- 1 cup sifted cake flour
- 1 cup chopped pecans
- Confectioners' sugar

Yield: 2 dozen
Preparation: 15 minutes
Baking: 30 minutes
Temperature: 300°

Cookies

Crust:
- 2 cups all-purpose flour
- 1 cup firmly packed brown sugar
- ½ cup (1 stick) butter, softened
- 2 cups whole pecans

Caramel Layer:
- ⅔ cup butter
- ½ cup firmly packed brown sugar

Topping:
- 1½ cups semi-sweet chocolate chips

Yield:	3–4 dozen
Preparation:	30 minutes
Baking:	22 minutes
Cooling:	30 minutes
Temperature:	350°

- ½ cup (1 stick) butter, melted
- 2 cups firmly packed brown sugar
- 2 eggs, beaten
- 1 cup chopped pecans
- 1 cup chopped dates
- 2 teaspoons vanilla
- 1 cup all-purpose flour
- 2 teaspoons baking powder
- ⅛ teaspoon salt
- Confectioners' sugar

Yield:	4½ dozen
Preparation:	35 minutes
Baking:	30 minutes
Cooling:	10 minutes
Temperature:	350°

Butter Pecan Turtle Cookies
Accolades galore.

Preheat oven to 350°.

Combine flour, brown sugar and butter in a 3-quart bowl. Beat with electric mixer at medium speed for 2–3 minutes, until well combined. Pat firmly into ungreased 9x13-inch baking pan. Sprinkle pecans evenly on top.

Combine butter and brown sugar in a heavy 1-quart saucepan. Cook over medium heat, stirring constantly until entire surface of mixture begins to boil. Boil about 1 minute, stirring constantly. Pour evenly over pecans and crust. Bake at 350° for 18–22 minutes until golden brown and bubbling. Remove from oven and sprinkle with chocolate chips. Swirl chocolate chips with spatula to cover evenly. Cool. Cut into squares.

Chinese Chews
A delicious surprise.

Preheat oven to 350°.

Grease a 9x13-inch baking dish.

Combine butter, brown sugar, eggs, nuts, dates and vanilla in large bowl; mix well. Stir in flour, baking powder and salt. Pour into prepared baking dish. Bake at 350° for 30 minutes.

Remove from oven and stir. Roll into 1-inch balls when slightly cool and then roll in confectioners' sugar. Cool.

Note: Mixture will not form into balls if allowed to get cold.

Peanut Butter Oatmeal Cookies

These cookies are not only delicious but reasonably nutritious.

Preheat oven to 350°.

Sift together flour, salt and baking soda in small bowl. Set aside.

Beat together butter, brown sugar and granulated sugar in large bowl. Beat in eggs and vanilla. Stir in peanut butter; mix well. Add dry ingredients and oats; stir. Mixture will be very stiff. Drop by rounded teaspoonfuls onto ungreased cookie sheet. Press flat with floured tines of fork in a crisscross pattern. Bake at 350° for 10 minutes. Let cool on cookie sheet 1–2 minutes before removing to cooling rack.

Note: Store in airtight container.

- 1 cup all-purpose flour
- ½ teaspoon salt
- 2 teaspoons baking soda
- 1 cup (2 sticks) butter, softened
- 1 cup firmly packed brown sugar
- 1 cup granulated sugar
- 2 eggs
- 1 teaspoon vanilla
- 1 cup smooth peanut butter
- 2 cups quick oats

Yield: 4 dozen
Preparation: 20 minutes
Baking: 10 minutes
Temperature: 350°

Crunchy Rich Chocolate Chips

You will love these.

Preheat oven to 350°.

Sift flour, baking soda and salt in large bowl; set aside.

Beat together margarine, brown sugar and granulated sugar in large bowl. Add egg, milk and vanilla. Mix thoroughly. Stir in dry ingredients alternately with oil. Mix thoroughly. Stir in corn flakes, oats and chocolate chips. Drop by teaspoonfuls onto an ungreased cookie sheet. Bake at 350° for 10–12 minutes.

- 3½ cups all-purpose flour
- 3 teaspoons baking soda
- 1 teaspoon salt
- 1 cup (2 sticks) margarine, softened
- 1 cup firmly packed brown sugar
- 1 cup granulated sugar
- 1 egg
- 1 tablespoon milk
- 2 teaspoons vanilla
- ¾ cup oil
- 1 cup corn flakes
- 1 cup quick oats
- 12 ounces semi-sweet chocolate chips

Yield: 6 dozen
Preparation: 30 minutes
Baking: 10 minutes
Temperature: 350°

Cookie Chip Chocolates
This is for hardcore chocolate lovers.

24 medium-size crisp plain butter or sugar cookies
24 ounces semi-sweet chocolate chips

Yield: 3 dozen
Preparation: 15 minutes
Microwave: 3 minutes
Chilling: 1 hour

Cover 2 cookie sheets with wax paper.

Break cookies into small chunks and place in medium-size bowl.

Melt chocolate chips in top of double boiler over low heat or in microwave. Pour chocolate over cookies. Fold cookie pieces gently into melted chocolate. Coat carefully without crushing cookie pieces. Drop by heaping tablespoonfuls on prepared cookie sheets. Chill until firm, about 1 hour. Layer chocolates in covered container; separate layers with sheets of wax paper. Store in cool place.

A NO Chocolate Brownie
Attention butterscotch lovers!

¼ cup (½ stick) butter, melted
1 cup firmly packed brown sugar
1 egg, beaten
½ teaspoon salt
¾ cup all-purpose flour
1 teaspoon baking powder
½ teaspoon vanilla
¼ cup shredded coconut
½ cup chopped nuts

Frosting:
¼ cup (½ stick) butter
¼ cup firmly packed brown sugar
2 tablespoons half and half
½ teaspoon maple extract
¾–1 cup confectioners' sugar

Yield: 16 (2-inch) squares
Preparation: 30 minutes
Baking: 25 minutes
Temperature: 350°

Preheat oven to 350°.

Grease and flour an 8-inch square baking pan.

Beat together butter and brown sugar until smooth. Add egg, salt, flour, baking powder, vanilla, coconut and nuts; mix well. Spread in prepared pan. Bake at 350° for 20–25 minutes. Cool.

Melt butter in medium-size saucepan over medium heat. Add brown sugar and cook over low heat for 3 minutes. Stir in half and half, mixing well. Cool slightly. Stir in maple extract. Beat in confectioners' sugar until mixture is of spreading consistency. Frost brownies. Cut into squares after icing has set.

Note: Recipe may be doubled and baked in a 9x13-inch pan.

Chocolate Rum Brownies
Double frosting never hurt anything.

Preheat oven to 350°.

Grease and flour a 7x11-inch or 8-inch-square baking pan.

Melt chocolate in top of double boiler over low heat.

Beat butter and sugar together in large bowl until creamy. Add eggs; beat well. Beat in chocolate and vanilla, with electric mixer at low speed, until well combined.

Combine flour, salt and baking powder in small bowl. Add to chocolate mixture. Pour into prepared pan. Bake at 350° for 20–25 minutes. Cool. Sprinkle with rum.

Beat together butter and sugar until creamy. Beat in vanilla. Spread on cooled brownies and chill to set frosting.

Melt chocolate and butter in top of double boiler over low heat. Remove from heat and cool slightly. Stir in corn syrup. Drizzle glaze over butter frosting and spread evenly. Chill. Cut into squares. Serve chilled.

Brownies:
- 2 (1-ounce) squares unsweetened chocolate
- ⅓ cup butter, softened
- 1 cup granulated sugar
- 2 eggs
- 1 teaspoon vanilla
- ⅔ cup all-purpose flour
- ¼ teaspoon salt
- ½ teaspoon baking powder
- 3 tablespoons rum

Butter Frosting:
- ½ cup (1 stick) butter, softened
- 2 cups sifted confectioners' sugar
- 1 teaspoon vanilla

Chocolate Glaze:
- 1 (1-ounce) square unsweetened chocolate
- 1 tablespoon butter
- ¼ cup light corn syrup

Yield:	3 dozen
Preparation:	1 hour
Baking:	25 minutes
Chilling:	6–8 hours
Temperature:	350°

Bars:
- 1½ cups graham cracker crumbs
- 1 cup chopped almonds, toasted
- ½ cup (1 stick) butter
- ¼ cup granulated sugar
- ⅓ cup cocoa
- 1 egg, slightly beaten
- 1½ teaspoons vanilla
- 3 tablespoons Kahlúa

Icing:
- 6 tablespoons unsalted butter, softened
- 1¾ cup confectioners' sugar
- 1 tablespoon cream or milk
- 3 tablespoons Kahlúa

Topping:
- 1½ tablespoons butter
- 4 ounces semi-sweet chocolate

Yield:	3 dozen
Preparation:	45 minutes
Freezing:	2 hours

Kahlúa Party Bars
Unique dark chocolate bars.

Combine graham cracker crumbs and almonds in large bowl.

Melt butter in small saucepan over low heat. Add sugar, cocoa, egg and vanilla. Cook slowly for 4 minutes or until thickened. Pour over crumb mixture; toss gently. Sprinkle Kahlúa over mixture and mix gently. Press into bottom of 7x11-inch pan. Place in freezer.

Beat together butter and confectioners' sugar in medium-size bowl. Add cream and Kahlúa; mix well. Spread over bar layer. Freeze until firm.

Melt butter and chocolate in small saucepan over low heat. Spread over icing. Cut into bars and freeze. Remove from freezer 30 minutes before serving.

Refrigerator Mint Bars
Nothing like mint after a meal.

Melt butter and chocolate in large saucepan over low heat. Remove from heat. Add sugar, vanilla, egg, coconut, oats and nuts; mix well. Add graham cracker crumbs. Press into ungreased 9-inch square baking pan.

Melt butter in large saucepan. Stir in milk, peppermint and food coloring. Add confectioners' sugar; mix well. Spread on bars.

Melt unsweetened chocolate and semi-sweet chocolate chips in small saucepan over low heat. Spread over icing. Chill to allow chocolate to harden. Bring to room temperature and cut into small bars. If cut while cold, chocolate will crack.

Note: Store in refrigerator.

Bars:
- ½ cup (1 stick) butter
- 1 (1-ounce) square unsweetened chocolate
- ¼ cup granulated sugar
- 1 teaspoon vanilla
- 1 egg, beaten
- 1 cup shredded coconut
- ¼ cup old-fashioned oats
- ½ cup chopped nuts
- 2 cups graham cracker crumbs

Icing:
- ¼ cup (½ stick) butter
- 1 tablespoon milk or cream
- 2 drops oil of peppermint (may substitute ½ teaspoon peppermint extract)
- 3 drops green food coloring
- 2 cups confectioners' sugar

Topping:
- ½ (1-ounce) square unsweetened chocolate
- ½ cup semi-sweet chocolate chips

Yield: 3 dozen
Preparation: 1 hour
Chilling: 1 hour

Apricot Spice Bars

Perfect for morning coffee or afternoon tea.

Preheat oven to 350°.

Grease and flour a 15x10-inch jelly roll pan.

Beat together butter, brown sugar and honey. Beat in eggs, mixing well. Stir in remaining ingredients. Spread into prepared pan. Bake at 350° for 20–25 minutes. Remove from oven. Cool for 15 minutes. Prepare glaze while apricot bars cool.

Combine lemon juice and confectioners' sugar. Spread over bars. Cut into bars before glaze sets.

Variation: Dried peaches, apples or other dried fruits may also be used.

- ⅓ cup butter, softened
- 1½ cups firmly packed brown sugar
- ½ cup honey
- 3 eggs
- 1¾ cups all-purpose flour
- 1 teaspoon baking powder
- 1 teaspoon salt
- 1 teaspoon ground cinnamon
- ½ teaspoon ground cloves
- 1 cup chopped walnuts
- 6 ounces (1 cup) dried apricots, chopped

Glaze:
- 1 tablespoon fresh lemon juice
- ¾ cup confectioners' sugar

Yield:	4 dozen
Preparation:	15 minutes
Baking:	25 minutes
Cooling:	15 minutes
Temperature:	350°

Champagne Sabayon

An easy and elegant dessert.

Hull and wash strawberries. Divide into 8 equal portions and place in sherbets or fruit dishes.

Beat egg yolks and sugar in top of double boiler until creamy. Stir in champagne gradually. Place over hot water and cook, stirring constantly until thickened. Pour over strawberries and serve.

Variations: May substitute 2 cups sliced fresh peaches, raspberries, blueberries or other fresh fruit.

- 1½ pints fresh strawberries
- 6 egg yolks
- 1 scant cup granulated sugar
- 1½ cups champagne

Serves:	8
Preparation:	15 minutes

Chocolate Dipped Strawberries
A match made in heaven.

Line a cookie sheet with wax paper.

Combine chocolate and oil in top of small double boiler over barely simmering water. Melt chocolate, stirring constantly until smooth and satiny. Remove chocolate from heat immediately after it is melted.

Hold each berry by the green cap and dip into chocolate, turning so that about ⅔ of the berry is coated. Allow excess chocolate to drip back into pan. Lay dipped berry on its side on prepared cookie sheet. Let coated strawberries stand at room temperature until chocolate hardens before removing from wax paper. (Do not store coated berries in refrigerator.) Use dipped strawberries within a few hours of coating, 12 hours at the most.

Note: Use only berries with fresh-looking green caps. The berries must be perfectly dry. The chocolate may not set quickly if it is very humid. Dipped berries may be placed briefly (10 minutes) in refrigerator to hasten hardening.

- 24 large fresh firm strawberries, washed and thoroughly dry (do not remove stems)
- 4 (1-ounce) squares semi-sweet chocolate, chopped into coarse pieces
- 1 teaspoon oil

Yield: 24 strawberries
Preparation: 20 minutes
Standing: 15 minutes

Viennese Torte
Always receives rave reviews.

A stationary mixer is recommended for this recipe.

Preheat oven to 325°.

Butter only the bottom of a 9-inch springform pan.

Melt chocolate in the top of double boiler over low heat. Remove from heat.

Beat butter and sugar in large bowl until creamy. Add 8 egg yolks, 1 at a time, beating after each addition. Add chocolate and beat for 25 minutes with electric mixer at low speed.

Beat egg whites in large bowl until stiff. Fold into chocolate mixture. Pour ¾ of batter into prepared pan. Bake at 325° for 30 minutes. Remove from oven and cool. Use remaining batter to fill in area where torte has fallen. Serve with whipped cream, if desired.

- 8 (1-ounce) squares semi-sweet chocolate
- 1 cup (2 sticks) unsalted butter
- 1⅓ cups granulated sugar
- 8 eggs, separated
- Whipped cream

Serves: 12
Preparation: 30 minutes
Baking: 30 minutes
Cooling: 1 hour
Chilling: 2–4 hours
Temperature: 325°

Chocolate Mousse Cups
Scrumptiously rich.

Melt chocolate and butter in small saucepan over very low heat, stirring constantly. Using a teaspoon, spread chocolate mixture over the inside of foil-lined paper cupcake liners until entire surface is covered. Chill until firm, then peel off paper.

Combine cream cheese, ¼ cup sugar and vanilla; mix well. Add egg yolks and melted chocolate.

Beat egg whites with remaining ¼ cup sugar; fold into chocolate mixture. Whip cream and fold into chocolate mixture. Spoon into chocolate cups. Refrigerate until served.

Garnish with additional whipped cream and/or shaved chocolate and a strawberry, if desired.

Note: When freezing, place filled cup into a fresh paper cup. Remove from freezer 45 minutes before serving.

Cups:
- 8 (1-ounce) squares semi-sweet chocolate
- 2 tablespoons butter

Mousse:
- 1 (8-ounce) package cream cheese, softened
- ½ cup granulated sugar, divided
- 1 teaspoon vanilla
- 2 eggs, separated
- 6 (1-ounce) squares semi-sweet chocolate, melted
- 1 cup heavy (whipping) cream

Suggested Garnishes:
- Whipped cream
- Shaved chocolate
- Strawberries

Serves: 8
Preparation: 1 hour, 30 minutes
Chilling: 15 minutes

Poires au Cointreau
An elegant light dessert.

Place sugar and 2 cups water in large saucepan. Bring mixture to a boil; boil for 5 minutes.

Combine remaining water and lemon juice in medium-size bowl. Peel, quarter and core pears. Immediately place in bowl of lemon water. Drain pears and add to syrup in saucepan. Cook pears 10–15 minutes or until barely tender. Pour pears and syrup into serving bowl. Cool. Add Cointreau and continue to cool, occasionally spooning syrup over pears. Chill before serving.

Serving Suggestion: A French wafer adds just the right crunch to this dessert.

- ¾ cup granulated sugar
- 4 cups cold water, divided
- Juice of 1 lemon
- 6 firm fresh pears
- ⅓ cup Cointreau

Serves: 6
Preparation: 30 minutes
Chilling: 3 hours

Kiwi Mousse

A light and wonderful alternative to chocolate mousse.

Break eggs into top of double boiler. Add ½ cup sugar and 4 tablespoons Grand Marnier. Cook over boiling water, whisking constantly until thick. Remove from heat and continue whisking for 3–5 minutes. Cool completely in refrigerator.

Whip cream in large bowl until thickened. Add remaining ¼ cup sugar and vanilla; continue beating until stiff. Gently fold in chopped kiwi and remaining 2 tablespoons Grand Marnier. Fold egg mixture into kiwi mixture. Spoon mousse into large cocktail glasses or tall parfait glasses. Top with slices of kiwi. Refrigerate until ready to serve.

Variation: Strawberries may be substituted for the kiwis.

- 3 eggs
- ¾ cup granulated sugar, divided
- 6 tablespoons Grand Marnier, divided
- 2 cups heavy (whipping) cream
- ¼ teaspoon vanilla
- 3 kiwis, peeled and finely chopped or grated
- 1 kiwi, peeled and sliced

Serves: 8
Preparation: 30 minutes
Chilling: 2 hours

Brandied Strawberry Fondue

Great fondue variation.

Crush strawberries in large saucepan. Combine cornstarch, sugar and water; add to strawberries. Cook and stir over medium heat until thick and bubbly. Pour into fondue pot. Add whipped cream cheese, stirring until melted. Gradually stir in brandy. Serve with dippers of choice.

- 2 (10-ounce) packages frozen strawberries, thawed
- ¼ cup cornstarch
- 2 teaspoons granulated sugar
- ½ cup water
- 4 ounces whipped cream cheese, softened
- ¼ cup brandy

Dippers:
- Pears
- Peaches
- Pineapple
- Pound Cake
- Marshmallows
- Bananas

Yield: 2–3 cups (6 servings)
Preparation: 30 minutes

 Desserts

Strawberry Meringue Croquembouche

An impressive dessert that transforms into a tree during the holidays.

- 8 egg whites, at room temperature
- ½ teaspoon cream of tartar
- ½ teaspoon salt
- 2 cups granulated sugar, divided
- ½ teaspoon almond extract
- ¼ cup sliced almonds
- 2½ cups heavy (whipping) cream
- 1 cup strawberries; hulled, washed and dried

Garnishes:
  Shaved chocolate
  Fresh mint leaves

Serves:	12
Preparation:	1 hour, 30 minutes
Baking:	1 hour
Chilling:	2–4 hours
Temperature:	250°

Preheat oven to 250°.

Butter and flour 2 large cookie sheets.

Beat egg whites in large bowl with electric mixer at medium speed until frothy. Add cream of tartar and salt; beat until soft peaks form. Add 1¾ cups sugar, 2 tablespoons at a time, gradually increasing mixer speed. Add almond extract. Beat until all sugar is incorporated and stiff peaks form. Fold in almonds. Drop meringue by large teaspoonfuls, 1 inch apart, on prepared cookie sheets. Bake at 250° for 1 hour or until meringues are pale tan and crisp. Remove carefully from cookie sheets. Cool on racks.

Arrange 10–12 meringues in a circle on round platter. Place a few meringues inside circle.

Beat cream until thick. Add remaining ¼ cup sugar, 2 tablespoons at a time, beating constantly. Spread a portion of the whipped cream over first layer of meringues. Arrange a second layer of meringues on top of whipped cream, making the second layer of meringues slightly smaller. Spread more whipped cream over second layer of meringues. Continue layering meringues and the cream, making each layer smaller until the dessert forms a pyramid. Fill spaces between meringues on outside of pyramid with whipped cream. Arrange strawberries on cream as decoration. Garnish pyramid with shaved chocolate and fresh mint leaves, if available. Chill in refrigerator 2–4 hours before serving.

Strawberry Trifle
A spectacular finish.

Preheat oven to 350°.

Grease and flour 2 (8-inch) round cake pans.

Sift cake flour, baking powder and salt in small bowl. Heat milk and butter in small saucepan until butter melts; keep hot.

Beat eggs with electric mixer at high speed, until thick and lemon-colored, about 3 minutes. Gradually add sugar, beating constantly at high speed for 4–5 minutes. Stir in flour just until blended. Stir in hot milk mixture and vanilla; mix well. Divide batter between prepared pans. Bake at 350° for 20 minutes or until done. Cool in pans for 10 minutes. Remove from pans and cool on rack.

Prepare pudding while cakes are baking. Combine sugar, cornstarch and salt in medium-size saucepan. Stir in milk. Cook and stir over medium heat until thickened and bubbly. Stir a small amount of hot mixture into egg yolks and return to saucepan, stirring constantly. Cook and stir 2 minutes more. Remove from heat; stir in butter and vanilla. Cover surface of pudding with wax paper. Chill.

Whip cream. Fold into chilled pudding.

Set aside 14 strawberries for garnish. Crush remaining berries. Add sugar. Measure 4 cups fruit. Reserve any remaining fruit for another use.

Split each cake in half to make 4 thin layers. Fit 1 layer into bottom of 2-quart soufflé dish or deep serving bowl. Spread 2 cups crushed berries over it. Top with second cake layer. Sprinkle ½ of the Cointreau over second cake layer. Spread with all of the pudding. Place the third cake layer on top of pudding. Spread with remaining berries. Sprinkle cut side of fourth cake layer with remaining Cointreau and place on top of berries cut side down. Cover and refrigerate overnight. Sift a heavy coating of confectioners' sugar over top of trifle. Garnish with whipped cream rosettes. Slice reserved strawberries and arrange around edge of trifle.

Variations: A mixture of fresh or frozen peaches and red raspberries may be used in place of strawberries. Sherry or other liqueurs may be substituted for Cointreau.

Desserts | 285

Cake:
- 1 cup sifted cake flour
- 1 teaspoon baking powder
- ¼ teaspoon salt
- ½ cup milk
- 2 tablespoons butter
- 2 eggs
- 1 cup granulated sugar
- 1 teaspoon vanilla

Pudding:
- ⅓ cup granulated sugar
- 1 tablespoon cornstarch
- ⅛ teaspoon salt
- 1 cup milk
- 2 egg yolks, beaten
- 1 tablespoon butter
- 1 teaspoon vanilla
- ½ cup heavy (whipping) cream
- 2 quarts fresh strawberries, divided [may substitute 2 (16-ounce) packages frozen strawberries]
- 3 tablespoons granulated sugar
- ⅓ cup Cointreau or Grand Marnier, divided
- Confectioners' sugar
- Whipped cream

Serves:	12
Preparation:	1 hour, 30 minutes
Baking:	20 minutes
Cooling:	30 minutes
Chilling:	Overnight
Temperature:	350°

Gâteau Rolla (Layered Chocolate Meringue Cake)

A truly unique birthday cake!

Meringue:
- 4 egg whites, at room temperature
- Pinch of salt
- ½ teaspoon fresh lemon juice
- 1 cup granulated sugar, divided
- 1 teaspoon vanilla

Chocolate Filling:
- 2 egg whites
- ½ cup granulated sugar
- 2 tablespoons unsweetened cocoa
- 4 (1-ounce) squares unsweetened chocolate
- 1 cup (2 sticks) unsalted butter, softened
- Shaved chocolate

Serves: 12–16
Preparation: 1 hour
Baking: 30 minutes
Temperature: 250°

Preheat oven to 250°.

Line 2 baking sheets with wax paper. Trace 2 (8-inch) circles on each baking sheet. Butter circles.

Beat egg whites with salt in medium-size bowl until stiff but not dry. Beat in lemon juice. Gradually add ¾ cup sugar, 1 tablespoon at a time, until meringue is thick and very satiny. Fold in remaining ¼ cup sugar and vanilla. Spread meringue thinly and evenly on wax paper circles. Bake for 20–30 minutes. Being careful that meringues do not color. Remove with spatula and peel paper from backs while still pliable. Place on cake racks to cool and crisp.

Beat egg whites in heavy enamel pan or double boiler until foamy. Place over low heat and beat in sugar and cocoa. Add chocolate. Stir until chocolate is melted and thoroughly blended. Remove from heat and cool for 5 minutes. Beat chocolate mixture into softened butter until filling is thick and smooth.

Assemble by placing 1 meringue on serving plate. Spread surface of meringue with ⅓ of chocolate filling. Repeat procedure with next 2 meringues, using all of filling. Top with remaining meringue. Garnish with shaved chocolate, if desired.

Note: Prepare cake ahead as much as 2 days. Store in a cool place.

Variation: This gâteau may also be made in the shape of a loaf pan for an elegant variation.

HINT:
Eggs separate better when they are cold.

Cherry Berry Delight
Heavenly.

Preheat oven to 275°.

Grease bottom and sides of 9x13-inch baking pan.

Beat egg whites, cream of tartar and salt in large bowl until frothy. Gradually beat in sugar. Beat until stiff and glossy, about 15 minutes. Spread in prepared pan. Bake at 275° for 1 hour. Turn off oven and leave meringue in oven until cool, about 12 hours or overnight.

Mix cream cheese, sugar and vanilla in large bowl until well combined. Whip cream in medium-size bowl. Gently fold whipped cream and marshmallows into cheese mixture. Spread over meringue crust and refrigerate for 12 hours or overnight.

Mix topping ingredients together until well combined. Cut dessert into serving pieces and spoon topping over each serving.

Note: Must be refrigerated.

Crust:
- 6 egg whites
- ½ teaspoon cream of tartar
- ¼ teaspoon salt
- ⅓ cup granulated sugar

Filling:
- 2 (3-ounce) packages cream cheese, softened
- 1 cup granulated sugar
- 1 teaspoon vanilla
- 2 cups heavy (whipping) cream
- 2 cups miniature marshmallows

Cherry Berry Topping
- 1 (1 pound, 5 ounce) can cherry pie filling
- 1 teaspoon fresh lemon juice
- 1 (16-ounce) package frozen strawberries, thawed

Serves: 12–16
Preparation: 45 minutes
Baking: 1 hour
Cooling: Overnight
Chilling: Overnight
Temperature: 275°

Desserts

Crème Brulée (Burnt Cream)
Rich and creamy.

Preheat oven to 300°.

Heat cream in top of double boiler over boiling water. Stir in sugar.

Beat egg yolks in large mixing bowl until light. Gradually pour hot cream over beaten yolks, whisking constantly. Stir in vanilla. Pour mixture into a 2½-quart baking dish. Place baking dish in pan and add hot water to a depth of 1 inch. Bake at 300° for 35 minutes or until knife inserted in center comes out clean. Do not overbake. Chill thoroughly.

Preheat oven to broil.

Sprinkle surface of cream with brown sugar. Set dish on bed of cracked ice and place under broiler until sugar is melted and browned. Serve at once or chill again and serve cold.

- 3 cups heavy (whipping) cream
- 6 tablespoons granulated sugar
- 6 egg yolks
- 2 teaspoons vanilla
- ½ cup firmly packed brown sugar

Serves:	6–8
Preparation:	15 minutes
Baking:	35 minutes
Chilling:	2–4 hours
Temperature:	300°

Cuban Blueberry Pudding
Great dessert for family and casual entertaining.

Preheat oven to 350°.

Grease and flour an 8-inch square metal baking pan.

Spread berries in prepared pan. Squeeze lemon juice over berries.

Beat together butter and ¾ cup sugar in large bowl.

Sift together flour, baking powder and ½ teaspoon salt. Add dry ingredients to sugar mixture alternately with milk. Spread batter over berries.

Combine remaining 1 cup sugar, cornstarch and remaining ¼ teaspoon salt. Sprinkle over cake batter. Pour boiling water over all. Bake at 350° for 1 hour. Serve warm or at room temperature with vanilla ice cream.

Variation: Other berries, cherries or peaches may be used.

- 2 cups fresh blueberries (may substitute frozen blueberries, thawed)
- Juice of 1 lemon
- 3 tablespoons butter, softened
- 1¾ cups granulated sugar, divided
- 1 cup sifted all-purpose flour
- 1 teaspoon baking powder
- ¾ teaspoon salt, divided
- ½ cup milk
- 1 tablespoon cornstarch
- 1 cup boiling water

Serves:	6
Preparation:	15 minutes
Baking:	1 hour
Temperature:	350°

Cranberry Pudding

A perfect finale for a Thanksgiving or holiday dinner.

Butter generously a 1-quart pudding mold.

Combine flour, salt, soda and cranberries in large bowl.

Combine molasses and boiling water in small bowl. Add to flour mixture; mix well. Pour into prepared mold. Cover mold and place in large kettle. Pour 3 inches of water into kettle. Bring water to a boil; reduce heat and cover kettle. Steam pudding for 3 hours. Remove pudding from mold. Serve warm with sauce.

Melt butter in medium-size saucepan over low heat. Add sugar and cream. Cook until slightly thickened. Stir in vanilla. Serve warm on pudding.

Note: Pudding may be made in advance, refrigerated or frozen and rewarmed in kettle before serving.

Pudding:
- 1½ cups all-purpose flour
- ½ teaspoon salt
- 2 teaspoons baking soda
- 2 cups fresh cranberries, each cranberry sliced in half
- ½ cup dark molasses
- ½ cup boiling water

Sauce:
- ½ cup (1 stick) butter
- 1 cup granulated sugar
- ¾ cup light (coffee) cream
- 1 teaspoon vanilla

Serves: 10
Preparation: 30 minutes
Cooking: 3 hours

Cinnamon Pudding

A favorite from Butler University sorority house.

Preheat oven to 350°.

Combine sugar, baking powder, cinnamon and flour. Add 2 tablespoons butter and milk; mix well. Place in 2-quart soufflé dish.

Combine brown sugar and remaining 2 tablespoons butter. Add water; mix well. Pour over flour mixture. Sprinkle with chopped nuts. Place soufflé dish on cookie sheet to catch any overflow. Bake at 350° for 45 minutes. The pudding rises to the top, separating from the sauce. Serve by spooning pudding first, then topping with sauce. Place dollop of whipped cream on each serving. Serve small portions for it is very rich.

- 1 cup granulated sugar
- 2 tablespoons baking powder
- 2 teaspoons ground cinnamon
- 2 cups all-purpose flour
- 4 tablespoons butter, melted (divided)
- 1 cup milk
- 2 cups firmly packed brown sugar
- 1½ cups cold water
- ½ cup chopped nuts
- Heavy cream, whipped

Serves: 8
Preparation: 30 minutes
Baking: 45 minutes
Temperature: 350°

3 cups milk
2 cups granulated sugar
½ cup sifted all-purpose flour
4 tablespoons (½ stick) butter, melted
Dash of salt
4 teaspoons freshly grated lemon peel
⅔ cup fresh lemon juice
6 egg yolks, beaten
6 egg whites, at room temperature
Walnut halves

Yield:	5–8 cups
Preparation:	20 minutes
Cooling:	10 minutes
Baking:	45 minutes
Temperature:	325°

Crumb Mixture:
½ cup (1 stick) butter, melted
2 cups vanilla wafer crumbs
½ cup firmly packed brown sugar

Topping:
1 cup chopped pecans
1½–2 cups caramel ice cream topping, warmed
½ gallon vanilla ice cream, softened

Serves:	12–15
Preparation:	15 minutes
Baking:	15 minutes
Cooling:	15 minutes
Freezing:	6–8 hours
Temperature:	350°

Lemon Cups

A complement to any entrée.

Preheat oven to 325°.

Requires 8 (5-ounce) custard cups or 5 (8-ounce) individual casseroles.

Heat milk in medium-size saucepan until bubbles form around edge. Remove from heat and cool slightly.

Combine sugar, flour, butter and salt in large bowl. Add lemon peel and lemon juice; mix well.

Stir egg yolks into cooled milk; add to lemon mixture. Mix well.

Beat egg whites until stiff; fold into custard. Fill ungreased custard cups or individual casseroles ⅔ full. Set dishes in a shallow pan. Fill the pan with 1 inch of hot water. Bake at 325° for 45 minutes or until cake top is done. Serve warm or chilled. Garnish with walnut half on top.

Note: Must be refrigerated.

Frozen Caramel Dessert

You will treasure this one.

Preheat oven to 350°.

Combine butter, wafer crumbs and brown sugar; mix well. Spread onto baking sheet and bake at 350° for 15 minutes or until browned; stir occasionally. Remove crumb mixture from oven; cool.

Sprinkle ¾ of the crumb mixture in bottom of 9x13-inch pan. Sprinkle pecans over crumb mixture. Drizzle caramel sauce over pecans. Spread ice cream on top of sauce; top with remaining crumb mixture. Freeze until solid.

Remove from freezer a few minutes prior to serving to ease cutting. Cut in squares and serve.

Fresh Peach Spectacular

The name says it all.

Preheat oven to 350°.

Stir butter and brown sugar with fork in 9x13-inch baking pan. Add flour and nuts; mix well. Spread evenly in bottom of pan. Bake at 350° for 10–15 minutes. Stir once. Be careful not to burn. Remove from oven. Set aside to cool.

Beat egg whites in large mixing bowl until soft peaks form. Add sugar gradually, beating well after each addition. Add chopped peaches and lemon juice. Beat at high speed until stiff peaks form and mixture is tripled in volume. May take up to 12–15 minutes with hand-held electric mixer. Whip cream and fold into peach mixture.

Place ½ of nut mixture in bottom of tube pan. Pour ½ of peach mixture over nut mixture. Repeat layers. Freeze until solid.

Run knife around outside edges of mold to loosen from sides of pan. Invert mold onto plate. Cover with towel dipped in hot water and wrung out. Lift off pan.

Peel and slice remaining peaches just before serving. Fill center of dessert. Slice mold and place fresh peaches on each serving.

Note: Fresh peaches must be used.

- ½ cup (1 stick) butter or margarine, melted
- ¼ cup firmly packed brown sugar
- 1 cup all-purpose flour
- ½ cup chopped pecans
- 2 egg whites
- 1 cup granulated sugar
- 1 cup peeled and chopped ripe peaches (4–5 medium-size peaches)
- 1 tablespoon fresh lemon juice
- 1 cup heavy (whipping) cream
- 2–3 fresh ripe peaches

Serves: 12
Preparation: 1 hour
Baking: 15 minutes
Freezing: 4–6 hours
Temperature: 350°

Frozen

Tortoni
An Italian coffee ice cream.

- ¼ cup almonds
- ¼ cup flaked or shredded coconut
- 1 egg white, at room temperature
- ½ cup plus 2 tablespoons granulated sugar, divided
- 1 cup heavy (whipping) cream
- 1 tablespoon instant coffee (powder or granules)
- 1 teaspoon vanilla

Serves:	8
Preparation:	15 minutes
Baking:	10 minutes
Freezing:	3 hours
Temperature:	300°

Preheat oven to 300°.

Place almonds and coconut on cookie sheet. Toast at 300° for 10 minutes or until lightly browned; watch carefully. Cool slightly. Crush toasted mixture in food processor or by placing between 2 pieces of wax paper and pressing with rolling pin.

Beat egg white in small bowl until stiff. Add 2 tablespoons sugar; beat until blended.

Whip cream in medium-size bowl. Add remaining ½ cup sugar, coffee, vanilla and beaten egg whites. Beat only to blend. Stir in ½ of the coconut-almond mixture. Spoon tortoni into parfait, sherbet or custard dishes or paper nut cups. Sprinkle remaining coconut-almond mixture on top. Place in freezer for at least 3 hours before serving. Serve directly from freezer. Will keep for several days in freezer. Tortoni is delicious even when not completely frozen.

Note: If unexpected guests are coming, may be prepared just before eating and placed in freezer while dinner is served. It will be ready to eat for dessert.

Fresh Peach Ice Cream
Deliciously light taste.

- 2 eggs
- 1¼ cups granulated sugar
- 1 cup milk
- ½ teaspoon vanilla
- ⅛ teaspoon almond extract
- 5 large ripe peaches; peeled, pitted and chopped
- 1 cup heavy (whipping) cream

Serves:	8
Preparation:	15 minutes
Freezing:	About 45 minutes

Recipe requires electric ice cream maker.

Beat eggs in a large bowl with wire whisk for about 5 minutes or until thick and lemon colored. Beat in sugar. Stir in milk, vanilla and almond extract; set aside.

Purée peaches in blender or food processor. Stir peaches into egg mixture; mix well. Stir in cream. Pour mixture into ice cream canister of electric ice cream mixer. Freeze in ice cream maker according to manufacturer's directions.

Variation: To make Strawberry Ice Cream, substitute 1 quart of strawberries, hulled and chopped.

Spumoni
What a showpiece.

Requires 3-quart bowl or mold.

Combine ingredients for Eggnog Layer in large bowl; mix well. Pour into 3-quart bowl and freeze.

Mix ingredients for Pistachio Layer in large bowl until well combined. Pour into 3-quart bowl over eggnog layer and refreeze.

Place cream and cocoa in medium-size bowl. Beat with electric mixer at high speed until peaks form. Pour into 3-quart bowl over eggnog and pistachio layers and refreeze.

Whip cream and sugar in medium-size bowl with electric mixer at high speed until stiff peaks form. Fold in berries and add food coloring. Pour over eggnog, pistachio and chocolate layers. Cover with foil and freeze, at least 6 hours. Invert bowl on platter. Cover with towel dipped in hot water and wrung out. Run hot knife around edge of bowl to loosen. Lift off bowl. Slice and serve immediately.

Eggnog Layer:
- 1 quart vanilla ice cream, softened
- Rum flavoring to taste
- 6 maraschino cherries, quartered

Pistachio Layer:
- 1 quart vanilla ice cream, softened
- Pistachio flavoring or almond extract
- Green food coloring
- ½ cup ground pistachios

Chocolate Layer:
- 2 cups heavy (whipping) cream
- 1 cup instant dry cocoa

Raspberry Layer:
- 2 cups heavy (whipping) cream
- 1 cup confectioners' sugar, sifted
- 2 (10-ounce) packages frozen raspberries, thawed and drained
- Red food coloring

Serves: 12–16
Preparation: 1 hour
Freezing: 6 hours

Luscious Lemon Mousse Freeze
A winner on all counts.

Cut ¾ inch from top of 8 lemons. Juice lemons, preserving shape. Reserve juice. Insert serrated spoon between rind and membrane to separate membrane from shell. Remove all membranes and pulp, taking care not to puncture bottom. Cut very thin slice from bottoms of lemons so they sit upright and level.

Melt butter in top of double boiler over hot water. Stir in lemon rind, lemon juice, sugar and salt. Stir until well combined. Gradually add eggs and egg yolks, stirring constantly. Cook over hot water, stirring constantly until thick and smooth. Remove from heat and cool completely.

Whip cream and fold into cooled lemon mixture. Spoon into lemon shells mounding mixture on top. Freeze for 6 hours. Remove from freezer 30 minutes before serving. Garnish with whipped cream and thin slice of lemon or sprig of fresh mint.

Note: These do not freeze well for much longer than 6 hours. They may pick up bitter taste from lemon shells if left longer. Reamed shells, however, can be frozen for several days and then filled 6 hours before using.

Variation: Lemon mousse may be served in individual meringue shells.

8 large lemons

Filling:
- ½ cup (1 stick) butter
- 1¾ teaspoons freshly grated lemon rind
- ¼ cup fresh lemon juice
- 1½ cups granulated sugar
- Dash of salt
- 3 whole eggs, beaten
- 3 egg yolks, beaten
- 1 cup heavy (whipping) cream

Suggested Garnishes:
- Whipped cream
- 1 lemon, thinly sliced
- Fresh mint sprigs

Serves: 8
Preparation: 45 minutes
Freezing: 6 hours

HINT:
One medium lemon yields about 3 tablespoons lemon juice and 1 tablespoon grated lemon rind.

Profiteroles with Chocolate Cognac Sauce
The grand finale.

Preheat oven to 450°.

Grease a cookie sheet.

Combine water, butter, sugar and salt in heavy medium-size saucepan. Bring to a boil. Remove from heat and add flour all at once. Stir vigorously until mixture forms a ball in middle of pan. Remove from heat; cool slightly.

Add eggs, 1 at a time, beating vigorously with wire whisk. Batter is ready when smooth and stiff. Drop rounded tablespoonfuls of dough onto cookie sheet. Set cookie sheet on middle rack on oven and bake for 5 minutes. Reduce heat to 350°. Continue baking until sides of puffs are completely firm and color is golden, about 25 minutes. Cool puffs on rack.

Cut off tops of puffs and set lids aside. Fill puffs with ice cream. Replace tops and arrange in large bowl or on individual plates.

Melt chocolate and butter in top of double boiler over low heat. Add sugar. Cook and stir until smooth. Add cream and cognac. Continue cooking, stirring constantly until warm. Spoon warm sauce over puffs. Serve immediately.

Note: Puffs can be filled with ice cream and frozen 1–2 hours in advance of serving time. Remove from freezer 15 minutes before serving.

Variation: Fill puffs with 1½ cups whipped cream; replace tops. Arrange in pyramid on plate. Cover with sauce and serve immediately.

Puffs:
- ⅔ cup water
- 4 tablespoons (½ stick) butter
- 1 tablespoon granulated sugar
- ½ teaspoon salt
- 1 cup sifted, unbleached all-purpose flour
- 4 eggs, at room temperature
- 1 pint vanilla or coffee ice cream

Chocolate Cognac Sauce:
- 4 ounces unsweetened chocolate
- 1¾ cups granulated sugar
- 4 tablespoons (½ stick) butter
- 1 cup heavy (whipping) cream
- 2 teaspoons cognac

Yield:	16–20 puffs
Preparation:	20 minutes
Baking:	30 minutes
Temperature:	450°

Filling:
- 4–5 medium-size apples; cored, peeled and sliced
- 1 tablespoon fresh lemon juice
- 2 tablespoons all-purpose flour
- ¼ teaspoon salt
- ¾ cup granulated sugar
- 2 eggs, slightly beaten
- 1 cup sour cream
- ½ teaspoon almond extract
- 1 (9-inch) deep dish pastry shell, unbaked

Topping:
- ⅓ cup granulated sugar
- ⅓ cup finely chopped almonds
- ¼ cup (½ stick) butter

Serves: 8–10
Preparation: 20 minutes
Baking: 50 minutes
Temperature: 350°

- 2 cups all-purpose flour
- 1 teaspoon salt
- ¾ cup shortening
- 1 egg, slightly beaten
- 1 teaspoon white vinegar
- Water

Yield: 2 (10-inch) crusts
Preparation: 15 minutes
Baking: 10 minutes
Temperature: 375°

Sour Cream Apple Pie
Deliciously different.

Preheat oven to 350°.

Toss sliced apples with lemon juice in large bowl. Set aside.

Mix flour, salt, sugar, eggs, sour cream and almond extract in large bowl. Stir in apples and pour into pastry shell. Bake at 350° for 30 minutes. Remove from oven.

Mix sugar and almonds in small bowl. Cut in butter until mixture resembles coarse crumbs. Spoon mixture over pie. Bake at 350° for 20 minutes or until light golden brown on top.

Note: Deep dish pastry shell is recommended to prevent pie from overflowing. Leftover pie must be refrigerated.

Never Fail Pie Crust
Trust us.

Preheat oven to 375°.

Combine flour and salt in medium-size bowl. Cut in shortening.

Place egg and vinegar in ½-cup measuring cup; add enough water to fill cup to top. Stir egg mixture into flour mixture; mix well. Divide dough in half. Roll out ½ of dough on floured surface. Fit pastry loosely onto bottom and sides of 10-inch pie plate. Trim ½ to 1 inch beyond edge; fold under and flute. Repeat process for remaining dough. Prick bottom and sides if baking unfilled pastry shell. Bake at 375° for 8–10 minutes or until golden.

Black Bottom Pie
Richly deserves the raves.

Preheat oven to 350°.

Mix crushed gingersnaps with butter and press into bottom and up the sides of a 9-inch pie pan. Bake at 350° for 7 minutes. Cool thoroughly.

Stir gelatin into water to soften. Set aside.

Combine ½ cup of sugar with salt and cornstarch in large saucepan. Stir in milk gradually, using a wire whisk. Bring to a boil and cook, stirring until thickened. Remove from heat.

Beat egg yolks in a small bowl and gradually stir ½ of the hot mixture into egg yolks. Combine yolk mixture with hot mixture in saucepan. Return custard to heat and cook for 2 minutes, stirring constantly. Remove from heat. Pour 1¼ cups of custard into a medium-size bowl. Stir in chocolate chips and vanilla. Pour into cooled pie crust. Chill while preparing rest of pie.

Add softened gelatin to remaining custard mixture, stirring until gelatin dissolves. Cool to lukewarm and add rum.

Beat egg whites with cream of tartar in medium-size bowl until stiff. Gradually beat in remaining ½ cup sugar. Fold egg whites into rum-flavored custard. Pour over chilled chocolate layer and chill until set.

Serve pie topped with whipped cream and garnish with shaved chocolate.

Note: *Must be refrigerated.*

HINT:
Egg whites will beat to a greater volume when at room temperature.

Crust:
- 36 gingersnap cookies, crushed
- 5 tablespoons butter, melted

Filling:
- 1 envelope (1 tablespoon) unflavored gelatin
- ¼ cup cold water
- 1 cup granulated sugar, divided
- ½ teaspoon salt
- ¼ cup cornstarch
- 2 cups milk
- 4 eggs, separated
- 6 ounces semi-sweet chocolate chips
- 1 teaspoon vanilla
- 1 tablespoon dark rum
- ¼ teaspoon cream of tartar
- Whipped cream
- Shaved plain chocolate bar (optional)

Serves:	8
Preparation:	45 minutes
Baking:	7 minutes
Chilling:	2–4 hours
Temperature:	350°

- 3 eggs, separated
- ½ cup granulated sugar
- 1¼ cups pumpkin (do not substitute pumpkin pie filling)
- ½ cup milk
- ½ teaspoon salt
- ½ teaspoon ground ginger
- ½ teaspoon ground cinnamon
- ½ teaspoon ground nutmeg
- 1 envelope unflavored gelatin
- ¼ cup cold water
- ½ cup granulated sugar
- 1 (9-inch) pastry shell, baked
- Whipped cream
- Almond extract

Serves: 8
Preparation: 30 minutes
Chilling: 3 hours

- ⅔–1 cup granulated sugar
- 2 tablespoons all-purpose flour
- ½ teaspoon salt
- 4 cups fresh sour cherries [may substitute 2 (10-ounce) packages frozen cherries]
- 1 (9-inch) double crust pastry shell, unbaked
- 2 tablespoons butter

Serves: 8
Preparation: 10 minutes
Baking: 55 minutes
Temperature: 425°

Pumpkin Chiffon Pie

A different twist to traditional pumpkin pie.

Place egg yolks in top of double boiler and beat slightly. Add sugar, pumpkin, milk, salt, ginger, cinnamon and nutmeg. Cook in double boiler over medium heat until thick. Remove from heat.

Soften gelatin in cold water in measuring cup. Add to hot pumpkin mixture and mix well. Set aside to cool.

Beat egg whites with sugar in medium-size bowl until stiff peaks form. Fold into cooled pumpkin mixture. Pour into pastry shell. Chill in refrigerator for at least 3 hours. Garnish with whipped cream flavored with almond extract.

Note: Must be refrigerated.

Mother's Fruit Pies

Tried and true.

Preheat oven to 425°.

Combine sugar, flour and salt in small bowl. Set aside. Place fruit in large bowl. (It is not necessary to thaw frozen fruit.) Sprinkle dry ingredients over fruit and toss until fruit is well coated. Let stand for 5 minutes. Pour into pastry shell. Dot with butter. Place crust on top. Tuck top crust under edge of lower crust and flute or crimp. Vent top crust by pricking with fork or making slits through pastry to allow steam to escape while baking. Bake at 425° for 10 minutes. Reduce heat to 350° and continue baking for 45 minutes or until crust is browned. Cool completely before cutting.

Variation: May substitute 4 cups fresh blueberries or 2 (10-ounce) packages frozen blueberries for the sour cherries.

Peach Pie
Easy and refreshing.

Preheat oven to 425°.

Place peach slices, pit side up, in pastry shell. Mix together remaining ingredients in medium-size bowl and pour over peaches. Bake at 425° for 10 minutes; reduce heat to 375° and continue baking for 40–50 minutes. Cool.

Note: Refrigerate leftover pie.

- 5–7 peaches; peeled, pitted and sliced
- 1 (9-inch) pastry shell, unbaked
- 1 cup granulated sugar
- ⅓ cup all-purpose flour
- ¼ teaspoon salt
- 1 egg
- ½ cup (1 stick) butter, melted

Serves: 8
Preparation: 15 minutes
Baking: 50 minutes
Temperature: 425°

French Silk Pie
Easy and very rich.

The use of a stationary mixer is recommended for this recipe.

Beat butter and sugar in large bowl until smooth and fluffy. Beat in chocolate and vanilla. Add eggs, 1 at a time, beating with electric mixer at medium speed for 5 minutes after each addition. Pour in pastry shell and chill overnight. Garnish with whipped cream.

Note: Superfine sugar can be made by processing granulated sugar in food processor until almost powdered.

- 1 cup (2 sticks) butter
- 1½ cups superfine granulated sugar
- 4 (1-ounce) squares unsweetened chocolate, melted and cooled
- 1 teaspoon vanilla
- 4 eggs, at room temperature
- 1 (9-inch) pastry shell, baked
- Whipped cream

Serves: 8–10
Preparation: 30 minutes
Chilling: Overnight

Pâte Brisée
- 1¾ cup all-purpose flour
- ½ cup (1 stick) unsalted butter, cut into small pieces
- 2 tablespoons granulated sugar
- ¼ teaspoon salt
- 1 tablespoon fresh lemon juice
- 1 egg yolk, beaten
- 2 tablespoons ice water
- Egg yolk

Filling:
- ¼ cup (½ stick) unsalted butter
- 5–6 cooking apples; pared, cored and thinly sliced (do not use Granny Smith)
- 1 teaspoon vanilla
- ⅛ teaspoon mace
- 2 eggs
- ½ cup granulated sugar
- 1 cup heavy (whipping) cream

Suggested Garnish:
- ½ cup heavy cream, whipped with ⅛ teaspoon mace

Serves:	6
Preparation:	1 hour
Chilling:	1 hour
Baking:	40 minutes
Temperature:	425°

Swiss Apple Tart

A pleasing variation of good ol' apple pie.

Recipe requires a 9-inch ceramic tart dish.

Place flour and butter in food processor. Process with on/off technique 8 times.

Combine sugar, salt, lemon juice, egg yolk and water in small bowl. Turn on processor and add liquid to processor. Process until mixture forms a ball. Chill dough for 1 hour.

Preheat oven to 425°.

Roll dough to ⅛-inch thickness and fit into 9-inch ceramic tart dish. Bake at 425° for 8 minutes; remove from oven. Brush with egg yolk to seal and bake for 2 minutes. Remove and reduce temperature to 325°.

Melt butter in heavy medium-size skillet. Add apples and cook gently until apples are just tender. Add the vanilla and mace. Arrange apple slices evenly in the partially baked shell.

Beat eggs and sugar until lemon colored. Stir in cream. Pour over apples and bake at 325° for 30 minutes or until custard has set and crust is golden. Serve warm with mace-flavored whipped cream.

Variation: Cinnamon or nutmeg may be used in place of mace.

Crumb Apple Pie

First place winner from 35 entries.*

Preheat oven to 350°.

Pare and thinly slice the apples to make about 12 cups. Place sliced apples in deep 9-inch pie plate. Combine lemon juice and water in small cup and sprinkle over apples.

Stir together sugar, cinnamon and nutmeg in small bowl. Sprinkle sugar mixture on top of apples and mix to coat all slices. Dot with butter.

Place brown sugar and butter in medium-size bowl. Beat together until creamy. Stir in flour until mixture is crumbly. Sprinkle on top of apples. Bake at 350° for 45–50 minutes. Let pie cool until only slightly warm. (If the pie is too warm, it is difficult to cut.)

Serving Suggestion: Top warm pie with ice cream, whipped cream or slices of Cheddar cheese.

*This pie won first place in the Governor's Favorite Apple Pie Recipe contest sponsored by Ladies' Home Journal. Although Governor Orr received the award, the recipe is actually Mrs. Orr's. It appeared in the October, 1984, Ladies' Home Journal.

- 8 tart apples (about 4 pounds)
- 2 tablespoons fresh lemon juice
- 2 tablespoons water
- ⅔ cup granulated sugar
- ½ teaspoon ground cinnamon
- ¼ teaspoon ground nutmeg
- 2 tablespoons butter

Crust:
- ½ cup firmly packed brown sugar
- ½ cup (1 stick) butter, softened
- 1 cup all-purpose flour

Serves: 8–10
Preparation: 30 minutes
Baking: 50 minutes
Temperature: 350°

Pâté Brisée

Use fingers and work together butter and 2 cups of the flour, until mixture resembles coarse crumbs. Mix in remaining ½ cup flour with a fork. Gradually add ice water to crumbs and mix until dough forms a ball. (Humidity affects the dough-making process, so amount of ice water will vary.)

Flour wax paper and wrap around dough. Refrigerate for 1 hour before rolling out.

- 2 sticks very cold butter, cut into 16 pieces
- 2½ cups all-purpose flour, divided
- ½ cup ice water

Yield: 2 (9-inch) crusts
Preparation: 10 minutes
Chilling: 1 hour

German Pudding Sauce
Versatile, rich sauce.

½ cup Marsala
2 teaspoons fresh lemon juice
¼ cup granulated sugar
3 egg yolks, beaten

Yield: 1 cup
Preparation: 15 minutes

Combine Marsala, lemon juice and sugar in medium-size saucepan over low heat. Cook until sugar is dissolved. Pour ½ of hot mixture into beaten yolks, whisking constantly. Return mixture to saucepan. Cook over low heat, whisking briskly until well thickened and highly frothed. Serve warm over puddings and cakes.

Chocolate Butternut Sauce
Crunchy and delicious.

12 ounces milk or semi-sweet chocolate chips
1 cup (2 sticks) butter
½ cup chopped pecans

Serves: 8–10
Preparation: 5 minutes
Cooking: 15 minutes

Place chocolate chips and butter in top of double boiler. Cook over simmering water until melted and hot. (May also melt in heavy saucepan over very low heat.) Stir in nuts just before serving. Serve warm over vanilla, coffee or peppermint ice cream. Sauce will harden on ice cream.

Note: Keeps in refrigerator for 1 month.

Lemon Sauce
Delicious topping for a variety of desserts.

1 cup boiling water
½ cup (1 stick) butter
1 cup granulated sugar
1 teaspoon ground nutmeg (or less to taste)
Juice and grated rind of 1 lemon (more, if desired)
1 egg, beaten
2 tablespoons cornstarch

Yield: 2 cups
Preparation: 15 minutes

Boil water in medium-size saucepan. Add butter, sugar, nutmeg, lemon juice and rind. Cook over medium heat until butter melts. Remove from heat.

Combine egg and cornstarch and stir until cornstarch is absorbed. Add to lemon mixture. Return to heat and cook until thick. Serve warm.

Chicken Stock

Place all ingredients in large stock pot. Fill pot with cold water to cover plus 2 inches. Bring to a boil; reduce to simmer. Simmer stock for 6–8 hours. (If chicken breasts are in pot, remove after 1 hour. Remove meat from bones and return bones to pot. Reserve breasts for another use.) When stock has finished cooking, place pot in refrigerator overnight.

Remove some but not all fat from top of stock next morning. Reheat slightly so fat is reabsorbed. Strain through colander. Place stock in glass or plastic containers. Use assorted size containers to accomodate a variety of quantities. Freeze. Should freeze well for up to one year. Stock improves with age.

- 3 pounds chicken parts, including necks, breasts, carcass, backs and wings (important for rich stock)
- 4–5 whole cloves garlic (optional)
- 2–3 carrots, skins intact
- 2–3 stalks celery, including leaves
- 1 onion (with skin on for flavor)
- 4 bay leaves
  Peppercorns to taste
  Salt
- 5–6 sprigs fresh parsley
  Pinch of basil
  Pinch of thyme
  Pinch of rosemary
  Pinch of sage

Yield: 4 quarts
Preparation: 30 minutes
Cooking: 8 hours
Chilling: Overnight

Best of the Basics

Beef Stock and a Meal

- 2 pounds veal bones
- 2 pounds beef bones
- 2 large yellow onions, studded with cloves
- 4 stalks celery, with leaves, divided
- Sprig of parsley
- 2 tablespoons whole peppercorns
- 4 bay leaves
- Sprig of thyme
- 1 bulb of garlic
- 1 (3-pound) top round roast

Preparation:	45 minutes
Cooking:	2 hours, 30 minutes
Chilling:	Overnight
Temperature:	400°

Preheat oven to 400°.

Distribute bones and onions evenly in roasting pan. Place in 400° oven for about 30 minutes. Stir occasionally until browned.

While bones are browning, make bouquet garni as follows: cut 1 celery stalk in half, fill celery with parsley, peppercorns, bay leaves and thyme; wrap with cheese cloth and tie together.

Place browned bones, onions, bouquet garni, remaining celery and garlic in stock pot. Place roast on top. Cover with cold water. Bring to a simmer and skim foam from top every 10 minutes until it stops appearing. Simmer for approximately 2 hours or until roast is done and registers 150° on a meat thermometer.

Remove roast and serve immediately or save for later use.

Remove stock pot from heat and strain stock through double layer of cheese cloth into a bowl; discard bones and extra vegetables. Refrigerate stock overnight. Skim congealed fat off top. Return stock to large saucepan over medium heat; bring to barest simmer. Let cook until stock is reduced by $2/3$. Pour stock into ice-cube trays or freezer containers and freeze for later use.

All-Purpose Crêpe Batter

Electric mixer method:

Combine eggs and salt in medium-size bowl. Gradually add flour alternately with milk, beating with mixer until smooth. Beat in melted butter.

Blender method:

Combine all ingredients in blender jar; blend for about 1 minute. Scrape down sides with rubber spatula and blend for another 15 seconds or until smooth.

Let either batter stand at room temperature for at least 1–2 hours. Batter may be strained if it seems lumpy.

Heat a 6-inch or 7-inch seasoned crêpe pan or upside down crêpe griddle over medium-high heat; brush lightly with butter or oil. Ladle a small amount of batter into pan and swirl pan around until bottom is thoroughly covered with thin coating. (If using an upside down griddle, quickly dip surface into top of batter. Flip over and return to heat.) Cook crêpe until lightly browned on one side, about 1 minute. Flip and cook briefly on other side but do not brown. (When using, upside down griddle, it is not necessary to flip crêpe.) Repeat process until all batter is used. Allow crêpes to cool on towels. (At this point, crêpes may be frozen. Place a sheet of wax paper between each crêpe and stack. Store in plastic bag until ready to use. Thaw before filling.) Fill crêpes by rolling, folding in half or by folding each side over center filling.

Variation: Dessert crêpes can be made by adding to the eggs, 2 tablespoons cognac or rum and 1 teaspoon vanilla or 1 teaspoon freshly grated lemon rind; and by sifting 2–4 tablespoons granulated sugar with dry ingredients. Proceed as above for making crêpes.

---

4 eggs
¼ teaspoon salt
2 cups all-purpose flour
2¼ cups milk
¼ cup (½ stick) butter, melted
Butter or oil

Yield: 32–36 crêpes
Preparation: 5 minutes
Standing: 1 hour
Cooking: 1 hour

Best of the Basics

10 cups bread flour (approximately), divided
⅓ cup granulated sugar
2½ teaspoons salt
2 packages dry yeast
3 cups milk
½ cup water
⅓ cup margarine

Serves: 12–16
Preparation: 20 minutes
Rising: 2 hours
Baking: 35 minutes
Temperature: 400°

Family White Bread

This recipe requires a candy thermometer.

Combine 1 cup of flour, sugar, salt and yeast in large mixing bowl. Place milk, water and margarine in medium-size saucepan. Heat to 120°–130°. Add to dry mixture and beat with electric mixer at medium speed for 2 minutes. Add 2 cups flour and beat 2 minutes. Stir in, by hand, enough remaining flour to make a soft dough. Knead 8–10 minutes until smooth and elastic. Place in greased bowl; cover with plastic wrap. Let rise in warm place until double, about 1 hour.

Grease 3 (9x5-inch) loaf pans.

Punch down and divide into thirds. Shape into loaves and place in pans. Let rise in a warm place until double, about 1 hour.

Preheat oven to 400°.

Bake for 30–35 minutes or until bottoms sound hollow when thumped. Remove from pans and cool on rack.

Pesto

12 blanched almonds, finely chopped
1 tablespoon pine nuts
12 walnut halves, blanched and finely chopped
1 clove garlic
2 cups chopped fresh basil
1 cup chopped Italian parsley
½ cup freshly grated Parmesan cheese
½ cup freshly grated Romano cheese
3 tablespoons butter
½ cup olive oil

Yield: 2 cups
Preparation: 10 minutes

Combine all ingredients in food processor. Process until a paste is formed. Serve with cooked pasta or as a spread on crackers.

Note: May be stored for several days in refrigerator and used as needed. Freezes well.

Sauce Vinaigrette (French Dressing)

Combine vinegar, oil, salt, pepper and mustard in a small jar. Garlic halves may be added to jar to impart flavor. Discard before serving. Cover and shake well to blend. You may adjust the vinegar, mustard, salt and pepper amounts to suit the salad or the individual palate. Pour over freshly washed and *thoroughly dried* greens of your choice. Toss gently but well, so leaves are lightly coated with dressing.

Note: The key to a superlative salad is using thoroughly dried and chilled greens, which have been torn not cut. Use fresh dressing and toss gently but very well, so that every leaf is lightly coated with dressing on both sides. There should be no excess dressing in the bottom of the bowl. A rule of thumb is about 1 tablespoon of oil, plus appropriate portions of other ingredients, per serving.

Variations: *Lemon Vinaigrette:* substitute an equal amount of fresh lemon juice for the vinegar and omit the mustard.

Mustard Vinaigrette: Increase the Dijon mustard to ½ teaspoon, or more if desired. For an even more pungent dressing, whisk in ⅛ teaspoon dry mustard.

Tarragon or Herb Vinaigrette: Use ⅛ teaspoon Dijon mustard and add ¼ teaspoon dried tarragon or 1 teaspoon chopped fresh tarragon or herb of your choice. (Basil is delicious with tomatoes and dill goes well with cucumbers.)

Watercress Vinaigrette: Wash, dry and remove thick stems from 1 bunch of watercress. Place watercress and a double recipe of the basic vinaigrette (1 cup) in a blender. Just before serving, whirl briefly until watercress is chopped. The bright green flecks will lose their color if the dressing is made in advance.

The variations for vinaigrette are countless, white wine or flavored vinegars, chopped green onions or chives, finely chopped fresh parsley, all are superb flavorings for salad.

- 3 large egg yolks
- ¾ teaspoon dry mustard
- ¾ teaspoon salt
- 2 tablespoons white wine vinegar or fresh lemon juice (more if desired)
- Dash of Tabasco sauce (optional)
- 1 cup vegetable oil
- ¾ cup olive oil
- 2 tablespoons boiling water

Yield: 2 cups
Preparation: 15 minutes

Best of the Basics

Mayonnaise

- 2 tablespoons red wine vinegar
- 6 tablespoons olive oil
- ½ teaspoon salt
- ¼ teaspoon freshly ground pepper
- Dash of dry mustard (may substitute ¼ teaspoon Dijon mustard)
- 1 clove garlic, halved (optional)

Yield: ½ cup (enough for 6 servings)
Preparation: 5 minutes

Bring ingredients to room temperature. Rinse large bowl with hot water and dry thoroughly. Add egg yolks, mustard, salt, vinegar and Tabasco. Beat well for 1–2 minutes. Combine oils. Add oil, 1 tablespoon at a time, beating after each addition until the last trace of oil has disappeared before adding another tablespoon. Continue in this manner until the yolks and oil have emulsified, then oil may be slowly drizzled into mixture. Continue beating until all the oil has been added and all traces of oil have disappeared. Taste to adjust seasonings. Beat in 2 tablespoons of boiling water to stablize the mayonnaise. Store in refrigerator.

Mayonnaise in the Food Processor

- 2 whole eggs
- 2 egg yolks
- ½ teaspoon dry mustard
- 1½ tablespoons white wine vinegar
- ½ teaspoon salt
- 2½ cups vegetable oil

Yield: 3 cups
Preparation: 10 minutes

Blend eggs, yolks, mustard, vinegar and salt for 30 seconds. Add oil, drop by drop, until the sound of the machine deepens, then begin to drizzle oil in steady stream. *Never add oil in large quanities. It must emulsify with the eggs.* When all the oil has been added, the mayonnaise is finished. Store in refrigerator.

Note: This recipe may be halved.

Variations: The flavor of the mayonnaise may be varied by using flavored vinegars, herbs, Tabasco, other oils (such as olive or peanut oil) or Dijon mustard.

Chocolate Whipped Cream

- 1 tablespoon cocoa
- 3 tablespoons granulated sugar
- 1 cup heavy (whipping) cream

Yield: 2–2½ cups
Preparation: 10 minutes
Chilling: 3–5 hours

Combine all ingredients in medium-size bowl and refrigerate for 3–5 hours, stirring occasionally. Whip chilled cream until thickened.

Party Pastiche

Good parties can meet virtually any description. They may be lavish or thrifty, sophisticated or simple, but the common thread insuring their success is an infusion of personal style, a little imagination and a lot of caring. We share with you some creative and successful party concepts and formats from our community. Copy them outright, cull only random ideas or use them to pique your own imagination. Our hints and menus, suggestions and recipes are offered as stepping stones to successful entertaining.

For a festive New Year's Eve celebration, set the scene well in advance by sending an invitation in the form of a foil-wrapped candy "kiss." Remove the strip of paper at the top and replace with a long narrow coil of paper, scripted on a typewriter or by hand with your party invitation. Set a glittery "silver table" centered with a handsome silver champagne bucket filled to the brim with a colorful profusion of flowers, paper streamers, noisemakers and plastic champagne glasses. At each table setting, place a tiny "favor," beautifully wrapped in silver paper and tied with a silver cord, to be opened at the stroke of midnight. (Gifts might take the form of men's and women's fragrances, or small calendars or appointment books for the year to come.) For festive toasting, tie tiny silver bells to the stems of wine glasses at each place setting. Plastic drink glasses lined with foil cupcake liners can become inexpensive, do-it-yourself votive candle holders to scatter across the table and around the room.

For a Christmas buffet, build an "apple tree." With wooden skewers, fasten shiny red apples and plaid taffeta bows to a styrofoam cone. Stand oversized gingerbread men, with frosting "clothing" and features, around the base of the tree. At each table setting, top individual apples with tiny two-inch gingerbread men (fasten with toothpicks), each holding a place card attached to his hand with a dab of icing. Tie additional gingerbread men to napkins with narrow red or green ribbon. (This basic "tree" concept adapts to a variety of other holidays and occasions with the use of differing trims.)

For imaginative brunch or luncheon centerpieces, make a "nest" of straw from packing material and top with a ceramic or wooden chicken or duck surrounded with a scattering of blown-out eggs. Another idea is based on a clay pot set on a mirror base. In it, anchor in plaster-of-Paris a small, bare, tree branch with abundant offshoots. Decorate branch according to the season—hang from its boughs: candy kisses and paper hearts on Valentine's Day; paper shamrocks and leprechauns for St. Patrick's Day; decorated, blown-out eggs for Easter; real or paper flowers for a springtime affair. (Keep your "tree" and use it for different events throughout the year.)

For a baby shower, fold napkins in diaper shapes and secure with diaper pins. Serve champagne or punch in individual baby food jars, each tied with a gingham ribbon bow. Set these at individual place settings, or for an impressive and delightfully incongruous serving, group on an oversized silver tray.

Use food as serving containers for other food. Scooped-out melons, coconuts and oranges can hold salads or desserts. Hollowed artichokes are ideal for dips and can double as candle holders, by anchoring candles with a bit of florist's clay. Remove the heart of a large head of Boston lettuce and fill with cold vegetables or seafood salads. A savoy cabbage serves the same purpose, or it may be lined with ice to hold a glass bowl of cold soup. A hollowed squash is a perfect container for herb butter.

For fall parties, select a pumpkin, cut a lid in the top and remove and discard the seeds and loose fibers. Season the center with salt and pepper, pour in $\frac{1}{2}$ cup chicken broth and replace lid. Rub exterior with oil and place in a well-greased, shallow pan. Bake at 375° for 1½–2 hours. The pumpkin will emerge from the oven with a rich, bronze gloss, and may be used as a tureen to serve autumn soups. To use pumpkin as a table centerpiece, repeat the cleaning procedure just described, but do not fill with chicken broth or bake. Pour melted paraffin into the center of the pumpkin and roll around to thoroughly coat the inner walls. Spray exterior with a light coating of clear shellac. When pumpkin has dried, fill with fresh or dried flower arrangements.

Tabletoppers unlimited: A wooden shoe filled with fresh flowers says, "Spring!" without speaking. Another spring notion—form a "maypole" of pastel ribbons strung from an overhead lighting fixture and secured at each table setting with a tiny "favor" for each guest. Table covers need not be confined to the usual assortment of linens—try woolen scarves, rag rugs, lovely old quilts, Mexican *rebozos*, wash-and-wear sheets, or lengths of yard goods. For a lovely color scheme, use a single hue in varying shades and intensities. For example, a deep rose cloth, with napkins in assorted tints of pale rose and mauve. Personalize your table decor with your family or personal treasures. Arrange center groupings of items you have collected—clay or ceramic figurines, miniature baskets, interesting rocks, wood carvings, seashells, stained or decorative glass pieces.

Flowers, flowers, flowers . . . Miniature assortments of cut flowers grouped or scattered on a table are often more impressive than a single imposing arrangement. Fill glass toothpick holders or pretty cordial glasses with fresh nosegays. Tall glass flasks, like those found in chemistry labs, are perfect holders for long-stemmed single blossoms. Flowering potted plants may be set at individual places or arranged in a pyramid at the center of the table. Keep in mind—fresh flowers make lovely decorations for trays and foods.

"She's the Berries" Bridal Shower

This lovely pre-nuptial event is ideally planned for warm weather when fresh berries are at their peak, but given the present availability of excellent fresh strawberries year-round, it is easily adaptable to any season.

Send handcrafted invitations in the form of giant crimson strawberries—purchase red cards from a paper-by-the-pound purveyor and fashion "berries" from these. Inscribe each: "Shower for____(bride's name)____—She's the Berries!"

Cover tables with candy-pink cloths and center with pink, white and red flowers and stem-on strawberries, all clustered in white wicker baskets. Center the buffet table with a pyramid tree of strawberries fastened with toothpicks to a styrofoam cone, or more simply, with quarts and quarts of huge, gorgeous, scarlet berries piled high on a silver tray.

Set tables with individual cashew baskets* at each place. (*Melt white chocolate and brush over the interiors of tiny fluted paper candy cups. When chocolate is partially set, insert two cashews in soft chocolate, one on each side of the cup, tilted to meet in the center. Make a tiny bow of narrow, colored ribbon and attach with a dab of icing where cashews meet.)

Our strawberry-saturated menu spotlights a spectacular Strawberry Meringue Croquembouche, a delectable variation of the classic French dessert, and augments it with an assortment of equally irrestible drinks and confections.

MENU
Chocolate-Dipped Strawberries
Strawberry Meringue Croquembouche
Peppermint Cookies   Russian Tea Cakes
Cashew Baskets
Strawberry Daiquiris   Iced Tea   Coffee   Tea

Country Fair Children's Party

For this innovative celebration for children, send invitations in the form of admission tickets. Enclose in each envelope, a roll of real tickets purchased from a novelty store, and include instructions to bring the tickets to the party to "buy" food, drink and game admissions. Have a clown at the door to greet each child and present him or her with an individually inscribed toy sandbucket, to be used to collect food, prizes and carry-home favors.

In your yard (on a warm, sunny day) or indoors, set up a "fairground" with individual food and game booths. (These can be easily constructed from oversized cardboard packing crates, begged from a friendly appliance store.) Set up each booth to dispense food or offer games, and man each with an adult or older child "helper."

Possibilities might include a sockball game (children throw a sock at an adult's head thrust through a cardboard frame); a fortune-telling booth; a "meet-the-monster" booth where children place their heads in the oversized, open mouth of a grotesque monster which is painted on a large square of cardboard, and have instant snapshots taken; a "horror-house" booth where blindfolded children are invited to dip their hands into bowls of "cats' eyes" (peeled grapes), "toads' eggs" (tapioca pudding), "giant's tongue" (cold, cooked beef tongue) and "monsters' brains" (cold spaghetti and oil).

Set up individual booths offering an assortment of typical carnival foods.

MENU
Popcorn   Elephant Ears
Golden Chicken Nuggets
Hot 'n Sweet Sauce
Ice Cream Cones   Cupcakes
Lemonade

Picnic Provençale

When you entertain a crowd, expand outdoors! Pick a mild, balmy evening, choose your locale (your own back yard or a convenient park or club site) and plan a delightful French alfresco supper.

Your invitations can be selected from the stock in your local art museum's giftshop or ordered by mail from a nearby museum. Choose notecards with a cover featuring a colorful, impressionistic garden scene. Handwrite your message in a flowing script inside the card.

Rent a decorative tent, if you wish, to insure against sudden showers—preferably in a sunny yellow and white color scheme. Cover the buffet table with a cloth in a bright, cheerful French country print. (Buy yard goods for this purpose and either "pink" or hem edges.) Create "still life" centerpieces, composed of huge wicker baskets overflowing with vividly colored fruits and vegetables. To complete your tabletop scheme, hollow out long baguettes (narrow loaves of French bread), fill with votive candles and place between fruit and vegetable baskets.

Round tables, seating six to eight persons, offer the best arrangement for dinner conversation. Cover tables with floor length white cloths, and top with overhanging squares of assorted, handblocked French print fabrics. Center each table with a hurricane lamp surrounded by rings of fresh flowers, leaves and grasses, or small bunches of white and green asparagus tied with ribbons picking up each table's colors. A string quartet, playing Renaissance music, makes a nice additional touch for the evening.

MENU

Chicken Liver Pâté   Sausage and Leek Tarts
Crab-Filled Pea Pods
Suprême de Volaille en Croûte   OR   Chicken Chaud-Froid
Marinated Green Beans   OR   Asparagus Vinaigrette
French Baguettes
Apricot Brie   Brandied Strawberry Fondue with Fresh Fruits

314 Luncheon Alfresco

This light luncheon is planned to honor teachers or volunteers at year end, or to serve as an award luncheon for an annual activity.

Inscribe "It's Been a Picnic of a Year" on invitation cards rimmed with a border design of walking ants. Set a festive color scheme of scarlet and saffron—red tablecloths topped with vivid yellow placemats and red checked napkins. Decorate the buffet table with a toy wheelbarrow filled with flowers, garden utensils and plants or with brightly colored helium balloons tied to the handle of an oversized sandbucket. Fill the bucket with flowers or with crushed ice and small bottles of wine.

Covered containers set in red sandbuckets or in miniature apple baskets are a fun way to serve this menu. To serve our chocolate mousse, choose small clay flowerpots, one per person. Fill hole in bottom with a "plug" of ladyfinger, or with a vanilla wafer, softened in a microwave oven. Fill each pot with prepared mousse and refrigerate. Just before serving, insert a drinking straw into each pot of mousse, and place a perky fresh flower in the straw.

MENU

Seasonal Fruit with Fresh Fruit Dip
Shrimp and Camembert en Croissant
24-Hour Cabbage Salad
Chocolate Mousse   Almond Butter Cookies

Sporty Tailgate Picnic

Autumn excursions to weekend football games require careful planning for the satisfying nourishment of hungry sports buffs. Nippy fall weather seems to beg for warming and filling sustenance. Our suggested tailgate menu fits the bill to a formation "T."

Begin with a piping hot, Bloody Mary Soup, poured directly from heat-retaining containers into waiting mugs. The hearty menu can be served buffet-style from your trunk, tailgate or portable table, or pre-packed in individual baskets. Mark your location with a cluster of helium balloons in team (or teams') colors, tied to a car aerial or door handle.

MENU

Bloody Mary Soup   Zesty Nibbles   Vegetable Grab Bag
Sauerkraut Salad   Pita Pockets with Steak and Mushrooms
No Chocolate Brownies   Cookie Chip Chocolates

Additional Menu Suggestions

PUTTIN' ON THE RITZ

Brie Soup au Sherry
Roast Pork with Plum Sauce
Almond Rice Pilaf   Asparagus Polonaise
Creamy Wilted Lettuce
Fresh Peach Spectacular   OR   Gâteau Rolla

AFTER THEATRE SUPPER

Spinach Balls   Boursin Cheese
B'Stilla (Moroccan Chicken Pie)
Greek Salad
Kiwi Mousse   Butter Pecan Turtle Cookies

ELEGANT SUMMER LUNCHEON

Champagne Punch   Crab Puffs Supreme
Mock Vitello Tonnato
Rice Salad   Eastwood Spinach Salad
Celery Rolls in a Loaf
Tortoni   Apricot Spice Bars

FESTIVE CELEBRATION BRUNCH

George's Mushrooms
Soufflé Roll with Ham Filling
Blueberry Bread
French Fruit Salad
Chocolate Rum Brownies

Pan Sizes

4 Cups:
9-inch pie plate
8-inch layer cake pan
7⅜ x 3⅝-inch loaf pan

8 Cups:
8 x 8-inch square pan
7 x 11-inch baking pan
9 x 5-inch loaf pan

6 Cups:
8 or 9-inch layer cake pan
10-inch pie plate
8½ x 3⅝-inch loaf

10 Cups:
9 x 9-inch square
11¾ x 7½-inch baking
10 x 15-inch jelly roll

9 x 13-inch (metal) 15 cups
8½ x 13½-inch (glass) 12 cups

Volume

Tube Pans:
7½ x 3-inch   bundt   6 cups
9 x 3½-inch   bundt   9 cups
9 x 3½-inch   angel   12 cups
10 x 3¾-inch bundt   12 cups
10 x 4-inch   tube   16 cups
10 x 4-inch   angel   18 cups

Springform Pans:
8 x 3-inch   12 cups
9 x 3-inch   16 cups

Ring Molds:
8½ x 2¼-inch   4½ cups
9¼ x 2¾-inch   8 cups

Equivalents and Metric Conversions

	Equivalents	Conversions
1 teaspoon	⅓ tablespoon	5 ml.*
1 tablespoon	3 teaspoons	15 ml.
2 tablespoons	1 fluid ounce	30 ml.
4 tablespoons	¼ cup	60 ml.
5⅓ tablespoons	⅓ cup	80 ml.
8 tablespoons	½ cup	120 ml.
16 tablespoons	1 cup or 8 fluid ounces	240 ml.
1 cup	½ pint or 8 fluid ounces	240 ml.
2 cups	1 pint	480 ml.
4 cups	1 quart	960 ml.
1 pint	16 ounces	480 ml. or .437 liter
1 quart	2 pints	960 ml. or .95 liter
4 quarts	1 gallon	3.8 liters
1 ounce	16 drams	28 grams
1 pound	16 ounces	454 grams
1 pound	2 cups liquid	

*ml = milliliter

Terms and Procedures

AU GRATIN: To cover top of scalloped or sauced dishes with a light but thorough coating of cheese, bread crumbs or other types of crumbs. Brown dishes in a 350° oven or under a preheated broiler 3 inches from the heat source, until a golden brown crust forms.

AU JUS: A French expression meaning "with the juice." Any dish containing only its own natural juices; it is a term usually applied to meat, such as roast beef, which is served in its own juice.

BAKE: To cook by means of dry heat, usually in an oven. Do not crowd things in the oven; free circulation of air is important. Always preheat the oven for 10–15 minutes unless otherwise indicated.

BARBECUE: To cook on a grill over intense heat or over open fire made with wood or charcoal. True barbecuing requires basting with a spicy sauce while the meat cooks.

BARD: To lay a piece of bacon or fresh pork fat over any part of meat you wish to keep from drying out while cooking. Tie in place with kitchen string. Barding fat is usually removed before serving, except in the case of game dishes.

BASTE: To moisten food with liquid or fat while cooking by means of a spoon, bulb baster or brush.

BATTER: A mixture containing flour and liquid, usually thin enough to pour. Batter is used for dipping, coating or for pancakes, cake, etc.

BEAT: To mix rapidly in order to make a mixture smooth and light by incorporating as much air as possible. By hand use a whisk, a fork or wooden spoon in a rhythmic, circular motion, lifting mixture up and over. Tip the bowl while beating. If using a rotary egg beater or electric mixer, use a rounded bowl for proper beating.

BEURRE MANIÉ: A mixture of butter and flour added at the end of the cooking process to thicken a hot sauce or soup. To make a beurre manié, mix equal parts of flour and soft butter, working them together quickly with your fingers. Add small bits to a hot liquid, stirring and cooking after each addition until they are blended and the sauce is thickened.

BLANCH: To plunge food into rapidly boiling water, a little at a time, so as not to disturb the boiling. Cook for the amount of time indicated in the recipe. Plunge food into cold water to arrest the cooking. Drain immediately.

BLANCHING ALMONDS: Pour boiling water over almonds. Drain. Press each almond between thumb and forefinger to remove skins.

BLEND: To combine two or more ingredients thoroughly; to mix by hand or with an electric mixer until smooth.

BOIL: To heat a liquid until bubbles break continually on the surface. Boiling temperature at sea level is 212°F. For a rolling boil, bubbles do not break on the surface.

BOUQUET GARNI: Herb mixture used to season food while cooking. Place sprigs of parsley, thyme, and a bay leaf (1 clove garlic, optional) on a square of cheesecloth. Tie cloth with a thin string, leaving a long end free. Tie string to saucepan handle. Immerse in soups or dishes that are being stewed. Remove at the end of the cooking process before serving.

BREAD CRUMBS: Easy and economical to make at home and a good way to use up bits and ends of bread. Whole-wheat and rye-bread crumbs add a robust flavor to recipes. *Dry Bread Crumbs:* Dry out bread in 250° oven, but do not brown. Do not use stale bread. Using a blender or food processor, blend bread until crumbs are desired texture. Crumbs can also be made using a rolling pin. *Fresh Soft Bread Crumbs:* Use unsweetened, coarse white bread without crusts. Using blender or food processor, blend bread, one slice at a time, until crumbs are desired texture. Bread can also be crumbled by gently pulling apart with a fork. Three slices of bread will make approximately 1 cup of fresh bread crumbs. *Toasted Buttered Crumbs:* Brown 1 cup bread crumbs (fresh or dry) in ¼ to ⅓ cup butter in a skillet or in the oven.

BROIL: To cook over or under direct heat, close to the fire or other source of heat. Pan broiling is like frying but with little or no fat.

BROWN: To sear or seal the juices into meat and to give it a good color. When browning meat, make sure it is absolutely dry, and turn so all sides are seared. Do not crowd pan or meat will steam in the pan rather than brown. Browning may be done under a broiler, in fat in a skillet or in a hot oven.

CARAMELIZE: To heat sugar in a heavy pan, over very low heat, stirring constantly with a wooden spoon until sugar turns to a golden syrup, about 5–6 minutes. Superfine sugar requires less time to caramelize.

CHILL: To place in refrigerator until cold.

CHOP: To cut solids into pieces with a sharp knife or other chopping device.

CLARIFY: To separate and remove solids from a liquid, thus making it clear.

CLARIFIED BUTTER: Melt butter, preferably unsalted, over low heat. Skim off foam. When completely melted, remove from heat and let stand to allow solids to settle to bottom. The butter fat skimmed from the top is the clarified butter, also called drawn butter.

COAT: To roll or shake in flour or sugar until lightly covered.

COOL: To let stand at room temperature until no longer warm to the touch.

CREAM: To blend together softened shortening or butter with any other ingredient by rubbing with the backside of a wooden spoon or using an electric mixer.

CRÈME FRAÎCHE: French version of fresh cream, which is thicker and tarter than regular cream. For a homemade version, add 1 tablespoon of buttermilk or 2 teaspoons of sour cream to 1 cup of heavy cream (not ultra-pasteurized, if possible). Put mixture in a jar (not metal); whisk it well; cover with plastic wrap and let stand at room temperature for at least 12 and up to 24 hours. The cream will become thick enough for a spoon to stand up in it and it will have a sour, nutty flavor. Stir when thickened, cover and refrigerate. It will keep for several weeks.

CROUTONS: Small cubes of buttered bread that have been browned in a 375° oven or sautéed in a skillet and then seasoned.

CUBE: To cut into small (about ½-inch) cubes.

CUT IN SHORTENING: To incorporate cold shortening into flour until it resembles coarse crumbs, uneven in size and texture. To mix shortening with flour, use a pastry blender, two knives or a food processor.

DEGLAZE: To remove and preserve the brown bits and dried juices that accumulate in a cooking pan. Add liquid to the pan in which meat, fish or poultry has been cooked, scraping up any remaining bits. Deglazing makes a small amount of natural sauce that can be poured over meat or used as a base for a more elaborate sauce.

DEGREASE: To remove grease from soup, stock, gravy or sauce. Skim the fat off the top with a spoon or skimmer, blotting out what remains with paper towels. If time allows, chill until the fat rises to the top and solidifies. Fat can then easily be lifted off.

DICE: To cut into very small (about ¼-inch) cubes.

DISSOLVE: To mix a dry substance with liquid until a solution forms.

DOT: To scatter small bits, as of butter or cheese, over surface of food to be cooked or baked.

DREDGE: To coat a solid food with sugar, flour, crumbs or dry mixture. Dredging can be done by dragging the solid food through the powdery substance, by shaking the food in a bag with the dry ingredient or by sifting dry ingredients over the food.

DRIPPINGS: The juices, fats and browned bits that collect in the pan after meat or poultry has been roasted. Unless burned or very greasy, the drippings are valuable for a sauce. (See DEGLAZE)

DRIZZLE: To slowly pour liquid in a fine stream over food.

DUST: To sprinkle food with dry ingredients. Use a strainer or jar with a perforated cover.

FILLETING: To remove the bones from meat or fish. The resulting pieces are called fillets.

FLAKE: To separate foods gently using a fork.

FLAMBÉ: To flame foods by dousing in any potable alcohol and igniting. Warm the alcohol beforehand to assure a flame. Alcohol content should be 80 proof or higher.

FLUTE: To make a decorative, scalloped or undulating edge on a pie crust or other pastry.

FOLD: To incorporate an aerated substance like whipped cream or beaten egg whites into a heavier substance. Using a spatula, gently cut through mixture, lift, and turn over. Repeat process, rotating bowl until ingredients are combined. The purpose of folding is to retain volume and lightness by taking care not to deflate the pockets of air.

FRY: To cook foods in hot oil or other fat. *Pan-frying* is done in a skillet. *Deep-frying* requires a deep heavy pan with 3–4 cups of hot fat into which the food is lowered until covered by the oil. Vegetable or solid shortening is recommended for deep frying. Do not use butter or olive oil.

GARNISH: Anything added to a dish after preparing. To decorate a dish, both to enhance its appearance and to provide a flavorful foil. Parsley, lemon slices, raw vegetables, chopped chives and other herbs are all forms of garnishes.

GLAZE: To apply a thickish liquid over the surface to give a final sheen. Vegetables cooked in butter combined with their own juices form a glaze. Sauce can be glazed by running it under a broiler until brown.

GRATE: To break up a solid into small particles, usually by rubbing against a metal object with sharp-edged holes. Small, medium or large particles may be grated. When grating a lemon rind, use only the colored part of the rind to avoid a bitter taste.

GRILL: To cook over open intense heat, indoors or outdoors.

JULIENNE: To cut into thin strips. A julienne of vegetables would be a mixture of vegetables that have been so cut. To julienne, make a stack of ⅛-inch thick slices about 2 inches long. Cut downward at ⅛-inch intervals to make match-stick pieces.

KNEAD: To work dough with hands or dough hook appliance until the gluten in the flour develops and the dough becomes smooth and elastic.

LARDING: To insert strips of fat under the skin or into meat with a hollow larding needle. Other fatty meats may be inserted in order to tenderize and add juiciness and flavor.

MARINADE: Liquid, usually containing vinegar or wine, spices, herbs and oil used for pickling, seasoning or tenderizing.

MARINATE: To cover foods in a seasoned liquid, always containing some acid, such as lemon juice, vinegar or wine, to tenderize and infuse the flavor.

MINCE: To chop very fine. If using a French blade, rock the blade back and forth from one end of roughly chopped pieces to the other, then repeat crosswise.

MIX: To combine two or more ingredients.

MOLD: To form into an attractive shape by filling a decorative container (a mold) and steaming, baking or chilling according to the recipe.

PARBOIL: To plunge food into boiling water for amount of time specified in the recipe; usually 5 minutes or longer.

PÂTÉ: A baked, well-seasoned loaf of various meats (usually ground), sometimes studded with strips of other meats, well lubricated with fat. Serve cold, cut into slices. Some recipes are referred to as pâtés because the consistency resembles a pâté, but they are uncooked.

PEEL: To remove the peels from vegetables and fruits.

PICKLE: To preserve meats, vegetables and fruits in brine.

PINCH: A trifling amount which can be held between the thumb and forefinger.

PIPE: To squeeze a soft, not runny, smooth food through a pastry tube in order to make a decorative shape or border.

PIT: To remove the pit or seeds from stoned fruits.

PLUMP: To soak dried fruits in liquid until they swell.

POACH: To cook in a liquid just below the boiling point; to simmer gently.

PROOF: To test yeast for freshness by creaming a small amount of cake yeast with an equal amount of sugar. If yeast is fresh, it will become liquid at once.

PUREÉ: To mash to a smooth blend, or press through a fine sieve or food mill. The result is also referred to as a pureé.

REDUCE: To boil down in order to reduce the volume.

REFRESH: To run cold water over something that has been boiled.

RENDER: To make solid fat into liquid by melting it slowly.

ROUX: A mixture of flour and fat, usually butter, blended gently and cooked over very low heat long enough to dispel the taste of raw flour. Roux is often used as a thickening agent.

SAUTÉ: To cook food quickly over a high heat in a small amount of oil. Sauté has come to mean in American terminology, cooking or browning food in small amount of fat over low or medium heat until food is tender, as in sautéing mushrooms and onions.

SCALD: To heat to just under the boiling point or until tiny bubbles appear at the edge of the pan.

SCALLOP: To bake in layers with a sauce, and if desired, to top with crumbs.

SCORE: To make shallow slits or gashes with a knife or fork on the surface of food. Scoring meat or fish will serve to both tenderize and help keep the shape. Process also applies to breads, cakes or pastries.

SEAR: *(SEE BROWN)*

SHRED: To cut or tear into shreds.

SIFT: To separate coarse pieces from fine by shaking through a sieve or sifter, thus removing lumps.

SIMMER: To boil gently so that bubbles come to the surface and just barely break.

SKEWER: To fasten with a wood or metal pin in order to hold something in place while cooking.

SLIVER: To cut or split into long, thin pieces.

SPIN A THREAD: To cook a syrup to 230°, at which point a thin brittle thread forms when a spoon filled with the boiling liquid is removed.

SOFT BALL: To cook a syrup to 234°, at which point a soft ball forms when a small amount of syrup is dropped into ice water. The ball will hold its shape.

STEAM: To cook by contact with steam in a covered container or in a perforated container placed over hot water. Sometimes foods are put into airtight molds, as in steamed puddings, and lowered into gently boiling water to cook. Also, food wrapped in tightly sealed foil and then baked will give a similar result to steaming.

STEEP: To pour boiling water over food, allowing it to sit until thoroughly saturated.

STEW: To cook slowly in a liquid for an extended period of time.

STIR: To rotate ingredients in a bowl or pan using a spoon or spatula, in order to mix, to ensure even cooking, or to prevent sticking.

SUPERFINE SUGAR: A finer grind of granulated sugar. Granulated sugar which has been pulverized in a food processor until light and powdery.

TEMPER: To prepare eggs for addition to a hot liquid. Pour small amount of hot liquid slowly into container with beaten egg; whisk continuously. Pour this mixture back into hot liquid, whisking at the same time. Cook until mixture thickens to desired consistency.

THICKEN: To add flour or cornstarch to a liquid to make it thicker. To make a thickening, measure the liquid to be thickened and for each cupful, mix 1½ tablespoons flour with 3 tablespoons of water until smooth. Stir mixture into hot liquid; cook until thickened. One tablespoon of cornstarch will thicken 1½ to 2 cups of liquid.

TOAST: To brown in a broiler, oven, toaster or over hot coals until crisp on the outside.

TOASTED ALMONDS OR SESAME SEEDS: Place nuts or seeds in a 325° oven and toast until golden, stirring frequently. Do not over brown.

TOSS: To mix lightly with two forks or with a fork and spoon.

TRUSS: To bind a bird so that it will keep its shape during cooking.

UNMOLD: To turn contents out of a mold so that it keeps its shape.

WHIP: To beat rapidly, with an electric mixer, hand beater or wire whisk, so as to incorporate air and to increase volume.

WHISK: To beat with a whisk or whip until well mixed.

HINTS

Peeling Tomatoes: Cover with boiling water for 1 minute or until skins begin to split. Drain and cover with cold water. Strip off skin with a small knife. This procedure may also be used for peaches and peppers.

Maître d'hotel butter: Work two teaspoons of strained lemon juice into 2 ounces of butter (unsalted preferred). Add pinch of cayenne pepper and 1 tablespoon chopped parsley. Form into roll; chill until firm and cut into pats.

Peeling prawns or shrimp: Pinch off head. Stretch prawn out fully, pinch off tail shell between finger and thumb. Remove body shell and any roe using thumb and forefinger.

Peeling onions: Onions should be peeled except when skin is left on to deepen the color of a stock. Chill onions in refrigerator first; the coldness will retard the volatile juices. To peel small onions, drop them first into boiling water for one minute; the skins will drop off easily. To keep onions intact, do not trim the root end, but pierce for even cooking.

Dicing onions: Cut peeled onion in slices from top to root without cutting through. Cut again in thin slices at right angles to other cuts. Turn onion on its side, hold and cut thin crosswise slices.

Storing brown sugar: Store in an airtight container in a cool place or refrigerator. A slice of apple in a small open bag in the container with the sugar will keep it soft. To soften hard brown sugar, put it in a covered bowl with a few drops of water and place in a 200° oven for 20 minutes.

Citrus fruit zest: Remove colored part of the rind with a potato peeler. Do not remove any of the white pitch as it causes a bitter taste.

Vegetables and fruits discoloring: To avoid discoloring of sliced onions, celery, mushrooms, avocados, peaches, pears or apples, sprinkle with lemon juice or douse with a solution of lemon juice and water.

Lining bowls, dishes or molds: To line a dish for soufflés, butter inside of dish. Add small amount of sugar for dessert soufflés or dry bread crumbs for savory soufflés, rotate bowl until it is coated and tip to discard excess. Wipe inside of gelatin molds with a thin layer of mayonnaise to facilitate unmolding. For chocolate cakes, grease pan and dust with unsweetened cocoa.

Index

A NO Chocolate Brownie . . . 276
All-Purpose Crêpe Batter . . . 305
Almond:
   Almond Butter Cookies . . . 271
   Almond Crumb Loaf . . . 244
   Almond Rice Pilaf . . . 222
   B'Stilla (Moroccan Chicken Pie) . . . 168
   Claire's Almond Punch . . . 36
   Granola . . . 34
   Redfish Antibes . . . 191
Anchovy:
   Caesar Salad . . . 73
   Mock Vitello Tonnato . . . 182
   Polly's Fancy Liptauer Cheese . . . 14
Appetizers: see also **Appetizer and Beverage** divider page 7
   Coquille St. Jacques . . . 202
   Crab Thermidor . . . 199
   Sautéed Scallops Provençale . . . 201
   Southern Barbecued Shrimp . . . 195
   Tijuana Tidbits . . . 69
   Torta Di Pasqua (Italian Easter Pie) . . . 114
Apple:
   Apple Butter Bread . . . 244
   Apple Chutney . . . 104
   Apple Cream Coffee Cake . . . 250
   Berry Good Hot Cider . . . 39
   Champagne Punch . . . 37
   Crumb Apple Pie . . . 301
   Glazed Apple Halves . . . 151
   Hot 'n Sweet Mustard Sauce . . . 25
   Raw Apple Cake . . . 264
   Sour Cream Apple Pie . . . 296
   Swiss Apple Tart . . . 300
Applesauce:
   Cupfins . . . 248
   Little Applesauce Muffins . . . 248
Apricot:
   Apricot Brandy Slush . . . 38
   Apricot Brie . . . 30
   Apricot Fingers . . . 265
   Apricot Spice Bars . . . 280
   French Toast Pockets . . . 256
Artichoke:
   Artichoke Appetizer . . . 32
   Artichoke Bottoms with Creamed Spinach . . . 206
   Carciofi Ripieni (Stuffed Artichokes) . . . 207
   Chicken Artichoke Élégante . . . 164
   Crab Salad Printanier . . . 90
   Eastwood Spinach Salad . . . 72
   Greek Salad . . . 83
   Ham and Artichoke Rolls . . . 155
   How to Prepare Artichokes and Bottoms . . . 205
   Seafood Ensemble . . . 204
   Vegetable Delight . . . 231
Asparagus:
   Asparagus à la Anne . . . 207
   Asparagus Polonaise . . . 208
   Asparagus Vinaigrette . . . 75
   Never Fail Asparagus . . . 208
   Party Roll-Ups . . . 20
   Sole Fillets with Asparagus . . . 190
   Springtime Soup . . . 45
   Westmoreland Asparagus Puff . . . 7
Aspic:
   Cucumber Aspic . . . 96
Au Gratin . . . 317
Au Jus . . . 317
Australian Fish . . . 188
Avocado:
   Avocado-Pita Sandwich . . . 70
   Fruit Salad Olé . . . 100
   Hot Avocado Crab Sandwich . . . 67
   New Orleans Salad Dressing . . . 102
   Orange and Avocado Salad . . . 99
   Tex-Mex Dip . . . 13

B'Stilla (Moroccan Chicken Pie) . . . 168
Bacon:
   Avocado-Pita Sandwich . . . 70
   Barbecued Green Beans . . . 209
   Blue Cheese Salad Dressing . . . 102
   Broccoli Salad Supreme . . . 75
   Brunch Eggs . . . 105
   Chicken-Broccoli Quiche . . . 112
   Country Noodles . . . 121
   Creamy Wilted Lettuce . . . 71
   Cucumbers with Bacon . . . 217
   Family Favorite . . . 68
   Fillet of Sole Meunière . . . 192
   Fresh Tomato Pie . . . 226
   Green Beans with Water Chestnuts . . . 208
   Herbed Pâté . . . 17
   Hot Bacon Potato Salad . . . 223
   Italian Vegetable Soup . . . 54
   Party Roll-Ups . . . 20
   Peas with Bacon and Mushrooms . . . 219
   Quiche Lorraine . . . 111
   Ratatouille Monterey . . . 228
   Shrimp Jambalaya . . . 196
   Spaghetti alla Carbonara . . . 120
   Zesty Tossed Salad . . . 74
Bake . . . 317
Baked Chicken Reuben . . . 177
Bamboo Shoots:
   Chinese Walnut Chicken . . . 174
   Hot and Sour Chicken . . . 163
Banana:
   Banana Bread . . . 245
   Banana Fruit Punch . . . 36
   French Fruit Salad . . . 101
   Fruit Salad Olé . . . 100
Bar Cookies: see also **Cookies**
   A NO Chocolate Brownie . . . 276
   Almond Butter Cookie . . . 271
   Apricot Spice Bars . . . 280
   Butter Pecan Turtle Cookies . . . 274
   Chinese Chews . . . 274
   Chocolate Pralines . . . 271
   Chocolate Rum Brownies . . . 277
   Cookie Chip Chocolates . . . 276
   Crunch Rich Chocolate Chips . . . 275
   Date Cookies . . . 273
   Kahlúa Party Bars . . . 278
   Peanut Butter Oatmeal Cookies . . . 275
   Peppermint Cookies . . . 272
   Refrigerator Mint Bars . . . 279
   Russian Tea Cakes . . . 273
Barbecue . . . 317
Barbecue:
   Barbecued Beef Brisket . . . 128
   Barbecued Chicken Broilers . . . 171
   Barbecued Green Beans . . . 209
   Barbecued Ribs . . . 154
   Leg of Lamb Barbecue . . . 145
   Southern Barbecued Shrimp . . . 195
Bard . . . 317
Barley:
   Hearty Mushroom Barley Soup . . . 47
Basic Popovers . . . 242
Basil:
   Pesto . . . 12, 93, 306
   Pesto Pasta . . . 93
   Pesto Torta . . . 12
   Summer Pasta with Basil, Tomatoes and Cheese . . . 94
Baste . . . 317
Batter . . . 317
Batter-Fried French Toast . . . 256
Bavarian Cheesecake . . . 267
Beans, Dry:
   Cuban Black Bean Soup . . . 63
   Hearty Vegetable Stew . . . 232
   Lamb and Bean Salad . . . 80
Beans, Green:
   Barbecued Green Beans . . . 209
   Green Beans with Water Chestnuts . . . 208
   Lamb and Bean Salad . . . 80
   Marinated Green Beans . . . 77
   Sour Cream Green Beans . . . 76
   Winter Soup . . . 46
Beat . . . 317
Béchamel Sauce . . . 206, 213

Beef: see also **Meats** divider page 123
Beef, Brisket:
  Barbecued Beef Brisket . . . 128
  Smoked Beef Brisket . . . 128
Beef, Chipped or Dried:
  Zippy Beef and Olive Spread . . . 15
Beef, Flank:
  Flank Steak . . . 127
  Stroganoff Steak Sandwich . . . 67
  Stuffed Flank Steak . . . 127
Beef, Ground:
  Beef and Noodle Casserole . . . 136
  Beef, Rice and Zucchini Skillet . . . 135
  Cannelloni Crêpes . . . 134
  Dressed-Up Hamburger . . . 136
  Pizza Fondue . . . 135
  Pizzaburger Meat Squares . . . 137
  Winter Soup . . . 46
Beef, Roast:
  Beef and Potato Salad in Sour Dough Round . . . 81
  Continental Goulash . . . 133
  Family Favorite . . . 68
  Individual Beef Wellingtons with Horseradish Sauce . . . 131
  Picnic Pot Roast . . . 129
  Sauerbraten with Gingersnap Gravy . . . 130
  Sweet and Sour Pot Roast . . . 129
Beef, Smoked:
  Ripe and Rye Appetizers . . . 20
Beef, Steak:
  Beef Curry . . . 132
  Pita Pockets with Steak and Mushrooms . . . 70
  Steak Roll . . . 125
  Steak with Mustard Sauce . . . 125
  Yuji's Teriyaki Kabobs . . . 126
Beef, Tenderloin:
  Chinese Tenderloin . . . 123
  Company Beef Tenderloin . . . 123
  J. B.'s Terrific Tenderloin . . . 124
  Sherried Beef Tenderloin . . . 124
Beef Curry . . . 132
Beef Stock and a Meal . . . 304
Beer:
  Fennel Breadsticks . . . 239
Beets:
  Pickled Beets . . . 103
Berry Good Hot Cider . . . 39
Best Ever Corn Bread . . . 242
Beurre Manié . . . 317
Beverages: see also **Appetizers and Beverages** divider page 7
  Apricot Brandy Slush . . . 38
  Banana Fruit Punch . . . 36
  Berry Good Hot Cider . . . 39
  Champagne Punch . . . 37
  Citrus Frappé . . . 40

Claire's Almond Punch . . . 36
Hummers . . . 40
Kahlúa . . . 39
Miss Ora's Mint Cooler . . . 38
Spiced Tea Special . . . 37
Wassail . . . 40
Biscuits:
  Hoosier Fried Biscuits . . . 238
  Monkey Bread . . . 250
Bisque:
  Shrimp Bisque . . . 42
  Tomato Bisque . . . 44
Black Beast Cake (Gâteau Bête Noire) . . . 260
Black Bottom Cupcakes . . . 264
Black Bottom Pie . . . 297
Black Forest Cherry Torte . . . 262
Blanch . . . 317
Blanching Almonds . . . 317
Blend . . . 317
Blitz Torte . . . 263
Bloody Mary Soup . . . 53
Blue Cheese:
  Blue Cheese Salad Dressing . . . 102
  Elegant Appetizer Tart . . . 11
Blueberries:
  Blueberry Bread . . . 243
  Blueberry Coffee Cake . . . 252
  Blueberry Layer Mold . . . 96
  Cuban Blueberry Pudding . . . 288
Boil . . . 317
Boothbay Chowder . . . 41
Bouquet Garni . . . 317
Boursin Cheese . . . 13
Braised Pork Chops with Orange and Mustard . . . 153
Braised Veal . . . 139
Brandy:
  Apricot Brandy Slush . . . 38
  Brandied Strawberry Fondue . . . 283
Bread: see also **Breads** divider page 233
  Sausage Bread . . . 154
Bread Crumbs . . . 317
Brie:
  Apricot Brie . . . 30
  Brie Soup au Sherry . . . 58
Broccoli:
  Broccoli Ring . . . 209
  Broccoli Salad Supreme . . . 75
  Coppelini Con Broccoli . . . 211
  Cream of Broccoli Soup . . . 57
  Feta Cheese and Broccoli Pie . . . 210
  Wild Rice—Vegetable Medley . . . 223
Broil . . . 318
Broiled Scallops . . . 201
Brown . . . 318
Brownies:
  A NO Chocolate Brownie . . . 276
  Chocolate Rum Brownies . . . 277
Brunch: see **Eggs, Cheese and Pasta** divider page 105

Brunch Eggs . . . 105
Burnt Cream (Crème Brulée) . . . 288
Butter Pecan Turtle Cookies . . . 274
Butterhorns:
  J. B.'s Famous Butterhorns . . . 236
Buttermilk:
  Grandma's Buttermilk Pancakes . . . 255
  L. S. Ayres Buttermilk Cake . . . 258
Butternut:
  Chocolate Butternut Sauce . . . 302
  Squash Soup . . . 63
Butterscotch Bon Bons . . . 265

Cabbage:
  Company Cabbage . . . 211
  24-Hour Cabbage Salad . . . 76
  Sue's Spinach Salad . . . 73
Caesar Salad . . . 73
Cakes: see also **Desserts** divider page 257
  Black Bottom Cupcakes . . . 264
  Black Forest Cherry Torte . . . 262
  Gâteau Bête Noire (Black Beast Cake) . . . 260
  L. S. Ayres Buttermilk Cake . . . 258
  One Hundred Dollar Chocolate Cake . . . 259
  Perfect Chocolate Cake . . . 257
  Pumpkin Roll . . . 261
  Raw Apple Cake . . . 264
Camembert:
  Shrimp and Camembert en Croissant . . . 69
Candy:
  Apricot Fingers . . . 265
  Butterscotch Bon Bons . . . 265
  English Butter Toffee . . . 266
  Grandmother's Caramels . . . 266
Cannelloni Crepes . . . 134
Capers:
  Caper Cheese Spread . . . 14
  Polly's Fancy Liptauer Cheese . . . 14
Caramel:
  Butter Pecan Turtle Cookies . . . 274
  Frozen Caramel Dessert . . . 290
  Grandmother's Caramels . . . 266
Caramelize . . . 318
Carciofi Ripieni (Stuffed Artichokes) . . . 207
Carrots:
  Carrot Puff . . . 212
  Carrot Purée in Mushroom Caps . . . 212
  Carrots and Celery with Herbs . . . 78
  Carrots in Horseradish Sauce . . . 214

Cold Carrot-Potato Soup . . . 65
Ginger Candied Carrots . . . 214
Sformata Di Verdura . . . 213
Spiced Carrots . . . 79
Sue's Spinach Salad . . . 73
Cashews:
 Asparagus à la Anne . . . 207
Casserole:
 Beef and Noodle
  Casserole . . . 136
 Chicken, Sausage and Wild Rice
  Casserole . . . 165
 Curried Sausage
  Casserole . . . 117
 Dilly Casserole Bread . . . 239
 E Leis' Grit Casserole . . . 117
 Ham and Spinach
  Casserole . . . 156
 Mexican Corn Casserole . . . 216
Cauliflower:
 Cauliflower-Cheese Soup . . . 48
 Cauliflower with
  Hazelnuts . . . 215
 Italian-Style Cauliflower . . . 215
 Wild Rice-Vegetable
  Medley . . . 223
Caviar Tart . . . 10
Celery:
 Carrots and Celery with
  Herbs . . . 78
 Celery Rolls in a Loaf . . . 240
 Celery Seed Dressing . . . 102
 New Orleans Salad
  Dressing . . . 102
Champagne:
 Champagne Punch . . . 37
 Champagne Sabayon . . . 280
 Chicken Cynthia à la
  Champagne . . . 159
 Lobster in Champagne
  Sauce . . . 200
Cheese: see also **Eggs, Cheese and Pasta** divider page 105
 Artichoke Appetizers . . . 32
 Cauliflower-Cheese Soup . . . 48
 Cheese and Potato Salad . . . 74
 Cheese and Wurst Salad . . . 84
 Cheese Dumplings in Tomato
  Soup . . . 45
 Cheese Pennies . . . 34
 Cheese Soufflé with Seafood
  Sauce . . . 109
 Cheese Squares
  Florentine . . . 23
 Chicken Cheese
  Chowder . . . 41
 Chicken Tostada Salad . . . 86
 Crab Stuffed Potatoes . . . 225
 Family Favorite . . . 68
 Fresh Tomato Pie . . . 226
 Gouda Wheels . . . 32
 Gourmet Potatoes . . . 225
 Ham and Spinach
  Casserole . . . 156
 Quiche Lorraine . . . 111
 Summer Pasta with Basil,
  Tomatoes and Cheese . . . 94
Cheesecake:
 Bavarian Cheesecake . . . 267
 Grasshopper
  Cheesecake . . . 269
 Old Fashioned
  Cheesecake . . . 268
 Pumpkin Cheesecake . . . 270
Cherries:
 Black Forest Cherry
  Torte . . . 262
 Cherry Berry Delight . . . 287
 Cherry Coffee Cake . . . 254
 Hungarian Cold Sour Cherry
  Soup . . . 66
 Mother's Fruit Pies . . . 298
 Wine Cherry Supreme . . . 98
Chestnut Dressing . . . 186
Chick Peas:
 Chicken Ceci . . . 167
 Hearty Vegetable Stew . . . 232
Chicken: see also **Poultry and Game** divider page 157
 B'Stilla (Moroccan Pie) . . . 168
 Baked Chicken Reuben . . . 177
 Barbecued Chicken
  Broilers . . . 171
 Chicken and Ham Bake . . . 180
 Chicken and Hearts of
  Palm . . . 173
 Chicken Artichoke
  Élégante . . . 164
 Chicken Bombay . . . 176
 Chicken Breast and Egg
  White . . . 169
 Chicken-Broccoli
  Quiche . . . 112
 Chicken Ceci . . . 167
 Chicken Chaud-Froid . . . 157
 Chicken Cheese
  Chowder . . . 41
 Chicken Cranberry Salad . . . 85
 Chicken Crescents . . . 177
 Chicken Curry . . . 178
 Chicken Cynthia à la
  Champagne . . . 159
 Chicken Dijonnaise . . . 171
 Chicken Enchiladas . . . 161
 Chicken Kabobs . . . 26
 Chicken Liver Pâté . . . 16
 Chicken Picata . . . 167
 Chicken San Marino . . . 166
 Chicken, Sausage and Wild Rice
  Casserole . . . 165
 Chicken Stock . . . 303
 Chicken Tostada Salad . . . 86
 Chicken-Wild Rice Salad . . . 87
 Chinese Walnut
  Chicken . . . 174
 Country Chicken Kiev . . . 173
 Crab Stuffed Chicken . . . 158
 Crispiest Fried Chicken . . . 175
 Curry Soup . . . 62
 Golden Chicken Nuggets . . . 25
 Hot and Sour Chicken . . . 163
 L. S. Ayres Chicken Velvet
  Soup . . . 56
 Lemon Coriander Chicken
  Pot-au-Feu . . . 172
 Lemon-Herb Chicken
  Breasts . . . 179
 Mandarin Chicken Salad . . . 84
 Marinated Chicken . . . 166
 Mexican Kiev . . . 181
 Mozzarella Chicken . . . 170
 "Oven Easy" Fried
  Chicken . . . 172
 Pecan Chicken with
  Mustard . . . 162
 Soufflé Roll with Filling . . . 110
 Suprêmes de Volaille en Croûte
  (Chicken Breasts in
  Pastry) . . . 160
 Sweet and Sour Chicken . . . 175
 Swiss Chicken
  Extraordinaire . . . 179
 Texas-Style Barbecue
  Chicken . . . 170
Chicken Liver Pâté . . . 16
Chili Egg Puff . . . 108
Chilies:
 Chicken Enchiladas . . . 161
 Chili Egg Puff . . . 108
 French Bread Appetizers . . . 28
 Gouda Cheese Round . . . 30
 Mexican Corn Casserole . . . 216
 Tortilla Soup . . . 59
Chili . . . 318
Chilled French Pea Soup . . . 66
Chinese Chews . . . 274
Chinese Fried Walnuts . . . 35
Chinese Mushrooms:
 Sour and Hot Soup . . . 61
Chinese Peas . . . 220
Chinese Sweet and Sour
 Meatballs . . . 27
Chinese Tenderloin . . . 123
Chinese Walnut Chicken . . . 174
Chocolate:
 Black Bottom Pie . . . 297
 Black Forest Cherry
  Torte . . . 262
 Chocolate Butternut
  Sauce . . . 302
 Chocolate Cognac
  Sauce . . . 295
 Chocolate Dipped
  Strawberries . . . 281
 Chocolate Mousse Cups . . . 282
 Chocolate Pralines . . . 271
 Chocolate Rum
  Brownies . . . 277
 Chocolate Whipped
  Cream . . . 308
 Cookie Chip Chocolates . . . 276
 Crunch Rich Chocolate
  Chips . . . 275
 English Butter Toffee . . . 266
 French Silk Pie . . . 299
 Gâteau Bête Noire (Black Beast
  Cake) . . . 260
 Gâteau Rolla (Layered
  Chocolate Meringue
  Cake) . . . 286
 Kahlúa Party Bars . . . 278
 One Hundred Dollar Chocolate
  Cake . . . 259
 Perfect Chocolate Cake . . . 257
 Refrigerator Mint Bars . . . 279
 Viennese Torte . . . 281

White Chocolate Party
   Mix . . . 35
Cookie Chip Chocolates . . . 276
Cookies: see also **Desserts** divider
   page 257
   A NO Chocolate
      Brownie . . . 276
   Almond Butter Cookies . . . 271
   Apricot Spice Bars . . . 280
   Butter Pecan Turtle
      Cookies . . . 274
   Chinese Chews . . . 274
   Chocolate Pralines . . . 271
   Chocolate Rum
      Brownies . . . 277
   Cookie Chip Chocolate . . . 276
   Crunch Rich Chocolate
      Chips . . . 275
   Date Cookies . . . 273
   Kahlúa Party Bars . . . 278
   Peanut Butter Oatmeal
      Cookies . . . 275
   Peppermint Cookies . . . 272
   Refrigerator Mint Bars . . . 279
   Russian Tea Cakes . . . 273
Chop . . . 318
Chowder:
   Boothbay Chowder . . . 41
   Chicken Cheese
      Chowder . . . 41
   Harvest Moon Chowder . . . 42
   Spicy New England Clam
      Chowder . . . 43
Christmas:
   Wassail . . . 40
Chutney:
   Apple Chutney . . . 104
Cider:
   Berry Good Hot Cider . . . 39
Cinnamon Pudding . . . 289
Citrus Frappé . . . 40
Claire's Almond Punch . . . 36
Clarify . . . 318
Clarified Butter . . . 318
Clams:
   Boothbay Chowder . . . 41
   Spicy New England Clam
      Chowder . . . 43
Cloverleaf Rolls:
   see J. B.'s Famous
      Butterhorns . . . 236
Coat . . . 318
Cock-a-Leekie Soup . . . 49
Coconut:
   Granola . . . 34
Coffee:
   Kahlúa . . . 39
Coffee Cake Supreme . . . 253
Cognac:
   Chestnut Dressing . . . 186
   Chicken San Marino . . . 166
   Chocolate Cognac
      Sauce . . . 295
Cointreau:
   French Fruit Salad . . . 101
   Poires au Cointreau . . . 282
Cold Carrot-Potato Soup . . . 65
Cold Cream of Cucumber
   Soup . . . 64

Cold Sole with Mustard
   Fruits . . . 187
Company Beef Tenderloin . . . 123
Company Cabbage . . . 211
Continental Goulash . . . 123
Cool . . . 318
Coppelini Con Broccoli . . . 211
Coquille St. Jacques . . . 202
Corn:
   Corn Pudding . . . 216
   Fresh Corn Sauté . . . 217
   Grilled Corn in Husks . . . 217
   Mexican Corn Casserole . . . 216
Corn Bread:
   Best Ever Corn Bread . . . 242
Cornish Game Hens:
   Tarragon Baked Cornish
      Hens . . . 184
   Wine Basted Cornish
      Hens . . . 183
Cottage Cheese:
   Country Noodles . . . 121
   Dilly Casserole Bread . . . 239
   Ham and Spinach
      Casserole . . . 156
   Presnutz . . . 106
   Three Cheese Casserole . . . 108
   Two-Layer Cranberry
      Salad . . . 97
Country Chicken Kiev . . . 173
Country Noodles . . . 121
Crab Meat: see also **Fish and
   Seafood** divider page 205
   Crab-Filled Snow Peas . . . 19
   Crab Meat Mold . . . 95
   Crab Meat Crêpes . . . 118
   Crab Meat Mornay . . . 200
   Crab Meat Wrapped in
      Phyllo . . . 31
   Crab Puffs Supreme . . . 22
   Crab Rangoon . . . 26
   Crab Salad Printanier . . . 90
   Crab-Shrimp Bake . . . 198
   Crab Stuffed Chicken . . . 158
   Crab Stuffed Potatoes . . . 225
   Crab Thermidor . . . 199
   Hot Avocado Crab
      Sandwiches . . . 67
   Ouefs avec Fruit de Mer . . . 106
Cranberry:
   Cranberry Pudding . . . 289
   Chicken Cranberry Salad . . . 85
   Glazed Apple Halves . . . 151
   Pears with Cranberry
      Dressing . . . 100
   Spiced Tea Special . . . 37
   Stuffed Crown Roast of
      Pork . . . 150
   Sweet and Sour Pot
      Roast . . . 129
   Two-Layer Cranberry
      Salad . . . 97
   Wassail . . . 40
Cream . . . 318
Cream Cheese:
   Boursin Cheese . . . 13
   Caper Cheese Spread . . . 14
   Caviar Tart . . . 10
   Elegant Appetizer Tart . . . 11

   Mushroom Spread . . . 15
   Polly's Fancy Liptauer
      Cheese . . . 14
   Pesto Torta . . . 12
   Tuna Cheese Ball . . . 16
   Zippy Beef and Olive
      Spread . . . 15
Creamy Wilted Lettuce . . . 71
Crème Brulée (Burnt
   Cream) . . . 288
Creole:
   Veal with Creole Sauce . . . 138
Crème Fraîche . . . 318
Creme de Menthe:
   Grasshopper
      Cheesecake . . . 269
Crêpes:
   All-Purpose Crêpe
      Batter . . . 305
   Cannelloni Crêpes . . . 134
   Crab Meat Crêpes . . . 118
   Crêpes . . . 134
Crescents:
   Chicken Crescents . . . 177
Crispiest Fried Chicken . . . 175
Croissant:
   Shrimp and Camembert en
      Croissant . . . 69
Croquembouche:
   Strawberry Meringue
      Croquembouche . . . 284
Croustades (Toast Cups) . . . 8
Croutons . . . 318
Crumb Apple Pie . . . 301
Crunch Rich Chocolate
   Chips . . . 275
Crustless Spinach Quiche . . . 111
Cuban Black Bean Soup . . . 63
Cuban Blueberry Pudding . . . 288
Cube . . . 318
Cucumber:
   Cold Cream of Cucumber
      Soup . . . 64
   Cucumber Aspic . . . 96
   Cucumber Sauce . . . 95, 193
   Cucumbers with Bacon . . . 217
   Miniature Cucumber
      Pinwheels . . . 18
   Salmon Loaf with Cucumber
      Sauce . . . 193
   Shrimp-Filled Cucumber
      Boats . . . 89
Cupcakes:
   Black Bottom Cupcakes . . . 264
Cupfins . . . 248
Currant:
   Chicken Bombay . . . 176
   Flank Steak . . . 127
   Medieval Parsley Bread . . . 233
   Sûpremes de Volaille en Croûte
      (Chicken Breasts in
      Pastry) . . . 160
Curry:
   Beef Curry . . . 132
   Chicken Curry . . . 178
   Curried Pea Soup . . . 49
   Curried Sausage
      Casserole . . . 117
   Curry Mix . . . 62
Cut in Shortening . . . 318

Dates:
    Chinese Chews . . . 274
    Date Cookies . . . 273
    Orange and Date Bread . . . 246
Deglaze . . . 318
Degrease . . . 318
Desserts: see **Dessert** divider page 257
Dice . . . 318
Dilly Casserole Bread . . . 239
Dip: see also **Appetizers and Beverages** divider page 7
    Hot 'n Sweet Mustard Sauce . . . 25
    New Orleans Salad Dressing . . . 102
    Pesto . . . 306
Dissolve . . . 318
Dot . . . 318
Dredge . . . 318
Dressed-Up Hamburger . . . 136
Dressings: see **Salad Dressings** and **Stuffings**
Drippings . . . 318
Drizzle . . . 319
Duck:
    Roast Wild Duck . . . 185
Dumplings:
    Cheese Dumplings in Tomato Soup . . . 45
    Potato Dumplings . . . 224
Dust . . . 319

E'Leis' Grit Casserole . . . 117
Eastwood Spinach Salad . . . 72
Easter Pie (Torta Di Pasqua) . . . 114
Eggplant:
    Eggplant Pie . . . 218
    Fresh Pumpkin Bake . . . 221
    Ratatouille Monterey . . . 228
    Ratatouille Pie . . . 9
Eggs: see also **Eggs, Cheese and Pasta** divider page 105
    Brunch Eggs . . . 105
    Eggs Continental . . . 107
    Ouefs avec Fruits de Mer . . . 106
Elephant Ears . . . 238
Enchiladas:
    Chicken Enchiladas . . . 161
English Butter Toffee . . . 266
English Muffins:
    Hot Avocado Crab Sandwich . . . 67
    Mushroom Delights . . . 68

Family Favorite . . . 68
Family White Bread . . . 306
Fennel Breadsticks . . . 239
Feta:
    Feta Cheese and Broccoli Pie . . . 210
    Greek Salad . . . 83
    Presnutz . . . 106
    Stuffed Zucchini . . . 231
Fillet of Sole Meunière . . . 192

Filleting . . . 319
Fish: see **Fish and Seafood** divider page 187 and specific listing
    Australian Fish . . . 188
    Cold Sole with Mustard Fruits . . . 187
    Fillet of Sole Meunière . . . 192
    Greek Fish with Lemon and Tomato Sauce . . . 190
    Heavenly Sole . . . 191
    Redfish Antibes . . . 191
    Salmon Loaf with Cucumber Sauce . . . 193
    Sole Fillets with Asparagus . . . 190
    Stuffed Sole Fillets . . . 189
Flake . . . 319
Flambé . . . 319
Flank Steak . . . 127
Flute . . . 319
Fold . . . 319
Fondue:
    Brandied Strawberry Fondue . . . 283
    Pizza Fondue . . . 135
Fontina:
    Ratatouille Pie . . . 9
    Summer Pasta with Basil, Tomatoes and Cheese . . . 94
French Baguettes . . . 235
French Bread:
    Family Favorite . . . 68
    French Bread Appetizers . . . 28
    French Toast Pockets . . . 256
    Pizza Fondue . . . 135
    Stroganoff Steak Sandwich . . . 67
    Surprise Sandwich Loaves . . . 19
    Swiss Chicken Extraordinaire . . . 179
French Dressing (Sauce Vinaigrette) . . . 307
French Fruit Salad Dressing . . . 101
French Silk Pie . . . 299
French Toast:
    Batter-Fried French Toast . . . 256
    French Toast Pockets . . . 256
Fresh Corn Sauté . . . 217
Fresh Fruit Dip . . . 12
Fresh Peach Ice Cream . . . 292
Fresh Peach Spectacular . . . 291
Fresh Pumpkin Bake . . . 221
Fresh Tomato Pie . . . 226
Frittata:
    Spinach Frittata . . . 115
Frog's Legs:
    Savory Frogs' Legs . . . 203
Frozen Desserts: see also **Desserts** divider page 257
    Fresh Peach Ice Cream . . . 292
    Fresh Peach Spectacular . . . 291
    Frozen Caramel Dessert . . . 290
    Luscious Lemon Mousse Freeze . . . 294
    Profiteroles with Chocolate Cognac Sauce . . . 295
    Spumoni . . . 293

Tortoni . . . 292
Fruit: see also specific listings
    Banana Fruit Punch . . . 36
    French Fruit Salad . . . 101
    Fresh Fruit Dip . . . 12
    Fruit Salad Olé . . . 100
    Orange and Avocado Salad . . . 99
    Pears with Cranberry Dressing . . . 100
    Summertime Melon Salad . . . 99
Fry . . . 319

Game:
    Roast Wild Duck . . . 185
    Quail in Casserole . . . 184
    Tarragon Baked Cornish Hens . . . 184
    Wine Basted Cornish Hens . . . 183
Garbonzo:
    Chicken Ceci . . . 167
    Hearty Vegetable Stew . . . 232
Garden-Style Seafood Salad . . . 92
Garnish . . . 319
Gâteau:
    Gâteau Bête Noire (Black Beast Cake) . . . 260
    Gâteau Rolla (Layered Chocolate Meringue Cake) . . . 286
Gelatin Salads:
    Blueberry Layer Mold . . . 96
    Chicken-Cranberry Salad . . . 85
    Crab Meat Mold . . . 95
    Cucumber Aspic . . . 96
    Pineapple-Lime Mold . . . 98
    Two-Layer Cranberry Salad . . . 97
    Wine Cherry Supreme . . . 98
George's Mushrooms . . . 24
German Pudding Sauce . . . 302
Ginger:
    Ginger Candied Carrots . . . 214
    Gingersnap Gravy . . . 130
Glaze . . . 319
Glazed Apple Halves . . . 151
Glazed Radishes . . . 220
Golden Chicken Nuggets . . . 25
Gouda Cheese Round . . . 30
Gouda Wheels . . . 32
Gougère with Ham and Mushrooms . . . 116
Goulash:
    Continental Goulash . . . 133
Gourmet Potatoes . . . 225
Granola . . . 34
Grandma's Bread and Butter Pudding . . . 241
Grandma's Buttermilk Pancakes . . . 255
Grandmother's Caramels . . . 266
Grapefruit:
    Fruit Salad Olé . . . 100
Grapes:
    Mandarin Chicken Salad . . . 84
Grasshopper Cheesecake . . . 269

Grate . . . 319
Great Day Pancakes . . . 255
Great Onion Rings . . . 218
Greek Fish with Lemon and Tomato Sauce . . . 190
Greek Salad . . . 83
Green Beans: see Beans, Green
Green Beans with Water Chestnuts . . . 208
Green chilies: see Chilies
Green Pepper Jelly . . . 103
Grill . . . 319
Grilled Corn in Husks . . . 217
Grits:
    E'Leis' Grit Casserole . . . 117
Ground Beef: see Beef, Ground
Gougère:
    Chicken San Marino . . . 166
    Gougère with Ham and Mushrooms . . . 116
    Individual Beef Wellingtons with Horseradish Sauce . . . 131

Ham: See also **Meats** divider page 123
    Chicken and Ham Bake . . . 180
    Chicken Ceci . . . 167
    Chicken San Marino . . . 166
    Cream of Parisian Vegetable Soup . . . 53
    Gougère with Ham and Mushrooms . . . 116
    Ham and Artichoke Rolls . . . 155
    Ham and Spinach Casserole . . . 156
    Ham Sensations . . . 23
    Herbed Pâté . . . 17
    Italian Vegetable Soup . . . 54
    Mommie Jewett's Ham Loaf . . . 156
    Mushroom Delights . . . 68
    Potato Salad Deluxe . . . 82
    Shrimp Jambalaya . . . 187
    Spinach Frittata . . . 115
    Surprise Sandwich Loaves . . . 19
Hamburger: see Beef, Ground
Hard Scramble Pancakes . . . 254
Harvest Moon Chowder . . . 42
Hazelnuts:
    Cauliflower with Hazelnuts . . . 215
Hearts of Palm:
    Chicken and Hearts of Palm . . . 173
Hearty Mushroom Barley Soup . . . 47
Hearty Potato Soup . . . 52
Hearty Vegetable Stew . . . 232
Heath Coffee Cake . . . 253
Heavenly Sole . . . 191
Hens: see Cornish Game Hens
Herb:
    Carrots and Celery with Herbs . . . 78
    Herb Toasted Pita Bread . . . 240
    Sesame Herb Toast . . . 241
Herbed Pâté . . . 17

Honey:
    Granola . . . 34
    Honey Butter . . . 255
    Honey Whole Wheat Bread . . . 234
Hoosier Fried Biscuits . . . 238
Horseradish Sauce . . . 131
Hot 'n Sweet Mustard Sauce . . . 25
Hot and Sour Chicken . . . 163
Hot Avocado Crab Sandwiches . . . 67
Hot Bacon Potato Salad . . . 223
Hot Mustard Sauce . . . 25
24-Hour Cabbage Salad . . . 76
How to Prepare Artichokes and Bottoms . . . 205
Hummers . . . 40
Hungarian Cold Sour Cherry Soup . . . 66
Hungarian Pork Chops . . . 153

Ice Cream:
    Fresh Peach Ice Cream . . . 292
    Hummers . . . 40
    Spumoni . . . 293
    Tortoni . . . 292
Indiana State Fair Peach Jam . . . 103
Italian Easter Pie (Torta Di Pasqua) . . . 114
Italian Mushroom Soup . . . 60
Italian-Style Cauliflower . . . 215
Italian Vegetable Soup . . . 54

J. B.'s Famous Butterhorns . . . 236
J. B.'s Terrific Tenderloin . . . 124
Jalapeño:
    Tex-Mex Dip . . . 13
Jam:
    Indiana State Fair Peach Jam . . . 103
Jambalaya:
    Shrimp Jambalaya . . . 196
Jelly:
    Green Pepper Jelly . . . 103
Julienne . . . 319

Kabobs:
    Chicken Kabobs . . . 26
    Yuji's Teriyaki Kabobs . . . 126
Kahlúa . . . 39
Kahlúa Party Bars . . . 278
Kidney Beans:
    Fresh Pumpkin Bake . . . 221
    Hearty Vegetable Stew . . . 232
    Italian Vegetable Soup . . . 54
Kielbasa Soup . . . 51
King's Arm Tavern Cream of Peanut Soup . . . 57
Kiwi Mousse . . . 283
Knead . . . 319
Knockwurst:
    Cheese and Wurst Salad . . . 84
Korean Salad Dressing . . . 101
Kugel:
    Noodle Kugel . . . 122

L. S. Ayres Buttermilk Cake . . . 258
L. S. Ayres Chicken Velvet Soup . . . 56
Lamb: see also **Meats** divider page 123
    Lamb and Bean Salad . . . 80
    Leg of Lamb Barbecue . . . 145
    Leg of Lamb with Parsley Crust . . . 145
    Marinated Butterflied Leg of Lamb . . . 144
    Marinated Leg of Lamb . . . 146
    Rack of Lamb Moutarde . . . 146
Larding . . . 319
Lasagne Florentine . . . 120
Layered Chocolate Meringue Cake (Gâteau Rolla) . . . 286
Leek:
    Cock-a-Leekie Soup . . . 49
    Sausage and Leek Tarts . . . 33
Leg of Lamb Barbecue . . . 145
Leg of Lamb with Parsley Crust . . . 145
Lemon:
    Greek Fish with Lemon and Tomato . . . 190
    Lemon Bread . . . 245
    Lemon Coriander Chicken Pot-au-Feu . . . 172
    Lemon Cups . . . 290
    Lemon-Herb Chicken Breasts . . . 179
    Lemon Sauce . . . 258, 302
    Luscious Lemon Mousse Freeze . . . 294
Lemonade:
    Apricot Brandy Slush . . . 38
    Champagne Punch . . . 37
Lentil:
    Spinach-Lentil Soup . . . 60
Lettuce:
    Creamy Wilted Lettuce . . . 71
    Caesar Salad . . . 73
    Zesty Tossed Salad . . . 74
Lime:
    Pineapple-Lime Mold . . . 98
Little Applesauce Muffins . . . 248
Lobster in Champagne Sauce . . . 200
Loin of Pork with Garlic and Herbs . . . 151
Luscious Lemon Mousse Freeze . . . 294

Macadamia Nuts:
    Tuna Cheese Ball . . . 16
Macaroni:
    Garden-Style Seafood Salad . . . 92
    Italian Vegetable Soup . . . 54
Mandarin:
    Eastwood Spinach Salad . . . 72
    Mandarin Chicken Salad . . . 84
    Summertime Salad . . . 99
Marinade . . . 319
Marinade:
    Yuji's Teriyaki Kabobs . . . 126

Marinate . . . 319
Marinated Butterflied Leg of
    Lamb . . . 144
Marinated Chicken . . . 166
Marinated Green Beans . . . 77
Marinated Leg of Lamb . . . 146
Marinated Mushrooms . . . 11
Mayonnaise . . . 308
Mayonnaise in the Food
    Processor . . . 308
Meat: see **Meats** divider page 123
    and specific listings
Meatballs:
    Chinese Sweet and Sour
        Meatballs . . . 27
    Spaghetti and Meatballs . . . 119
Medieval Parsley Bread . . . 233
Melon:
    Summertime Melon
        Salad . . . 99
Meringue:
    Blitz Torte . . . 263
    Gâteau Rolla (Layered
        Chocolate Meringue
        Cake) . . . 286
    Strawberry
        Croquembouche . . . 284
Meunster:
    Crustless Spinach
        Quiche . . . 111
Mexican Corn Casserole . . . 216
Mexican Kiev . . . 181
Mince . . . 319
Miniature Cucumber
    Pinwheels . . . 18
Mint:
    Miss Ora's Mint Cooler . . . 38
    Peppermint Cookies . . . 272
    Refrigerator Mint Bars . . . 279
Miss Ora's Mint Cooler . . . 38
Mix . . . 319
Mock Vitello Tonnato . . . 182
Mold . . . 319
Mold:
    Blueberry Layer Mold . . . 96
    Broccoli Ring . . . 209
    Crab Meat Mold . . . 95
    Cucumber Aspic . . . 96
    Pesto Torta . . . 12
    Pineapple-Lime Mold . . . 98
    Polly's Fancy Liptauer
        Cheese . . . 14
    Spinach Noodle Ring . . . 121
    Two-Layer Cranberry
        Salad . . . 97
Mom's Wild Rice Stuffing . . . 186
Mommie Jewett's Ham
    Loaf . . . 156
Monkey Bread . . . 250
Monterey Jack:
    Chicken Artichoke
        Élégante . . . 164
    Chicken Enchiladas . . . 161
    Chili Egg Puff . . . 108
    French Bread Appetizer . . . 28
    Mexican Corn Casserole . . . 216
    Presnutz . . . 106
    Ratatouille Monterey . . . 228
    Spicy Tomato Salad . . . 79

Tijuana Tidbits . . . 69
Wild Rice-Vegetable
    Medley . . . 223
Mousse:
    Chocolate Mousse Cups . . . 282
    Kiwi Mousse . . . 283
    Luscious Lemon Mousse
        Freeze . . . 294
Mozzarella:
    Mozzarella Chicken . . . 170
    Three Cheese Casserole . . . 108
    Torta Di Pasqua (Italian Easter
        Pie) . . . 114
Muffins:
    Cupfins . . . 248
    Little Applesauce Muffins . . .
        248
    Orange Crunch Muffins . . . 247
    Pumpkin Tea Muffins . . . 246
    Quick Yeast Muffins . . . 237
Mushrooms:
    Carrot Pureé in Mushroom
        Caps . . . 212
    George's Mushrooms . . . 24
    Gougère with Ham and
        Mushrooms . . . 116
    Hearty Mushroom Barley
        Soup . . . 47
    Italian Mushroom Soup . . . 60
    Marinated Mushrooms . . . 11
    Mushroom Croustades . . . 8
    Mushroom Delights . . . 68
    Mushroom Spread . . . 15
    Peas with Bacon and
        Mushrooms . . . 219
    Stuffed Mushrooms . . . 24
    Vegetables 3-Way . . . 232
Mustard:
    Braised Pork Chops with
        Orange and Mustard . . . 153
    Chicken Dijonnaise . . . 171
    Hot 'n Sweet Mustard
        Sauce . . . 25
    Hot Mustard Sauce . . . 25
    Mustard Sauce . . . 125, 150
    Pecan Chicken with
        Mustard . . . 171
    Rack of Lamb Moutarde . . . 146
    Steak with Mustard
        Sauce . . . 125

Navy Beans: see Beans, Dry
Never Fail Asparagus . . . 208
Never Fail Pie Crust . . . 296
New Orleans Salad
    Dressing . . . 102
Noodles: see also **Eggs, Cheese and
    Pasta** divider page 105, see
    also Pasta
    Beef and Noodle
        Casserole . . . 136
    Coppelini Con Broccoli . . . 211
    Country Noodles . . . 121
    Lasagne Florentine . . . 120
    Noodle Kugel . . . 122
    Noodles and Swiss
        Cheese . . . 122
    Spinach Noodle Ring . . . 121

Oatmeal:
    Granola . . . 34
    Peanut Butter Oatmeal
        Cookies . . . 275
Okra:
    Shrimp Jambalaya . . . 196
Old-Fashioned
    Cheesecake . . . 268
Old-Fashioned Vegetable
    Soup . . . 55
Olive:
    Chicken Enchiladas . . . 161
    Eastwood Spinach Salad . . . 72
    Greek Salad . . . 83
    Herbed Pâté . . . 17
    Ratatouille Pie . . . 9
    Ripe and Rye Appetizers . . . 20
    Tex-Mex Dip . . . 13
    Zippy Beef and Olive
        Spread . . . 15
Onion:
    Great Onion Rings . . . 218
    Spinach in Onion Shells . . . 219
One Hundred Dollar Chocolate
    Cake . . . 259
Orange:
    Braised Pork Chops with
        Orange and Mustard . . . 153
    French Fruit Salad . . . 101
    Fruit Salad Olé . . . 100
    Orange and Avocado
        Salad . . . 99
    Orange and Date Bread . . . 246
Oriental Chicken Wings . . . 28
Ouefs avec Fruits de Mer . . . 106
"Oven Easy" Fried Chicken . . . 172
Oyster Crackers:
    Zesty Nibbles . . . 33

Pancakes:
    Grandma's Buttermilk Pancakes
        . . . 255
    Great Day Pancakes . . . 255
    Hard Scramble Pancakes . . . 254
Papillote:
    Shrimp and Pesto "en
        Papillote" . . . 197
Parboil . . . 319
Parfait:
    Citrus Frappé . . . 40
Parmesan:
    Scott's Parmesan
        Spinach . . . 229
Parsley:
    Leg of Lamb with Parsley
        Crust . . . 145
    Medieval Parsley Bread . . . 233
    Pesto and Pasta Salad . . . 93
Party Pastiche . . . 309
Party Roll-Ups . . . 20
Pasta: see also **Eggs, Cheese and
    Pasta** divider page 105, see
    also Noodles
    Garden Style Seafood
        Salad . . . 92
    Pesto and Pasta Salad . . . 93
    Spaghetti alla Carbonara . . . 120
    Spaghetti and Meatballs . . . 119
    Summer Pasta with Basil,

Tomatoes and Cheese . . . 94
Pastry:
　Crab Meat Mornay . . . 200
　Eggplant Pie . . . 218
　Elegante Appetizer Tart . . . 11
　Gougère with Ham and
　　Mushrooms . . . 116
　Never Fail Pie Crust . . . 296
　Pâté Brisée . . . 300, 301
　Pâté Choux . . . 116
　Ratatouille Pie . . . 9
　Sausage en Croûte . . . 115
　Suprême de Voille en Croûte
　　(Chicken Breasts in
　　Pastry) . . . 160
　Westmoreland Asparagus
　　Puffs . . . 7
Pâté . . . 319
Pâté:
　Chicken Liver Pâté . . . 16
　Herbed Pâté . . . 17
Pea Pods:
　Chinese Tenderloin . . . 123
　Crab-Filled Snow Peas . . . 19
　Shrimp Tomato
　　Vinaigrette . . . 91
Peach:
　Fresh Peach Ice Cream . . . 292
　Fresh Peach Spectacular . . . 291
　Indiana State Fair Peach
　　Jam . . . 103
　Peach Pie . . . 299
Peanut Butter:
　Butterscotch Bon Bons . . . 265
　King's Arm Tavern Cream of
　　Peanut Soup . . . 57
　Peanut Butter Oatmeal
　　Cookies . . . 275
Peanuts:
　Crispiest Fried Chicken . . . 175
　Eastwood Spinach Salad . . . 72
Pears:
　French Fruit Salad . . . 101
　Pears with Cranberry
　　Dressing . . . 100
　Poires au Cointreau . . . 282
Peas:
　Chilled French Pea Soup . . . 66
　Chinese Peas . . . 220
　Curried Pea Soup . . . 49
　Peas with Bacon and
　　Mushrooms . . . 219
　Vegetable Delight . . . 231
Pecans:
　Chocolate Butternut
　　Sauce . . . 302
　Granola . . . 34
　Pecan Chicken with
　　Mustard . . . 162
Peel . . . 319
Peppermint:
　Miss Ora's Mint Cooler . . . 38
　Peppermint Cookies . . . 272
　Refrigerator Mint Bars . . . 279
Pepperoni:
　Chicken Ceci . . . 167
　Stuffed Mushrooms . . . 24
Perfect Chocolate Cake . . . 257
Perfect Rice . . . 222

Pesto:
　Pesto . . . 197, 306
　Pesto and Pasta Salad . . . 93
　Pesto Torta . . . 12
　Shrimp and Pesto "en
　　Papillote" . . . 197
Petal Bread . . . 237
Phyllo:
　Apricot Brie . . . 30
　B'Stilla . . . 168
　Crab Meat Wrapped in
　　Phyllo . . . 31
　Feta Cheese and Broccoli
　　Pie . . . 210
Pickle . . . 319
Pickled Beets . . . 103
Pickles:
　Surprise Sandwich
　　Loaves . . . 19
Picnic Pot Roast . . . 129
Pie: see also **Desserts** divider page
　257
　Eggplant Pie . . . 218
　Elegant Appetizer Tart . . . 11
　Ratatouille Pie . . . 9
Pie Crust:
　Never Fail Pie Crust . . . 296
Pinch . . . 320
Pineapple:
　Banana Fruit Punch . . . 36
　Chicken-Wild Rice Salad . . . 87
　Claire's Almond Punch . . . 36
　Company Beef
　　Tenderloin . . . 123
　French Fruit Salad . . . 101
　Hot 'n Sweet Mustard
　　Sauce . . . 25
　Pineapple-Lime Mold . . . 98
　Summertime Melon
　　Salad . . . 99
Pipe . . . 320
Piquant Pork with Spiced Apple
　Rice . . . 147
Pit . . . 320
Pita:
　Avocado-Pita Sandwich . . . 70
　Herb Toasted Pita Bread . . . 240
　Pita Pockets with Steak and
　　Mushrooms . . . 70
Pizza Fondue . . . 135
Pizzaburger Meat Squares . . . 137
Plum:
　Roast Pork with Plum
　　Sauce . . . 152
Plump . . . 320
Poach . . . 320
Poires au Cointreau . . . 282
Polly's Fancy Liptauer
　Cheese . . . 14
Popovers:
　Basic Popovers . . . 242
Poppy Seed Dressing . . . 101
Portia's Bay Scallops . . . 203
Pork: see also **Meats** divider
　page 123
Pork, Chops:
　Braised Pork Chops with
　　Orange and Mustard . . . 153
　Hungarian Pork Chops . . . 153

Pork, Ground:
　Chinese Sweet and Sour Meat
　　Balls . . . 27
　Herbed Pâté . . . 17
　Mommie Jewett's Ham
　　Loaf : . . 156
Pork, Roast:
　Loin of Pork with Garlic and
　　Herbs . . . 151
　Pork Loin with Orange
　　Glaze . . . 149
　Real Italian Spaghetti
　　Sauce . . . 152
　Roast Pork with Plum
　　Sauce . . . 152
　Stuffed Crown Roast of
　　Pork . . . 150
Pork, Ribs:
　Barbecued Ribs . . . 154
Pork, Tenderloin:
　Piquant Pork with Spiced Apple
　　Rice . . . 147
　Pork Tenderloin with Wine
　　Sauce . . . 148
Potato:
　Beef and Potato Salad in Sour
　　Dough Round . . . 81
　Cheese and Potato Salad . . . 74
　Cold Carrot-Potato Soup . . . 65
　Crab Stuffed Potatoes . . . 225
　Gourmet Potatoes . . . 225
　Hearty Potato Soup . . . 52
　Hot Bacon Potato Salad . . . 223
　Potato Dumplings . . . 224
　Potato Salad Deluxe . . . 82
　Ranch Potatoes . . . 224
　Sweet Potatoes with
　　Topping . . . 226
Pot Roast: see Beef, Roast
Praline:
　Chocolate Praline . . . 271
Presnutz . . . 106
Profiteroles with Chocolate
　Cognac Sauce . . . 295
Proof . . . 320
Prosciutto:
　Chicken San Marino . . . 166
　Torta Di Pasqua . . . 114
Pudding:
　Cinnamon Pudding . . . 289
　Cranberry Pudding . . . 289
　Cuban Blueberry
　　Pudding . . . 288
　German Pudding Sauce . . . 302
　Grandma's Bread and Butter
　　Pudding . . . 241
Puff Pastry:
　Individual Beef Wellingtons with
　　Horseradish Sauce . . . 131
　Westmoreland Asparagus
　　Puffs . . . 7
Pumpkin:
　Fresh Pumpkin Bake . . . 221
　Pumpkin Cheesecake . . . 270
　Pumpkin Chiffon Pie . . . 298
　Pumpkin Roll . . . 261
　Pumpkin Soup . . . 56
　Pumpkin Tea Muffins . . . 246
Punch: see also **Appetizers and**

Beverage divider page 7
  Banana Fruit Punch . . . 36
  Champagne Punch . . . 37
  Claire's Almond Punch . . . 36
Pureé . . . 320
Purée:
  Carrot Purée in Mushroom Caps . . . 212

Quail in Casserole . . . 184
Quiche:
  Crustless Spinach Quiche . . . 111
  Quiche Lorraine . . . 111
  Seafood Quiche . . . 113
  Chicken-Broccoli Quiche . . . 112
Quick Spinach Soup . . . 65
Quick Yeast Muffins . . . 237

Rack of Lamb Moutarde . . . 146
Radishes:
  Glazed Radishes . . . 220
Raisins:
  Broccoli Salad Supreme . . . 75
  Granola . . . 34
Ranch Potatoes . . . 224
Raspberry:
  Berry Good Hot Cider . . . 39
Ratatouille:
  Ratatouille Monterey . . . 228
  Ratatouille Pie . . . 9
Raw Apple Cake . . . 264
Real Italian Spaghetti Sauce . . . 152
Red Snapper:
  Redfish Antibes . . . 191
Reduce . . . 320
Refresh . . . 320
Refrigerator Mint Bars . . . 279
Relish: see also **Salads** divider page 71
  Apple Chutney . . . 104
  Pickled Beets . . . 103
  Uncooked Cucumber Slices . . . 104
Render . . . 320
Ribs:
  Barbecued Ribs . . . 154
Rice:
  Almond Rice Pilaf . . . 222
  Beef, Rice and Zucchini Skillet . . . 135
  Chicken Artichoke Élégante . . . 164
  Chicken-Wild Rice Salad . . . 87
  Perfect Rice . . . 222
  Rice Salad . . . 88
  Wild Rice-Vegetable Medley . . . 223
Ricotta:
  Presnutz . . . 106
  Torta Di Pasqua . . . 114
Ring-A-Lings . . . 249
Ripe and Rye Appetizers . . . 20
Roast Beef Wellington with Horseradish Sauce . . . 131

Roast Leg of Lamb with Parsley Crust . . . 145
Roast Pork with Plum Sauce . . . 152
Roast Wild Duck . . . 185
Rolls:
  Celery Rolls in a Loaf . . . 240
  J. B.'s Famous Butterhorns . . . 236
  Ring-A-Lings . . . 249
Romaine:
  Caesar Salad . . . 73
  Roquefort-Stuffed Shrimp . . . 10
Rotini:
  Pesto and Pasta Salad . . . 93
Round Steak: see Beef, Steak
Roux . . . 320
Rum:
  Chocolate Rum Brownies . . . 277
  Hummers . . . 40
Russian Tea Cakes . . . 273

Sabayon:
  Champagne Sabayon . . . 280
Salad: see **Salads** divider page 71
Salad Dressing: see also **Salads** divider page 71
  Blue Cheese Salad Dressing . . . 102
  Celery Seed Dressing . . . 102
  French Fruit Salad Dressing . . . 101
  Korean Salad Dressing . . . 101
  New Orleans Salad Dressing . . . 102
  Poppy Seed Dressing . . . 101
Salmon:
  Salmon Loaf with Cucumber Sauce . . . 193
  Shrimp-Filled Salmon Rolls . . . 7
Sandwich: see also **Soups and Sandwiches** divider page 41
  Avocado-Pita Sandwich . . . 70
  Cream Cheese Spread . . . 71
  Family Favorite . . . 68
  Hot Avocado Crab Sandwiches . . . 67
  Mushroom Delights . . . 68
  Pita Pockets with Steak and Mushrooms . . . 70
  Shrimp and Camembert en Croissant . . . 69
  Stroganoff Steak Sandwich . . . 67
  Tijuana Tidbits . . . 69
Sauce:
  Chocolate Butternut Sauce . . . 302
  Cucumber Sauce . . . 95, 193
  German Pudding Sauce . . . 302
  Horseradish Sauce . . . 131
  Sauce Vinaigrette (French Dressing) . . . 307
  Hot 'n Sweet Mustard Sauce . . . 25
  Hot Mustard Sauce . . . 25
  Lemon Sauce . . . 302

Sauerbraten with Gingersnap Gravy . . . 130
Sauerkraut:
  Baked Chicken Reuben . . . 177
  Sauerkraut Salad . . . 77
  Sausage Surprise Balls . . . 21
Sausage:
  Chicken Breasts in Pastry (Suprême de Volaille en Croûte) . . . 160
  Chicken, Sausage and Wild Rice . . . 165
  Curried Sausage Casserole . . . 117
  Italian Vegetable Soup . . . 54
  Piquant Pork with Spiced Apple Rice . . . 147
  Sausage and Leek Tarts . . . 33
  Sausage Bread . . . 154
  Sausage en Croûte . . . 115
  Sausage Surprise Balls . . . 21
  Spinach Frittata . . . 115
  Stuffed Crown Roast of Pork . . . 150
Sauté . . . 320
Sautéed Scallops Provençale . . . 201
Savory Frogs' Legs . . . 203
Scallop . . . 320
Scallops:
  Broiled Scallops . . . 201
  Coquille St. Jacques . . . 202
  Portia's Bay Scallops . . . 203
  Sautéed Scallops Provençale . . . 201
Scald . . . 320
Scampi Delectable . . . 194
Score . . . 320
Scott's Parmesan Spinach . . . 229
Seafood: see also **Fish and Seafood** divider page 187
  Cheese Soufflé with Seafood Sauce . . . 109
  Garden-Style Seafood Salad . . . 92
  Seafood Ensemble . . . 204
  Seafood Quiche . . . 113
Sear . . . 320
Sesame:
  Granola . . . 34
  Sesame Herb Toast . . . 241
Sformata Di Verdura . . . 213
Sherbet:
  Citrus Frappé . . . 40
Sherry:
  Sherried Beef Tenderloin . . . 124
  Brie Soup au Sherry . . . 58
Shread . . . 320
Shrimp: see also **Fish and Seafood** divider page 187
  Crab-Shrimp Bake . . . 198
  George's Mushrooms . . . 24
  Ouefs avec Fruits de Mer . . . 106
  Roquefort-Stuffed Shrimp . . . 10
  Scampi Delectable . . . 194
  Seafood Ensemble . . . 204

Shrimp and Camembert en Croissant . . . 69
Shrimp and Pesto "en Papillote" . . . 197
Shrimp Bisque . . . 42
Shrimp Jambalaya . . . 196
Shrimp Newburg Sauce . . . 158
Shrimp Tomato Vinaigrette . . . 91
Shrimp-Filled Cucumber Boats . . . 89
Shrimp-Filled Salmon Rolls . . . 7
Southern Barbecued Shrimp . . . 195
Sift . . . 320
Simmer . . . 320
Skewer . . . 320
Slaw:
   24-Hour Cabbage Salad . . . 76
Sliver . . . 320
Smoked Beef Brisket . . . 128
Snow Peas
   Potato Salad Deluxe . . . 82
   Crab-Filled Snow Peas . . . 19
Snacks: see also **Appetizers and Beverage** divider page 7
   Cheese Pennies . . . 34
   Chinese Fried Walnuts . . . 35
   Granola . . . 34
   White Chocolate Party Mix . . . 35
   Zesty Nibbles . . . 33
Soft ball . . . 320
Sole: see also **Fish and Seafood** divider page 187
   Australian Fish . . . 188
   Cold Sole with Mustard Fruits . . . 187
   Fillet of Sole Meunière . . . 192
   Greek Fish with Lemon and Tomato . . . 190
   Heavenly Sole . . . 191
   Sole Fillets with Asparagus . . . 190
   Stuffed Sole Fillets . . . 189
Soufflé Roll with Filling . . . 110
Soup: see **Soups and Sandwiches** divider page 41
Sour and Hot Soup . . . 61
Sour Cream Apple Pie . . . 296
Sour Cream Green Beans . . . 76
Sour Dough:
   Beef and Potato Salad in Sour Dough Round . . . 81
Southern Barbecued Shrimp . . . 195
Spaghetti:
   Real Italian Spaghetti Sauce . . . 152
   Spaghetti alla Carbonara . . . 120
   Spaghetti and Meatballs . . . 119
Spareribs:
   Barbecued Ribs . . . 154
Spiced Apple Rice . . . 147
Spiced Tea Special . . . 37
Spicy New England Clam Chowder . . . 43
Spicy Tomato Salad . . . 79
Spin a Thread . . . 320

Spinach:
   Artichoke Bottoms with Creamed Spinach . . . 206
   Cheese Squares Florentine . . . 23
   Chicken Artichoke Élégante . . . 164
   Crustless Spinach Quiche . . . 111
   Eastwood Spinach Salad . . . 72
   Herbed Pâté . . . 17
   Lasagne Florentine . . . 120
   Pita Pockets with Steak and Mushrooms . . . 70
   Presnutz . . . 106
   Quick Spinach Soup . . . 65
   Scott's Spinach Parmesan . . . 229
   Soufflé Roll with Filling . . . 110
   Spinach Balls . . . 22
   Spinach Frittata . . . 115
   Spinach in Onion Shells . . . 219
   Spinach-Lentil Soup . . . 60
   Spinach Noodle Ring . . . 121
   Springtime Soup . . . 45
   Strawberry Spinach Salad . . . 71
   Stuffed Zucchini . . . 231
   Sue's Spinach Salad . . . 73
   Three Cheese Casserole . . . 108

Spreads: see also **Appetizers and Beverages** divider page 7
   Caper Cheese Spread . . . 14
   Polly's Fancy Liptauer Cheese . . . 14
   Mushroom Spread . . . 15
   New Orleans Salad Dressing . . . 102
   Zippy Beef and Olive Spread . . . 15
Spumoni . . . 293
Squash:
   Squash Soufflé . . . 229
   Squash Soup . . . 63
Steak: see Beef, Steak
Steak Roll . . . 125
Steak with Mustard Sauce . . . 125
Steam . . . 320
Steep . . . 320
Stew . . . 320
Stews:
   Hearty Vegetable Stew . . . 232
Stir . . . 320
Stir Fry:
   Hot and Sour Chicken . . . 163
Stock:
   Beef Stock and a Meal . . . 304
   Chicken Stock . . . 303
Strawberry:
   Brandied Strawberry Fondue . . . 283
   Chocolate Dipped Strawberries . . . 281
   French Fruit Salad . . . 101
   Strawberry and Spinach Salad . . . 71
   Strawberry Meringue Croquembouche . . . 284

Strawberry Trifle . . . 285
Summertime Melon Salad . . . 99
Stroganoff Steak Sandwich . . . 67
Stuffed Artichokes (Carciofi Ripieni) . . . 207
Stuffed Chicken in Pastry (Suprême de Volaille en Croûte) . . . 160
Stuffed Flank Steak . . . 127
Stuffed Mushrooms . . . 24
Stuffed Crown Roast of Pork . . . 150
Stuffed Tomatoes with Two Fillings . . . 227
Stuffed Zucchini . . . 231
Stuffing:
   Chestnut Dressing . . . 186
   Mom's Wild Rice Stuffing . . . 186
   Walnut Rice Stuffing . . . 227
   Zucchini Stuffing . . . 227
Sue's Spinach Salad . . . 73
Summer Pasta with Basil, Tomatoes and Cheese . . . 94
Summertime Melon Salad . . . 99
Sunflower Kernels:
   Granola . . . 34
   Broccoli Salad Supreme . . . 75
   Zesty Tossed Salad . . . 74
Superfine Sugar . . . 320
Sweet and Sour:
   Sweet and Sour Chicken . . . 175
   Sweet and Sour Pot Roast . . . 129
Sweet Potatoes with Topping . . . 226
Swiss:
   Baked Chicken Reuben . . . 177
   Cheese and Potato Salad . . . 74
   Cheese and Wurst Salad . . . 84
   Coquille St. Jacques . . . 202
   Crab Meat Mornay . . . 200
   Eastwood Spinach Salad . . . 72
   Family Favorites . . . 68
   Noodles and Swiss Cheese . . . 122
   Swiss Chicken Extraordinaire . . . 179
   Westmoreland Asparagus Puff . . . 7
Swiss Apple Tart . . . 300

Tarragon Baked Cornish Hens . . . 184
Tart:
   Elegant Appetizer Tart . . . 11
   Swiss Apple Tart . . . 300
Tenderloin: see Beef, Tenderloin and Pork, Tenderloin
Tea:
   Spiced Tea Special . . . 37
Temper . . . 320
Teriyaki:
   Yuji's Teriyaki Kabobs . . . 126
Tex-Mex Dip . . . 13
Texas-Style Barbecue Chicken . . . 170
Thicken . . . 320

Three Cheese Casserole . . . 108
Tijuana Tidbits . . . 69
Toast . . . 320
Toast:
   Batter-Fried French Toast . . . 256
   Croustades (Toast
      Cups) . . . 8, 33
   French Toast Pockets . . . 256
   Herb Toasted Pita Bread . . . 240
   Sesame Herb Toast . . . 241
Toasted Almonds . . . 320
Toffee:
   English Butter Toffee . . . 266
Tomato:
   Bloody Mary Soup . . . 53
   Cheese Dumplings in Tomato
      Soup . . . 45
   Elegant Appetizer Tart . . . 11
   Fresh Tomato Pie . . . 226
   Greek Fish with Lemon and
      Tomato . . . 190
   Ratatouille Monterey . . . 228
   Ratatouille Pie . . . 9
   Shrimp Tomato
      Vinaigrette . . . 91
   Summer Pasta with Basil,
      Tomatoes and Cheese . . . 94
   Stuffed Tomato with Two
      Fillings . . . 227
   Tex-Mex Dip . . . 13
   Tomato Bisque . . . 44
Torta Di Pasqua (Italian Easter
   Pie) . . . 114
Torte:
   Black Forest Cherry
      Torte . . . 262
   Blitz Torte . . . 263
   Viennese Torte . . . 281
Tortilla:
   Chicken Enchiladas . . . 161
   Tortilla Soup . . . 59
Tortoni . . . 292
Toss . . . 320
Tostada:
   Chicken Tostada Salad . . . 86
Trifle:
   Strawberry Trifle . . . 285
Tuna:
   Mock Vitello Tonnato . . . 182
   Tuna Cheese Ball . . . 16
Turkey:
   Family Favorite . . . 68
   Lasagne Florentine . . . 120
   Mock Vitello Tonnato . . . 182
Two-Layer Cranberry Salad . . . 97

Uncooked Cucumber
   Slices . . . 104
Unmold . . . 320

Veal: *see also* **Meats** divider page
   123
   Braised Veal . . . 139
   Veal a l'Orientale . . . 142
   Veal Balls and Sour
      Cream . . . 143
   Veal Blanchette . . . 139
   Veal Forester . . . 141

Veal Tarragon . . . 140
Veal with Creole Sauce . . . 138
Wiener Kalbseinmachsuppe
   (Veal Soup) . . . 50
Vegetables: *see also* **Vegetables**
   divider page 205 and specific
   listings, *see also* **Vegetable
   Salads** divider page 71
   Cream of Parisian Vegetable
      Soup . . . 53
   Harvest Moon Chowder . . . 42
   Italian Vegetable Soup . . . 54
   Old Fashioned Vegetable
      Soup . . . 55
   Springtime Soup . . . 45
   Vegetable Delight . . . 231
   Vegetable Grab Bag . . . 18
   Vegetables 3-Way . . . 232
   Winter Soup . . . 46
Velouté Sauce . . . 120
Vermicelli:
   Country Noodles . . . 121
Viennese Torte . . . 281
Vinaigrette:
   Asparagus Vinaigrette . . . 75
   Shrimp Tomato
      Vinaigrette . . . 91
   Sauce Vinaigrette (French
      Dressing) . . . 307
Vitello:
   Mock Vitello Tonnato . . . 182

Walnut:
   Chinese Fried Walnuts . . . 35
   Chinese Walnut
      Chicken . . . 174
   Walnut Rice Stuffing . . . 227
Wassail . . . 40
Watercress Soup . . . 58
Westmoreland Asparagus
   Puff . . . 7
Whip . . . 320
Whipped Cream:
   Chocolate Whipped
      Cream . . . 308
Whisk . . . 320
White Bread:
   Batter-Fried French Toast . . . 256
   Family White Bread . . . 306
   Miniature Cucumber
      Pinwheels . . . 18
   Party Roll-Ups . . . 20
White Chocolate Party Mix . . . 35
Whole Wheat:
   Honey Whole Wheat
      Bread . . . 234
Wiener Kalbseinmachsuppe (Veal
   Soup) . . . 50
Wild Duck:
   Roast Wild Duck . . . 185
Wild Rice:
   Chicken-Wild Rice Salad . . . 87
   Mom's Wild Rice
      Stuffing . . . 186
   Wild Rice-Vegetable
      Medley . . . 223
Wine:

Wine Basted Cornish
   Hens . . . 183
Pork Tenderloin with Wine
   Sauce . . . 148
Wine Cherry Supreme . . . 98
Winter Soup . . . 46

Zesty Nibbles . . . 33
Zesty Tossed Salad . . . 74
Zippy Beef and Olive
   Spread . . . 15
Zucchini:
   Beef, Rice and Zucchini
      Skillet . . . 135
   Hearty Vegetable Stew . . . 232
   Mozzarella Chicken . . . 170
   Ratatouille Monterey . . . 228
   Ratatouille Pie . . . 9
   Stuffed Zucchini . . . 231
   Wild Rice-Vegetable
      Medley . . . 223
   Zucchini Alfredo . . . 230
   Zucchini Coffee Cake . . . 251
   Zucchini Creole . . . 230
   Zucchini Stuffing . . . 227

Contributors

Roxanne Brooks Acheson
Linda Swanson Adams
Beth Goodwin Aldrich
Kathryn Norris Allen
Pamela Cornwall Andrews
Linda Lons Appel
Mary Tone Atkins
Jennifer A. Bailey
Charlene Sarka Barnette
Jean Stacy Barthelmes
Audrey Hofelich Beckley
Lizette Daggett Bennett
Harriet Dahlstrom Berg
Mary Lou Burgett Berns
Kathryn Gloin Betley
Patty Dissette Bledsoe
Mary Jo Albright Bradley
Kathy Worster Brant
Gina Nessler Bremner
Janice Hartsough Brennan
Patricia Abbitt Brinegar
Elizabeth Dickerson Brown
Dorothy Sheerin Brown
Suzette Scheib Brown
Nancy Faison Bryson
Mary Ann Gunter Buckley
Linda Dougherty Burks
Nancy Sternberger Burris
Donna Terry Butcher
Susan Emrich Butz
Mary Jo Steuernagel Campbell
Moira Monaghan Carlstedt
Anne Englehart Carpenter
Joan Malcolm Carr
Ann Farrell Chaney
Anne Clark
Diana Collins Cochran
Dinny Trubey Cochran
Elizabeth Skinner Cochran
Rachel Cornell Cohen
Brooke Scott Collins
Pamela Rauch Comer
Laurie Grimme Cook
Lynda Skogan Cook
Anne Plummer Corr

Jacqueline Hare Cox
Patricia Norquest Cracraft
Bonnie Coyner Craig
Caterina Griner Cregor
Karen McKee Crossland
Gayle Geisler Crouse
Suzanne Fortier Cunningham
Kathryn Moore Dannels
Janet Gallas Dann
Betty Dawson Darko
Mary Alice Graves Dawson
Kathryn Shook Diener
Judith Ford Dolphin
Nancy Flynn Dorris
Nancy Schaefer Drake
Susan Landrum Due
Anne Goodyear Dustman
Christine Coleman Elmore
Margaret Cambell Emerson
Julia Sloan Evans
Patricia DePrez Ewing
Mary Ann Crahan Fagan
Deborah Mitchell Falk
Jane Seastrom Farber
Ann Scott Farkas
Marni Ransel Fechtman
Carol Elmes Ferguson
Pamela Walker Ferree
Nanci Smucker Feurer
Cynthia Winters Fisher
Judy Johnson Fisher
Janet Wupper Fox
Susan Blickman Frank
Judy Canada Fraps
Nancy Milligan Frick
Pamela Demuth Fry
Sandra McLean Gordner
Carol Garefana
Betty Ison Garland
Elizabeth Steiner Garrett
Caresss Stalker Garten
Joyce Cunningham Gellenbeck
Lois Hilkene Gibson
Glass Chimney
Polly Cochran Grabow
Polly Shipley Grafton
Mary Bennett Graub
Sally Calwell Gray
Mary Prendergast Grein
Leslie Gronauer
Sue Borton Gustin
Ginny Sittler Hacker
M. Elizabeth Hackl
Linda Dayhuff Hale

Sharon Kline Hamilton
Emily Cramer Hancock
Margaret Sullivan Harms
Priscila Bortz Harrington
Kathleen Martin Harrison
Suzanne Northam Hazelett
Susan Schrader Heath
Jane Teixler Hebert
Karen Tucker Hebert
Connie Bloyd Held
Martha Duran Hennessey
Kathy Kerwin Hiatt
Deborah Bartley Hilburn
Portia Conn Hirschman
Ginny Hall Hodowal
Sarah Smith Hofheinz
Suzanne Weir Hogan
Kathryn Cox Hoover
Rae Gettle Horrigan
Ann Fairchild Hulett
Patricia Huddleston Huse
Suzanne Sims Huse
Marsha Tucker Hutchinson
Maude Glore Hux
Darlene Isenberg
Katherine Kelly Ivcevich
T.Y. Iwamoto
Jill Foddrill Jackson
Elizabeth Duncan Jenkins
Kathryn Nolte Jenkins
Susan Hertzberg Johnson
Betsy Warner Jones
Mary Belting Jones
Anne Gilmore Jordan
Mary Dowd Jordan
Linda Jones Kammen
Cynthia Berg Kamples
Eleanor Reed Kassebaum
Rochelle Meyer Kelley

Janet Faires Kendall
Barbara Bates Kern
Jeannine Godfrey Kirby
Susan Rosenthal Kleinman
Anne Beekman Kraege
Carryl Wischmeyer Krohne
Chris Garrott Krok
Susan Garrison Kruse
Linda Shytle Lacy
Sandy Schwomeyer Lamb
Margaret Montgomery Land
Marno Manson Lane
Janet Preheim Lautzenheiser
Laura Dickerson Lehman
Mary Kay Conaty Leicht
Hazel Francis Lemen
Joy Neese Leppert
Kathyrn Wilsey Lerch
Ann Lurie Levinsohn
Jennie Lichtenauer
Suzanne Weir Logan
Susan Logsdon
Lois Richardson Lohse
Sally Schnaiter Lugar
Cheryl Longardner Lynn
Barbara Mayse MacDougall
Marilyn Mahoney
Suzanne Bauman Maine
Kay Pierson Manion
Andrea Shuff Marshall
Suzanne Tardy Maxwell
Jane Judkins McCabe
Thomas J. McCabe
Carolyn Kubec McClamroch
Scott McCrea
Kathy McKinney
Gayle Torian Meyer
Marjorie Teetor Meyer
Nancy Helm Miller
Barbara S. Monn
Suzanne Traylor Moore
Candace Porter Morrison
Weezie Fisk Morris
Michelle Laughery Moss
Susan Engel Naus

Margaret McKinney Neal
Deborah Berg Nell
Susie Puett Nicely
Nancy Ryan Nyhart
Mary Foster Orben
Cynthia Garrett O'Connor
Elaine O'Sullivan
Mildred Penn Ogle
Marilyn Benninger Olsen
Josie Orr (Mrs. Robert D. Orr)
Barbara White Parker
Janet Neal Patton
Helen Moser Peterson
Ellen Federspiel Poffenberger
Anne Davis Polestra
Lois A. Poteet
Frances Bernstein Prince
Ruth Meyer Purcell
Susan Brink Quebe
Lydia Meloy Quilhot
Andrea Caperell Quinn
Jean Heidt Quinn
Jane Hamilton Radcliffe
Anne Donnellan Rafferty
Kathleen Drewes Ramsey
Roberta Everett Recktenwall
Sophie Weiss Richardson
Laura Nahmias Rich
Julia Irwin Richter
Anne Ehrich Riley
Cynthia Sheehan Rogers
Charlene Capps Roth
Ann Bowman Ruebeck
Ann Greenlee Rugg
Susan Rogers Sams
Jane Wessels Schlegel
Nancy J. Schuman
Sue Williams Scott
Donna Segal
Maribeth Gramelspacher Seger
Marcia Miles SerVaas
Anne Korb Shane
Celestine Donnelly Sipe
Pat Markey Slama
Sally Chamberlain Slaughter
Suzanne Smart
Anne Ewing Smith
Katherine Spong Smith
Lianne Somerville
Marilyn Wells Sprague
Elizabeth Sechrist Stanford
Mary Miller Stanley
Barbara Feck Stayton
Kate Lee Steele

Pamela Wasson Steele
Anita Booth Stewart
Lynn Kinsey Stokely
Jane Polivka Stone
Penny McClevey Stone
Joyce Stout
Cheryl Williamson Strain
Janet Allenmeier Strawbridge
Emily Moore Sturman
Judy Arnott Stusrud
Joy Myers Sullivan
Mary Moody Sutherland
Anne Koch Swengel
Martha Irby Talyor
Hannah Hofherr TenEyck
Linda Clark Theobald
Marla Sue Theurer
Susan Spahr Thomas
Susan Deems Tittle
Deborah Ricketts Tolley
Margie Reed Tomlinson
Sue Crowder Townsend
Andrea Polzin Tremain
Patricia Tussing
Susan Peck Van Huss
Constance Frigstad Vickery
Wythe Denby Vyverberg
Ann Irwin Warden
Amy Karatz Weisz
Emily Stallings Weldon
Kathy Waite Whitmore
Caryl Fernandes Wilhoite
Erva C. Williams
Evelyn Nixon Williams
Nancy Nichols Williams
Betsy Karch Wilson
Ann Cluley Wishard
Julie Davis Wood
Nancy Meider Wood
Sue Rosebrough Worthington
Linda Brubaker Wright
Beth Brodrick Yakey
Andrea Hilburn Yates
Roberta Martin Yencer
Janet Shelton Yockey
Mary Ann Thomison Zink

Winners

**3050 North Meridian
Indianapolis, IN 46208**

Please send me ____ copies of Winners at $14.95 each $_____
plus shipping/handling at $ 2.00 each $_____
add sales tax for delivery in Indiana at $ .75 each $_____
please gift wrap at $ 1.00 each $_____
please furnish gift enclosure card at $ .50 each $_____
TOTAL $_____

Name _____

Address _____

City _____ State _____ Zip _____

All copies will be sent to the same address unless otherwise specified. If you wish one or any number of books sent as gifts, furnish a list of names and addresses of recipients. If you wish to enclose your own gift card with each book, please write name of recipient on outside of envelope, enclose with order, and we will include it with your gift.

Make checks payable to JLI Publications. Prices subject to change.

Winners

**3050 North Meridian
Indianapolis, IN 46208**

Please send me ____ copies of Winners at $14.95 each $_____
plus shipping/handling at $ 2.00 each $_____
add sales tax for delivery in Indiana at $ .75 each $_____
please gift wrap at $ 1.00 each $_____
please furnish gift enclosure card at $ .50 each $_____
TOTAL $_____

Name _____

Address _____

City _____ State _____ Zip _____

All copies will be sent to the same address unless otherwise specified. If you wish one or any number of books sent as gifts, furnish a list of names and addresses of recipients. If you wish to enclose your own gift card with each book, please write name of recipient on outside of envelope, enclose with order, and we will include it with your gift.

Make checks payable to JLI Publications. Prices subject to change.

Winners

**3050 North Meridian
Indianapolis, IN 46208**

Please send me ____ copies of Winners at $14.95 each $_____
plus shipping/handling at $ 2.00 each $_____
add sales tax for delivery in Indiana at $ .75 each $_____
please gift wrap at $ 1.00 each $_____
please furnish gift enclosure card at $ .50 each $_____
TOTAL $_____

Name _____

Address _____

City _____ State _____ Zip _____

All copies will be sent to the same address unless otherwise specified. If you wish one or any number of books sent as gifts, furnish a list of names and addresses of recipients. If you wish to enclose your own gift card with each book, please write name of recipient on outside of envelope, enclose with order, and we will include it with your gift.

Make checks payable to JLI Publications. Prices subject to change.